Complete Book of

American Kitchen
and Dinner Wares

Lois Lehner

ISBN 0-87069-320-4
Library of Congress Catalog No. 79-67716

Photographs:

Wayne Cubberly of Cubberly's Studios in Delaware and Marion, Ohio.

Cover photograph:

Gorham Division of Textron, Inc., Providence, Rhode Island.

Published by

Wallace-Homestead Book Company
1912 Grand Avenue
Des Moines, Iowa 50309

Acknowledgments

The list of credits for the help I have received in writing this book is so tremendous that it would make a book of its own. A sincere thank you is not enough for all who helped, so I only hope the book lives up to their expectations and will repay them in part. First and foremost is my thanks to editor, Don Brown of Wallace-Homestead Book Co., who helped me to organize my thinking in dealing with a huge mound of material. What I wanted to put into a single volume was impossible. He helped me to understand what could go into a book and what would have to be dealt with in magazine articles. He encouraged me several times when I felt absolutely "bogged down" by the enormity of the dinnerware field.

Secondly, the companies now in business were very helpful. Not only did they furnish information about their own companies, but several times they helped to find the history of those out of business by answering my questions and furnishing names of people who might be able to help me. Most of the companies sent advertising material and pictures which we just couldn't get squeezed into one volume, but which were used in various ways to compile the lists, etc. for the book. You will find many references to magazine articles in this book from which some of this material was derived. Copies of marks and company-furnished information and pictures all remain the property of the various companies and are used here with their permission. A special thanks to these companies: American Fine China; Terrace Ceramics (formerly owned by John Bonistall who also helped with Shawnee and American Pottery Company of Marietta); Arita Tabletop; Brush Pottery; Buffalo China Company; W.C. Bunting Company; Canonsburg Pottery; Chatham Potters; Conrad Crafters; H.F. Coors Company, Inc., of Inglewood, California; Charles S. Ryland of Coors Porcelain in Golden, Colorado; Cordey China; Crest Studios; Cumbow China; Gorham Fine China (Flintridge); Hadley Pottery; Haeger Potteries, Inc.; Hall China; Heath Ceramics; Hoffman China; Hull Pottery; the Interpace Companies (especially Shenango China); Maddux of California; Mayer China; Marsh Industries, and Franciscan (formerly Gladding, McBean and Co. Also Iron Mountain Stoneware; Jackson China; and, at Homer Laughlin China Company, Mr. E.S. Carson, who was a great help. Lenox furnished the pictures of their workers along with a wealth of other material. Gorham, Lenox, and Pickard, our three most well-known fine china makers in the country today, deserve special attention. Others include Lewis Brothers Ceramics; Nelson McCoy Pottery; Metlox Potteries; Pfaltzgraff; Red Cliff Company; Ridgewood Industries, Inc.; Royal China Company; Robinson-Ransbottom; Sabin Industries; Salem China; Scio Pottery; Stangl Pottery; Sterling China Company; Syracuse China; Taylor, Smith and Taylor (Anchor Hocking); Treasure Craft; Vohann of California; Walker China; and Western Stoneware. Former employees of the companies no longer in business were one of the greatest sources of information. They patiently answered questions and sometimes sent newspaper clippings, etc., particularly Charles Ryland on Coors Porcelain and Douglas Butler whose family worked at McCoy. In the Bibliography and notes throughout the book, you will find that many authors were very generous in granting permission to use their material. A special thanks to Seymour and Violet Altman and Crown Publishers for the material reprinted from *The Book of Buffalo Pottery*, and Harvey Duke, author of *Hall China, A Guide for Collectors*. Others who furnished information are Barbara Hayes, author of *Bauer—The California Pottery Rainbow*; Don Hoffman, author of *Why Not Warwick?*; A.W. Friedley, author of *Catalina Pottery—The Early Years*; Paul Evans, *Art Pottery in the United States*; Grace Allison, author, who contributed information and the Lotus Ware picture; but most of all, Annise Heaivilin, who researched many hours to help me. Also a special thanks to the fine portrait photographer with many awards in that field, who entered the realm of photographing dishes as a special favor to this author. Our splendid pictures are the work of Wayne Cubberly of Cubberly's Studios in Delaware and Marion, Ohio.

Librarians from many states took the time to do research and to copy directories for this book. This is not part of the work they are paid to do, nor do they really have the time, but many were willing to help. To them, a sincere thanks from the china collectors and this author. Annagayle Harvey spent evenings researching the files in the West Virginia secretary of state's office for me. Mrs. E.A. Reiter of the Trenton Free Public Library in Trenton took the time to copy the whole run of *Trenton City Directories*, without which the book could not have been written, because so many factories were in Trenton.

Editors, writers, and readers from the various collectors' magazines all helped in various ways with pictures, information, artwork, the marks drawings, etc. Sophia Papapanu and Barbara Mizirach, writers for *Depression Glass Daze* both sent very helpful material. Jo Cunningham, editor of *Glaze* sent pictures. Jean Fowles copied a whole run of Sears catalogs for me and contributed artwork. June Kass Jackson sent directories and furnished information about various potteries. Martha B. Brisker, a special dealer friend, searched and searched to help me to acquire the dishes pictured. Lois Finnerty and Helen Montgomery researched on a local level. In fact, Helen covered most of Texas trying to find dinnerware companies. Sometimes it is harder to uncover the very few that existed in a single state than it is to research the companies in a state where potteries were numerous.

Contents

PART ONE

A Word about the Book

The vastness of the undertaking to write this book was almost overwhelming when I began to realize the monumental mound of material that would encompass the scope of our American dinnerware and kitchenware industry and that very little of the story had ever been told before. The story was there, in the dishes themselves, so we proceeded to literally fill the garage with dishes. The rest of the story was in various places, in little bits and pieces, such as in catalogs, advertisements, magazines, and in many people's heads. Little of it was in books or in any piece of organized writing. My goal was to present a comprehensive history of the American dinnerware and kitchenware industry in the United States in such a way that it would not only be a great aid to the collector, but, also be a well-documented historical recording. To achieve my goal within one moderately priced, easy-to-handle, single volume, I would have to have a tremendous organization of the material. I discovered that I could not possibly cover all facets of the dinnerware field in one book, so I chose the marks and history for main coverage in this first book in preference to pattern information. I did get many decorations and shapes into lists and company information. This is a book to be studied and searched; one to come back to many times, and one which will reward the reader with many answers. I have tried to include study helps and suggestions with the various sections.

The writing of this book might be compared to trying to find the needle in a haystack, then trying to cram the haystack inside the eye of the needle! To present an overall comprehensive view of the industry, I ended up by writing a paragraph on companies that should, and will, have whole books written about them. In a very few instances you will find a great deal of space devoted to a single factory, not because it was a favorite of the author, but because it was chosen to typify a group or to illustrate a problem faced by all of the potteries or to give an understanding of how a particular type of dinnerware was made. Examples of this are William Bloor, representing the very early pottery industry; Lenox, representing fine china manufacture; Shenango, and Gladding, McBean and Company representing the growth of big business along with the other Interpace companies. The complete picture is here in the history of the companies. The discovery that there are only three makers of fine china left in the Fine China Guild in this country today might lead some reader to study the various reasons given in the company histories for individual potteries closing, one after another.

The first colonists to this country brought some dinnerware with them, which could have been Delft from Holland, slipware from England, or Faience from France. But they ate from wooden plates, pewter dishes, or very early handmade, hand-thrown dishes made in the colonies. Even the Europeans weren't able to make porcelain yet, but they knew what it was because they were bringing it from China. Then in the mid-1700s Europe started making porcelain. About 1800, Josiah Spode perfected the formula for bone china. But it was due to the efforts of Joseph Wedgwood of England, who perfected cream-colored earthenware, that matched sets of dishes, priced within the means of most families, were finally made. In the course of time, Americans began trying to make their own china. These early efforts were feeble attempts on the whole. Surprisingly enough, these companies failed, not because they couldn't make fine china, not because they couldn't find capital or raw materials, but because the people in this country wouldn't buy our own dishes. At first the ties to the old country were ethnic, foreign dishes were something from back home. Then and later, owning foreign china became a prestige thing, the thing to do. This attitude was fought all through the years as revealed in the histories of many of the companies.

The problem of limitation, which companies to include, which to leave out, was the major problem I encountered in writing this book. The factory period started in the United States around 1830. In 1828, the American Pottery Manufacturing Company, Jersey City, New Jersey, finally made some dinnerware comparable to that made by the English. This book deals mainly with the companies that follow the mechanization of the dinnerware and kitchenware industry. The reader will find crocks, jugs, stoneware dishes, etc., all mentioned somewhere in the book, but they are included because the company that manufactured them operated on a large scale. For instance Western Stoneware made sets of stoneware dishes just as heavy as any older stoneware jug as late as 1975. But as a general rule, hand-thrown pottery on a wheel is excluded from the book. Rockingham, yellowware, and redware are discussed only if they were the early products of a company that went on and on for years and finally ended up making semiporcelain. A few companies that made almost all artware are included if they were a big enough company so that the few dinnerware items made by them may be easily found. In other words, if they made a lot of that dinnerware in a short time. Roseville Pottery Company's Raymor, is an example, or Weller's kitchenware and apple ware. The same thing applies to the sanitary manufacturers who made dinnerware for awhile; Mercer, Maddox, etc., for instance. They made mostly sanitary ware while they existed, but enough of their dishes are around to still be found. A few individuals (not only big companies) are listed if they produced enough to make a significant contribution to the industry as a whole and if their products might be readily found. The products of the very earliest makers were never easily found. Only a few examples have ever existed. So these makers have been included to give an understanding of how the early industry progressed. From "William Bloor," *American Ceramic Society Bulletin*, XVI, January 1937, p. 25, the following was found which tells the important dates and the men who contributed to the production of whiteware in the United States. Whiteware in its broadest sense includes cream-colored ware, white granite or ironstone, semiporcelain, and porcelain ware.

Chronology of Whiteware Production Developments

1671 John Dwight, England. (patented porcelain fluxed with glass)

1695 M. Chicanneau, France. (soft-paste porcelain)

1710 John Frederic Böttger, Germany. (hard porcelain)

1749 Thomas Frye, England. (patented bone china)

1768 William Cookworthy, England. (patented hard-paste porcelain)

1769 Gousse Bonnin, Philadelphia, Pa. (bone china)

1789 John Curtis, Philadelphia, Pa. (queensware)

1799 William McFarland, Cincinnati, Ohio. (earthenware)

1800 Josiah Spode, England. (began production of bone china)

1801 James and Robert Caldwell, Cincinnati, Ohio. (earthenware)

1808 Alexander Trotter, Philadelphia, Pa. (earthenware)

1809 Thomas Vickers & Sons, Downington, Pa. (queensware)

1810 Daniel Freytag, Philadelphia, Pa. (earthenware and bone china)

1816 Dr. Mead, New York, N.Y. (hard-paste porcelain)

1816 Abraham Miller, Philadelphia, Pa. (queensware)

1816 David G. Seixas, Philadephia, Pa. (cream-colored earthenware)

1825 Jersey Porcelain & Earthenware, Jersey City, N.J. (hard-paste porcelain)

1825 William Ellis Tucker, Philadelphia, Pa. (hard-paste porcelain)

1829 D. and J. Henderson, Jersey City, N.J. (porcelain)

1829 Lewis Pottery Co., Louisville, Ky. (cream-colored earthenware)

1830 Smith Fife & Co., Philadelphia, Pa. (porcelain)

1832 Joseph Hemphill, Philadelphia, Pa. (porcelain)

1833 American Pottery Mfg. Co., Jersey City, N.J. (porcelain)

1837 Thomas Tucker, Philadelphia, Pa. (porcelain)

1840 Charles J. Boulter, Philadelphia, Pa. (soft-paste porcelain)

1845 Norton and Fenton, Bennington, Vt. (earthenware)

1846 Edwin Bennett, Baltimore, Md. (queensware)

1848 Charles Cartlidge & Co., Green Point, L.I. (porcelain)

1853 Charles Hattersley, Trenton, N.J. (earthenware)

1853 Charles Kurbaum and J.T. Schwartz, Philadelphia, Pa. (porcelain)

1853 Morrison and Carr, New York City. (white granite)

1854 American Porcelain Mfg. Co., Gloucester, N.J. (soft-paste porcelain)

1857 William Young & Sons, Trenton, N.J. (whiteware)
1857 George Allen, Philadelphia, Pa. (porcelain and Parian ware)
1858 Southern Porcelain Co., Kaolin, S.C. (porcelain)
1859 Trenton China Co., Trenton, N.J. (vitrified ware)
1859 Rhodes and Yates, Trenton, N.J. (white granite)
1859 Millington, Astbury, & Poulson, Trenton, N.J. (whiteware)
1859 Fenton and Clark, Peoria, Ill. (white granite)
1860 H. Speeler, Trenton, N.J. (whiteware)
1860 American Pottery Co., Peoria, Ill. (white granite)
1861 James Tams and J.P. Stephens, Trenton, N.J. (white granite)
1863 Bloor, Ott, & Booth, Trenton, N.J. (creamware and white granite)
1863 Coxon & Co., Trenton, N.J. (creamware and white granite)
1865 Frederick Dallas, Cincinnati, Ohio. (common white)
1865 Trenton Pottery Co., Trenton, N.J. (earthenware)
1868 Greenwood Pottery Co., Trenton, N.J. (white granite)
1868 James Moses, Trenton, N.J. (earthenware)
1869 S.M. Kier, Pittsburgh, Pa. (earthenware)
1869 Astbury and Maddock, Trenton, N.J. (whiteware)
1870 John Wyllie, Pittsburgh, Pa. (earthenware)
1870 Knowles, Taylor & Knowles, East Liverpool, Ohio. (whiteware)
1870 John Goodwin, Trenton, N.J. (earthenware)
1870 Thomas Maddock, Trenton, N.J. (sanitary ware)
1871 Yates, Bennett, & Allen, Trenton, N.J. (white granite)
1874 H. & S. Laughlin, East Liverpool, Ohio. (white granite)
1875 Thomas Gray & L.W. Clark, Boston, Mass. (white earthenware)
1876 American Crockery Co., Trenton, N.J. (white bisque and granite)
1876 Morris and Willmore, Trenton, N.J. (Belleek)

A Few Definitions

I had a long list of definitions to include in this book which were excluded in preference to adding just one more picture or a little more company history. Definitions for pottery terms can be found in many books in any good library and also in the dictionary. The following is a concise, oversimplified, discussion of a few of the terms you will encounter in this book.

Ceramics is the broadest of all terms which we must consider. It embraces the production and decoration of all objects formed from clay by molding, modeling, and baking—from bricks to the finest art pottery and porcelain. As long as it's made from clay, it is ceramic. Next we have to consider glass versus clay products, and that isn't necessarily a simple distinction, either. Have you ever tried to tell whether a dish is fine porcelain or a milky glass? In fact the "Report of the Committee on the Definition of the Term Ceramics" as printed in the *American Ceramic Society Bulletin*, III, July 1920, p. 26, includes all varieties of glassware, including quartz glass, glazes, enamels, and even many artificial stones under the term ceramics. Perhaps this is the reason that old glass factory directories also listed the potteries.

The study of ceramic chemistry is a field in itself. (One which I cannot even begin to understand.) But the whole process of making the various kinds of ware from clay depends on what the mixture of clay and other products is and how high the ware is heated, both of which results in the formation of the various grades of chinaware. The more of the elements which are used to make glass that are added to the pottery mixture and the higher the pottery is heated, the more vitrified or harder the product becomes and the better it is considered to be, and, accordingly, the more expensive the ware is to make. In this book are detailed accounts given by some of the potteries about how their ware is made, which are provided for the readers who have a talent for understanding this part of ceramics. (See Lenox.) American dinnerware has taken many forms over the years. *Yellowware* was the cheapest, plainest form of common pottery. Made of yellow clay, it was mostly undecorated, but it sometimes had simple bands of pale blue or smoke-colored scrolls with a colorless glaze over a buff body. *Mocha ware* was cream-colored, thinner, lighter, more easily broken than yellowware. *Redware* was made from surface clays throughout the eastern United States, especially in Pennsylvania and Ohio, and was made until after 1900. It is soft, fragile, often gaily colored, and in Pennsylvania it was slip-decorated. *Brown ware* has a dull, stony, opaque glazing which gave the ware its name. *Earthenware* was a broad term that included all pieces made of clay, but in use came to mean a type of pottery not as hard as ironstone or stoneware. Much of the dinnerware that didn't fit into the category of ironstone, or of the others mentioned, was just dubbed earthenware, which came to mean a more porous, softer, off-colored type of ware. By burning pottery clay much longer to a greater degree of hardness, stoneware, the most durable of the potteries, was made. *Stoneware* was refined for cups, plates, etc. It approaches the qualities of porcelain in some respects when highly refined, and is sometimes called *stone china.* Stoneware has a compact texture and its hardness is resistant to penetration or pressure. Stone china was generally gray or cream-colored. *Ironstone* is a heavy duty, off-white ware, sometimes called opaque porcelain or semiporcelain. Gray-white ironstone was made in the United States from about 1870 to 1910; the plates were plain and heavy. **Hotel china** is a hard vitreous ware produced in three different weights. The old ironstone chipped and scratched, as is evidenced in old pieces found today, but it stood tremendous wear which is proved by the fact that it is still found at all after receiving such wear. Porcelain is of two kinds, hard paste and soft paste. **Porcelain** is a hard, thin, translucent, delicate ware. The term **china** today has come to mean whatever the plate on the table happens to be, but it was once meant to be identified only with porcelain. The type which most of the china in this book will be is **semiporcelain** or **semivitreous** ware. This is a good grade of china, not too heavy to handle, not translucent, not too easy to break—a grade of pottery that lent itself to all types of decoration and lasted a long time with a little care. **Parian** is such a true, hard-paste porcelain that it doesn't have to be glazed. It will hold water like glass. **Paste**, incidentally, is just another name for the material used to make the body of the ware. **Hard paste** is made with kaolin and other ingredients and **soft paste** is bone ash plus other materials. My problem with real porcelain is that I don't ever expect to handle enough of it to tell the difference between hard-paste porcelain and soft-paste porcelain, which some experts can do. However, if the piece of porcelain had a broken edge, the body underneath would be smooth and glossy like glass. It is hard to tell when the **glaze** (a coating of glass) on a real piece of porcelain ends and the body starts. This is certainly no problem with semiporcelain; underneath the semiporcelain piece's glaze is a dull, soft body (dig your fingernail into it) which absorbs stains if the glaze becomes cracked or crazed. **Crazing** is the development of the hundreds of tiny lines or breaks in the glaze that run every which way on a crazed plate. But to get back to true porcelain for just one more statement: Barber said there were so many degrees of hard- and soft-paste porcelains that it is really hard to tell where one ended and the other started. I am sure this is true of what became known as semiporcelain. Semiporcelain ranges in degrees just as porcelain does, from some that is soft and chips so easily that it is almost like a chalk figure to semiporcelain that is so hard or vitrified that if it were translucent, it might almost be considered to be porcelain. Semiporcelain is opaque. Fine, thin porcelain is translucent unless, like fine hotel china, the ware is very thick, then it is no longer translucent, yet it is porcelain. The **hardness** that keeps being mentioned in connection with porcelain is simply a superior resistance to penetration by liquids and a resistance to pressure. **Short sets**, so often referred to in this book were sets made by the factory without all of the pieces found in a full set. Perhaps there were no egg cups or dessert dishes or deep dishes made. Any of these missing would make it a short set.

Transfer printing is a method which was brought over from England by the very early potters. It involved engraving from a copper plate. The copper plate was warmed and the color worked into the engravings. The excess color was cleaned off the copper plate. A piece of thin, tissue-type paper was brushed with a soft soap solution. This paper was then laid on the engraved plate and run through a roller press to transfer the color to the paper. The pattern was transferred to the dish and rubbed down into place. Hand work could then be added by filling in the design with color or trimming the piece with gold. There was a decorating kiln, and some of the ware went through that kiln many times. These old transfer designs are delicate and have the look of something engraved. The color, hand painted in, is irregular and runs out of the lines.

Decalcomania or the use of decals started in the early 1900s in Europe. First the potters tried just heating the ware and pressing the decal into place. By the mid-1930s the application of decals was done by machine. Royal China, for instance, had regular printing presses to do the work. Germany made most of the pottery decals used in the United States by the late 1930s. Americans tried to make their own decals at first, but the potters insisted the decal manufacturers use English-made duplex paper, so it never paid to manufacture the paper here. By the time the decal manufacturers imported their paper and paid a high labor rate, they couldn't compete with the Germans, so they went back to making decals for things other than dishes such as furniture, which did not require heat for application. (McKee, Floyd W., *A Century of American Dinnerware Manufacture*, privately printed, 1966, pp. 11-12.)

Front row: salt and pepper set, Harker Pottery; pie server and rolling pin unidentified as to maker, probably Harker Pottery, also. ***Back row:*** pie plate, Harker Pottery; platter, cream and sugar, Hall China Company; cookie jar, "Kitchen Craft" by Homer Laughlin China Company; ball pitcher, Universal Potteries, Inc.

Left to right: Cronin China Company, Salem China Company, Sabin Industries.

14

Some Points to Keep in Mind

Many times dishes did not have a decoration or pattern name, only numbers. Sometimes I might refer to a decal such as a "wheat" decal meaning it was not the pattern name but just a description of the way it was decorated. I added "like" to some names, such as "leaflike," because the real name for the ware might have little to do with what it looked like. Steubenville Pottery's leaflike pattern was called "Woodfield" which is closer than some of the names came.

When a collector finds two plates of exactly the same shape with the same pattern type of name on the back and those two plates have different decorations on the front, then the name is a shape name. Some potteries, like Harker Pottery and Royal China Company, used the word "series" for a shape or a line of ware.

Study the shapes of the dishes in the pictures; *shape is the key to the identification of all dinnerware and kitchenware.* Many companies used the same decals. See the picture of the tulip decal products that were made by four different companies, all using the same decal. (Decals were bought from specialty companies by the potteries.) The cookie jar in the picture is Homer Laughlin's "Kitchen Kraft"; the ball pitcher is marked "Universal Potteries"; the pie plate and salt and pepper are by Harker Pottery; the cream sugar and platter are part of a full set of dishes marked Hall China.

Rule number one in identifying pottery is never to assume anything! The next picture shows three plates with identical decals, very similar gold trims, similar shapes, and two of the three even have marks which are very much alike, but all of them were made by different companies. The plate in the center is a service plate by Salem China Company, the plate on the right is decorated by Sabin Industries, and the plate on the left was made by Cronin China Company, Minerva, Ohio. Sabin Industries at one time around the 1940s used an S mark on a paint palette. This is the one that tricked this author. Because of the similarity of the Sabin and Salem plates, I thought the S mark was a Salem mark. As I said, one can never assume anything in identifying pottery marks and products.

Understanding Practices of the Potteries

If we could knock out all hard and fast rules in dealing with pottery products and information, it would help tremendously. Every rule, idea, and practice had an exception. I found that I could finally begin to understand what the potteries did after I learned one lesson: that lesson was to put myself in the place of the pottery, to try to think like a businessman, not a collector. Only then did I begin to understand the use of marks, the kinds of pottery made, the various business practices, the selling (including retailing and wholesaling), the combinations and mergers the potteries went through, etc. None of this was designed to make life difficult for the collector; it was a matter of survival for the pottery.

For instance, the collector can better understand marks if he realizes why the pottery used them at all. What does make the understanding difficult, is that each company had its own reason or combination of reasons for using or not using marks. Scio Pottery, a very successful pottery, has never identified thier ware. They do not feel it is necessary, and it must not be for them, because they really sell many dishes and that is why they are in business. Anytime in the Marks Section that a pottery has at least ten marks shown, it is almost safe to assume that they liked to use marks and that somewhere out there in collectors' land are at least ten more marks they have used that have not been attributed to the company by various authors. (Notice I said "almost safe" to assume, because, as I said, assuming anything about dinnerware is never completely safe.) Many marks have shown up for some of the companies listed in the Barber book of 1904 that were not listed in his book. The same will be true of this book.

As to the dates involved in giving the history of a pottery, potteries didn't just begin and end. It would seem that it would be an easy thing to set a starting and stopping date for any given pottery. That is not so. First there were organization dates, then first production dates, and then incorporation dates. Any one of these gives a clue to the approximate date the pottery really got going, unless one of the following happened: the company organized and never did produce a product; or the company may not have incorporated for years after it had been formed; or a business may have started as a hobby and produced pottery for years before it was acknowledged as a business. For all practical purposes, a factory may have been out of business for a year or more and not producing one thing before a liquidation or bankruptcy sale took place. Name changes cause trouble in placing specific dates.

As you read the various histories of the companies, you will find they changed products over the years many times. Some switched from dinnerware to sanitary ware. Some made art pottery and then for a short time made dinnerware. Some made electrical porcelain and dinnerware at different times in their history. Some started as brick factories and worked up to dinnerware. Universal Potteries, Inc. switched to tile. The factories were in business to make money, and they attempted to make a product that would make money. The state of New Jersey had almost as many potteries, maybe more, than Ohio did, making dinnerware. They were operating earlier than the Ohio potteries. The New Jersey factories made a fine grade of ware either in porcelain or semiporcelain, but on the whole it was better than that made in Ohio later. When Ohio potteries really got going in the first quarter of the twentieth century, they made a cheaper product and undersold New Jersey, so many of the New Jersey factories switched to sanitary ware. Any time a given factory can turn out a good porcelain bathtub, you know they can also make a set of dishes of fine quality. Secrets surrounding the manufacture of ware by various companies are sometimes guarded with the greatest care, even today.

Names were given to lines and products for advertising and identification purposes. If they could be sold with only a number identification, many times a number was all that they were given. (See Warwick.) Even Lenox, which gave hundreds of names to decorations and shapes, had some identified only by number. A lot of this name business depended upon how the pottery attempted to sell their dishes. Some sold through retail concerns, dime stores, chain stores; some sold to the catalog companies; some potteries attempted to retail their own products. All of this determined how much identification had to be assigned to the ware. A big advertising promotion meant a big fancy name (possibly linked to the name of the designer, etc.).

If by this time you are having a little trouble mastering the terminology involved in pottery making, consider the following paragraph taken from "Symposium Held at the 48th Annual Meeting of the American Ceramic Society in Buffalo, New York, April 30, 1946," as recounted in the *American Ceramic Society Bulletin*, XXV, October 1946, p. 376. Mr. Gould is speaking and lecturing the other pottery owners and some designers on the usage of terms:

> There is a lot of talk here about foreign imports. I was quite surprised also to hear the different terms which are used. The department-store buyers, for example, call earthenware "semiporcelain" or "chinaware." They call china "porcelain." I have heard all the rest of you call porcelain "chinaware." There is little interest on the part of the manufacturer, and certainly no help from the buyer, to explain the difference. The American earthenware, which we call semiporcelain, is an absolute misnomer. It has certain advantages from the cost standpoint and has definite inherent beauty in itself. We attempt to compete with this product against a true porcelain, which we call "china," and we do not get down to fundamentals. We do not know what we are talking about.

A Note about Cookie Jars

Cookie jars have been a great moneymaker for the various potteries over the years, and this continues to be true. Potteries that made mostly decorative type ware like Abingdon for example, oftentimes made cookie jars also. If a company made practically all kitchenwares, cookie jars fit into that type of production, too. Even the companies that classed themselves as dinnerware makers made cookie jars. There is a distinction between dinnerware and kitchenware manufacturers, especially today, when the unions require a higher scale for dinnerware workers than for kitchenware labor. At any rate, almost all of the potteries made some cookie jars and this is a collecting field all in itself. Pictured are a variety of cookie jars made by companies not pictured elsewhere in this book. There are additional cookie jars pictured throughout the book.

The corn cookie jar is by Stanford Pottery in Sebring, Ohio. The clock cookie holder came from Abingdon Pottery. The big red apple is now being made by Holiday Designs in Sebring. The jar made of stoneware with raised apples and leaves is a recent product of Robinson Ransbottom of Roseville, Ohio. The cookie container with gold band trim and the word "Cookie" was made by Acme Craftware, Inc.

Front row: Stanford Pottery, Acme Craftware, Inc. **Back row:** Abingdon Pottery, Holiday Designs, Robinson Ransbottom.

18

Various Aspects of the Pottery Industry

For each aspect of the industry I have named a few examples to study. There will be more that illustrate these various points throughout the text.

American Potteries as Family Businesses. See Metlox Potteries, Harker Pottery, Hadley Pottery, and Treasure Craft.

American Pottery as a Part of Big Business. See Anchor Hocking Corporation, Jeannette Corporation, Interpace, Maddux of California.

Aspects of Art in Dinnerware Industry. See Russel Wright, Vernon Kilns, and Viktor Schreckengost.

Decorators Who Use Their Mark on China Made by Others. See Bunting, Crest Studios, Pickard, Inc. (in the early years), Kettlesprings Kilns, and Sabin Industries.

Difficulties Encountered by the Potteries in This Country. See Lenox, Inc., Shenango Pottery, and Canonsburg Pottery.

Effects of Tariffs on the Industry. See Canonsburg Pottery, Lenox, Inc., Maddux of California.

How Dinnerware Is Made. See Lenox, Inc., Gladding, McBean and Company, and Knowles, Taylor, Knowles.

How Porcelain Is Made. See United States Pottery, Bennington, Vermont.

How Pottery Is Marketed. See Maddux of California.

Late Manufacture of Pennsylvania-type Ware. See Purinton Pottery and Hoffman China.

Manufacturers Who Manufacture Exclusively for Decorators and Other Outlets. See American Fine China.

Retailers Who Use Their Own Mark. See Terrace Ceramics, Sears and Roebuck (as discussed under American Fine China), Atlas China in New York City.

Shapes in Dinnerware. Study the W.S. George picture.

Special Runs and Whimsy-type Material. Read Imperial Porcelain Works.

The Beginning of Dinnerware As We Know It Today. See the potteries in Trenton, Lenox, Inc., Harker Pottery, William Bloor, and the Bennett Pottery.

Trenton As the "Staffordshire of America." See International Pottery.

What Fine Porcelain China Is. See Lenox, Inc., Gorham Co., Pickard, Inc., U.S. Pottery at Bennington, Vermont, and the definitions in front.

PART TWO

Kitchenware and Dinnerware Manufacturers from A to Z

ABINGDON POTTERY in Abingdon, Illinois, was known mainly for the decorative pottery that was made there from the time the pottery started around 1934 until ending in 1950. However, the firm did make a variety of cookie jars, such as the "Cookie Time Clock" shown in the picture on page 18. The names given to the cookie jars in the advertising promotion were most intriguing, such as "Hobby Horse," "Choo-Choo," "Money Bag," "Jack-in-the-Box," "Hippo," "Grandma," "Little Ol' Lady," etc. The names in themselves should send collectors scurrying to find the jars. In "Abingdon, U.S.A.," *Glaze*, June, 1977, p. 6, is an article by Betty Latty which is very informative.

ACME CRAFTWARE, INC. was a pottery which operated in Wellsville, Ohio, from 1946 to 1970 making what was termed artware pottery, ceramic vases, nut bowls, etc. They went out of business when their property was taken for a highway. The owners, John Bryen and Roland Leonard, retired from making pottery. They made some pieces that would be considered accessory pieces for table use. A small turquoise teapot with a gold spout was found. See Marks Section for marks. See the cookie jars in the picture on page 18.

Acme Pottery.

ACME POTTERY (or PORCELAIN) COMPANY was in business only two years in Crooksville, Ohio, from 1903 to 1905. *(Second Annual Crooksville-Roseville Pottery Festival Booklet*, 1967, p. 38.) They were makers of semiporcelain dinnerware. See picture of plate marked "Acme Porcelain/Crooksville" on a scroll. (See Marks Section.)

AKRON CHINA COMPANY was located in Akron, Ohio, 1894 to 1908. In 1905 they employed two-hundred people to make china which included white granite or ironstone, hotel ware, decorated dinnerware, and toilet wares. Their marks involved the initials "A.C.Co." and sometimes they used the word "Revere" without their initials. (Source: Blair, C. Dean, *The Potters and Potteries of Summit County, Ohio, 1828-1915*, published by the Summit County Historical Society, Akron, 1965, p. 25, and *Factory Inspection Report* for Ohio, 1905.) See picture of plate marked "Revere China."

Akron China Company.

AKRON QUEENSWARE COMPANY was located in Akron, Ohio, between 1890 to 1894. According to Blair they were the first ones to make white granite in Summit County, Ohio. Clay was imported by this company because the clay in Springfield Township, Summit County, Ohio, where the factory was located, burns to a buff color. Ball clay was brought in from Georgia, Tennessee, and England. The mark used was "A.Q.W. Co. Warranted Iron Stone China, Akron Ohio" in a circle stamped underglaze. (Blair, p. 26.)

THE ALAMO POTTERY, INC. in San Antonio, Texas, was established in 1944. They made a hand cast tableware with fiestalike colors. Texas made a lot of pottery and has received little recognition in the books so far. It was mostly hand thrown type, and, even though they made a lot of table items, hand thrown ware is mostly excluded from this book. The Texan stoneware and Mexican looking handmade pottery they produced will receive its proper recognition very soon.

ALBRIGHT CHINA COMPANY was located in Carrollton, Ohio, from 1910 to the early 1930s. They had a second plant at Scio, Ohio, which later became the home of Scio Pottery. They made dinnerware of semiporcelain marked "Albright China Company," also "Albright/Carrollton, Ohio." The plant in Scio operated from around 1920 to 1927. A reader writing to *Collector's News* sent a photograph of a plate made by this company, marked "Celebron/Albright/Carrollton, Ohio, U.S.A." It was described as a beautiful dinnerware and the picture showed a sailing ship decal. (See picture of Albright semiporcelain plates.) In *Crockery and Glass Journal*, December 18, 1924, p. 153, the Albright China Company advertised three shapes, "Glendere," a fancy shape; "Highland," a plain shape; and "Pilgrim," an octagon shape. They advertised factories at Carrollton, Ohio, and Scio, Ohio, with sales offices in Chicago, Illinois.

Albright China Company.

ALLEGHENY CHINA COMPANY, in Warren, Pennsylvania, is a wholly owned subsidiary of Buffalo China, Inc., at present. It was founded in 1952 by a Mr. Chitchester who in turn sold to Buffalo China in 1962. The Allegheny operation was not of great potential until it was completely renovated by Buffalo China Company. At the present time, almost one-fouth of Buffalo China's output comes from the factory.

ALLIANCE CHINA COMPANY. See Cunningham and Picket for history and picture of a plate with a wheat pattern and broad yellow bands around the shoulder made by Homer Laughlin for this company. "Goldcrest" was the name of this pattern. Alliance China Company was a jobbing concern. Do not confuse them with Alliance Vitreous China Company. Both companies existed in Alliance, Ohio.

ALLIANCE VITREOUS CHINA COMPANY operated around the turn of the century in Alliance, Ohio, and ran until the beginning of the depression. They made a fine grade of hotel china and china bathroom accessories. Do not confuse them with the Alliance China Company. (See Alliance China Company.) Most of the stock of this company was sold to George H. Bowman Company of Cleveland in 1919.

ALLIED POTTERS at 490 Bay Street, San Francisco, were listed in the 1940s and early 1950s *California Manufacturers' Directory* as making tableware and decorative accessories.

ALPAUGH AND McGOWAN. See the Trenton Potteries Company.

AMERICANA ART CHINA COMPANY in Sebring, Ohio, started in 1949 to decorate only, but now they manufacture pottery as well as decorate it. They were listed in 1978 for china and glass novelties, earthenware, stemware, tumblers, mugs, ceramic and glass decorative and serving accessories. They use a paper label for a mark.

AMERICAN ART CHINA WORKS owned by Rittenhouse & Evans was established in 1891 in Trenton in the old Washington Pottery. Their specialty was a thin artware resembling Belleek which was called "American China," in plain, white, and decorated. They were short-lived and out of business before 1900 (when my New Jersey Directories began). (Barber, E.A., *Pottery and Porcelain of the United States*, p. 241.) See the American China Works of Trenton, New Jersey.

AMERICAN BELEEK COMPANY (spelled with one l) was listed in business in 1954 in the Trenton, New Jersey, directory, at 213 Bunting Avenue. In a fairly complete run of the directories, this was the only listing I found for them. In Time-Life's book, *Encyclopedia of Antiques*, Vol. B, p. 36, American Beleek Company is said to have made Belleek of lesser quality in the 1950s.

AMERICAN BISQUE COMPANY, Williamstown, West Virginia, was started in 1919 to supply the shortage of china dolls which originally came from Germany until World War I. American Bisque turned to making other products—cookie jars, salad bowls, serving dishes of various kinds, ashtrays, etc.—all have been made by this company in huge quantities.

In 1922, B.E. Allen who started Sterling China Company in Wellsville, started to invest in American Bisque, and in order to protect his interests, he finally purchased all of the stock. The company is still owned by the Allen family. Charles M. Allen, grandson of B.E. Allen, presently owns the controlling interest and is active in the operation. (Information furnished by A.N. Allen, son of B.E. and father of Charles M.)

American Bisque Company has had its share of hardships so typical of our American Glass factories and potteries. They are in the high water area of the Ohio river and in 1937, ten and one-half feet of water covered the factory floor. On July 28, 1945, the factory burned completely. After rebuilding, all products were made by Ram press only; these use no casting. They have two large kilns operating; one is one-hundred feet long, the other is thirty-five feet in diameter. A sixty-foot decorating kiln is also used. They employ around one-hundred people in the peak of the season. American Bisque uses two trademarks. "Sequoia Ware" is sold in gift shops, and "Berkeley" is sold in chain stores, etc. At one time their cookie jars bore a label which looked like a child's blocks with A. B. C. on them. Another mark this company used on cookie jars was "Design Patent/A.B. Co." (See Marks Section.)

AMERICAN CERAMIC PRODUCTS, INC. in Los Angeles, California, was started by Tom Hamilton and for a short time the company was very successful, but the operation faded and was liquidated according to Floyd McKee in *A Century of American Dinnerware*, p. 49. (Repeated letters brought only a very few *California Manufacturers' Directories*; I didn't get the exact beginning and ending dates for this company.) The company started sometime before 1940, because the book by Helen E. Stiles, *Pottery in the United States*, New York: E. P. Dutton, 1941, p. 149, speaks of a fire suffered by the American Ceramic Products, Inc. in April, 1940. At that time they moved to a new location. I found them listed in the 1951 and 1954 *California Manufacturers' Directory*, at 1825 Standford, Santa Monica, California, under the heading of Chinaware, with twelve sales outlets for their products. "Tiger Iris" was listed as a pattern made there in 1954. In 1955 they were no longer listed. Stiles (p. 150) states that bowls and vases were their principal products; they added a line of figurines, smoking equipment, and fruit bowls with a beautiful glaze of transparent crackle called "La Mirada" ware. Cecil Jones, an Englishman, was responsible for the fine glazes developed by this company. See Winfield Pottery for a possible connection.

AMERICAN CHINA COMPANY was organized in 1894, in Toronto, Ohio, went into receivership and was reorganized in 1897. The plant closed in 1910. In *The History of Toronto, Ohio, 1900 to 1914*, by Walter M. Kester, published 1969, is this description of the wares of this factory: "The ware was slightly off white made from models or molds gracefully designed, plates were jiggered in various sizes, cups were pressed in a plaster mold and finished in a cup machine." The *1902 Glass Factory Directory* listed American China Company as making semiporcelain dinner sets, toilet sets, and short sets of odd dishes, some decorated. They also made a good grade of white granite and the plant was referred to as the Toronto Whiteware factory by the local people. Pictured are three beautiful, decaled, semiporcelain plates made by American China Company. (See "American China Company," in The *Antique Trader*, July 4, 1979, p. 70, by this author, for more on American China Company.) One interesting fact that I just found about this company is why a company that made so many beautiful dishes lasted for such a short time and was closed at the peak of production. The town objected to the smell, dirt, etc. and caused the town council to take action to close it.

American China Company, Toronto, Ohio.

AMERICAN CHINA COMPANY, Trenton, New Jersey, was described in Barber's *Pottery and Porcelain of the United States*, p. 240, as making stone china by chromo-lithographic process which he defined as "applying vitrifiable decalcomania designs to the surface of the ware, either under or over the glaze." (Collectors cannot tell the age of a piece by whether the decal is under or over the glaze as some writers have indicated.) Barber is telling us the decals were fired on. See Warwick in the back of this book for pictures of actual decals. Since there was no mention of the name American China Company in Barber's *Marks of American Potters* or no listing in the *Trenton Directories* for this exact name, this author is assuming that Barber was referring to the American Crockery Company of Trenton (see American Crockery Company for history), because they used the mark American China.

AMERICAN CHINA CORPORATION, 1929 to about 1934, was made up of the following companies: Knowles, Taylor, Knowles of East Liverpool; National China Company, East Liverpool; Smith-Phillips China Company, East Liverpool; Carrollton Pottery Company, Carrollton, Ohio; The Pope-Gosser Company, Coshocton, Ohio; the E.H. Sebring Company, Sebring; The Sebring Manufacturing Company, Sebring; and Morgan Belleek China, Canton, Ohio. They failed due to the depression.

AMERICAN CHINA MANUFACTORY. See William Ellis Tucker.

AMERICA CHINA PRODUCTS COMPANY. See Ohio Pottery.

AMERICAN CROCKERY COMPANY in Trenton, New Jersey, was mentioned by Barber as in business in 1876 making white granite wares, and he shows marks they used in 1890. I had a very complete run of *New Jersey Industrial Directories*, and I didn't find American Crockery Company listed in 1900 or after that. American Crockery made stone china, bisque, and white granite goods. (Barber, p. 305.) In *China Classics*, by Larry Freeman, published by Century House, New York , 1959, p. 78, is an advertisement for this company showing "Yedda" dinnerware, a "Wheat" jug, "Cable" dinnerware and jug, a "Rose" jug, also chamber sets in "Bamboo," "Rustic," and "Bullion," etc. In "Pottery in the United States," from *Harper's New Monthly Magazine*, February 1881, and reprinted in *Hobbies*, February, 1949, p. 104, is this paragraph about "Yedda" dinnerware:

> This dinner service, called "Yedda" with its quaint forms and all over Daisy pattern painted in deep underglaze blue heightened by gold, is at once clear, dark, and brilliant, and wonderfully well defined, considering the intense heat which the color requires—a heat in which not less than half the pieces are destroyed.

AMERICAN FINE CHINA COMPANY started in business in May, 1977, in Warrington, Pennsylvania. They are a type of company which exists in the United States today, namely they manufacture dinnerware, kitchenware, and accessory pieces under private label for other people who have sales and marketing organizations. There is a great amount of china and ceramics sold in the United States under the names of companies which do not manufacture. Actually just when this arrangement began in our country is uncertain. Homer Laughlin made a lot of china for the various companies in Alliance, Ohio (see Cunningham and Pickett), dating from the 1930s. The decorating of blanks has been a long established practice in both glass and pottery. It is only one more step to have one company make a product and another company to sell it in our specialized society. Salem China Company is now a distributing organization. A sales organization which we can all understand that has its products made by different factories under its own name is Sears, for many years called Sears and Roebuck. "Harmony House" sold by Sears has consistently been a good grade of dishes, manufactured by a large number of companies with the Sears mark rather than the manufacturers' mark. For all practical purposes, the chinaware that Sears sells is theirs. The fact that someone else manufactures it for them is just a means to an end, in that the design is theirs and the style is theirs, and the type of quality is theirs.

AMERICAN HAVILAND. See Shenango China Company.

AMERICAN PORCELAIN MANUFACTURING COMPANY of Gloucester, New Jersey, was mostly considered a failure according to Barber's *Pottery and Porcelain of the United States*, p. 183. The factory lasted only a few years from 1854 to 1857 and then became *THE GLOUCESTER CHINA COMPANY* which closed around 1860. In 1893 when Barber wrote his book, he said that few pieces could be found at that time that could be positively identified, so think what the chances to find any of the ware would be now. The company made an all white china or porcelain of good quality, but Barber said the workmanship and glazing were inferior. However, this very same crudeness is what would make any piece of this precious porcelain dear to the heart of today's collectors. The Gloucester China Company's porcelain was semitransparent and very strong. "A.P.M. Co." is found impressed in some ware made by American Porelain Manufacturing Company.

AMERICAN PORCELAIN MANUFACTURING COMPANY of Greenpoint, New York, in 1854 until 1856, were successors to Charles Cartlidge who had operated from 1848-1854 making bone china. (Jervis, W.P. "A Dictionary of Pottery Terms," *The Pottery, Glass and Brass Salesman*, October 4, 1917, p. 13.)

AMERICAN POTTERY COMPANY was incorporated in the state of Ohio on March 21, 1942, in the name of Stoin-Lee Pottery Company with principal offices in Byesville, Ohio. In December, 1942, the name was changed to the American Pottery Company, and in October, 1944, the principal offices were moved to Marietta, Ohio. During 1944, J.B. Lenhart acquired a majority of the outstanding stock and acted as treasurer and general manager until he resigned in 1961. In 1961, R. J. Braden became the new owner of the land and buildings which he leased to the American Pottery Company. Braden also acted as chairman of the board of directors and treasurer. Then in 1962 until 1964, John F. Bonistall became president and general manager of the American Pottery Company of Marietta. In 1965, the American Pottery Company went out of business. Mr. Bonistall has a continuing history in the management of various potteries. He was president and general manager at Shawnee from 1955 until 1961 when Shawnee closed (see Shawnee for history). Bonistall was president of Terrace Ceramics which was the sales organization through which the products made at the American Pottery Company in Marietta were sold. He owned Terrace Ceramics. (See Terrace Ceramics.) In addition to that, John F. Bonistall was vice-president and general manager at the Stangl Pottery in Trenton, New Jersey, a position he has held since July, 1977. (Information furnished by J.F. Bonistall for all the above potteries mentioned.) American Pottery Company of Marietta made a line of ware which was sold through Terrace Ceramics.

AMERICAN POTTERY COMPANY of Peoria, Illinois. See Peoria Pottery for history.

AMERICAN POTTERY COMPANY of Jersey City. See Jersey City Pottery for history.

AMERICAN POTTERY WORKS was purchased in East Liverpool, Ohio, in 1887 by the Sebring brothers. There were six brothers, who by working very hard, acquired enough money to purchase a one-kiln pottery which employed ten men in East Liverpool. Their business prospered, and by the 1893 and 1894 *Factory Inspection Reports*, they were employing close to one-hundred people. In these reports, the name was simply SEBRING POTTERY at East Second Street in East Liverpool, making white and decorated ware. By the 1902 *Factory Inspection Report*, the Sebring Pottery had been moved to the town of Sebring which the brothers founded around 1889 or 1890. George, Jr. went to buy land for the town of Sebring as early as 1888, for $1.25 per acre. The sole purpose for founding Sebring was to make a pottery manufacturing town. A pottery was one of the first buildings built, then followed a

American Pottery Works, Sebring, Ohio.

succession of potteries. By the end of two years the town of Sebring was pretty well established. See French China, French Saxon China, Limoges China Company, Oliver China, Sebring China, Sebring Manufacturing Company, Saxon China, Royal China, for more on various Sebring, Ohio, potteries. Pictured is a bowl made in East Liverpool by the Sebrings with the Sebring Brothers' mark. Also pictured is an attractive leaf-shaped dish with some hand trim in gold and old-fashioned decals typical of the time. The dish is marked "Stone China" but it is an inferior grade of soft semiporcelain. According to Wilbur Stout in *Clay Industry in Ohio*, p. 72, the factory made some bone china, but judging from the texture of these two pieces, this factory didn't seem to have the skill or technique.

ANCHOR HOCKING CORPORATION Lancaster, Ohio, has a long, well-known history in the field of glassmaking, but their interests in pottery making is less well known. Anchor Cap Corporation was incorporated September 13, 1928, and as of December 31, 1937, was consolidated with Hocking Glass Company which had already merged with General Glass and Standard Glass and the name became Anchor Hocking Glass Corporation. From that time on company after company was consolidated, controlled, merged, or was formed by or with Anchor Hocking. Included were American Metal Cap of Brooklyn; Salem Glass Works, Salem, New Jersey; Gas Transport, Inc., Ohio; Maywood Glass Company, Los Angeles; Carr-Lowrey of Baltimore, Maryland; Glass Crafters, Inc., Baltimore; Tropical Glass and Box Company, Zanesville Mould Company, Zanesville, Ohio; Anchor Hocking Inter America, Ltd. (to purchase distributorship in Puerto Rico); Plastics, Inc., St. Paul; Lindner Industries, Netherlands. Moldcraft, Inc., was acquired, and Ravenscroft, Ltd. was a formed company. This is a very sketchy outline of the formation of the present corporation and is mentioned here only to give an indication of the complexity of the corporation that has also become a part of the pottery industry in America.

In March, 1973, Anchor Hocking Corporation acquired Taylor, Smith, and Taylor of Chester, West Virginia, a manufacturer of stoneware and ceramic dinnerware. (See Taylor, Smith, and Taylor.) Then in 1975 the Taylor, Smith, and Taylor company was dissolved and has since been operated as a division of Anchor Hocking Corporaton. The name Taylor, Smith, and Taylor is now phased out.

ANCHOR POTTERY of Trenton, New Jersey, was founded in 1893. In the *1902 Glass Factory Directory* they were listed as making dinner sets and toilet sets. They were listed in the *Trenton City Directories* until 1927 as Anchor Pottery, but they were purchased by Fulper Pottery in 1926. Pictured is a saucer with an intricate design in a greenish blue color marked with an Anchor Pottery mark which is shown in Barber's book. In the Stangl Company booklet is the following statement regarding Anchor Pottery: "In 1926 the company (Fulper) had also taken over the Anchor Pottery Company, Trenton, New Jersey, which had been owned by the Grand Union Tea Company and was used to manufacture premiums that Grand Union gave away in its house-to-house sales program." (Barber, *Pottery and Porcelain of the United States*, p. 161, and the *1902 Glass Factory Directory* listing: *Stangl, A Portrait in Progress*, privately printed by Stangle Pottery Company 1965.)

Anchor Pottery.

ANGELUS POTTERIES at 2300 East 52nd Street, Los Angeles, California, were listed in the *1924 California Manufacturers' Directory* as making dinner and hotel ware.

ARITA TABLETOP COMPANY was founded in Anaheim, California, in 1976, as a wholly owned subsidiary of International Air Services of Burlingame, California. They are presently a fast-growing dinnerware firm supplying many fine stores in the United States. Arita Tabletop used one mark as shown. The company's products include fine porcelain and an excellent grade of stoneware, beautifully decorated. Arita Tabletop Company's "Country Kitchen" stoneware includes, "Blue Gingham,"

"Buttermilk," "Nutmeg," and "Peach Cobler." Arita Tabletop's "Arabesque" stoneware includes dinnerware patterns "Brocade," "Chantilly," and "Desert Snow." The Arita "Brushstrokes Stoneware" includes "Butter Blossom," "Ebb Tide," "Forest Glade," "Lavender Blue," "Petite Point," "Pirouette," "Poppies Please," and "Windstraws." Arita "Dimension" stoneware includes "Horizons," "Variations," "Symmetry Blue," "Symmetry Brown," and "Symmetry Gray." Arita "Syncopation" which is a line of fine porcelain includes "Caprice," "Flower Shower," "Honeycomb," "Irish Fern," "Waterfalls," and "Windmills." Arita "Imari," another line of fine porcelain, includes "Imari Fan," "Imari Garden," and "Imari Royal." (Information furnished by company.)

ARSENAL POTTERY was referred to by Barber as the Arsenal Pottery of the Mayer Pottery Manufacturing Company, with Joseph S. Mayer as president, making decorated porcelain underglaze and Majolica in 1893 in Trenton, New Jersey. Jervis said the Trenton, New Jersey, Arsenal Pottery was not in business in 1917. The pottery had Toby pitchers and jugs at the Chicago Fair. (Barber, *Pottery and Porcelain of the U.S.*, p. 241, and Jervis, "A Dictionary of Pottery Terms" in the *The Pottery, Glass and Brass Salesman*, October 11, 1917, p. 11.)

ASTBURY AND MADDOCK. See Thomas Maddock and Sons for history.

ATHISON POTTERY COMPANY. See Chittenango Pottery Company.

ATLAS CHINA COMPANY, Niles, Ohio. See Bradshaw China Company for history.

ATLAS CHINA COMPANY listed at Fifth Avenue in New York City in a 1940 directory used the mark found on the back of the plate pictured. Also see Marks Section. Do not confuse this retailer with the Atlas China Company in Niles or the Atlas-Globe China Company in Cambridge. This plate could have been made almost anyplace and marked by the retailer with his mark.

ATLAS-GLOBE CHINA COMPANY. See Various Cambridge Potteries listing for history. Also see Bradshaw China Company.

AVALON CHINA. See Chesapeake Pottery.

BAGLEY AND ROBERTS began business in Zanesville, Ohio, in 1893 and were listed as late as 1906. Stout said they quit around 1905 and were makers of cooking utensils from local clays for many years. He stated that this firm had a reputation for quality and good workmanship. (Stout, Wilbur, *History of the Clay Industry in Ohio*, p. 61.)

JOHN BAHL was a known and respected name in the pottery industry in East Liverpool, Ohio, for many years. While he worked for Edwin M. Knowles as a decorator, he designed the original "Bluebird" calendar plate when he was just twenty-one years old. Finally, in the years 1940 and 1941, John Bahl, with his son

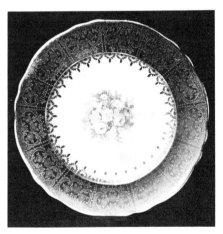

Atlas China Company, New York City.

Bahl Potteries, Inc.

27

Jack, was operating a pottery of his own, **BAHL POTTERIES, INC.**, when John died suddenly of a heart attack at the age of fifty-two. Jack soon left the business to work for Cronin China Company, and the pottery-collecting world was left with a very limited supply of the Bahl pottery. John patterned his ware after the old yellowware he had seen in his youth in East Liverpool. He made his ware from the yellow local clay and and painted some of the pieces. Pictured is a saucedish marked "Nova Rose, Sandela Ware" which is hand painted on yellowware. The plate is marked just "Sandela Ware" with the Bahl Pottery mark. (See the Marks Section.)

BAILEY WALKER CHINA COMPANY. See Walker China Company in marks and history section.

BARBERTON POTTERY was located in Barberton, Ohio, from 1901 to 1905. In 1905 they employed one-hundred ninety-nine people to make semiporcelain. They made a full line of dinner and hotel ware, both plain and decorated. Blair states that at one time they employed three hundred people, also that they made porcelain as well as the semiporcelain found listed in the factory report.

BAUER POTTERY operated in Los Angeles from before 1914 until a strike closed the plant in the 1950s. There has been differing opinion as to location and dates on this pottery. In the 1948 and 1952 *California Manufacturers' Register*, the J.A. Bauer Pottery was listed at 415 West Avenue, Los Angeles. Bauer was not listed in the 1955 or 1957 *Registers* and therefore went out of business some time in the 1950s. Oftentimes it is much easier to find the products and to know what a company made than it is to establish a few basic facts about its operation. This seems to be the case with Bauer, because the building reportedly has been torn down. John Andrew Bauer made jugs in Paducah, Kentucky, before going to Los Angeles where, according to Barbara Hayes, he was in business on Avenue 33 making redware and flower containers. J.A. Bauer died in 1923, but the plant continued to operate. By 1930, under the management of W.E. Bockmon, the Batchelder Tile Company was acquired to become the second plant of the Bauer Pottery. The Ring pattern was the first dinnerware made in 1932 by a casting process. Bauer Pottery was also making hand thrown items at this time. Not until the late 1940s did Bauer Pottery turn solely to dinnerware. A 1940 mark for Bauer crockery was "Bockmon's Quality Pottery" named for W.E. Bockmon the manager. Some lines in the 1950s were "Contempo" and "Al Fresco Ware" and were marked "Brusche" for Herb Brusche who was the husband of Bauer's granddaughter. Herb Brusche worked at the pottery. In the 1951 *California Manufacturers' Register*, a Brusche Ceramics was listed at 4960 South Workman Mill Road, Whittier, California, making tableware and dinnerware. My next *Register* was 1955 and Brusche Ceramics were no longer listed. According to Jim Bloesser, writer for *Depression Glass Daze*, the Ring pattern was very similar to Homer Laughlin's "Fiesta." He lists the colors for the Ring pattern as orange, yellow, light green, cobalt blue, maroon, blue gray, pink, black, ivory, and gray. (Information from the *California Manufacturer's Registers*; Hayes, Barbara, *Bauer— The California Pottery Rainbow*, Venice, California; Salem Witch Antiques, 1975; Bloesser, Jim, " The Mysterious Bauer," *Depression Glass Daze*, November, 1977, p. 43.)

J. H. BAUM operated from 1880 (Ramsay) or from 1888 (Stout) until 1895 (Ramsay) or to 1897 (Barber) or to 1898 (Stout). At least the old writers agree Baum existed in Wellsville, Ohio, making white granite and cream-colored ware. I couldn't resist this because we research writers are supposed to get a completely factual account from conflicting data.

A.M. BECK potter. See Crown Pottery, Evansville, Indiana.

R.K. BECK was a wildlife painter whose name appears on plates with scenes he has created. The scenes were applied by decal in faithful reproduction of his paintings.

BEDFORD CHINA COMPANY. See Walker China Company.

L.B. BEERBOWER AND COMPANY had operated the old pottery works in Elizabeth, New Jersey, for several years by the time Barber published *Marks of American Potters* in 1904. This pottery was started in 1816 to make stoneware. A Mr. Pruden started the manufacture of yellowware and Rockingham at the pottery. Beerbower and Company made ironstone china, semigranite, cream-colored ware and print decorated ware here. From 1877 to 1879 Beerbower and Griffin had operated in the Phoenix Pottery. See Phoenix Pottery, Phoenixville, Pennsylvania. W.P. Jervis in "World's Pottery Marks," *China, Glass and Brass Salesman*, December 16, 1917, said that L.B. Beerbower closed prior to 1902.

BEERBOWER AND GRIFFIN. See Phoenixville Pottery for history.

THE BELL POTTERY COMPANY started in Findlay, Ohio, in 1888 or early 1889, to make vitreous tableware. The company moved to Columbus, Ohio, around 1903 to make hotel ware and went bankrupt in 1906. The company was listed in the directory as making semiporcelain dinner sets, toilet sets, and short sets of odd dishes. Barber lists the products for this company as vitreous translucent china and hotel ware. *The Complete Directory of Glass Factories and Potteries* for 1902-1903, listed the same production for Findlay and Columbus, except some of the ware was decorated in the Findlay listing. Barber shows three marks. The building in Findlay later housed the U.S. Electrical Company which made porcelain insulators. The building in Columbus was sold to the Sanitary Earthenware Company in 1911 after standing idle for a while. (Stout, W., *History of Clay Industry in Ohio*, pp. 86, 88. Also a letter from Don E. Smith, who researched the Findlay area and wrote the book, *Findlay Pattern Glass.)*

VARIOUS BENNETT POTTERIES. The first Bennett, whose name was James, began in the pottery business in this country by starting the first pottery that was in East Liverpool, Ohio, in 1839. From 1839 to 1841, he operated alone. Then from 1841 to 1844 he was joined by his brothers, Daniel, Edwin, and William. In 1844, Edwin, Daniel, and James moved to Birmingham, Pennsylvania, where they started a small pottery. In 1846, Edwin went on to Baltimore, Maryland, where he operated the E. Bennett Chinaware Factory until 1848. In 1848, William left Birmingham to join Edwin in Baltimore, and the name became E. & W. Bennett until 1856. Meanwhile, back in Pittsburgh James had retired, and Daniel carried on alone until 1849. From 1856 to 1890 the name of the factory was the Edwin Bennett Pottery and from 1890 to 1936 the title was Edwin Bennett Pottery Company. The Bennett products evolved through the various types familiar to this country. From stoneware, yellowware, Rockingham, and majolica in the earliest years, to cream-colored ware, stone china, or granite earthenware in the late 1800s, to Parian, some fine china and artware, before they started back down the scale to plain, semiporcelain and common china prior to closing their doors in 1936. Bennett's products were beautiful and outstanding in the early years. He even made a Belleek (fine, thin china) and a Rebekah-at-the-Well Rockingham teapot. Thelma Shull in "American Scenes for the China Collector" in *Hobbies*, June, 1942, p. 66, said that Bennett made tableware from transfer prints as the medium for picturing historical scenes. Also see "Bennett Pottery," staff written, in *Spinning Wheel*, November, 1958, p. 22.

BENNINGHOF, UHL, AND COMPANY. See Crown Pottery, Evansville, Indiana, for history.

BERGSTROM AND FRENCH. See La Solana Potteries, Inc.

BLACK AND BEACH POTTERY COMPANY. See New Milford Pottery Company.

BLOOR, OTT & BOOTH. See the Etruria Pottery for history.

WILLIAM BLOOR. The history of William Bloor is an intricate part of the pottery industries' history in East Liverpool, Ohio. The following excerpt is from "It All Started in East Liverpool" by W. A. Betz, *Crockery and Glass Journal*, April, 1955, and it gives such a vivid picture of the pottery industry in 1850 that is included here as written:

> Potting in 1850 was a rugged operation; all work was done by hand and "throwing" on a potter's wheel was the only method of forming the ware. The "boss" participated in all processes, from mining the clay to packing the finished ware. He would then market it in wagons around the countryside or on trading boats down on the Ohio. An attempt would be made to dispose of the ware for cash but a scarcity of this medium of exchange would not discourage him from exchanging his wares for anything which he felt he could dispose of back home. Upon returning from a successful trip the "help" would be paid off and work would begin on another kiln of ware. This then was the beginning, the start of the uphill battle of another American industry. Progress did not come easily; it was trial and error and then try again. Everything was crude, from the clay pits to the marketing methods. But the man of pottery had ideas and dreams just as have other men in other walks of life.
>
> Soon they began dreaming of making white ware. These dreams first came true when William Bloor, in partnership with William Brunt, Jr., purchased the old Woodward, Blakely & Co. plant in 1859 and made the first white ware in East Liverpool the following year. It was an exceedingly white Parian Ware, quite translucent and thoroughly vitrified. Much of it was unglazed on the outside and had only a thin covering of glaze on the inside; and much of it was decorated with artistic designs which were painted by hand. The color scheme most used was a light blue background with the design in relief in clear white.
>
> Mr. Bloor made staple goods, hotel ware and such novelties as vases, mugs, fancy dishes, curtain knobs, fancy butter dishes and Parian busts of noted statesmen.
>
> Practically everything made in this plant was by the "casting" method; liquid clay (or "slip") was poured into two-part plaster molds. After awhile, when the mold had absorbed some of the water in the slip, causing the slip to adhere to sides of the mold, the excess slip was poured off. What remained was allowed to dry further. Then the mold was opened and the ware removed for further decorating, glazing and firing. Mr. Bloor was about 50 years ahead of the revival of this process which is still being used today.

BOCKMAN, W.E. See Bauer Pottery.

H.R. BODINE in Zanesville, Ohio, made pottery cookware from 1878 until around 1900. The following quote is from W. Stout's *Clay Industry in Ohio*, p. 60:

> G.H. Bodine & Co. are manufacturers and sole controllers of Bodine's patent cooking utensils. Especially worthy of notice are those evidences of skill which have contributed appliances for home utilities among which are the peculiar devices invented and patented by H.R. Bodine, which since his death in 1883 have been entirely controlled by the present firm, G.H. Bodine & Co. This business had its inception in 1878 by H.R. Bodine, soon after which letters patent were secured on various utensils for culinary use, which have had such a high degree of excellence as to merit general approval and to secure large sales in various parts of the country. Among the articles manufactured and controlled by this company are Bodine's patent cooking crocks, coffee pots, bean pots, griddles, milk boilers, etc., which are finely finished and far superior to iron utensils. Such business was conducted by this firm until about 1900.

BONNIN AND MORRIS. The china works of Gousse Bonnin and Anthony Morris operated only from 1769 to 1772 or 1773 in Philadelphia. They made dinner services, dessert services, tea services and small table accessories. The shapes were patterned after the English china of the time and the patterns were those used by Bow, Chelsea, and Worcester. They had great financial difficulty, sold the property and Bonnin went back to England. Barber gave their only known mark as a "P", and he wasn't certain about what it should stand for. (Eberlein, Harold and Ramsdell, Roger, *The Practical Book of Chinaware*, p. 294.) See the listing in the introduction for other very early makers of whiteware.

BOULTER, CHARLES J. Worked for Abraham Miller. See W.E. Tucker.

GEORGE H. BOWMAN COMPANY. See Cleveland China Company for history. See George H. Bowman for marks.

BRADSHAW CHINA COMPANY started in 1901 (date from Grace Allison) in Niles, Ohio, became *TRITT CHINA COMPANY* in 1912 until 1922 when it became the *ATLAS CHINA COMPANY* until 1925. In 1925 a fire destroyed most of the plant. The remainder of the plant was moved to Cambridge and consolidated with the Globe China Company and called the *ATLAS-GLOBE CHINA COMPANY*. Both the Globe and the Atlas were owned by a man named O. C. Ahrendts at the time of consolidation. (See Oxford Pottery at Cambridge for history of the Globe Pottery.)

This series of potteries made semiporcelain dinnerware, and Bradshaw China made ironstone or granite of a superior quality, with decorations of the decalcomania style (Barber). Tritt China made some porcelain. In 1934, Atlas-Globe was reorganized in Cambridge to become Universal Potteries which operated in Cambridge making semiporcelain dinnerware and serving pieces until 1956, when the plant was changed over to make floor and wall tile, at which time that plant was called the *OXFORD TILE COMPANY DIVISION OF UNIVERSAL POTTERIES.* The name became just the *OXFORD TILE COMPANY* around 1960 and was known by that name until its closing in March, 1976.

BREWER, HART, POTTERY COMPANY. See Trenton Pottery Company for history in Trenton. See also Brewer Pottery Company, Tiffin, Ohio.

BREWER POTTERY COMPANY was built in Tiffin, Ohio, in 1899, when the captalists connected with the Trenton Pottery Company decided to build a plant there because of the natural gas that was available. The plant was built to make chinaware and earthenware products, but by 1892 the production had turned solely to sanitary ware. In May, 1899, the building was sold to the Great Western Pottery Company which also made plumbers' earthenware. (Stout, Wilbur, *History of the Clay Industry in Ohio*, p. 87.)

BRIGHTON POTTERY in Cincinnati, Ohio, was started by William Bromley around 1843 and operated until 1860. Bromley became associated with a man named Bailey, according to Ramsay, in 1857 until 1860. After 1860 until around 1870, Bromley was joined by his son, as *BROMLEY AND SON.* Stoneware, yellowware and Rockingham were made by the Bromleys. On p. 119, of *American Country Antiques* by Katherine McClinton is described a six-paneled pitcher with a floral design marked "W. Bromley and Co. Brighton Pottery, Cin., Ohio."

BRIGHTON POTTERY of Zanesville, Ohio, was started around 1905. Brighton Pottery was listed in the *1905 Factory Inspection Report* for the state of Ohio as making clay cooking ware, which doesn't begin to express the beauty of the little spattered teapot pictured which is marked "Brighton Pottery Company, Zanesville, Ohio," in a circle. This company apparently operated for only a couple of years, according to the Purviances. (See Bibliography.)

Brighton Pottery.

B.J. BROCK COMPANY was listed at 4513 W. 153rd Street, Lawndale, California, in the 1950s and was apparently gone by 1955. At the same address in the 1951 and 1948 *California Manufacturers' Directory* was the Southern California Pottery Company with no mention of B.J. Brock Company at that time. Whether there was a connection between the two companies was not established. Brock may have purchased Southern California Pottery, or simply have started in the same building at a later date. (Southern California Ceramic Company in Santa Monica, California, was a separate company in the late 1940s and early 1950s.) Some pattern names found listed for Brock were "Horizon Pattern," "Harvest," "Country Lane," and "Country Meadow." Either of the last two names would have been appropriate for the plate pictured, but it is unidentified as to pattern names. Also see Southern California Pottery for patterns.

BROCKMAN POTTERY COMPANY, Cincinnati, Ohio, was listed in the *1902 Glass Factory Directory* as making white granite and some porcelain dinner sets, toilet sets, and short sets of odd dishes, decorated. This pottery had its origin in 1854 when Brewer and Tempest operated as partners until 1856, then Tunis Brewer operated alone until 1859. Tempest became a part of Tempest, Brockman and Company from 1862 until 1881. From 1881 to 1888, the pottery was owned by Tempest, Brockman and Sampson. From 1888 to 1912, the pottery was listed as the C.E. Brockman Company. Products made here, besides those already listed, were cream-colored ware and ironstone.

B.J. Brock Company.

BROWN'S POTTERY in Arden, North Carolina, started in 1924 and are operating at present. They make flameproof, earthen cooking ware, dishes, and all types of kitchen pottery as well as garden pottery and artware, many made to custom order. All pieces are marked "Brown's Pottery/Arden, N.C./Handmade." Not everything is handmade, but the handmade pieces are so marked. The history of the Brown's Pottery goes back for seven generations of Browns to John Henry Brown who came from England. His son was Bolden, born in South Carolina, who worked with a wheel run by foot power and a horse-drawn clay mill. His mixture for glaze was just sand and ash. Thomas O. Brown, the son of Bolden, moved to Georgia where he applied salt and glass glazes to improve the pottery. Another one of Bolden's sons, James, added chemicals which brought color to the glaze. The fifth generation of Browns was represented in the pottery business by Davis P. Brown the son of James, who left Atlanta and started the pottery in Arden, North Carolina, around 1924, where the business is still located. From that time on methods were constantly improved with better kilns, wheels, and clays. Electric power brought a great difference and the wares were then shipped abroad. Davis is said to have made the largest handmade vase in the world at six feet, two inches tall and nine feet, eight inches around. Son of Davis, Louis, was the sixth generation of Browns who owned and operated the pottery from 1967 to 1976, when his sons Charlie and Robert became the owner-operators. These seventh generation Browns were asked by the Smithsonian Institute to represent the United States in the Festival of American Folklife held at the Exposition in Montreal in 1971. One of their current products is a French style earthenware (1978).

BRUNT POTTERY COMPANY, East Liverpool, Ohio. The Brunt family was so interwoven with the pottery industry that their name became involved in more than six potteries making a variety of wares from Rockingham to porcelain insulators spanning a period from 1858 to 1903. (See, Lehner, Lois, *Ohio Pottery and Glass, Marks and Manufacturers*, p. 42, for a detailed history of this family's associations.) For the purposes of this book we are concerned with the granite and porcelain dinnerware made by the Brunts. **WILLIAM BRUNT, SON, AND COMPANY** was in business from 1879 to after 1902 in East Liverpool where they made ironstone with the various marks shown. This same company was listed as just **WILLIAM BRUNT POTTERY COMPANY** in the *1902-1903 Complete Directory* making white granite dinner sets, toilet sets, short sets of odd dishes, and hotel ware. Some wares were decorated. By 1926 the pottery building was one of the buildings used by Hall China Company. Also see Dresden Pottery, East Liverpool, Ohio. A semiporcelain plate made by the Brunt Pottery Company, which has the "Alpine China" mark may be seen in the picture with the Dresden Pottery history. See Dresden Pottery, East Liverpool, Ohio.

BRUSCHE CERAMICS were listed in 1951 at 4960 South Workman Mill Road, Whittier, California, as making tableware and dinnerware in the *California Manufacturers' Directory*. Barbara Hayes, author of the book, *Bauer—The California Pottery Rainbow*, said by letter that Herb Brusche, who was the husband of Bauer's granddaughter, made his own line at the Bauer plant. Some of it was marked "Brusche" and some "Brusche Bauer." The only piece of this I have seen is in a rather heavy in weight saucer nicely glazed in gray, marked "Brusche" and "Made in U.S.A."

BRUSH POTTERY has been operating in Roseville since 1925. They are one of the very few companies that have kept information and catalogs of their products. They have a listing of catalogs on file in the Brush Pottery office for various years between 1899 to 1978. Numbers are missing in the 1930s and 1940s but they have much more material documented than a majority of the potteries. Also E. Lucille Barnett who grew up with the pottery has been very generous with information for writers.

Brush Pottery has not made a great number of table items but the ones they did make are very nice. The "Cherry Line" of accessories including the piece shown is just beautiful with a soft glaze finish and hand-painted recessed design. The cream and sugar (1957) pictured has a very hard, shiny glaze and is marked only U.S.A. Many potteries marked some ware only with U.S.A. at various times; don't try to identify by this. Brush made between forty and fifty designs in cookie jars. Incidentally, this is the second Brush Pottery; the first was in Zanesville, Ohio, 1907 until it burned to the ground in 1908. The first Brush Pottery made mostly artware. (See Brush-McCoy Company, also.)

Brush Pottery, Roseville, Ohio.

BRUSH-McCOY POTTERY operated in Roseville from 1911 to 1925. They also had a plant in Zanesville at that time. According to Lucille Barnett, the artware was made in Zanesville and other products were made in Roseville. Just recently the Huxfords, Sharon and Bob, photographed the Brush-McCoy catalogs and released them in book form. (See Bibliography.) All types of kitchenware items are shown; crocks, mixing bowls, pitchers, teapots, butter crocks, a ceramic rolling pin, "Nurock" ware similar to old English Rockingham, and a "Corn" line in pitchers, mugs, and various covered jars. The J.W. McCoy plant also made a corn line.

THE BUFFALO POTTERY COMPANY was organized in 1901 in Buffalo, New York, and the first kiln was fired in 1903. The pottery was built to supply the pottery needs of the Larkin Soap Company. Production was completely molded, either by jiggering or casting, and was decorated both underglaze or overglaze. (See Evans, Paul, *Art Pottery in the United States*, pp. 34-37.) According to Evans the company made its own underglaze colors and used decalcomania as well as hand decorating. Until around 1916 the company made semivitreous ware, and that year they changed to vitrified china. In the *1902-1903 Complete Directory*, Buffalo Pottery was listed as manufacturers of semiporcelain dinner sets and toilet sets. The Buffalo China mark was first used in 1915 but the name of the pottery was not officially changed to Buffalo China Company until 1956. Buffalo China now makes only hotel and institutional type of ware, beautifully decorated. The following list of dinnerware patterns includes some made as late as 1922 by the company as listed in the excellent book, *The Book of Buffalo Pottery*, by Seymour and Violet Altman published by Crown Publishers, New York, in 1969, pp. 157-158. It is reprinted with the authors' and publisher's permission. (This book is a "must" for all pottery collectors, dinnerware collectors included.)

Buffalo Pottery Company. **Front row:** *children's plate, "Vassar" plate, "Lamare" platter.* **Back row:** colorful decaled and hand-painted bowl.

Given below are the names of the dinnerware patterns, the years in which they were offered in the catalogs, and details about them taken from the catalog descriptions. It is not known whether any of this ware was offered through other distribution outlets of the pottery.

Lamare, 1904 through 1908:
  Sprays of poppies, choice of dove, dark blue, green, or brown. Embossed work in pure gold.
Modjeska, 1904 through 1909:
  Pink roses or blue forget-me-nots. Pure gold trim.
Wild Poppy, 1905 through 1908:
  Borders of wild poppies in olive green.
Bonrea (named for Louis Bown and William Rea), 1905 through 1916:
  Ornate scroll border in myrtle green with pure gold trim.
Old Blue Willow Ware, 1905 through 1917.
Color Band, 1909 through 1910:
  Plain with wide color band and two pure gold lines bordering each piece. Comes in apple green, turquoise, or maroon.
Miana, 1909 through 1910:
  Border pattern of Persian design in Oriental colors, dark and light blue and green predominating.
Kenmore, 1909 through 1911:
  Art Nouveau and floral border in green decor, illuminated in gold and gold trim.
Buffalo, 1909 through 1914:
  Sprays of roses and altheas in natural colors. Full gold trim.
Maple Leaf, 1909 through 1914:
  Small border of green maple leaves and pink flowers with full gold trim.
Princess, 1909 through 1914:
  Green floral border with full gold trim.
Seneca, 1909 through 1914:
  Border of flowers. Choice of green or dark blue. Gold handles and embossed work.
Tea Rose, 1909 through 1914:
  Small border of pink roses and green leaves with full gold trim.
Gold Band, 1909 through 1915:
  Plain white with a wide pure gold band.
Forget-Me-Not, 1909 through 1917:
  Forget-me-nots in border pattern with full gold trim.
Florence Rose, 1910:
  Double border of pink roses and green leaves with edges and embossed work in gold.
Gold Lace Border, 1911 through 1914:
  Gold border in a lace design. Edges and embossed work in gold.
Pluto, 1911 through 1916:
  Wide border of pink roses and green leaves, in natural colors. Edges and embossed work in pure gold.
Queen, 1911 through 1917:
  Narrow border of pink roses and green leaves in natural colors, edges and embossing in gold.
Minerva, 1913 through 1916:
  Sprays of pink roses and spring beauties. Full gold trim.
Vienna, 1915:
  Designs in dark blue underglaze. Full gold trim.

34

Vassar, 1915 through 1916:
 Designs in conventional dark green underglaze.
Empress, 1915 through 1917:
 Green conventional border. Full gold trim.
Fern Rose, 1915 through 1917:
 Border design of small pink roses and green leaves with full gold trim.
Wild Rose, 1915 through 1917:
 Wild roses and spring flowers in natural colors with gold trim.
Gold Line, 1916 through 1917:
 Plain white, decorated with two narrow gold lines.
Rosebank, 1917:
 Wide border of pink roses and green leaves in natural colors. Edges traced in gold.
Spray Decor Tea Set, 1919 through 1920:
 Vitreous china. Sprays of pink roses. Very realistic and can hardly be told from
 hand-painting.
Blue Bird Tea Set, 1919 through 1922:
 Vitreous china. Bluebird decor in full natural colors.
Bungalow, 1920 through 1921:
 Vitreous china. Fine latticework alternated with a fine floral decoration in red, green, or
 yellow. Blended and dotted beneath with little flowers. Full gold trim.
Dresden, 1920 through 1921:
 Vitreous china. Delicate pink roses and blue flowers intertwined and arranged in panels on
 a dainty ivory background. Edges and handles traced in coin gold.
Glendale, 1920 through 1921:
 Vitreous china. Comes in green, golden brown, turquoise blue. An unusual festoon design
 surrounding pink roses. Edges and handles traced in coin gold.
Pink Rose, 1920 through 1922:
 Vitreous china. Sprays of pink roses almost like hand-painting. Gold border.
Beverly, 1921:
 Vitreous china. Conventional border interspersed with pink roses and green leaves. Pure
 coin gold handles.
Coin Gold Band, 1921:
 Vitreous china. Single band of coin gold 3/16th inch wide. Pure gold handles.

There are many of these patterns pictured in *The Book of Buffalo Pottery* by the
Altmans. They also picture, and list with dates, many serving pieces including a
chocolate pot, salad or fruit bowls, cake plates, oatmeal sets, cracker jars, fruit sets,
teapots, butter tubs, and much more that was used as tableware. Annise Heaivilin
who has made a study of Tea Leaf pattern has a piece of Vassar (so marked) and
verified by the company as Buffalo China Tea Leaf in the Vassar shape. A Buffalo
pottery item pictured is a child's dish made around 1913 to 1918, according to the
Altmans, p. 164. The platter pictured is marked "Lamare" and was made between
1904 and 1908 according to the Altmans' list. The plate in the picture is marked
"Vassar." The large bowl with roses is very colorful, almost to the place of being
gaudy.

According to an article in *China, Glass, and Lamps* entitled "American Pottery
Trade Marks," September 3, 1923, p. 15, Buffalo Pottery, in 1905, produced the first
underglazed blue willow ware ever made in America. The article went on to say that
demand for the product increased so steadily that another plant was built in 1914
adjoining the original pottery, with each plant operating independently. In 1923
both plants were producing hotel and dinnerware with no semiporcelain having been
made since 1917. In 1923, Buffalo Pottery had fourteen general kilns and eight
decorating kilns occupying eight acres of ground. The article mentions "Deldare," an
original production with olive green body and hand decorations after old English
subjects. In *Pottery Glass and Brass Salesman*, "The Man Who Saw," May 31, 1917,
p. 16, is an interesting item for the collectors of "Bluebird" china.

 Arlington H. Ledden, 16 West Twenty-third Street, has just received from the Buffalo
 Pottery Company a fetching addition to his popular baby plate line. The decoration is a flock
 of bluebirds of various sizes in flight. The decoration is also brought out on butter tubs, jugs,
 covered jugs and other specialties, making altogether a quite interesting collection of items for
 spring trade.

W.C. BUNTING COMPANY in Wellsville, Ohio, from 1946 to present did not manufacture dishes; they are decorators only, but their mark is found very often on a variety of ware with no other mark added for the maker. Bunting buys blanks for decoration from Taylor, Smith, and Taylor, Homer Laughlin China, Sterling China, and Hall China, according to a letter from the Bunting Company. Any piece found with a Bunting mark can be dated after 1946.

BURFORD BROTHERS POTTERY was in business in East Liverpool, Ohio, from 1879 until after 1906. They made a variety of products including semivitreous porcelain ware, which was plain white (as shown in the picture), also decorated. They also made cream-colored ware, hotel ware, and granite or ironstone. In 1902, they were listed as making semiporcelain dinner sets, toilet sets, short sets of odd dishes, hotel ware, plain and decorated. *(Complete Directory of the Glass Factories and Potteries of the United States and Canada for 1902 and 1903*, published by Commoner Publishing Company, Pittsburg, Pennsylvania.)

BURGESS AND CAMPBELL. See International Pottery, Trenton.

BURLEY AND WINTER POTTERY COMPANY operated in Crooksville, Ohio, from 1872 to 1932. They have now become well-known for their "Heart Brand" stoneware which included kitchen accessories such as bowls, pitchers, mugs, etc. There were actually more garden items in the kitchenware line, but the kitchenware makes very nice collectibles. See the picture of the "Heart Brand" mug.

Burley and Winter Pottery Company.

BURROUGHS AND MOUNTFORD COMPANY were in business only a few years in Trenton, New Jersey, from 1879 to 1882 (Ramsay). They produced artware according to Ramsay, but Barber says they also produced a large line of table and toilet wares. They made various grades of white granite and cream-colored wares, some with printed decorations. A variety of marks were shown in Barber. (Ramsay, John, *American Potters and Pottery*, p. 183; Barber, E.A., *Marks of American Potters*, p. 60.)

CALDWELL, JAMES & ROBERT. They made earthenware in Cincinnati, Ohio, in 1801.

CALIFORNIA BELLEEK COMPANY was listed at 527 West Seventh Street, Los Angeles, in the *1948 California Manufacturers' Directory*.

CALIFORNIA CERAMICS at 2318 E. 52nd Street, Los Angeles, was listed in 1948 and in 1954. They were not listed in 1955. Dinnerware pattern names found for this company would indicate that they operated on a large scale while they may not have lasted too long. "Orange Blossom," "Orchard," "Cherry," "Lava," "Mandalay," "Country Gentleman," and "Hawaiian Star" were listed.

VARIOUS CAMBRIDGE POTTERIES. The glass that came from Cambridge, Ohio, has overshadowed the fact that potteries operated there from 1895 to 1976 under various names, making a variety of products. The **CAMBRIDGE ART POTTERY** was the first to start (1895 until 1909). According to Barber they made a fine line of faience vases, jardinieres, pedestals, and clay specialties. But they were also listed in the *1902-1903 Complete Directory* as making dinner sets, short sets of odd dishes, and novelties. From 1909 to 1923, the name of the pottery became the **GUERNSEY EARTHENWARE COMPANY.** The **OXFORD POTTERY** operated from 1914 to 1925. (See Oxford Pottery for history.) In 1925, for one year, the **GLOBE CHINA COMPANY** operated in the old Oxford Pottery. Then from 1926 to 1934 the name was **ATLAS-GLOBE POTTERY.** (See Bradshaw Pottery, also Atlas Pottery for history.) Pictured is an assortment of ware made in Cambridge, Ohio. The old brown water jug was made by Oxford Pottery; the two teapots are marked "Guernsey Earthenware." The cup and saucer have the Atlas-Globe mark. Also see Universal Potteries, Inc. for more pottery made in Cambridge.

Various Cambridge, Ohio, Potteries. Two teapots, Guernsey Earthenware Company; water jug, Oxford Pottery; cup and saucer, Atlas-Globe China Company.

CAMERON POTTERIES COMPANY in Cameron, West Virginia, was listed as the Cameron Clay Products Company in the *1902-1903 Complete Directory.* In the *American Ceramic Society Bulletin,* XXIII, May, 1946, p. 78, was the note that in 1907, Cameron Potteries Company was acquired by the Eljer Company of Ford City, Pennsylvania. The article stated that Cameron Potteries had made tableware before 1907. Eljer was strictly a sanitary ware maker as far as I can determine, so while Eljer owned the Cameron Pottery, sanitary ware would be made there. The article stated that Eljer subsequently sold the Cameron plant but no exact date was given. Evidently, the plant went back to tableware before 1958, because in the 1958 *Crockery and Glass Journal Directory Issue,* Cameron Clay Products were listed as making "Sevilla" earthenware which was sold through J. & I. Block Company in New York City. In the *1962 West Virginia Manufacturing Directory,* Cameron Clay Products, Inc. were listed as making semivitreous pottery. They were not listed in the *1967 West Virginia Manufacturing Directory.* In 1935, either a reorganization took place or a separate company formed. A Cameron China Company was started in April, 1935, and was dissolved in February, 1937, according to the office of the secretary of state of West Virginia. This short-lived company may have been a part of the Cameron Pottery Company. It was formed to make clay novelties.

Canonsburg Pottery.

CANONSBURG POTTERY operated in Canonsburg, Pennsylvania, from 1901 to 1978, when a public sale dispersed the property. Just before 1900, when W.S. George was induced to help start a pottery in Canonsburg, Pennsylvania, he was also operating a pottery in East Palestine, Ohio, known as the East Palestine Pottery Company, which had been formed in 1884. (See East Palestine Pottery Company for history.) As early as 1899, George explored the possibility of locating a plant in Canonsburg. By October, 1899, an organization had been formed and a board of directors elected. In April, 1900, construction began on a $50,000 building, and the pottery was in operation by the beginning of 1901, operating as the Canonsburg Plant of the East Palestine Pottery Company. In 1902 the company was listed in the *1902-1903 Complete Directory* as the Canonsburg China Company making semiporcelain dinner sets, toilet sets, and short sets of odd dishes, some decorated. Evidently around 1909, W.S. George sold his interests or the interests of the East Palestine Pottery Company that were held in the Canonsburg Pottery. There was some sort of a reorganization that year and a charter was granted to the Canonsburg Pottery Company. John George, brother of W.S. George, was elected president. He served in that capacity until his death in 1920, when he was succeeded by Willard C. George, John's son. In 1931, Canonsburg Pottery employed three-hundred six people. In 1948, W.C. George was followed by John George II, who was Willard's son. John II had a brother William R. George, and in 1976 the last two Georges in the pottery business sold the Canonsburg Pottery to Angelo Falconi. Then on May 18, 1978, a complete dispersal bankruptcy sale of all machinery and equipment was held. The plant had stood idle following a fire around 1975. Prior to 1975, for a period of four or five years, the pottery had been making crock-pot inserts. A "Regency" gravy server which was made at the pottery around 1970, is shown in the picture. This had the name "Regency Ironstone." Pictured is a very old platter with an old (prior to 1913) mark found in the W.P. Jervis book. The plate with the Currier and Ives scene underglaze has the "American Traditional" shape. (See the Leigh Potters, Inc., plate which is pictured with the Crescent China Company.) The two little plates are "Keystone" shape with different flowered decals. The three-tiered serving tray is marked "Simplicity."

CARILLON CERAMICS CORPORATION with a pottery in Metuchen, New Jersey, was a part of General Ceramics Company until 1944 when it became a separate company. Then in 1945 the Carillon Ceramics Corporation was sold to the Richmond Radiator Company of New York, New York. In *House & Garden*, December, 1940, p. 16b, was an advertisement for a "Carillon China" bowl for table use. The advertisement said "hear its bell-like ring so characteristic of Carillon China whose gorgeous glazed and deeptoned hues might well have been made by fairy hands," etc. General Ceramics Company had manufactured plumbing fixtures after 1931, but evidently some dishes were made at the Carillon Ceramics division in Metuchen, New Jersey. These dishes would be of excellent quality porcelain, even though they looked fairly heavy in the picture, because any company that could produce the fine quality porcelain required for bathrooms would be capable of producing excellent porcelain for dishes. The 1940 advertisement lists the General Ceramics Company at 30 Rockefeller Plaza, New York, N.Y., which would be a sales outlet and office address for the company.

CARR CHINA COMPANY was chartered on June 7, 1916, the principal office was in Grafton, West Virginia. In 1938, they employed two-hundred thirty people to make hotel ware. The pottery was started by Thomas Carr, son of a potter who learned the trade in England, then moved to this country. Seeing the advantages of the Monongahela Valley region for operating a pottery, Thomas Carr moved from the New York area where his father had operated, to Grafton. (James Carr operated in the New York City Pottery for years. Thomas may have been his son.) William Frey developed a color application that helped the already successful plant to do even better. The floor space of the plant covered 75,000 square feet, kilns were fired day and night and several shifts of employees maintained. The plant operated until July, 1952. Pieces described by a Carr china collector were a "Blue Willow" pitcher, "Washington" plate, "Blue Onion" ice cream dish, "Rho-Dendra" mug with yellow, blue, green slip color application, a miniature Toby mug of George Washington made for the 1939 World's Fair in New York, a cream and sugar in marbleized pink and white. Pictured for Carr China in this book is a hotel platter. Several marks sent to this author, which are not shown in the Marks Section, are as follows: "Grafton/Carr China Co."; Onion/Carr China/Grafton/W.Va."; "Blue Willow/Carr China Made in U.S.A." on a leaf; "Rho Dendra/Carr China"; most of the output was marked "CarrChina/Grafton, W.Va." (Information furnished by Imelda Dowden, Grafton, West Virginia.)

Carr China Company.

JAMES CARR. See New York City Pottery, also the International Pottery, and the Lincoln Pottery in Trenton.

CARR AND CLARK. See the Lincoln Pottery in Trenton and International Pottery.

CARR AND MORRISON. See the New York City Pottery.

CARROLLTON POTTERY COMPANY was organized in January, 1903, and by August of that same year a building was built and wares were being made. By 1915 they were operating nine kilns and eight decorating kilns. In June, 1914, fire destroyed half the plant which had to be rebuilt and was also enlarged at that time. They made a high-grade semivitreous porcelain. In 1915 they employed three-hundred fifty people with an annual output of one-half million dollars. In 1929 they merged with seven other companies to form the American China Corporation. In *Crockery and Glass Journal*, December 18, 1924, p. 153 they advertised "Superior," a pattern name for a semisquare, plain edged dinnerware service. In 1934 the corporation failed due to the depression. Pictured are some very attractive dishes made by Carrollton Pottery in very good quality semiporcelain.

Carrollton Pottery Company.

Cartwright Brothers.

CHARLES CARTLIDGE AND COMPANY of Greenpoint, New York, from 1848 to 1854 (Stout's date) made tableware of bone porcelain. They made many objects both useful and ornamental. They employed fine china painters, but Barber said they apparently did not mark their wares because no marks had been identified. (Barber, *Marks of American Potters*, p. 79.) It became American Porcelain Company. (See American Porcelain Company.)

CARTWRIGHT BROTHERS. There were Cartwrights in the pottery business in East Liverpool from 1864 until 1924. The early Cartwrights made Rockingham, yellowware and creamware. In 1880 the name became *CARTWRIGHT BROTHERS* and continued under that name until operations were suspended in 1924. Cartwright Brothers made white granite and semiporcelain. They started making Tea Leaf pattern in 1881. The *1902-1903 Complete Directory* lists the Cartwright Brothers as making white granite, common china dinner sets, short sets of odd dishes and jardinieres, some decorated. They were the makers of the Garfield Drape plates in mottled blue and light green glaze copied from a pressed ware pattern according to Ramsay. (Hutchinson, Jeanette Ray, "Story of Tea Leaf," *Antiques Reporter*, November, 1973, p. 1; Ramsay, John, "American Majolica," *Hobbies Magazine*, May, 1945, p. 45.) Pictured is a little leaf-shaped plate.

CASTLETON CHINA. See Shenango Pottery.

CATALINA POTTERY is located on the island of Santa Catalina off the coast of California. The following information is from *Catalina Pottery – The Early Years* by A.W. Fridley. The Catalina Pottery was started around 1927 to make clay building products. Around 1930 decorative and functional or utilitarian type pottery was added to the line. Between 1931 and 1937, the company made a full line of color-glazed dishes in whiteware and brownware. In 1937 the plant was sold to Gladding, McBean and Co. at which time the pottery was made only on the mainland and the island plant closed. (See Gladding, McBean and Co. for history.) Gladding, McBean and Co. continued some of the Catalina lines and used the Catalina trademark until 1947, at which time the ownership of the trademark returned to the Catalina Island Company as was originally agreed. In 1963, the Catalina Island Company attempted a limited production but was unsuccessful. The Fridley book gives an extensive history, product lists, pictures of products, etc. Besides decorative pieces, a large amount of dinnerware was made under the name of Catalina, including plates, cups, coffee servers, saucers, mugs, tumblers, casseroles, pitchers, servers, relish and vegetable dishes, etc. The items pictured in Mr. Fridley's book were bright solid colors with fine glazes in bright and dark blue, reddish orange, yellow, green, etc.

CEMAR PRODUCTS produced pottery housewares at 3024 Rosslyn Street in Los Angeles, California, in the 1940s and 1950s. I found them listed as late as 1957. In 1954 they made "Lanaware" serving bowls and "Pennsylvania Pantryware."

CENTURY SERVICE CORPORATION. See Cunningham and Picket for picture and history. The "Yellow Wheat" pattern with a wide yellow band that is pictured was manufactured by Homer Laughlin and was called "Autumn Gold." Production number CSC-34, was manufactured by Homer Laughlin China Company under the Century Service Corporation name in "untold thousands of dozens" as stated by the Homer Laughlin China Company. This extremely popular pattern was manufactured early in the years between 1953 and 1968, the years the Century Service Corporation name was in use. Another pattern in wheat without the wide yellow band made for Century Service by Homer Laughlin China was "Golden Wheat" in the Rhythm shape. "Autumn Gold" was made with Nautilus shape cups and a Cavalier shape sugar and creamer as pictured and Brittany plates. (Information from the Homer Laughlin China Company.) Also made for this company was the "Empire Green" pattern which was also made by H.L.C. in the Brittany and Cavalier shapes with a pink rose in center and very dark green, wide band border. Another pattern in this same shape was "Emerald."

CERAMIC ART COMPANY, Trenton, New Jersey. See Lenox.

CHAMBERLAIN AND BAKER. See Hampshire Pottery.

CHATHAM POTTERS, INC. started in 1941 by Frank and Margie Goss in Chatham, New Jersey. The plant was moved to its present location in Oswego, Kansas, in June 1976, with sales offices in Chatham, New Jersey, and Oswego at the factory site. This is an example of real American ingenuity and a promising garage hobby that grew into a full-fledged business that even outgrew its location and had to move to another state for room to expand. Before World War II, the Gosses were both working full time for the Telephone Laboratories in Berkeley Heights, New Jersey. They started making pottery in their garage. The business grew until they both had to give up their jobs to devote full time to the pottery business. In 1964, they incorporated under the name of Chatham Potters, Inc., and the company continued to grow because of the high quality product it manufactured. In 1965, Costas Kalogirou who came from Greece where his family had been potters for four generations, was appointed manager of the plant in New Jersey, at which time new shapes and designs were introduced. In 1967, Kalogirou purchased the company. The search for room to expand and a better supply of gas caused the company to relocate in Oswego, Kansas, in 1976. The initials "CP" as shown in the Marks Section is impressed on each piece of pottery. The oldest pattern is "Country Harvest" or "Fruit" (two names for the same pattern), used when the company first started. "Anthony," "Bouquet," and "Cane" were first made about 1967. "Bird of Paradise" was started in 1976 and "Country Craft" and "Mimosa" in 1977. Chatham Potters make a very fine grade of stoneware high-fired at a temperature of 2300 degrees for superior strength. The dinnerware is handcrafted by hand painting and each piece bears the artist's signature. For today's living the stoneware can go from the freezer to the oven, and is at ease with any life-style because of its timeless designs and softly muted colors.

CHELSEA CHINA COMPANY in New Cumberland, West Virginia, started in 1888 to make white graniteware. This must have been a short-lived company. The secretary of state's office in West Virginia did not find a listing and this factory was not in the *1902-1903 Complete Directory*. Both sources seemed to furnish very complete information on those factories which existed after 1900. See Marks Section for Chelsea marks.

CHELSEA CERAMIC ARTWORKS. See Dedham Pottery.

CHELSEA POTTERY, Dedham, Massachusetts. See Dedham Pottery.

CHESAPEAKE POTTERY was started at the corner of Nicholson and Decatur streets in Baltimore, Maryland, in 1880 by Henry and Isaac Brougham and John Tunstall. In 1882, C.F. Haynes and Company purchased the Chesapeake Pottery. In 1879, **D.F. HAYNES AND COMPANY** had been jobbers located at 347 West Baltimore Street in Baltimore, Maryland. After enthusiastic expansion, the Chesapeake Pottery experienced some financial difficulties and was put up for sale in 1887 and purchased by Edwin Bennett. Edwin Bennett already owned one pottery at Canton and Central Avenues. (See Bennett Pottery Company.) So just a few years later, Bennett sold the Chesapeake Pottery to his son, E. Huston Bennett and David F. Haynes, then the name became **HAYNES, BENNETT AND COMPANY.** E. Huston Bennett retired in 1895 and his interest was purchased by Frank R. Haynes son of D.F. Haynes, and the firm became **D.F. HAYNES AND SON** in 1896. When David died in 1908, his son Frank assumed complete control. In 1914 the American Sugar Refining Company purchased the property and the pottery business was discontinued at the Chesapeake Pottery site. The Maryland Queensware Factory also made a pottery for D.F. Haynes. (See Maryland Pottery Company.) In a *1902-1903 Complete Directory* D.F. Haynes was listed as making semiporcelain toilet sets, odd sets of dishes, jardinieres, and novelties. Ramsay listed them as making Majolica between 1881 and 1890 and Parian after 1895, then some white granite and semiporcelain. Barber said a product belonging to the Majolica family was marked "Clifton." He also describes "Avalon" with a fine body, ivory tint, and soft rich glaze ornamented with sprays of flowers in relief. "Calvertine" was similar to Avalon but decorated differently, turned on a lathe with spaces for bands, over which were laid relief ornaments. Other products made at the Chesapeake Pottery were jugs, plates, cups, lamps, vases, clocks, etc., and much that would be considered artware. "Severn" ware made around 1885 had a fine vitreous body of a subtle grayish-olive tint. There are many pieces of this pottery pictured in the Barber book. From about 1887 to 1890, or perhaps a little later according to Barber, three intertwining circles were used to indicate the shapes of dinner services made at Chesapeake Pottery, such as the "Arundel" shape. "Home Flowers," "Coreopsis," "Poppy," and "Glen Rose," were all decorations. The letters C.C.P. stood for Chesapeake Pottery and H.B.H. for Haynes and Bennett. These marks were printed on the glaze in the same colors as the overglaze decorations. The "Avalon" mark was used on toilet wares and may have been used on other wares, too, according to Barber. (Fitzpatrick, Nancy, "The Chesapeake Pottery Company," *Spinning Wheel*, September, 1957, p. 14; also Barber's *Pottery and Porcelain of the U.S.* p. 323.)

CHESTER POTTERY. See Phoenixville Pottery Company.

CHINA WORKS OF PHILADELPHIA. See Bonnin and Morris.

CHITTENANGO POTTERY COMPANY in Chittenango, New York, started in 1897 to make white granite (Ramsay) and only lasted a short time due to disastrous fires. They were still in business in 1901 because Barber said they furnished china for the Buffalo Exhibition. Then in the *1902-1903 Complete Directory* listing the only pottery listed in Chittenango was the Athison Pottery Company making china dinner sets and short sets of odd dishes. W. P. Jervis in "Chittenango Pottery Company," a listing in "A Dictionary of Pottery Terms" in *Pottery, Glass and Brass Salesman,* December 13, 1917, p. 99, said the pottery was established to manufacture porcelain, but was abandoned after the fire and the works were converted to the manufacture of terra-cotta.

CITY POTTERY in Trenton, New Jersey, which made white granite and cream-colored ware, began in 1859 and ran under a succession of owners until sometime before 1900. They were not listed in the directories that I had, which started with 1900. The first owners were **RHODES AND YATES** in 1859, followed by **YATES AND TITUS** in 1865, then **YATES, BENNETT, AND ALLEN** in 1871.

THE CLEVELAND CHINA COMPANY or the **GEORGE H. BOWMAN COMPANY** was one distributing company that marked many pieces of china with the distributor's name. Bowman operated a jobbing and import concern in connection with a large retail store on Euclid Avenue in Cleveland. At one time the company had fifty men selling on the road. From the 1890s until sometime in the 1930s, the Bowman Company or Cleveland China Company was in operation and an influence in the pottery industry. Iroquois China of Syracuse, New York, Summit China of Akron, Alliance Vitreous China of Alliance, Ohio, all made pottery products for Bowman at some time in that period. A variety of marks is shown for Bowman, and he no doubt used a great many more. Imported china may be found with a Bowman mark and that of a foreign maker. (See George H. Bowman for marks.) In 1939, Iroquois China was sold at bankruptcy. It had been under the control of George H. Bowman. George H. Bowman went to work selling for Homer Laughlin China Company and retired around 1950. In 1954, George H. Bowman and Son were listed in business in Salem, Ohio. Illinois China Company must have made products for Bowman too. Two plates identical in shape, clay body color, and decals were found; one was marked "Cleveland China," the other was marked "Illinois China." Pictured is a sugar and creamer and large rose decaled plate bearing Bowman's marks.

Cleveland China Company.

CLEWS, JAMES. See Indiana Pottery Company.

CLINCHFIELD POTTERY. See Southern Potteries, Inc.

THE VARIOUS COLONIAL COMPANIES. The first business that must be considered by the name Colonial is the **COLONIAL POTTERY.** The name of the building was the Colonial Pottery and had various owners in East Liverpool, Ohio, from the time of Benjamin Harker through Wallace and Chetwynd in 1881, and on until Wallace and Chetwynd became part of the East Liverpool Potteries Company in 1900. When the East Liverpool Potteries Company dissolved in 1903, a new Colonial was formed in the Colonial Pottery building. Their products were ironstone and semiporcelain (W.P. Jervis, "Dictionary of Pottery Terms," *Pottery, Glass, and Brass Salesman,* May 20, 1915, p. 13.) This **COLONIAL COMPANY** operated until 1929 according to Vodrey (Vodrey, William H., "Record of the Pottery Industry in East Liverpool District," *Bulletin of American Ceramic Society,* XXIV, August 1945, p. 284.) Another **COLONIAL COMPANY** was listed in Pittsburgh, Pennsylvania, at 4835 Flamingo Drive, in the 1956, 1959, and 1968 *Industrial Directories for Pennsylvania.* They were not listed in 1954 or 1970, so this gives us something of a beginning and ending date for their existence. The story of these three businesses has been recounted together to avoid confusion of the newer Colonial marked plates with the older Colonial Company products. A plate was found marked "Spruce" with the newer Colonial mark shown in the Marks Section. See the East Liverpool Potteries picture for a picture of a saucedish made by Colonial Company in East Liverpool.

COLUMBIA CHINA. See Harker Pottery Company's marks.

COLUMBIAN ART POTTERY COMPANY was founded in 1893 by W.T. Morris and F.R. Willmore, according to Barber, at Trenton for the manufacture of table and toilet china and artwares in a Belleek body. "Thin Belleek china and ivory ware of a fine quality are made here in original forms and decorations and include articles of utility and ornamental pieces, such as candlesticks, umbrella holders, tea pots and specialties." (Barber, *Pottery and Porcelain of the U.S.,* p. 242.) This company was listed under general pottery wares in the *Trenton City Directories* for the years 1901 and 1902. I found no further listings. They used a shield mark on Belleek as shown. On opaque china, Barber said they used a miniature copy of the Liberty Bell.

COLUMBIAN POTTERY on South Street between Twelfth and Thirteenth streets in Philadelphia, Pennsylvania, made queensware (a type of cream-colored ware) with Alexander Trotter as the proprietor in 1808 (Barber, *Pottery and Porcelain of the U.S.,* p. 111).

CONRAD CRAFTERS, INC. in Wheeling, West Virginia. At the time that Warwick quit business there were many people with half-completed sets of dishes and no way to buy the rest of a set. The American Hostess Corporation and the Dean and Kite Company offered four of the Warwick employees a plan to stay employed for a while. These two companies purchased the entire stock of the remaining Warwick whiteware and hired Charles Conrad, Ralph Knight, Albert Lewis, and Carolyn Conrad to decorate the dishes as they did when they worked for Warwick. Albert Lewis operated the kiln. This led to the starting of the Conrad Crafters, a souvenir and gift business which was incorporated in 1957. At the present time it is possible to buy Bavarian blanks decorated by Conrad Crafters to match the old Warwick china for replacement pieces. See the Marks Section for marks.

CONTINENTAL CHINA COMPANY. See W.S. George Pottery Company, East Palestine, Ohio, for history.

CONTINENTAL KILNS, INC. was chartered on October 16, 1944, with the principal office on Carolina Avenue in Chester, West Virginia. The company was dissolved on June 28, 1957. (Information furnished by AnnaGayle Harvey of the secretary of state's office in West Virginia.) The company was formed, according to

McKee, p. 37, with Vincent Broomhall, former art director of the E.M. Knowles Company as the "leading light," with James Robson, Howard Scweitzer, and Alf Duhrssen furnishing part of the capital. Their plan was to manufacture a Belleek-type body and to produce a high art article. McKee did not say whether they accomplished their purpose. Collectors will have to find the products first to find out. Pictured is one very pretty hand painted plate by Continental Kilns but it is semiporcelain, which is far from a Belleek-type body.

COOK CHINA COMPANY was founded by Charles Howell Cook in Trenton, New Jersey, in 1893 or early 1894, in the building formerly owned by Ott and Brewer called the Etruria Pottery. (See Etruria Pottery.) In the *1902-1903 Complete Directory.* Cook Pottery was listed as making semiporcelain, hotel ware, white granite dinner sets, toilet sets, short sets of odd dishes and jardinieres, some being decorated. According to Barber, Cook made Belleek on which he used a three feather mark, and also produced a good grade of Delft ware. Cook also had a plant at Trenton, New Jersey, called the Prospect Hill Works of the Cook Pottery. (See Prospect Hill Pottery.) Cook stayed on as head of the Cook Pottery until illness caused him to quit in 1926. ("Charles Howell Cook," *American Ceramic Society Bulletin*, XIII, February 1925, p. 48.) In the *Trenton City Directories*, Cook China Company was listed by this name through 1929. In the 1930s the company became ***COOK CERAMICS*** makers of electrical hardware. So for the purposes of this book the dates for Cook China Company would be 1893 to 1929. Cook Ceramics was no longer listed after 1959. Cook Pottery used Mellor and Co. in its marks because F.G. Mellor was one of the original founders and early owners.

H.F. COORS COMPANY, INC. was founded by Mr. and Mrs. Herman F. Coors in 1925 at 8729 Aviation Boulevard, Inglewood, California. The owner in 1978 is their son, Robert M. Coors. This company has made many ceramic products since its beginning, including doll heads, wall tile, soap dishes, handles, faucets, and shower heads. But they are currently making a fine grade of hotel china called "Alox" and a line of hotel porcelain cooking ware called "Chefsware." This company was in no way connected with the Coors Company in Golden, Colorado. Some collectors are not aware of this company's existence and are confusing their products with those of the Golden, Colorado company. (Information furnished by company.)

COORS PORCELAIN in Golden, Colorado, is still in business but stopped making dishes in 1939. There has been so much conflicting information on the Coors companies – H.F. Coors and Coors Porcelain – that this author was very happy to get information directly from both companies to correct the errors. The following information was given in a letter of May 19, 1978, from Charles S. Ryland of Golden, Colorado, who worked for Coors Porcelain for thirty-five years and is preparing a book about the company.

45

The Coors Porcelain Company was founded as the Herold China and Pottery Company in 1910 by Mr. J.J. Herold. There were never any records lost in a fire as the plant has never had a severe fire. Many of the records were just destroyed because of lack of room. The company became the Coors Porcelain Company in 1920, though it had been so in fact since 1915. (Herold returned to Ohio in 1914.) It is still in business and is making chemical porcelain, electronic ceramics, and mechanical ceramics. No dinnerware has been made for public sale since 1939. Coors stopped making dishes, etc., because of W.W. II, as they needed the facilities to make other things.

CORDEY CHINA COMPANY. There are many people who would say Cordey China has no real place in a dinnerware book because it is art pottery. Porcelain sculptures of the most beautiful kind were the main output at Cordey. Marcia Ray mentions coffee sets marked Cordey, and Chester Davis in the article "Cordey China" in *Spinning Wheel*, January/February, 1973, p. 10, said that the output of Cordey's tableware was phased out around 1949. Imagine porcelain lace and ribbons, and tiny flowers, all on covered dishes and coffee sets. Cordey China was founded in Trenton, New Jersey, in 1942 by Boleslaw Cybis, a Polish painter who had come to the World's Fair in New York in 1939 to paint murals for the Polish Pavilion. (Davis.) Marcia Ray in *Collectible Ceramics*, pp. 49 and 50, said that Cybis was headed home to Poland when it was invaded by the Germans. He returned to the states and has stayed since. The first actual listing that I could find in the *Directory of New Jersey Manufacturers* for Cordey China was in 1948, so the factory must have started slowly and quietly at 356 Enterprise Avenue in Trenton. Cordey China was listed continuously until 1963. After World War II, the gift shop production ceased when the Japanese started sending giftware again and the production became artistic porcelains marked only Cybis. In the directories the first listing I found for Cybis, Inc. was 1960 until 1971. There was an overlapping of three years from 1960 to 1963 when both Cordey China and Cybis, Inc. were operating. In 1969, Cordey China Company was acquired by Lightron Corporation. Lightron also purchased Schiller Bros., and in 1970 the two were combined to form Schiller Cordey, Inc. which is currently making beautiful porcelain hand-decorated lamps.

COXON AND COMPANY of Trenton, New Jersey. See Trenton Potteries Company.

COXON POTTERY existed in Wooster, Ohio, from 1926 to around 1930 and failed due to the depression. Prior to that time Fred Coxon had operated a pottery for a short time in Fredericksburg, Ohio. When Fred Coxon moved to Wooster, he was joined by his brother, Edward Coxon, Sr., and Edward's son, Edward Coxon, Jr., to make a fine china called "Coxon Belleek," a rich ivory, thin, high-fired porcelain. See picture of Coxon marked plate. Also see the Morgan Belleek Company.

CRESCENT CHINA COMPANY. In the *Stark County Story*, Vol. IV, p. 743, Part II, by Edward T. Heald is the story of a plant built in Alliance, Ohio, by one of the Sebring brothers which was operated under the name Crescent China from 1920 until 1926. At that time the name was changed to the **LEIGH POTTERY COMPANY** and was operated until 1931 under that name when the depression put them out of business. The examples of the ware that I have found with the marks of this company, and also the many other companies owned by the Sebrings, show that they were the makers of only a fair grade of semiporcelain, with decals over the glaze, a lightweight porous body that didn't last too long but which was attractively decorated and no doubt moderately priced. Pictured for Crescent China is a very thin vegetable dish and platter in "Martha Washington" shape with an attractive monogramed design. Also pictured is an Indian pattern piece from Crescent called "Indian Tree" which incidentally is really a peony tree according to Marcia Ray, author of *Collectible Ceramics*, p. 94. According to Gerald D. Barnett in "Leigh Potters, Inc.," *National Glass, Pottery and Collectables Journal*, March 1979, p. 22, Leigh Potters, Inc. made

Coxon Pottery. Plate marked "Belleek."

a "Corinthian" line and an "Ultra" shape with a green wheat decoration. Leigh Potters also made a line of what they called artware including "Jazz" bookends shown by Barnett. The small plate in the picture is by Leigh Potters. Notice the similarity in shoulder trim to a plate pictured for Canonsburg called "American Traditional." "Aristocrat" shape by Leigh had three concentric lines impressed around the shoulder of the plate as shown in Sears 1936 catalog with Devon Point decoration.

CRESCENT POTTERY COMPANY. See Trenton Potteries Company for history.

CREST STUDIOS started in business in 1950 in New York City. They are decorators of china manufactured by Pickard, Inc. See the Crest Studio mark.

CRONIN CHINA COMPANY was founded in 1934 in Minerva, Ohio, and manufactured a very nice grade of semiporcelain dinnerware until 1956 when the United States Ceramic Tile Company acquired all the stock of Cronin China. The plant still operated under the Cronin name manufacturing wall and floor tile as was listed in the *1960 Directory of Manufacturers for Ohio.* Pictured are plates made by Cronin; the small plate in the right-hand lower corner is marked "Romance," and the plain colored plate in the back row is a rose brown "Cronin Casual" plate. The two large plates with flowers have the Brotherhood of Co-operative Potters mark, but no pattern name. Colorama and Cronin Casuals are the same plate. Some are found marked with both names. Cronin used the mark "Bake Oven" on some kitchenware. The small plate with the maroon and gold border and flowers in the middle is "Royal Rajah Maroon." Also see p. 14 for picture of plate.

Cronin China Company.

Crooksville China Company. **Front row:** *"Sun Lure" plate, very old bowl, "Stinthal" plate.* **Back row:** *"Pantry Bak-in Ware" round platter, "Stinthal" gravy boat.*

CROOKSVILLE CHINA COMPANY in Crooksville, Ohio, started in 1902 and ran until the late 1950s. They started in business employing one-hundred twenty-five people and by 1931 were employing two-hundred fifty, and at the time of closing – three hundred people. Crooksville Pottery products are of a good grade of semiporcelain that at times comes close to a fine vitrified ware. They used quaint, old country-type decorations that will have tremendous appeal to collectors. Crooksville "Pantry-Bak-in" ware had a smooth, hard body with attractive decalcomania. The line started in a small way with a waffle set before 1930 which was greatly extended in 1932. Bowls in five sizes, two different teapots, two sizes of covered jugs, a fruit juice set, coffepots, three sizes of baking dishes, cookie jars, four spice jars, stands for baking dishes, and three different covered baking sets were just some of the items in the line. (*China, Glass and Lamps*, November, 1923, p. 19.) The finest, thinnest semiporcelain of Crooksville's ware is marked "Stinthal China." There is no mention of Crooksville Pottery on it. (See the marks in the Marks Section.) Stinthal was a special ware made by the pottery which was thin, highly vitrified, and very pretty. Crooksville's "Pantry Bak-in Ware" had many different decals for decoration, one of which was a very attractive type of needlepoint. "Sun Lure" is a mark which refers to the light cream-to-yellow color of the ware. Hardly any pattern names may be found on the Crooksville ware; it is going to be very hard to identify as to pattern. This is a pottery that a whole book needs to be written about. Pictured is a plate marked "Sun Lure" with a cream-to-yellow color and bird decals, a smaller, thinner plate with flowers in the center marked "Stinthal," and a large "Pantry Bak-in Ware" plate with cross-stitch flowers for a design. Also pictured is a large, old bowl with a mark shown in the Barber book (before 1904) and a raised design.

CROWN POTTERY COMPANY. In 1882, A.M. Beck came from England and started a pottery in Evansville, Indiana, to make majolica. In 1884, Beck died and the pottery was sold to **BENNIGHOF, UHL, AND COMPANY,** who began the manufacture of whiteware. (Barber.) By 1891 the pottery was organized as Crown Pottery Company by the Flentke family (McKee) until 1902 when Crown Pottery Company took over the Peoria Pottery Company in Peoria, Illinois, and the two companies assumed the name of **CROWN POTTERIES COMPANY.** In 1904, Peoria Pottery was closed for good. (See Peoria Pottery.) Barber gives a variety of marks for

Left to right: mug, Uhl Pottery; plate with raised design which matches dish on the end, Crown Potteries Company; second large plate from left and small plate, Crown Pottery Company.

Crown Pottery and if you will notice, they look very much like English marks, as they were intended to do. Crown Pottery made ironstone china, "Crown Porcelain" dinnerware, toilet ware, semiporcelain, and in the *1902-1903 Complete Directory* they were listed as making semiporcelain and white granite dinner sets, toilet sets, and short sets of odd dishes, some decorated. According to McKee, Crown had been one of the plants selling a good part of its production to jobbers in plain white when Scio cut in. Being hemmed in by city streets with no room for expansion for proper kilns added to Crown's troubles in the 1950s. Crown Potteries went out of business between 1954 and 1958. The last listing I had for them was 1954. I did not have the directories for the years between 1954 and 1958, but they were no longer listed in 1958.

It has been suggested that there was some connection between Crown Pottery and the Uhl Pottery Company. I find none except that eventually Crown took over the building when Uhl Pottery moved to Huntingburg, Indiana. Uhl Pottery originated in Evansville in 1854 when August Uhl and his brother started a pottery in Vanderburgh County. In 1879 the pottery became **LOUIS UHL AND SON.** In 1884 it was called **BENNIGHOFF, UHL AND COMPANY** according to Barber. Then in 1891 the name was changed to the **UHL POTTERY COMPANY** and was moved from Evansville to Huntingburg for easier access to clay. In 1891 Crown Pottery was organized in the Uhl Pottery building in Evansville. In searching the *Indiana Directories* for an ending date for Uhl Pottery, I didn't find them listed after 1941, but the building was leased for awhile to the Louisville Pottery in the 1940s, then closed. Uhl Pottery Company made stoneware kitchen items.

An interesting paragraph follows which was taken from "Clay and Clay Industries," the *Indiana Department of Geology and Natural Resources Twentieth Annual Report, 1895,* p. 173, which sheds some light on why Crown Pottery was forced to consolidate with the Peoria Pottery to stay in business.

> The Crown Pottery Co., of Evansville, was organized in 1891, for the purpose of making ironstone china and decorated tableware. The materials used are none of them obtained in Indiana, and consist of feldspar, flint, ball-clay and kaolin, the latter from Florida and North Carolina. On account of the removal of the tariff on such goods, the market became flooded with similar wares of English make, and the factory was compelled to close down four months in 1894, and three months in 1895. Of the 160 hands employed, 50 are girls who receive $3.00 to $4.00 a week; 60 are boys at $4.00 per week, and the remainder are men at $2.00 per day. The capital stock of the company is $75,000, and the value of the annual output, when run steadily, is $100,000.

CROWN POTTERY. Brand name used by Robinson-Ransbottom. Sometimes used with or without the pottery's name.

CROWN POTTERIES COMPANY. See Crown Pottery, Evansville, Indiana.

CROXALL POTTERY COMPANY of East Liverpool, Ohio, was listed in the *1902-1903 Complete Directory* as making white granite in short sets of odd dishes. From 1898 until around 1912, (Vodrey) John W. Croxall and Sons operated a pottery which had been in the Croxall family under various names since 1844. From 1856 to 1898 it was owned by Croxall and Cartwright. (See *Ohio Pottery and Glass Marks and Manufacturers*, p. 44.) The early Croxalls made yellowware, Rockingham, and Rebecca at the Well teapots. No marks were shown in Barber for this company, and I haven't found any of their ware, but they did make white granite dinnerware and some should still be around. In 1914, American Porcelain Company purchased the Croxall Pottery of G.W. Croxall and Sons to make electrical porcelain products. (Vodrey, William H., "Record of the Pottery Industry in East Liverpool District," *Ceramic Bulletin*, XXIV, August 1945, pp. 282-288, gave the ending date for Croxall Pottery, and Stout, W., *History of the Clay Industry in Ohio*, printed around 1921, p. 86.)

CUMBOW CHINA AND DECORATING COMPANY in Abington, Virginia, started in 1932, and is still in busines (1978), at present decorating beautiful china pieces and dinnerware sets. A few of the patterns include Tea Leaf, Ruskin, Margaret, Louis XV, Old School, Early American Home, Wedding Ring, Abingdon, etc.

CUNNINGHAM INDUSTRIES INC. See Cunningham and Pickett.

CUNNNINGHAM AND PICKETT and associated companies. Years of searching for information on what I had come to term my "Alliance, Ohio, mess" were brought to a happy ending with a letter from E.S. Carson of the Homer Laughlin China Company, October 19, 1977. "The Homer Laughlin China Company produced many thousands of dozens of dinnerware items for Cunningham and Pickett and associated companies from 1938 to 1969 as noted on the attached enclosure. All of these companies to our knowledge were owned by Mr. Alfred Cunningham; however, in the earlier years there was also a Pickett involved." The following dates were supplied by Homer Laughlin China and E.S. Carson even went back and substantiated the material with copies of order sheets.

Customer (jobber or retailer)	First Purchased	Last Purchased
Cunningham and Pickett, Inc.	1938	1968
Alliance China Company	1958	1968
Century Service Corporation	1953	1968
Laughlin International China Co.	1961	1964
International China Company	1958	1968
International D.S. Co.	1961	1968
Lifetime China Co.	1953	1968
Cunningham Industries, Inc.	1967	1969

These names represent marks found on the backs of dishes, sometimes alone, and once in a great while the mark of Homer Laughlin China may also be found on the dish. Alfred Cunningham was a distributor who sold dishes through many outlets; some of them were grocery store premiums, etc. Cunningham, in any of his above company names, did not manufacture china; he was a distributor only. One thing that made me very happy with the various company names used by Mr. Cunningham is that most of his marks included the pattern name. Pictured is a variety of dishes sold under various jobbers' names, and they are so marked. The cereal bowl is by International D.S. Company. The plate with the bouquet of flowers in the center and gold trimmed edge is "Stratford" with a Liberty shape and marked Cunningham and Pickett. The shape is not marked on these plates, only the pattern name. The shape

names were given to me by Homer Laughlin China Company. In the picture the dessert plate is marked "Lifetime China," the wheat plate is marked "Century Service Corporation," the largest platter is "International China," and the wheat platter has Alliance China Company's mark.

Other patterns in the following shapes were made for Cunningham and Pickett by Homer Laughlin China Company: "Avon," Republic shape; "Petipoint," Virginia Rose shape; "Greenbrier," Liberty shape; "Wayside," Brittany, Republic shape; "Embassy," "Flamingo," "DuBarry," "Wheat Spray," "American Beauty," "Melody," the last six in Rhythm shape. In the Nautical Ivory shape and color we have "Heirloom" and "Magnolia" patterns for Cunningham and Pickett, and "Harvest Gold" in the Republic shape. (Information furnished by Homer Laughlin from order sheets.)

CURTIS, JOHN. 1791 to 1811 at 10th and Filbert streets in Philadelphia; made queensware.

DALE AND DAVIS. See Prospect Hill Pottery.

DALLAS, FREDERICK operated in the Hamilton Street Pottery from 1865 until before 1910 making white granite. This pottery operated as a center for the ladies when the china painting craze, which gave us a lot of beautiful hand-painted plates and art pottery, hit Cincinnati. At one time Hamilton Street Pottery was firing hand-painted ware for two hundred women. The pottery produced the common whiteware.

DAVIDSON PORCELAIN COMPANY was chartered on April 12, 1920, in Chester, West Virginia, and was dissolved September 27, 1935. (Information from Annagayle Harvey, office of the secretary of state of West Virginia.)

DAVIDSON POTTERY COMPANY was listed in Wheeling, West Virginia, as being established in May, 1897, to make porcelain china and pottery products, and inspected on November 11, 1897, in a two-story brick building. (Report of the commissioner of labor of the state of West Virginia for 1897-1898.)

DAVIDSON, TAYLOR & COMPANY. Jobbing concern. Around the turn of the century they sold dishes to Sears made by Homer Laughlin China Company. They were located on Wheeling, West Virginia.

DEDHAM POTTERY of East Dedham, Massachusetts, from 1895 to 1943 (Evans p. 83), was preceded by Chelsea Pottery formed in 1891. The products of this

Dedham Pottery as pictured in
***House Beautiful**, 1933.*

company are considered to be art pottery, but according to Paul Evans in *Art Pottery in the United States*, New York: Scribner's, 1974, p. 84, they did produce over fifty patterns of tableware "spanning the gamut of any zoo and greenhouse" (in decoration). Rabbits, ducks, grapes, azaleas, magnolias, turkeys, clover, elephants, etc. (See Evans for more.) Stiles, p. 193, said they specialized in crackleware with freehand decorations in cobalt blue. The designs were unusual and the crackle pattern, sometimes in the form of a spider web was most interesting. She also stated that the Rabbit decoration was designed by Joseph Linden Smith and was the best known design of the Dedham Pottery, and was adopted as their trademark. James Robertson, the founder, was the fourth in line of a family of Scottish potters and was followed in this country after 1853 by seven more generations of Robertsons in that business. Frederick W. Allen in "More About Dedham Pottery," *Hobbies*, September, 1952, p. 80, gave us the spelling "Craquleware" for the popular ware made by Robertson. This author had a letter from J. Milton Robertson in which he told how a drawing of a rabbit would vary so much from decorator to decorator, that at first the company put a raised design on the plate so that all the artist had to do was to follow the design and the rabbits would be alike. However, in the drying and shrinking process in the mold, frequently the plate did not release from the mold without cracking. By the time this raised decoration was eliminated from the molds, the decorators were used to the design. The fact that the early plates had a raised design and the later plates did not has great significance for the collector. However, any of this ware today has a great value.

DELAWARE POTTERY. See Trenton Potteries Company for history.

DENVER CHINA AND POTTERY COMPANY, 1901 to 1905, was organized by William A. Long in Denver, Colorado. This was primarily an art pottery but Paul Evans said they made three classes of ware. The ordinary flint blue line included table pieces such as bowls, mugs, and baking dishes. In the line of colored glazes were pitchers. The third line was the artware. (See Evans, Paul, *Art Pottery of the United States*, p. 88, for a complete history and fine discussion of the company's products.)

DERRY CHINA COMPANY in Derry Station, Pennsylvania, operated for what was apparently a short time around 1900. In the *1902-1903 Complete Directory* they were listed as starting in 1902 with seven kilns to make semiporcelain and hotel ware, dinner sets, toilet sets, and short sets of odd dishes. Barber also listed them as in operation making semivitreous china around 1904. My next listing was for 1916 and there was no listing of a pottery in Derry after that, so they had either moved or quit.

DICKOTA POTTERY started as the Dickinson Fire and Pressed Brick Company in 1892, in Dickinson, North Dakota. The company was purchased by the Dickinson Clay Products Company in 1934, and pottery production was started to give the men work when the brickyard could not operate in the cold winter months. While most of the pottery made at the Dickota Pottery was of the decorative type, a line of pottery dishes was introduced in 1938, just before the pottery closed. Their mark was "Dickota" scratched on the article, also sometimes paper labels were used. (Dommel, Darlene, "Dickota Pottery," *Antique Trader Annual of Articles for 1974*, p. 337.)

DORCHESTER POTTERY WORKS at 101 Victory Road in Boston, Massachusetts, has been in business since 1895. (Company information.) They are makers of high-fired stoneware for acid proof use in seventeen hundred items for medical, jewelry, and food companies. They used a lead stamp for a mark until 1941. This pottery is not to be confused with the Dorchester Pottery of Millville, New Jersey, which was in fact a division of the Stangl Pottery and which was in existence only a few months in 1976 when a fire destroyed the plant before the first dinnerware was made. They did make a few crockpots in the building. (Later information from Edna Mae Hicks, secretary to Frank H. Wheaton, owner of Stangl Pottery.)

DRESDEN CHINA COMPANY of Salineville, Ohio, was started in 1902. When National China Company of East Liverpool moved to Salineville, they purchased the Dresden China Company in 1910. In the *1902-1903 Complete Directory*, Dresden China was listed as making semiporcelain dinner sets and short sets of odd dishes. In the *1904 Factory Inspection Report*, they employed sixty-five people.

Front row: "Alpine China" plate, Brunt Pottery Company; small plate, Dresden Pottery. **Back row:** gravy boat (1895) Potter's Co-operative (Dresden Pottery); large, gold-trimmed bowl, Potter's Co-operative; cracker jar, Potter's Co-operative (Dresden Pottery).

DRESDEN POTTERY. BRUNT, BLOOR, MARTIN AND COMPANY operated in the Dresden Pottery from 1875 to 1892 in East Liverpool, Ohio (Ramsay dates). There is a variety of marks shown for this company as they were recorded by Barber. This company became a member of the Potters' Co-operative Association which Ramsay dates 1892 and McKee says around the turn of the century. William H. Vodrey's "Record of the Pottery Industry in East Liverpool District," *American Ceramic Society Bulletin* XXIV, August 1945, p. 282, dates the Potters' Co-operative as 1882. The pieces pictured all have one of the old marks shown in Barber's book which was written in 1904. The little plate is semiporcelain of a good quality and is marked with "Dresden Semi-porcelain" in a wreath. The plate is thin, has a nice vitrified ring to it, and is trimmed with decals of pink roses and green leaves. The cracker jar has the vitreous porcelain mark, is thick, heavy, with no ring to it at all. The larger plate is a Brunt Pottery plate with the "Alpine China" mark. See the Brunt Pottery Company history.

DRYDEN POTTERY was mainly artware pottery in Ellsworth, Kansas, from 1946 until 1956 when the factory moved to Hot Springs, Arkansas, until present. Eight months after starting in business it was reported that James Dryden, founder and owner, was making plans to make complete sets of dishes. Around 1948 a way to make thinner, harder ware was perfected and the local clays were perfect for a "Fiesta" type of dinnerware. There are some marks shown for Dryden Pottery in the Marks Section, but they may not be the ones used on dinnerware.

DUCHÉ, ANTHONY was manufacturing a stoneware product akin to porcelain in Philadelphia by 1730. Rudolf Hommel in his article, "Colonial Master Potters" in *Hobbies*, May 1949, p. 80, felt that Duché had been neglected by the historians in telling the whiteware story in this country. (As you can see he was left out of the list on page 9 that came from an American Ceramic Society Bulletin.) The son of Anthony Duché settled in Savannah, Georgia, in 1735, and made a porcelain which was described to be as good as Chinese porcelain. Another son of Anthony, James Duché, made stoneware in Massachusetts according to the article.

THE EAGLE POTTERY in Trenton, New Jersey, was started in 1876 by Richard Millington, passed through several owners, and was listed as late as 1900 in the *Trenton City Directories* but was not listed after that. Other owners were Burroughs and Mountford (see that listing), also Astbury and Maddock. (See that listing.) (Barber.)

EAST END POTTERY COMPANY began in 1894 at the north side of Railroad Street in East Liverpool. In 1900, East End Pottery joined the East Liverpool Potteries Company, which was dissolved July 7, 1903. (See East Liverpool Potteries Company.) By 1905 they were back on their own operating as the *EAST END CHINA COMPANY.* The plant was taken over by Gus Trenle who filed to change the name to Trenle China Company in January, 1909 *(Secretary of State Report for 1910).* See Trenle China. The East End China Company made a very fine grade of semiporcelain. According to Annise Heaivilin, this company also made ironstone in a Tea Leaf pattern.

EAST LIVERPOOL POTTERY COMPANY in East Liverpool, Ohio, made a good quality of semiporcelain ware from around 1884 to 1903. They became one of the six companies to join the East Liverpool Potteries Company. (See that listing.)

EAST LIVERPOOL POTTERIES COMPANY was formed by a group of potteries in East Liverpool, Ohio, who were having trouble competing on their own. The combination was of short duration lasting only from 1900 to 1903. See Colonial, Globe, East Liverpool Pottery Company, George C. Murphy, East End Pottery, and the United States Pottery at Wellsville. In the *1902-1903 Complete Directory*, the East Liverpool Potteries Company was listed as making white granite, semiporcelain, and Rockingham ware in dinner sets, toilet sets, and short sets of odd dishes and jardinieres, some decorated. Pictured are semiporcelain products made by some of the different factories that were part of the East Liverpool Potteries Company. The footed, fancy vegetable dish is by the George C. Murphy Company; the very large

*East Liverpool Potteries Company. **Front row:** small plate with raised design, Globe Pottery; large plate, East End Pottery; large platter, United States Pottery of Wellsville, Ohio; small plate, East Liverpool Potteries Company; saucedish, Colonial Pottery. **Back row:** round serving dish, East Liverpool Pottery Company; footed serving or vegetable dish, George C. Murphy Company.*

platter is from the United States Pottery at Wellsville, Ohio. The other small plate in the picture was marked East Liverpool Potteries Company and could have come from any of the six plants. The medium-sized plate with the decal of babies in the center and raised design is from Globe Pottery. The decal on the East End Pottery larger plate is worn, but it shows sheep and a barn in the center and gold trim on a raised, beaded edge trim. (This was the hardest to find of these companies, and this poor example is all I have.) The little saucedish was made by the Colonial Pottery with a decal of tiny pink roses. None of these dishes are discolored with age; they are still a bright bluish white. The glaze is not crazed, only the decals over the glaze seem to have suffered. The perfectly round serving dish with a decal of roses was marked East Liverpool Pottery Company.

THE EAST MORRISANIA CHINA WORKS of D. Robitzek on 150th Street, in New York City, was making white granite, cream-colored, and decorated ware around 1893. (Barber)

EAST PALESTINE POTTERY COMPANY was one of the early names of the W.S. George Pottery in East Palestine. (See W.S. George Pottery Company for history.) From 1884 to 1909 the pottery was called the East Palestine Pottery Company. The pitcher in the photograph has the "Lafayette Porcelain" mark. It is decorated with an overglaze flowered decal and a shading of blue at the top and bottom. Despite the mark "porcelain" it seems just like all of the rest of the semiporcelain made in this country—medium thick, little ring, with a fairly porous, lightweight body of white clay. The little saucedish is marked "Iris" and "E.P.P. Co." and is of the same composition as the pitcher. The platter is also "Iris." These pieces are typical of the semiporcelain wares made by the potteries around 1900 in an attempt to give the housewife something attractive that she could afford to buy. The quality of the clay body was poor, but the decorations were very nice, making them better to collect now, than to use then.

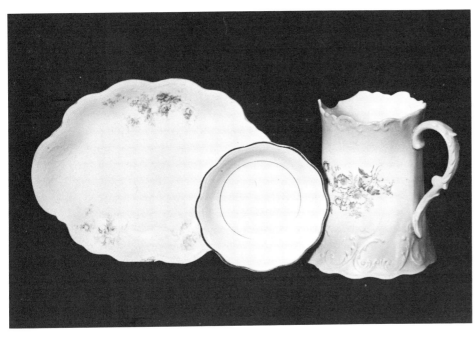

East Palestine Pottery Company.

EAST TRENTON POTTERY COMPANY. Barber in *Pottery and Porcelain of the United States*, p. 47, mentions this company as being in business in 1888. They made plates with portraits of the presidents in the 1888 presidential year. The last listing in the *Trenton City Directories* was in 1905. There were several marks for this company as shown. They made white granite, opaque china.

55

EGYPTIAN POTTERY COMPANY in Trenton, New Jersey, is just mentioned in Barber's *Pottery and Porcelain of the U.S.* as being in business around 1893. They were listed in the *Trenton City Directories* through 1902 making sanitary ware. This was true of so many of the early Trenton, New Jersey, potteries. Some of them made a few dishes, always of fine porcelain, in their early years. Then when East Liverpool, Ohio, really got into the competition, these factories switched to sanitary ware and many times to electrical porcelain.

ELVERSON POTTERY COMPANY. The Elverson name in pottery had a long history in New Brighton, Pennsylvania. Thomas Elverson made yellowware and Rockingham from 1862 to 1880 according to Ramsay. Elverson and Sherwood made stoneware around 1870. Before 1904, W.H. Elverson purchased what had been the old Enterprise Pottery in New Brighton. (The Enterprise Pottery made stoneware and was listed in 1895 and in 1900 as employing forty-five people.) In the 1931 and 1935 *Industrial Directories for New Jersey*, Elverson Pottery Company was listed as making pottery and chinaware employing fifty people. Through 1950 they were listed the same way, but by 1953 they had become Friedle-Elverson Pottery as they were listed on through 1975, making pottery products not classified under dinnerware.

EMPIRE CHINA COMPANY in Burbank, California, was listed in the *1924 California Manufacturers' Directory* as making semivitreous china.

EMPIRE CHINA COMPANY, of Greenpoint, New York, made some hotel ware in the early days of its existence before the Civil War, but then went on to electrical porcelain and insulators before 1870. (Watts, Arthur, S., "Early History of the Electrical Porcelain Industry in the United States," *American Ceramic Society Bulletin* XVIII, October 1939, pp. 404-408.)

EMPIRE POTTERY COMPANY of Syracuse, New York. See Syracuse China Company for history.

THE EMPIRE POTTERY was established in Trenton, New Jersey, in 1863 by Coxon and Thompson. Around 1884 the pottery passed on to Alpaugh and McGowan who made thin porcelain dinnerware, tea and toilet sets. (Barber, *Marks of American Potters*, p. 63.) This pottery was later owned by a Wood and Barlow who used the "Imperial China" mark. (See the Trenton Potteries Company for the rest of the Empire history and see Marks Section for marks.)

ENTERPRISE POTTERY COMPANY. See Trenton Potteries Company for history.

EQUITABLE POTTERY COMPANY. See Trenton Potteries Company for history.

THE ETRURIA POTTERY was built in 1863 by Bloor, Ott, and Booth. In 1865 the firm became *OTT AND BREWER* when John Hart Brewer entered the firm. In 1893 the firm was followed by Cook Pottery Company. ("Charles Howell Cook," *American Ceramic Society Bulletin*, August 1925, p. 415.) This company is especially well known for at least two things that they did. One was to hire Isaac Broome who modeled some famous Parian portrait busts and figure vases that were exhibited in the 1876 Centennial Exposition. They were also the first American company to make the famous thin eggshell china with the lustre glazes called Belleek. Opaque china tablewares were made at the Etruria Pottery and marked with a Maltese Cross surrounded by a ribbon, or occasionally a circular rising sun device containing the firm name of Ott and Brewer. According to the marks shown in Barber, the company also made semiporcelain and ironstone china. Much is to be learned from the marks used by a company, because they often classify their product by the mark. (Barber.)

EXCELSIOR POTTERY, Trenton, New Jersey. See William Young and Sons.

FAIENCE MANUFACTURING COMPANY, Greenpoint, New York, operated 1880 to 1890 and made mainly art-type wares. They made some majolica but that seemed to be in fancy pieces also. They dipped ware in colored glazes to get blended, mottled, or marbled effects. There may be some pitchers, etc.

CALEB FARRAR established a pottery in Middlebury, Vermont, to manufacture earthenware and white tableware in 1812, and operated until 1850 when Farrar sold to James Mitchell. James Mitchell sold to Nakum Parker, and before 1900 the building had been converted to a home. (Barber, E.A., *Pottery and Porcelain in the United States.* New York: G.P. Putnam's Sons, 1893, p. 438.)

WILLIAM FARRAR. See Southern Porcelain Manufacturing Company, Kaolin, South Carolina.

FELL AND THROPP. See Trenton Pottery Company for history.

FENTON, CHRISTOPHER. See the United States Pottery, Bennington, Vermont.

FENTON, AND CLARK. See Peoria Pottery Company.

FEUSTAL AND WALTZ, also FEUSTAL AND NOWLING. See W.S. George Pottery, East Palestine.

FLINTRIDGE CHINA COMPANY was started in Pasadena, California, in 1945 by two men who had worked at Gladding, McBean and Co. (Tom Hogan and Milton Mason). They manufactured a thin china using a high Nepheline syenite body. A series of outstanding china designs came along that rapidly expanded the plant to a full city block in 1963 with three and one-half million dollars in sales. One original design was "Black Contessa" which is still highly popular today. See Gorham for more. (Information furnished by Robert W. MacDonald, sales promotion manager at Gorham Division of Textron.)

FLORENCE POTTERY, 1920 to 1941, Mount Gilead, Ohio, was originally one of the old potteries. McGowan started two potteries in the town, with one on each end of town at various times. Florence Pottery became of interest to collectors when it was learned that Rum Rill was made there in the late 1930s and until the pottery burned in 1941. See Rum Rill for more on this. Lawton Gonder managed the Florence Pottery from 1938 to 1941 and from there he went to Zanesville, Ohio, and started the Gonder Ceramic Arts Company. See Gonder Ceramic Arts for more information.

THE FORD CHINA COMPANY in Ford City, Pennsylvania, manufactured a fine grade of semiporcelain in toilet and tableware marked with various pattern names as shown in Marks Section. In the *1900 Factory Inspection Report for Pennsylvania* they employed six-hundred twenty people. In the *1902-1903 Complete Directory* they were listed as making semiporcelain dinner sets, toilet sets, and short sets of odd dishes and jardinieres, some decorated. Around 1912, the Pennsylvania China Company was operating in Ford City and in Kittanning. In the *1916 Industrial Directory for Pennsylvania*, W.S. George was in Kittanning and there was no pottery listed in Ford City. Pictured for Ford China are four pieces all marked with shape names.

Ford China Company. **Left to right:** "Turin" plate, "Derby" plate, "York" soup bowl, "Derby" small plate.

FOSTER POTTERY COMPANY, Lexington, North Carolina. Jobbers of pottery for years prior to World War II. Owners, Foreman and Foster became principal stockholders in Southern Potteries at Erwin, Tennessee. (McKee, p. 35)

FRANKLIN POTTERY COMPANY, Franklin, Ohio, from 1880 to 1884, made semi-porcelain and graniteware dishes.

FRANKOMA POTTERY started in 1936 and operating at present in Sapulpa, Oklahoma (1978), is the result of the efforts of one truly remarkable family. John Frank, the founder, died in 1973 and the control of the pottery passed into the hands of his daughter Joniece Frank. John had a B.A. degree from the Chicago Art Institute and Joniece graduated from Hockaday College Preparatory School in Dallas, Texas, then received a degree from the University of Oklahoma and later studied two months in Europe. John Frank served as an instructor of Art and Ceramics at the University of Oklahoma from 1927 until he started Frankoma Pottery in 1936. Joniece grew up in her father's shadow and in the pottery business. It is no wonder that with such artistic talent and such business understanding that Frankoma Pottery has continued to grow by leaps and bounds, surviving the very early financial difficulties which seem to go along with starting almost any business. Also the pottery was practically wiped out by fire in 1943, then rebuilt. Another daughter of John's, Donna Frank, has written an interesting and informative book about John and the factory called *Clay in the Master's Hands*, New York, New York: Vantage Press, 1977, which affords an insight into the pottery business that is seldom seen. An article in The *Antique Trader*, July 20, 1976, p. 46, entitled "Collectables for Tomorrow from Frankoma Pottery," tells a story in the title alone. These will be the collectibles of tomorrow because of design and quality, and this pottery is very nice to have around today. One line introduced in the 1940s was Mayan-Aztec. Besides the beautiful lines of dinnerware, Frankoma is well known for a series of Christmas plates, sculptured items designed by John's wife, Grace Lee Frank, flower containers, and all sorts of novelty items. (Information furnished by company.)

FRAUNFELTER CHINA COMPANY. See Ohio Pottery, Zanesville, Ohio.

FREDERICK, SCHENKLE AND ALLEN COMPANY, East Liverpool, Ohio. See Globe Pottery.

FRENCH CHINA COMPANY founded around 1900 in Sebring, Ohio, was a separate company from **SAXON CHINA** founded in Sebring, Ohio, around the same time. French China and Saxon China both became part of the Sebring Manufacturing Company from 1916 to 1934 when the name became **FRENCH SAXON CHINA COMPANY.** Jervis mentions a merger of the two companies as early as 1907 with each retaining their original names, but the fact is that the two companies were closely related throughout the years, so that it is not surprising we find them making the same shaped china marked by the separate companies. All of these companies made the "Martha Washington" shaped dinnerware which came with many decals. In 1964 the French Saxon China Company was purchased by Royal China Company and operated as a wholly owned subsidiary. All of the companies mentioned above made semiporcelain dinnerware. Four small-sized plates made by these companies are pictured. The

Front row: cream and sugar set, French China Company. **Back row:** *"Martha Washington" shaped plate, French China Company; plate, French China Company; plate, Saxon China; plate, French-Saxon China.*

58

plate with the bird decal on either side is the "Martha Washington shape"; this particular plate was made by French China. Also by French China is the plate with the old transfer hand-painted decals. (They applied the decals, then painted a little over them.) The cream and sugar set with a Dutch scene is by French also. Some would call this set "flown" or "flow" blue; some would not. American blue just did not flow very much in any I can find. The plate with a border and flowers is by French-Saxon; the other small plate with chrysanthemums in the center is Saxon China Company's.

FRENCH SAXON CHINA. See French China Company, Sebring, Ohio.

DANIEL FREYTAG at South Fifth Street, Philadelphia, Pennsylvania, from around 1810 to 1830 (Ramsay) made a fine white earthenware which was elaborately decorated and might have made bone china according to Spargo, page 180. He used silver and gold ornamentation and bright colored overglazes.

FULPER POTTERY was founded in 1814 (Evans date) in Flemington, New Jersey, at the corner of Main and Mine streets by Samuel Hill. (Evans, Paul, *Art Pottery of the United States*, p. 108.) Abraham Fulper acquired the pottery in 1860. After his death his sons operated the pottery under various names involving Fulper. By 1911, J. Martin Stangl was working for Fulper. Between 1915 and 1920, Stangl left Fulper to work for Haeger Potteries. When he came back in 1920 it was to head the pottery, according to company history. In 1926 Fulper acquired Anchor Pottery Company of Trenton, New Jersey, and by 1929, Fulper had two plants operating in Flemington. In 1930 Stangl acquired the Fulper firm, following a disastrous fire in the Flemington plants in 1929. (For a discussion of the beautiful Fulper art pottery see the Paul Evans' book, which also includes a much more detailed history of the company.) In 1920, Fulper Pottery introduced solid color glazed dinnerware. For many years they used only green, but in 1930 other colors were added to the dinnerware line. (*Stangl: A Portrait of Progress in Pottery*, company history, 1965.) See Stangl Pottery for more.

McKee described Fulper-made dinnerware as an Italian type of decoration on dinnerware with a red body and white englobe applied over the face or outside of the unfired ware. The outlining of decorative design or scrollwork was scratched on by hand, colors painted on, then the item glazed and fired. He said they centered their production on three or four well chosen patterns and prospered. This was marked as "Stangl" Ware. See Stangl for marks. (IMPORTANT NOTE: Fulper dinnerware was marked Stangl. But to clear up a bad misconception that is evidently a typesetters' error in an early Thorn book of marks—Kenneth, Pluto, Cupid, Tiger, Greek, and Lygia are not Fulper marks. They belong to French China, Sebring, Ohio. The tragedy is that by mislocating one little number the error occurred and modern authors are perpetrating the mistake. See French China.)

GEIJSBEEK POTTERY COMPANY at Golden, Colorado, started in 1899 (Barber, p. 165). Also according to Barber in *Marks of American Potters*, some marks used said Denver, Colorado. See Marks Section. Marcia Ray, p. 248, called the Geijsbeek Pottery "a commercial venture where three kilns turned out whiteware said to be very much like modern Delft without the blue decoration."

GENERAL CERAMICS. See Carillon Ceramics Corporation.

W.S. GEORGE POTTERY OF CANONSBURG. (See also W.S. George Pottery in East Palestine.) The W.S. George Pottery that was listed in Canonsburg was actually in Strabane, Pennsylvania, about a mile from the Canonsburg Pottery. (See Canonsburg Pottery in Canonsburg.) W.S. George started his own pottery in Canonsburg in the very early 1900s. One source said 1905, one said 1909, when the reorganization took place at the Canonsburg Pottery and W.S. George sold his interests there. I would be inclined to believe he had his own pottery underway before he sold his interests in Canonsburg. At any rate we are safe in saying this pottery started in the very early 1900s and operated until it burned in 1955. At this time W.S. George Pottery was in bankruptcy. George died a millionaire in 1925. W.S. George had a second pottery in Pennsylvania at Kittanning which employed ninety-one in the 1931 and 1935 *Industrial Directories for the State of Pennsylvania.* In those same years he employed one-hundred seventy-six at his Canonsburg pottery. The offices for all three of W.S. George's potteries were in East Palestine, Ohio. The story of W.S. George, the man, is an American success story. In 1897 he was a very young man when he was hired to head the decorating department of the Ohio China Company in East Liverpool. In 1898 he accepted management of the East Palestine Pottery Company and by 1904 he owned the controlling interest in that company. (*Daily Leader*, East Palestine daily paper, "East Palestine's First Pottery," staff-written, February, 1960, p. 1.)

By 1909 this company and Continental China which he had built in East Palestine carried the name of W.S. George Pottery. The Kittanning Pottery of W.S. George was owned by him very early in the 1900s also. I haven't been able to determine that the dinnerware made in the different states, Pennsylvania and Ohio, had any mark to designate the place they were made. The marks shown just involve the name George. See W.S. George in East Palestine, Ohio.

W.S. GEORGE POTTERY OF EAST PALESTINE. Around 1880 a pottery was started in East Palestine, Ohio, by **FEUSTAL AND WALTZ** to make yellowware and Rockingham. By 1881 the pottery was operating under the name **FEUSTAL AND NOWLING POTTERY COMPANY.** In 1884 it became known as the **EAST PALESTINE POTTERY COMPANY.** A group of potters from East Liverpool had purchased the plant to make white and decorated ware. In the *1902-1903 Complete Directory* they were listed as making semiporcelain dinner sets, toilet sets, and short sets of odd dishes, some decorated. The plant was near bankruptcy several times but was finally put on a paying basis by George E. Sebring who was hired to manage the plant in 1893. By 1904, the controlling interest in the pottery was owned by W.S. George who had started another pottery in Pennsylvania. (See Canonsburg Pottery.) Also at this time W.S. George built a new building in East Palestine and the new plant was called **CONTINENTAL CHINA COMPANY.** In 1909 the name of the East Palestine plant was changed to the **W.S. GEORGE POTTERY COMPANY.** In 1912

W.S. George Pottery. Left to right. **Front row:** *"Lido" shaped plate, melonlike-shaped plate, "Elmhurst" shape, blue-bird decaled plate, "Rainbow" shape.* **Back row.** *"Argosy" shaped plate, "Astor" shaped plate, coupe-shaped plate with large cherry decals, "Bolero" shaped plate, "Radison" shaped plate.*

60

the first building to house the East Palestine Pottery Company burned and wasn't replaced until 1924. The pottery was listed through 1961 in the East Palestine telephone directories as W.S. George Pottery. The building was sold before that, because in 1960 the building was used as plant No. 4 of Royal China. Royal sold all of their interests to Jeannette Glass company of Jeannette, Pennsylvania, and Jeannette idled the old East Palestine plant but kept the Sebring plants of Royal China running. (Be sure to see Canonsburg Pottery history for more on W.S. George.) W.S. George made a great variety of semiporcelain dishes that are already being widely collected. The most advantageous fact that could be passed on to readers in one picture seemed to be the various shapes of W.S. George. Pictured are plates that show these different shapes.

WILLARD C. GEORGE. This mark as shown with the Canonsburg Pottery marks, was found on a very nice set of dishes. I found no evidence that this was a separate company. Willard C. George was president of Canonsburg Pottery from 1920 until 1948 when Willard died. I am only assuming (which is never really safe) that this was some special production of his or in his honor. They are very attractive semivitrified dishes, thin and well styled. See Canonsburg Pottery for history.

GLADDING, McBEAN AND COMPANY was organized to make sewer pipe in 1875 by Charles Gladding, Peter McGill McBean, and George Chambers, all of Chicago, who had been attracted to California by the discovery of fire clay deposits at the little foothill town of Lincoln in Placer County. In 1884, terra-cotta for buildings was manufactured for the first time and today Gladding, McBean and Company's products, particularly terra-cotta, are well known worldwide. Other products followed: hollow tile in 1890, face brick in 1891, roof tile in 1893, enamel brick in 1899, vitrified brick in 1902, and coated brick in 1915.

Tropico Pottery which started in 1904 to make faience and floor tile on Los Angeles Boulevard, Los Angeles County, later made a line of Garden Ware. Gladding, McBean and Co. acquired Tropico Pottery in 1923 and combined the garden line with one made at the Lincoln plant; which is now the Glendale plant, where the facilities were greatly expanded by Gladding, McBean and Co. From April 15, 1935, to December 31, 1937, Tropico Pottery also produced a line of artware and mixing bowls which became part of the Franciscan products.

Catalina Ware and Catalina Art Ware were originally made by Santa Catalina Island Co., Pottery Division, Avalon, California. The product is identified by numbers with the prefix "C". Catalina glazes are identified by numbers with the prefix "CA". (See Marks Section.) In 1937 Gladding, McBean and Co. purchased the Catalina Island Company. Early Catalina Pottery is also identified by the name "Catalina" inscribed in the ware. After 1937 the impressions were replaced with a stamped inscription. In 1947 the use of the Catalina trademark was relinquished as was previously agreed. Catalina products were sold under various names identifying lines patterns.

In 1933, Gladding, McBean and Co. acquired the West Coast properties of the American Encaustic Tiling Company, which for many years has been the largest manufacturer of floor and wall tile in the world. In December, 1943, Gladding, McBean and Co. acquired the plants of the Stockton Fire Brick Company at Pittsburg, California. This was followed in September, 1944, by the addition of the two plants to make silica brick of the Emsco Refractories Company.

In 1934, the company began the manufacture of dinnerware and art pottery which is marketed under the name of Franciscan Ware. The first dinnerware was made in plain shapes and bright colors, reminiscent of the old Spanish days. Later on, other graceful shapes and subdued or pastel colors were added. This style of dinnerware, together with the beautifully modeled underglaze patterns that recently were developed, have won national acclaim. In 1942, the first china was manufactured at the Glendale plant and also marketed under the Franciscan name. This transulucent vitrified china is inspiring. Typically American in body and decoration, it was accepted with great response in the field of fine chinas.

The following is a quote about Franciscan Ware obtained from company-furnished information:

Franciscan Ware is the general name applied to the earthenware type of body which is used by Franciscan in such lines as the Apple, Desert Rose, Fruit, Ivy, Coronado, El Patio and Metropolitan. The composition of this earthenware differs from the usual formulas for such bodies in that its basic ingredient is talc, or magnesium silicate, instead of the conventional clay, or aluminum silicate, and the use of talc in casting and jiggering bodies was first perfected by Gladding, McBean & Co. and was covered by a very strong patent known as the "Prouty Patent" which the Company purchased a number of years ago from Mr. Willis Prouty. This patent expired in May, 1945, but before its expiration many firms were using talc and infringing the patent rights.

The Franciscan body is protected by another series of patents called the "Malinite Patents." These will remain in force for a number of years and as infringers are discovered they will be prosecuted heavily. The name "Malinite" comes from the inventor, Dr. Malinowsky, who improved the Prouty talc body by adding a small quantity of amorphous flux, such as ground glass. This flux can be adjusted to make a very tight and strong body at temperatures much lower than the maturing temperatures of ordinary earthenware bodies.

The great benefits of talc in a body is to prevent crazing of the glaze, both when first fired and after a lapse of years. The exact reasons for this harmony with glazes are not certain, but it is a chemical fact that when clay is fired above 900F. there is a molecular change and a loss of water, or crystallization, which is not the case when talc is subjected to any high temperatures. In our twelve years of production, there has never been a piece of Franciscan Ware craze, even after it has been in constant household use for years.

The use of the glass flux in the body also helps to bind the glaze to the body. This action can be seen in a cross section of glazed body under a good microscope. Because of the chemical formula of the Franciscan Malinite body it is possible to obtain glazes of an unusual satin texture in color tones that are exceptionally clear. Glazes of high lustre can also be obtained and these have a surface hardness as great as can be found on any other types of earthenware, domestic and imported.

The Apple, Desert Rose, Ivy and Fruit patterns are hand decorated with underglaze stains on an embossed body. The stains are blended in our own laboratory and are further treated by passing through a colloid mill, a piece of apparatus that by means of surface tension and terrific centrifugal force reduced the size of stain particles to an absolutely impalpable powder.

The decorated pieces are covered with a transparent glaze of high brilliancy which is compounded to bring out the best shades in the underglaze stains and also to show the body in a rich, creamy tone. The body color is derived from the talc, but with the wrong type of glaze it could easily appear quite muddy.

Franciscan Ware cannot be decorated with gold or low-fired overglaze colors, and any artists or decorators wishing to buy ware for redecorating should be told frankly they will not be successful. At the very low temperatures used for overglaze decoration the Franciscan glazes will blister and scum.

Thus, from the starting plant in 1875, Gladding, McBean and Co. had grown to eleven plants. It is a far different concern from the co-partnership formed in 1875. Its products exhaust every conceivable "shape of clay." Its assets have grown from $12,000 to over $17,000,000.

In 1962 Gladding, McBean and Company merged with Lock Joint Pipe Company to form International Pipe and Ceramics Corporation. Then in 1968, the name was changed to Interpace Corporation. (See Interpace Corp.)

Franciscan consisted of three distinct lines: Masterpiece China, a fine quality translucent china; Earthenware, a cream-colored ware in a variety of decal and hand-decorated patterns; and Whitestone Ware, a white earthenware. "Desert Rose" and "Apple Blossom" are two early and very popular patterns in Franciscan earthenware.

Gladding, McBean and Company.

Stiles describes Franciscan pottery as consisting of "tableware, pitchers, bowls, and many novelties designed in lovely shapes and simple lines with glazes of rich, deep coloring." She states that many of the early designs (book written, 1941) were inspired by Spanish California of the Mission period and thus the name Franciscan. (Stiles, Helen, *Pottery in the U.S.*, New York: E.P. Dutton & Co., Inc., 1941, p. 143, and company furnished information.) Pictured is a dinnerware marked G.M.B. in solid colors of green, red, yellow, and blue. Also pictured is an "apple" bowl marked "Franciscan." In the *Buten Museum of Wedgwood Bulletin*, Merion, Pa., April, 1979, vol. 3, no. 2, is the following statement:

> The directors of Josiah Wedgwood and Sons Ltd. have announced that agreement has been reached with Interpace Corporation whereby Wedgwood will acquire the assets of the Franciscan dinnerware and architectural tile pottery in Glendale, California for a consideration of 13 million dollars. The agreement is subject to contract and to any necessary exchange control approval being obtained.

Chronological Chart of Products
Manufactured by
Franciscan Dinnerware Division
(Gladding, McBean and Company until 1962)

(The pattern names, marks, etc. shown are the property of the Interpace Corporation
at the time of the writing of this book.)

Year	Shape or Pattern	Product
1934	Cielito Art Ware	Franciscan
	Cocinero	Franciscan
	El Patio Table Ware	Franciscan
	Garden Ware	Tropico
	Miscellaneous Ware	Special
	Special Ware	Special
1935	Coronado Art Ware	Franciscan
	El Patio Nuevo	Franciscan
	Franciscan Ruby Art	Franciscan
	Tropico Ware	Tropico
1936	Capistrano Art Ware	Franciscan
	Coronado Table Ware	Franciscan
	Florist Special	Franciscan
	Flower Pots & Saucers	Tropico
1937	Aurora Art Ware	Catalina
	Avalon Table Ware	Catalina
	Catalina Art Ware	Catalina
	Del Mar Table Ware	Franciscan
	Del Oro Table Ware	Franciscan
	Encanto Art Ware	Franciscan
	Lamp Bases	Special
	Mango Table Ware	Franciscan
	Montecito Table Ware	Franciscan
	Padua Table Ware	Franciscan
	Pueblo Table Ware	Franciscan
	Rancho Table Ware	Catalina
	Terra Cotta Specials	Catalina
	Tiger Flower Table Ware	Franciscan
	Willow Table Ware	Franciscan
1938	Fruit Table Ware	Franciscan
	Hawthorne Table Ware	Franciscan
	Hotel Ware (1000)	Franciscan
	Kitchen Ware	Franciscan
	Ox Blood Art Ware	Catalina
1939	Geranium Table Ware	Franciscan
	Hotel Ware (1100)	Franciscan
	Max Shonfeld Art Ware	Franciscan
	Nautical Art Ware	Catalina
	Silver City Special	Special
1940	Apple	Franciscan
	Duotone Table Ware	Catalina
	Floral Art Ware	Catalina
	Merced Shape	Masterpiece
	Metropolitan Service	Franciscan
	Montebello Art Ware	Catalina
	Reseda Art Ware	Catalina
	Saguaro Art Ware	Catalina
	Victoria Service	Franciscan

Year	Shape or Pattern	Product
1941	Arden	Masterpiece
	Arcadia Blue	Masterpiece
	Arcadia Gold	Masterpiece
	Arcadia Green	Masterpiece
	Arcadia Maroon	Masterpiece
	Beverly	Masterpiece
	Cherokee Rose Green	Masterpiece
	Cherokee Rose Palomino	Masterpiece
	Dainty Bess	Masterpiece
	Del Monte	Masterpiece
	Desert Rose	Franciscan
	Gold Band 302	Masterpiece
	Laguna	Masterpiece
	Mountain Laurel	Masterpiece
	Wishmaker Table Ware	Franciscan
	Woodside	Masterpiece
1942	Angeleno Art Ware	Catalina
	Arcadia Cobalt	Masterpiece
	Balboa	Masterpiece
	Beverly Cobalt	Masterpiece
	Carmel (turquoise)	Masterpiece
	Cherokee Rose Gold	Masterpiece
	Crinoline	Masterpiece
	Desert Blossom	Masterpiece
	Fremont	Masterpiece
	Gold Band 101	Masterpiece
	Gold Band 201	Masterpiece
	Gold Band 202	Masterpiece
	Gold Band 302	Masterpiece
	Larchmont	Masterpiece
	Monterey Cobalt	Masterpiece
	Northridge	Masterpiece
	Ovide or Redondo Shape	Masterpiece
	Polynesian Art Ware	Franciscan
	Shasta	Masterpiece
	Westwood	Masterpiece
	Wild Flower Table Ware	Franciscan
	Wilshire	Masterpiece
1943	Blue Jessamine	Masterpiece
1944		
1945	Rossmore	Masterpiece
1946	Blossom Time	Masterpiece
	Chinese Yellow	Masterpiece
	Cobalt	Masterpiece
	Del Rey Shape	Masterpiece
	Elsinore	Masterpiece
	Emerald Green	Masterpiece
	Fuchia	Masterpiece
	Lorraine Green	Masterpiece
	Lorraine Maroon	Masterpiece
	Maroon	Masterpiece
	Peacock Green	Masterpiece

Year	Shape or Pattern	Product
1947	California Manor	Masterpiece
	California Wheat	Masterpiece
	Lorraine Grey	Masterpiece
1948	Cameo Pink	Masterpiece
	Domino Black	Masterpiece
	Dove Grey Gold	Masterpiece
	Encanto Shape	Masterpiece
	Huntington 401	Masterpiece
	Ivy	Franciscan
	Jade Green	Masterpiece
	Jasper Green	Masterpiece
	Platinum Band 606	Masterpiece
	Primrose Yellow	Masterpiece
	Robin Egg Blue	Masterpiece
1949	Breakfast Sets	Masterpiece
	California Rose	Masterpiece
	Cimarron	Masterpiece
	Dove Grey Platinum	Masterpiece
	Encino Shape	Masterpiece
	Fruit (1400 line)	Franciscan
	Gold Band 101 (E)	Masterpiece
	Gold Band 301 (B)	Masterpiece
	Mariposa	Masterpiece
	Monterey	Masterpiece
	Platinum Band (E)	Masterpiece
	Renaissance Grey	Masterpiece
	Ridgewood	Masterpiece
	Sonora	Masterpiece
	Tiempo	Franciscan
1950	California Poppy	Franciscan
	Canton	Masterpiece
	Chelan	Masterpiece
	Granada	Masterpiece
	Mesa	Masterpiece
	Olympic	Masterpiece
	Palo Alto	Masterpiece
	Tahoe	Masterpiece
	Sierra	Masterpiece
1951	Franciscan Wheat	Franciscan
1952	Appleton	Masterpiece
	Aragon	Masterpiece
	Birchbark	Masterpiece
	Carmel	Masterpiece
	Celadon (Flambeau)	Masterpiece
	Claremont	Masterpiece
	Concord	Masterpiece
	Magnolia	Masterpiece
	Maroon (Flambeau)	Masterpiece
	Renaissance Crown	Masterpiece
	Sandalwood	Masterpiece
	Spruce	Masterpiece
	Starry Night	Masterpiece
	Teak	Masterpiece
	Willow	Masterpiece
1953	Franciscan Wheat	Franciscan
	Regency	Masterpiece
1954	Echo	Franciscan
	Eclipse Shape	Franciscan
	Eclipse White	Franciscan
	Flair Shape	Franciscan
	Flair White	Franciscan
	Dawn	Masterpiece
	Encanto Rose	Masterpiece
	Pomegranate	Franciscan
	Starburst	Franciscan
	Twilight	Masterpiece

Year	Shape or Pattern	Product
	Willow Bouquet	Masterpiece
	Winter Bouquet	Masterpiece
	Woodlore	Franciscan
	Trio	Franciscan
1955	Autumn	Franciscan
	Contours Art Ware	Masterpiece
	Huntington Rose	Masterpiece
	Oasis	Franciscan
	Silver Pine	Masterpiece
1956	Ballet	Masterpiece
	Brentwood	Masterpiece
	California Wheat	Masterpiece
	Del Rio	Masterpiece
	Encore	Masterpiece
	Duet	Franciscan
1957	Ferndel	Franciscan
	Gold Leaves	Masterpiece
	Montecito	Masterpiece
	Sunset	Masterpiece
1958	Acacia	Masterpiece
	Debut	Masterpiece
	Family China	(3000 line)
	Indian Summer	Family China
	Larkspur	Franciscan
	Radiance	Family China
	Spring Song	Family China
	Sycamore	Family China
	Winsome	Family China
1959	Arabesque	Masterpiece
	Cameo	Masterpiece
	Capri	Cosmopolitan
	Cosmopolitan China	(NTK Japan)
	Crown Jewel	Masterpiece
	Happy Talk	Whitestone
	It's a Breeze	Whitestone
	Lucerne	Cosmopolitan
	Malaya	Cosmopolitan
	Nassau	Cosmopolitan
	Merry go Round	Whitestone
	Newport	Cosmopolitan
	Pink a Dilly	Whitestone
	Sommerset	Masterpiece
	Swingtime	Whitestone
	Tapestry	Masterpiece
	Tara	Cosmopolitan
	Trianon	Cosmopolitan
	Twice Nice	Whitestone
	Valencia	Cosmopolitan
	Whitestone Ware	(TTK Japan)
1960	Daisy	Franciscan
	Cloud Nine	Whitestone
	Cortina	Cosmopolitan
	Interlude	Masterpiece
	St. Moritz	Cosmopolitan
	Whirl a Gig	Whitestone
1961	Corinthian	Masterpiece
	Glenfield	Porcelain
	Fan Tan	Whitestone
	Melrose	Porcelain
	Patrician	Masterpiece
	Platina	Porcelain
	Porcelain	(NTK Japan)
	Simplicity	Porcelain
	Snow Pine	Porcelain
	Spice	Franciscan
	Swirl Shape	Masterpiece
	Talisman	Porcelain

Year	Shape or Pattern	Product
1962	Cypress	Franciscan
	Dusty Rose	Regal China
	Medallion	Family China
	Platinum Swirl	Regal China
	Renaissance Gold	Masterpiece
	Renaissance Platinum	Masterpiece
	Rondelay	Masterpiece
	Silver Mist	Masterpiece
	Silver Wheat	Regal China
	Simplicity	Regal China
	Wedding Band	Regal China
1963	Blue Fancy	Whitestone
	Fruit (2200 line)	Franciscan
	Sierra Sand	Franciscan
	Snow Crest	Franciscan
	Tulip Time	Franciscan
	2200 Shape	Franciscan
1964	Classic	Regal China
	Hacienda	Franciscan
	Malibu	Franciscan
	Merry Mint	Whitestone
	Ring A Ling	Whitestone
1965	Cantata	Whitestone
	Emerald Isle	Discovery
	Hacienda (green)	Franciscan
	Pickwick	Whitestone
	Tahiti	Discovery
	Terra Cotta	Discovery
	Topaz	Discovery
	Walden	Whitestone
	Discovery (new name)	Family China
1966	Antique Green	Masterpiece
	Antigua	Whitestone
	Brown Eyes	Whitestone
	El Dorado	Earthenware
	Martinique	Masterpiece
	Midnight Mist	Masterpiece
	Moon Glow	Masterpiece
	Nightingale	Masterpiece
	7000 Shape	Masterpiece
1967	Constantine	Masterpiece
	Chalice	Masterpiece
	Garland	Earthenware
	Hawaii	Whitestone
	Madeira	Earthenware
	Montago	Earthenware
	Zinnia	Earthenware
1968	Applique	Masterpiece
	Bird 'N Hand	Whitestone
	Monaco	Masterpiece
	Regalia	Masterpiece
	Royal Renaissance	Masterpiece
1969	Gabrielle	Masterpiece
	Kasmir	Masterpiece
	Pebble Beach	Earthenware
1970	Indigo	Masterpiece
	Medallion Plate	Masterpiece
	Millbrook	Ironstone
	Nut Tree	Earthenware
	Peacock Plate	Masterpiece
	Yellow Bouquet	Ironstone
1971	Ariel	Masterpiece
	Castile	Masterpiece
	Golden Gate	Whitestone
	Happenstance	Whitestone
	Larami	Stoneware
	Petals & Pods	Whitestone

Year	Shape or Pattern	Product
	Quadrille	Masterpiece
	Sequoia	Stoneware
	Silver Lining	Masterpiece
	Taos	Stoneware
	Yuma	Stoneware
	Zanzibar	Earthenware
	Cimmaron	Stoneware
	Floral	Earthenware
1972	Abstract	Gourmet
	Apache	Ind. Stoneware
	Brush	Gourmet
	Cane	Ind. Ironstone
	Circles	Gourmet
	Crinoline	Masterpiece
	Dotted Stripe	Ind. Porcelain
	Yellow Zebra	Ind. Porcelain
	Flame	Ind. Porcelain
	Gold Plate	Ind. Porcelain
	Gourmet	Gourmet
	Gray Wave	Ind. Porcelain
	Kachina	Ind. Stoneware
	Lariat	Ind. Stoneware
	Moondance	Earthenware
	Nouelle Ebony	Masterpiece
	Nouelle Ivory	Masterpiece
	Nuts and Bolts	Ind. Porcelain
	Petalpoint	Masterpiece
	Plain White	Ind. Porcelain
	Pueblo	Earthenware
	Rimrock	Earthenware
	Rodeo	Ind. Stoneware
	Silver Plate	Ind. Porcelain
	Sonora	Ind. Stoneware
	Stripes	Gourmet
	Sundance	Earthenware
1973	Amapola	Earthenware
	Creole	Earthenware
	Jamoca	Earthenware
	Madrigal	Masterpiece
	Mandalay (Neptune)	Masterpiece
	Mary Jane	Ironstone
	Minaret	Masterpiece
	Natchez	Masterpiece
	Ondine	Masterpiece
	Picnic	Earthenware
	7700 Line	Masterpiece
	2600 Line	Earthenware
	2700 Line	Earthenware
	Shalimar	Masterpiece
	Yankee Doodle	Ironstone
1974	Garden Party	Earthenware
	Ginger Snap	Earthenware
	Limerick	Ironstone
	Madrigal	Masterpiece
	Mandalay	Masterpiece
	Minaret	Masterpiece
	Maypole	Earthenware
	Ondine	Masterpiece
	Picnic	Earthenware
	Shalimar	Masterpiece
1975	Crown Daisy	Earthenware
	Dogwood	Earthenware
	Fallbrook	Ironstone
	Greenhouse Series	Earthenware
	Mirasol	Earthenware
	Pillowtalk	Ironstone
	Swirl	Masterpiece
	Wrightwood	Masterpiece

GLASGOW POTTERY. John Moses started the Galsgow Pottery in Trenton, New Jersey, in 1893. (His brother, James Moses started Mercer Pottery, Trenton, in 1858, and John and James were both associated with James Carr and Edward Clark for a few months in 1879 in the International Pottery.) This firm made a great variety of articles and used several marks. They started with Rockingham and yellowware in the early years and then later made cream-colored ware, white granite or ironstone, thin hotel ware, a completely vitrified china, and steamboat china. They made ware for the armed forces stamped Q.M.D. and U.S.M.C. At the Centennial Exhibition they exhibited stone china, decorated ware, and majolica. A plate, decorated with "Philadelphia" in a circle around "1873," then in a larger circle "Centennial Commemorative of the Boston Tea Party, Dec. 1773" all of this on the front, was pictured in "Memo from Marcia," *Spinning Wheel*, January-February, 1973, p. 72. The plate was backstamped "Glasgow Pottery Company, Trenton, New Jersey." The Glasgow Pottery was listed only until 1900 in the *Trenton City Directories*. Between 1901 and 1905 the company was listed as **JOHN MOSES AND SONS** making general pottery. The *1902-1903 Complete Directory* listed the company as making semiporcelain, white granite, in common china dinner sets, toilet sets, and short sets of odd dishes, some decorated. Pictured is a plate made by Glasgow Pottery with the old transfer design decals and some hand painting on the blue and pink flowers and brown leaves. The other plate with the fancier shape is marked only with the word "Trilby." What might be conceived to be small handles protrude on either side.

Glasgow Pottery.

GLIDDEN POTTERY, INC. was located at 100 North Main, Alfred, New York. In an ad in *Better Homes and Gardens*, March 1947, is shown a rounded square bakeware dish made by Glidden which is hand painted in green and blue. They were included in the *Crockery and Glass Journal Directory* issue in March, 1954, under dinnerware. The following pattern names were listed in 1954: "Menagerie," "Mexican Cock," square Gliddenware, and a modular casserole.

GLOBE CHINA COMPANY operated for just one year in Cambridge, Ohio, in 1925. See the listing Various Cambridge Potteries and Bradshaw China Company for more.

GLOBE POTTERY COMPANY succeeded Frederick, Schenkle, Allen and Company (1881-1888) in 1888 in East Liverpool, Ohio. Around 1900 Globe Pottery joined the East Liverpool Potteries Company. That company dissolved in 1903. See the East Liverpool Potteries Company for dishes made by all six companies that went together to form the group, including a plate made by Globe Pottery Company. The Globe Pottery was listed last in 1912. They continued for a while after the combination was dissolved.

GLOUCESTER CHINA COMPANY. See American Porcelain Manufacturing Company of Gloucester, New Jersey, for history.

GOLDSCHEIDER POTTERY was listed in the *Trenton City Directories* from 1943 through 1950 as the Goldscheider Everlast Corporation. While I feel certain this pottery was mainly involved in the making of art pottery, they undoubtedly made some items which could be used on the table. From the *American Ceramic Society Bulletin*, "Goldscheiders Produces New Porcelain Base," vol. 25, no. 12, 1946, p. 494:

> The Goldscheider family, famous for three hundred years as Viennese craftsmen, has discovered a new porcelain base.
>
> The Goldscheiders, refugees from their native Vienna from the day Hitler invaded it, are producing their products in Trenton, N.J., and Goldscheiderware has obtained a higher production level here than in the non profitable days of old Vienna.
>
> Erwin F. Goldscheider, vice-president of the company in charge of production, is responsible for the ceramic discovery. The direct result will be an immediate change from the present china body to an additional and stronger porcelain body. The porcelain base is a combination of American air-floated and magnetically purified kaolin feldspathic rock, and silica.
>
> The Goldscheider's new fine-china body apparently assumes extra hardness when fired to vitrification, retaining the highest possible degree of pure whiteness. This permits the most delicate underglaze decoration to be applied on its surface, as well as unlimited nuances of color shading. Since it is leadless, it will retain its original sheen, a goal of ceramists for hundreds of years.
>
> These new translucent porcelains will be decorated exclusively in gold, platinum, and overglaze colors for extreme delicacy of ornament, and in unlimited colors and shades for general production. Production has begun at once for early shipment to American stores first, then global exportations to follow.

Gonder Ceramic Arts Company.

GONDER CERAMIC ARTS POTTERY was founded by Lawton Gonder in 1941, and the pottery operated until 1957. Gonder had worked at the Ohio Pottery and the American Encaustic Tiling Company both in Zanesville. Before 1941, Gonder was employed by the Florence Pottery in Mount Gilead, Ohio, during the time they were manufacturing pottery for Rum Rill, a distributing agency in Little Rock, Arkansas. Exact pieces may be found marked with either "Gonder" or "Rum Rill." Either Gonder brought the Rum Rill molds with him to Gonder Ceramic Arts, or perhaps Gonder was yet another company that manufactured for Rum Rill besides Red Wing, Shawnee, and Florence. Gonder Ceramic Arts did make dinnerware in a square shape with a mottled appearance as is shown in the picture. They also made a variety of pitchers, teapots, and bowls that could be used for decoration or service in the kitchen, but their main output was of a decorative type of ware.

GOODWIN POTTERY, East Liverpool. The Goodwin family was involved in the pottery business in East Liverpool, Ohio, and Trenton, New Jersey, starting as early as 1844. John Goodwin made the old yellowware and Rockingham in East Liverpool from 1844 to 1853, sold to the Baggott Brothers, moved to Trenton until 1863, then came back to East Liverpool at various potteries. In 1872 John Goodwin purchased the old Broadway Pottery of T. Rigby and Company. It was here that he began preparations to make whiteware. He died in 1875. James, son of John, began whiteware production in 1876. The firm became the Goodwin Brothers until 1893 when it became the Goodwin Pottery until 1912 (Jervis). The building was purchased by Hall China Company in 1919, but between 1912 and 1919 it may have been vacant for quite a time. Goodwin Pottery Company made a pear-white, a cream-colored ware, and some decorated ware. In 1902 they were listed in the *1902-1903 Complete Directory* as making semiporcelain and common china dinner sets, toilet sets, and short sets of odd dishes. ("James H. Goodwin," *Ceramic Society Bulletin*, VII, February 1925, p. 34.)

GORHAM COMPANY. The Gorham Company was established in Providence, Rhode Island, in 1831 by Jabez Gorham. Jabez's son, John, was primarily responsible for developing the manufacturing techniques that enabled the company to become the world's leading silversmiths, famous for sterling flatware as well as silver hollow-ware. In 1967, Gorham became a division of Textron, Inc. of Providence, and then began developing the total tabletop marketing approach by acquiring the Reizart

Crystal Company. In March 23, 1970, it acquired the Flintridge China Company of Pasadena, California. Flintridge had begun operations in 1945 as a partnership of Thomas Hogan and Milton Mason. Their manufacturing skills helped to build Flintridge into a small but highly respected china company. Beginning with a top quality product, Gorham added its design and marketing strengths and within eight years expanded from 30,000 square feet of manufacturing space and four kilns to over 80,000 square feet and eight large quality-designed kilns. (Company furnished information by the Gorham Division of Textron of Providence, Rhode Island.)

Black Contessa

Royal Buttercup

Fairmeadows

Gorham Company fine china. (Also see cover photograph.) Photographs: Gorham Company.

Towne Garden

Chantilly Lace

69

GRAY AND CLARK. See New England Pottery.

GREAT WESTERN POTTERY was for some reason a popular name for potteries. The one that is of concern to this book is the one founded by the Brunts in East Liverpool in 1867 and which was taken over by John Wyllie in 1874. This pottery made Rockingham and yellowware, but they also made ironstone in the various dinnerware patterns of the time. See John Wyllie and Son for details. Incidentally, about the name Great Western Pottery, there was a pottery in Tiffin by that name listed in directories for 1894 as employing one-hundred twenty-seven people to make earthenware, but in the 1907 listing, the earthenware turned out to be plumbers' goods. There was also a Great Western Pottery in Kokomo, Indiana, in 1922, but I found no further listing.

GREENWOOD POTTERY in Trenton, New Jersey, was organized in 1868 out of a pottery which had been started in 1861 by Stephens, Tams, and Company. In 1886 the name "Greenwood China" was first impressed on ironstone or white granite according to Barber. Before that time the company used a mark showing the coat of arms of the state of New Jersey. Sometimes the initials of the company were used. The *1902-1903 Complete Directory* listed Greenwood Pottery as making hotel ware, sanitary ware, dinner sets, toilet sets, and short sets of odd dishes, some decorated. One pattern made by Greenwood Pottery was the "Onion" pattern. The Greenwood Pottery is discussed in several places in Barber's *Pottery and Porcelain of the United States*. He mentions Greenwood Pottery's use of the "Greenwood China" mark. Nowhere in Barber's books is Greenwood China and Greenwood Pottery discussed as being two separate companies, but they may have been. In searching for an ending date for the Greenwood Pottery, I had the *Trenton City Directory* listings from 1900 to 1975; I didn't have the ones before 1900. From before 1900 to 1924, the Greenwood China Company was sometimes called Greenwood Porcelain Company. Greenwood China Company (or Greenwood Porcelain Company) was listed as doing business at North Clinton Avenue opposite Oak. The Greenwood Pottery was listed at East Canal and North Grand streets until 1933. In the *Industrial Directories* for the state of New Jersey, these were also listed as two completely separate companies doing business at the addresses already given, making general ware. There may have been two separate companies. W.P. Jervis in "A Dictionary of Pottery Terms" in the *Pottery, Glass, and Brass Salesman*, February 21, 1918, p. 43, said the following:

> Greenwood Pottery Company, Trenton, N.J.–Incorporated in 1863, the original officers being Charles Brearley, president: James P. Stephens, treasurer, and James Tams, superintendent. After many failures and disappointments, a body was produced combining the best qualities of procelain and earthenware. *This highly vitrified ware became known as hotel china, its peculiar toughness rendering it suitable for rough usage, and may be regarded not only as an independent American invention, but as a decided advance in ceramics.* Mr. James Tams, the present president, is largely responsible for the success attained. (Italics added for emphasis.)

GRIFFIN CHINA COMPANY. See Phoenix Pottery, Phoenixville, Pennsylvania, for history.

GRIFFIN, SMITH, AND HILL. See Phoenix Pottery, Phoenixville, Pennsylvania, for history.

GRIFFIN, SMITH, AND COMPANY. See Phoenix Pottery, Phoenixville, Pennsylvania, for history.

GUERNSEY EARTHENWARE. See Cambridge Potteries for history and marks.

THE M.A. HADLEY POTTERY in Louisville, Kentucky, got its initial start in 1939 when Mary Alice Hadley brought home pieces of pottery to hand decorate. After she decorated them she took them to the Louisville Pottery Company for glazing and firing. The demand for her pottery increased, so she hired help to decorate, then rented a room at the Louisville pottery in which to work. The business grew, and in 1944 the Hadleys were looking for a small pottery to buy. They bought the building at 1570 Story Avenue in Louisville, Kentucky, in October of that year. By December they had the first kiln ready to fire. In 1948 they added a second kiln and new processing equipment. Until 1969, the ware was either cast (in molds) or jiggered (thrown on a wheel by hand). In 1969 a Ram Press was put into operation for making plates and similar items.

The Hadley Pottery Company was always operated by George and Mary Alice Hadley as a cooperative effort. In the early years the business had grown so rapidly George had to quit his job to devote full time to the pottery. In 1960 the name was changed from the Hadley Pottery to Hadley Pottery, Inc. In 1965, Mrs. Hadley died. The same attractive, hand-decorated pieces of kitchenware and pottery are still available at the pottery, using the patterns that were originated by M.A. Hadley.

Mrs. Hadley painted in water colors and oils long before she became involved in pottery decorating. She had received awards and recognition and had exhibited paintings in New York, Boston, Los Angeles, and other cities. The Hadley designs used on the pottery were unique. Hadley pottery is made from native clays with a modified stoneware body similar to ironstone. The decoration is applied on the unfired pieces, which are then sprayed or dip-glazed and fired in a single-fire process at 2300 degrees. This produces maximum bond between the body and decoration which is under the lead-free glaze, making a very durable product.

The Hadley Pottery produces a complete line of dinnerware and numerous ornamental and incidental pieces. Open stock is maintained in eight patterns and marketed as "M.A. Hadley Designs" in all fifty states and Canada. The Hadleys also made attractive pottery lamps. By 1950 the list of dinnerware patterns had grown to eight designs. "Pear and Grape," "Green Bird," "Fisherman," and "Country Scene" which came in eight scenes (a farmer and wife, son, daughter, horse, cow, pig, etc.), were all introduced before 1943. Others were "Blue Horse" in deep blue and white and "Ship and Whale" (also called "Three Masted Schooner and Whale"). By 1950 a "Scalloped Edge" was listed in solid white or green glaze. "Three Leaf Clover" was another, but wasn't listed for very many years. In 1952, "Brown Fleck" with a straightedge design was chosen by the Selection Committee of the Museum of Modern Art of New York for the museum's "Good Design" Exhibition. "Brown Fleck" is a favorite that is still made.

The list of kitchenware items made by Hadley is extensive: saltbox, matchbox, coffee urns, canister type jars for tea, coffee, sugar, etc., a little dipper to use in canisters, a syrup pitcher, cinnamon shaker, mustard jar, even a dish for the dog and one for the cat. There were also many figure pieces made at Hadley Pottery.

HAEGER POTTERIES, INC. In 1871, David H. Haeger purchased an interest in the Dundee Brick Yard in Dundee, Illinois. Before passing away in 1900, Mr. Haeger added two other brick and tile factories to his holdings, which earned him a comfortable fortune. After 1900 the management fell to his sons who added flowerpots to the products in 1912. In 1914 they began to glaze pottery and Haeger Potteries, Inc. was really given birth. A few days before World War I the pottery launched its artware efforts, sending the first shipment to Marshall Field and Company of Chicago. The ware was widely accepted, and in July, 1919, Edmund H. Haeger purchased the pottery at Dundee from the family corporation and doubled the factory output by constructing another kiln. Output and sales kept gradually increasing as the years went by until, in 1939, Haeger Potteries, Inc. took over the Macomb Pottery at Macomb, Illinois, to convert the plant exclusively to artware. A second tunnel kiln was built at Dundee in 1941. In 1934 the Haeger Potteries exhibited at the Century of Progress in Chicago in a separate building which housed a complete pottery plant. Marshall Field and Company catalogs show Haeger luncheon and tea sets made in 1938 in four colors, blue, rose, yellow, and green, with attractive shapes and a fine glaze. Also pictured in an ad for 1976, was the "Country Classics," a hand-decorated tabletop collection in early American tradition which were made of ironstone in Leather Brown and Orange Peel. (Company information. Also the *American Ceramic Society Bulletin*, "History of Haeger Potteries, Inc.," XXIV, October 1945, p. 356.) According to *China Glass and Tableware*,

"Newsletter," August 1979, p. 17, Haeger Potteries, Inc. will be introducing a new dinnerware line in the fall of 1980. The new line will be named "Cherokee Stoneware" and was designed by Ben Seibel.

Hall China Company "Rose Parade" pattern pieces. Photograph: Martha Brisker's Antiques, Richwood, Ohio.

Hall China Company "Autumn Leaf" pitcher. Photograph: Jo Cunningham.

HALL CHINA COMPANY was founded August 14, 1903, and is still in business. The company was started at East Fourth and Walnut streets in East Liverpool by Robert Hall and his son, Robert T. Hall in the plant formerly operated by the East Liverpool Potteries Company. It was a hard beginning for a new company suffering from lack of capital and stiff competition. Whiteware, bedpans, mugs, and jugs were the early products. From 1908 to 1914 dinnerware was added to the line but discontinued until later. The company's ultimate success hinged on Mr. Hall's determination to perfect an economical, single-firing process for making a product with a leadless glaze. In 1911, Robert Hall was successful on both counts and produced a ware that is hard, non-porous, craze proof, and beautiful. The company labeled this line of one-fire ware, "Secret Process" and it is still a most important part of their production. From then on the Hall story is one of growth, constant need for new facilities, etc. In 1920, soon after the death of Robert T. Hall, Malcolm W. Thompson joined the company. In 1930 they built a complete new factory in the East End section of East Liverpool and abandoned their original plant. Hall became a leader in the line of teapots, making them in all conceivable sizes, shapes, gold-decorated, etc. My favorite is the one that looks like Aladdin's lamp. A much collected pattern is Autumn Leaf (see photograph of pitcher). Poppy pattern and Red Poppy pattern, Crocus, and Blue Bouquet, are a few of the patterns. I believe Hall China Company products have been more closely documented than any pottery that ever existed in the United States, between the very fine books by Harvey Duke and Jo Cunningham. (See the Bibliography for books on Hall.) See several marks in Marks Section. Pictured is a range set consisting of a drip bowl and shakers in Hall's Rose Parade pattern. Also pictured is a casserole, sugar, and creamer in Rose Parade. In *China, Glass and Lamps*, June 18, 1923, p. 21, Hall China Company's ad read "Forty-eight different teapots, no two alike. Every pot is craze proof, non-absorbent fireproof china from the largest manufacturer of fireproof cooking china in the world."

In the Sears and Roebuck catalogs during the 1940s, dishes made by Hall China Company were advertised. These contained the "Harmony House" mark seeen in the Marks Section. Pattern or decoration names were "Richmond," "Monticello," and "Mount Vernon." All of these were the same shape, thin, fine china, handsomely decorated. Pictured is a pitcher, identified by Harvey Duke as "Daffodil/Squiggle J-Sunshine," (p. 91). "Russet Ware," as shown in Sears and Roebuck in the 1930s, had an ivory, smooth interior and a surface which looks painted but is undoubtedly baked on. There is a shaker of "Russet Ware" pictured. Also pictured is an Irish Coffee Mug number 1273. The sugar bowl is "Red Poppy." See the picture in the introduction for a tulip decal used by Hall China. The small pitcher in the photograph is "Harlequin." The Hallcraft Line designed for Hall China by Eva Zeisel includes many beautiful designs or decorations. The "Hallcraft White" was left very plain to accent the shape of the dishes. "Spring" had blossom clusters in pink, turquoise, and violet, with soft green leaves. "Dawn" was a stylized sunburst in fine black lines. "Flair" had turquoise blossoms with scroll decor. "Fantasy" had a slender black abstraction accented with yellow dots. "Arizona" featured golden yellow leaves and traces of black. "Frost Flowers" was floral sprays in turquoise blue. Wildflowers in gay multicolors was called "Bouquet." "Holiday" had sprays of flowers in red and black. "Buckingham" was a decoration of wrought iron grillwork and trees. "Caprice" featured flowers in pinks, grays, and yellows with accents of blue and black that filled most of the plate. "Romance" consisted of floral sprays in tangerine, ochre, and black. Pieces in the Hallcraft Line included three sizes of platters, two sizes of jugs or pitchers, a covered onion soup, different sizes of covered dishes, a fruit bowl, coffeepot, teapot, and many other accessory pieces in addition to the regular pieces such as plates, cups, etc. (Taken from material sent by the company.)

THE HAMPSHIRE POTTERY operated in Keene, New Hampshire, from 1871 to 1923. Started by J.S. Taft; at first they made very ordinary wares such as stone jugs, crocks, flowerpots, milk pans, and pitchers. Then in 1878 the firm started making Majolica in green, brown, yellow, and blue colors with raised decorations. The early pieces were not marked. In 1883, Wallace L. King was hired to run a department

73

which was to produce decorative pottery. A line of art specialties requiring as many as five firings was developed called Royal Worcester. Several artists were hired and the emphasis was on art pottery right up to the First World War when the plant was closed temporarily. In 1916, Taft sold the factory to George Morton of Boston. When the factory opened again after the war, white hotel china and mosaic floor tile were added to the line. In 1923 the factory closed. A mark (not shown in Marks Section) used by this pottery was an M inside an O designating Emoretta, wife of Cadmon Robertson who entered the business in 1904. In the *Complete Directory of Glass Factories and Potteries of the United States and Canada*, 1902 and 1903, J.S. Taft and Company were listed as making dinner sets, toilet sets, short sets of odd dishes, some decorated. Evans mentions another pottery that was purchased by Hampshire Pottery by 1874 in Keene. The second pottery was begun in 1871 by *STARKEY AND HOWARD*, later purchased by *W.P. CHAMBERLAIN AND E.C. BAKER* before being purchased by Hampshire Pottery. ("First Hampshire Pottery Was Made One Hundred Years Ago," staff written, *Tri State Trader*, December 21, 1971, p. 2; and Evans, Paul, "Hampshire Pottery," *Spinning Wheel*, September, 1970, p. 22.)

HARDESTY CHINA COMPANY, New Brighton, Pennsylvania, at some time in the 1930s, was formed by Eugene Hardesty to produce a fine, thin, translucent dinnerware at a reduced cost. Production of this ware was based on Hardesty's patent application for a quick firing innovation which produced a vitrified dinnerware. He was also a consultant at Paden City Pottery and worked for a number of years as a ceramic engineer at Mayer China Company in Beaver Falls. Hardesty died accidentally in November, 1947, at age 41. I was unable to determine the exact dates for the pottery. It was not listed in the *1947 Industrial Directories* for Pennsylvania so it was probably out of business before his untimely death. ("Eugene Hardesty," *Bulletin of American Ceramic Society*, XXVII, March 1948, p. 147.)

HARKER POTTERY. In 1839, an Englishman, Benjamin Harker, Sr., sold whatever he owned in England, came to Ohio, bought a patch of ground, erected a log cabin, built a beehive kiln, moved his clay down off a big hill by mule, ground it by hand and, in 1840, started a pottery business which lasted until 1972 and culminated in the Harker Pottery. The pottery researchers do not agree at all on the dates of the early meanderings and partnerships of the Harkers, and I can't imagine Benjamin and his successors worrying very much about record-keeping as they fought the weather, primitive methods, and bone weary tiredness, just trying to get that clay off the big hill and made into usable products. They probably never dreamed that in 1979 somebody would be trying to figure out what they were doing back then. There were no good roads and no railroads, but the timber was uncut and served as a source of fuel, even though that meant a lot more work to cut it. A few weeks after Harker arrived, James Bennett came to town and started his pottery in East Liverpool which is considered the first operable pottery in the district. Harker furnished clay to Bennett which gave Harker a little capital. It was after seeing Bennett take the first pottery out of his kiln that Harker got the idea to make pottery too. Up until then he had intended just to farm his ground. Benjamin Harker didn't live too long. From 1844-1847 his two sons, Benjamin, Jr., and George operated the pottery now called the *ETRURIA POTTERY.* Some sources say George died as early as 1851, but it seems, perhaps, he lived until around 1864. Anyhow during this period Benjamin, Jr. had to go to the Civil War, partners and operators came and went, and confusion reigns in the history books. From 1846 or 1847 to 1851, the name was *HARKER (George) TAYLOR (James) AND COMPANY.* From 1851 to 1854, it was *HARKER, (George) THOMPSON, AND COMPANY.* The companies just listed operated on the River Road east of what became the Homer Laughlin Pottery. When Benjamin and George separated, Benjamin took a partner, William G. Smith, and operated as *HARKER AND SMITH* at the Northeast corner of Second and Washington streets from 1853 to around 1857 when the pottery became *FOSTER AND GARNER.* When

Benjamin came back from the Civil War he was in the Wedgwood Pottery which was sold to Wallace and Chetwynd in 1881. When George died, his sons William W. Harker and Harry N. Harker were very young. A brother-in-law, David Boyce, filled in until the boys were old enough to take over. In 1877, Benjamin, Jr. sold any interest he still retained in the original Harker pottery and it was George's boys who became responsible for the founding of the pottery that concerns the collectors of dinnerware. In July, 1889, the firm incorporated, and from 1890 on it was known as the Harker Pottery with George's son, W.W. Harker as the first president.

The name Boyce runs through the Harker Pottery history. We have mentioned the first Boyce named David who came to the pottery when Benjamin, Jr. went to the Civil War and who then stayed on until George's sons grew up enough to take over the business. David had a son, Charles R. Boyce, and the sons of Charles Boyce were executives in the pottery around 1940. Their names were David and Robert. Finally in 1959, David G. Boyce became president. No doubt part of Harker's huge success for so very many years was the fact that not only did the family stay with the business, but a line of faithful employees also stayed, giving the company a certain pride in their products. By 1965, Harker was employing three hundred people to turn out twenty-five million pieces annually, with tunnel kilns and the latest equipment. Harker developed a special engraving process which gave us "Cameoware." They featured a Russel Wright designed dinner service from 1953 to 1958. (Sources: Ramsay, Jervis, and Barber's books, as well as the "Oldest Pottery in America Marks Its 125th Anniversary" reprinted from *China, Glass and Tablewares*, January, 1965, no page given. Also "Centenary Anniversary of Harker Pottery Company" from the *American Ceramic Society Bulletin*, XX, June 1941, p. 25.)

According to Harvey Duke in the *Depression Glass Daze*, January, 1978, Columbia China was a separate sales agency set up by Harker Pottery. He said they used different names and marks so that more than one outlet in a given town might think they were handling Harker Pottery's wares on an exclusive basis. Duke said this didn't fool anyone for long and the marks were dropped. He cited "Hotoven," "Columbia China Company," "Oven Ware," and "Sun Glow Bakerite" as examples.

Harker Pottery. **Front row:** *"Pate Sur Pate" pitcher, "Fruits" cake plate and servers.* **Back row:** *"Deco Dahlia, Hot Oven" casserole, "Fruits" water bottle, "Cameoware, Provincial Tulip" plate.*

All we can do is to give a suggestion here as to the many lines developed by Harker Pottery. A special ware made by this company was "Cameoware" which came in many different designs. The design was recessed in a white color. The older Cameoware had a much deeper design than the later Cameoware. Pattern names were "Provincial Tulip" (see the picture of a plate in this design), "Wheat," "Blue Rhythm," "Lotus," and "White Rose" to name only a few. These were found advertised in the 1950s and early 1960s. "Quaker Maid" by Harker had a dark brown glaze with drips and blotches of lighter colored glaze around the edges. This was a full line with plates, cups, accessory pieces, etc. "Bakerite" was a line of kitchen accessories including bowls, water bottles, rolling pins, spoons and forks for serving, cake plates, casseroles, etc. This line came with many different decorations. Pictured is a water bottle, cake plate, and serving tools in "Fruits" design. "Pate Sur Pate" ware was part of the Chesterton Series; the ware had vivid solid coloring in blue, green, gray, etc. and had an attractive raised edging. See the photograph of the cream pitcher in Pate Sur Pate; these pieces were marked with this name. Also, see the photograph with Russel Wright history for a handled cake plate designed for Harker Pottery by Wright. Harker also had a line of kitchen accessories called "Hot Oven" which came in various designs or decorations. Pictured is a casserole in "Deco Dahlia" marked "Hot Oven."

In the *National Glass, Pottery Collectables Journal,* vol. I no. 1, December, 1978, p. 12, is information about how Harker Pottery made Cameoware. The ware was first glazed with color, a template placed over it, then sand blasted. The sand blasting left the pattern of the template. Then the ware was given another coat of glaze. This is the only pottery that I have found so far that has made this type of ware. This was an expensive and time consuming process. Harker didn't make as much Cameoware as they did of their other lines. Considering these facts plus the attractiveness of Cameoware, we know another great collectible is born.

HARMONY HOUSE was not a company but a brand or trade name used by Sears and Roebuck for their products produced by many different companies. This will be found as the only mark on many dishes; also may be found in combination with a maker's mark.

HATTLERSLEY POTTERY. See City Pottery, Trenton, New Jersey.

D.F. HAYNES AND COMPANY. See Chesapeake Pottery.

HAYNES, BENNETT, AND COMPANY. See Chesapeake Pottery.

HEATH CERAMICS, INC. of Sausalito, California, is closely tied to the history of Edith Kiertener Heath who studied at the Chicago Art Institute for six years, was a supervisor in a federal art project, and who began working in ceramics in 1941 and 1942 by making dinnerware on a potter's wheel. Then in 1947 she designed and began production of Heath dinnerware with ten employees and Brian Heath as manager. From that almost humble beginning, the Heath Ceramics business grew until in 1960 they moved into a beautiful new building built and designed for their individual company's needs. In 1961 a "Gourmet Line" was developed, and in 1963 the company also started making architectural tile as well as the other products. One great accomplishment was a tile mural two-hundred twenty feet long by ten feet high in the Occidental Center in Los Angeles. (This is mentioned in a dinnerware and accessory book only to show the scope of the work of the company.) This is a small resume of the work done by Edith Kiertener Heath and the Heath Ceramics, both of which will be known as an integral part of the American Ceramic Industry. (Information, dates, etc. furnished by company.)

HEATHER HALL in Beaver County, Pennsylvania, was a pottery which made restaurant and hotel ware in the 1950s.

HEMPHILL, JOSEPH. See W.E. Tucker.

HENDERSON, D. & J. See the Jersey City Pottery.

HEROLD POTTERY in Golden, Colorado, was started in 1910 by John Herold, chemist and potter from Roseville, when he was forced to go to Colorado for his health. He made porcelain tablewares and ornamental objects as well as chemical porcelain. Money or capital seemed to be Herold's greatest problem, and by 1914 he had sold out and was back in Ohio to work. (Evans, Paul, "Artware of the Ohio Pottery," *Spinning Wheel*, December, 1976, p. 15.) According to a letter from Charles S. Ryland, an employee of Coors Porcelain, the Herold plant belonged to Coors as early as 1915 but the name wasn't changed to Coors Porcelain until 1920. (See Coors Porcelain.)

RICHARD P. HOFFMAN CHINA COMPANY has been in Columbus, Ohio, since 1946. They make handcrafted dinnerware and related items in the old Pennsylvania Dutch style. The following are patterns of dinnerware made by Hoffman: "Sunburst," yellow with shaded edges; "Meadow," light gray with shaded edges; "Turquoise," a vibrant blue with shaded edges; "Forest Green," a dark bright green; "White Satin," waxy textured as a gardenia; "Grape," a single bunch of deep blue grapes and vine at the side of a plate with mottled gray background; "Sunflower," green and yellow sunflower on light gray background; "Sand," a cream-colored matt glaze breaking to amber; "New Age," modern design of orange and brown on gray; "Fruit," a cluster of fruits on white satin background with a green border; and "Daisy," a daisy pattern on white satin background. Hoffman also makes personalized plates with Dutch-type inscriptions such as family tree plates, birth plates, children's sets, etc. (See picture.) Of interest was the interpretation of the Pennsylvania Dutch art given to Hoffman by a knowledgeable lady. I have repeated it here because many of the dinnerware companies used similar designs as may be noted in the photographs for the various companies. (1) Open Lilies surrounding figures means Peace and Love. (2) Ground Line means the earth from which all life springs. (3) Wheat signifies prosperity. (4) The Dove indicates peace. (5) Continuous Lines mean eternal life. (6) A flower above figures means fertility. (7) Laurel signifies honor. (8) The Evergreen Tree for good health. (9) Scallops for the ups and downs of life. (10) Dots mean daily prayers. (11) Winged Leaves denote God's goodness.

Richard P. Hoffman China Company.

HOLIDAY DESIGNS, INC. operating in Sebring, Ohio, at present (1979) are manufacturers of very attractive cookie jars and ceramic canister sets. This company started in 1964. See the Marks Section for marks. See the picture of apple cookie jar on page 18.

HOLLYDALE POTTERY COMPANY in Hollydale, California, was listed in 1948 (my earliest California directory for that period) through 1954. They were not listed in 1955. They were makers of dinnerware and earthenware. I found one pattern name listed for them—"Holly Stone" dinnerware.

HOLLYWOOD CERAMICS, Los Angeles, California, were manufacturers for Maddux of California. (See Maddux.) Hollywood Cermics were listed at 3061 Riverside Drive in 1954. A change of ownership for Hollywood Ceramics in 1976 is explained in the Maddux of California history.

HOPEWELL CHINA COMPANY in Hopewell, Virginia, was started in 1922 by Sol Ostrow and became the **JAMES RIVER POTTERIES** around 1929 to 1930 (it was still listed Hopewell China in 1929), which continued in operation until shortly after 1938. Floyd McKee in *A Century of Dinnerware*, p. 37, said that some of the buildings that had been used in the World War I work in Hopewell were purchased to house the new pottery. Other owners that followed Ostrow were Joe Thorley and later, Sol Slobodkin. I think it is a safe statement to say this was the only semiporcelain dinnerware manufacturer in any of the southern states around that time. By the succession of owners, the plant must have had a difficult time surviving. McKee says, "One of their desperate moves was to try to run a theatre give-away deal whereby initialed dinnerware was given out a piece at a time." *A Survey of Hopewell*,

Hull Pottery. Plaid Ware.

Virginia, put out by the Hopewell Chamber of Commerce in 1938, tells another story, "A new and modern kiln, of the continuous process type, was constructed last year (1937) at the plant. The James River Potteries employed some 200 people, all highly skilled. They found that Hopewell was a good location because of its nearness to large centers of population and its excellent rail and water transportation facilities." McKee said they were closed in the 1930s but it must have been very late in the 1930s because the pottery was still operating in 1938. In *China, Glass, and Lamps*, May 21, 1923, p. 3, Hopewell China Corporation advertised pattern number 322, "Oriental Pagoda" as dinnerware of distinction. In *American Home*, December, 1937, p. 72, is an advertisement for the James River Potteries featuring "Rappahannock," "Powhatan," "Isle of Palms," and "Pocahontas." This was called the new "Commonwealth" line with many patterns and was created by J. Palin Thorley for leading department stores.

Hull Pottery. "Hull Art" marked tea set.

Hull Pottery. **Front row:** *"Sun Glow" pitcher, Ⓗ pitcher.* **Middle row:** *"Sun Glow" grease bowl and shaker, H container or cookpot (probably had a lid).* **Back row:** *Ⓗ handled beanpot or cookpot (this one did have a lid).*

HULL POTTERY started in Crooksville, Ohio, in 1905 by Addis E. Hull, and is still in business at present. Hull Pottery did not make any dinnerware, but they have manufactured a great quantity of kitchenware over the years. While the company is best known among collectors for the Hull Art Pottery, they are well known to the wives of America who have used and appreciated their very usable kitchenware products. As the real beauty that is in these products is discovered, the Hull kitchenware will become widely collected also. Tall handsome coffeepots, attractive cookie jars, and well designed and beautiful lines like "Sun Glow" have made Hull a real success in this field. "Heritageware" and "Just Right" were other kitchenware lines. Pictured are three pieces of the "Sun Glow" line with flowers. The other pieces are marked H in a circle. In *Pottery, Glass, and Brass Salesman*, May 31, 1917, p. 16, is the following item on the A.E. Hull Pottery:

Hull Pottery. Five-banded line.

> The popularity of cereal sets still continues. The demand is growing every day and the manufacturers are hard pressed to keep abreast of it. In spite of this, the A.E. Hull Pottery, of which Guy Cooke, 200 Fifth Avenue, is the New York representative, has found time to work on four new decorations–a parrot in dark blue in a yellow panel, with dark blue bands on either side; a scroll effect in terra cotta color on both the top and bottom of the jars; a vine treatment in a combination of colors, including dark blue and green; and a classic design in green, blue and golden brown. In these new decorations the concern has gotten away from the old stereotyped forms usually seen on cereal sets. The ware is white, high fired and sanitary. Each set contains fifteen pieces, including large and small jars, vinegar and oil jugs, and salt box.

HUNTINGTON CHINA COMPANY was chartered September 4, 1904, in Huntington, West Virginia, and was dissolved August 7, 1911. (Secretary of state's office of West Virginia.) Herford Hope, born in London, apprenticed at Mayer Pottery in Beaver Falls at age fifteen, became a foreman for Mayer Pottery in 1904, and in 1906 became superintendent of the Huntington China Company. *(American Ceramic Society Bulletin*, vol. 8, no. 2., p. 47.)

HYALYN PORCELAIN was started in the 1940s by two potters from Zanesville, Ohio, one by the name of Moody. In 1975, Cosco of Columbus, Indiana, bought Hyalyn Porcelain. The company now operates as Hyalyn Cosco in Hickory, North Carolina, manufacturing decorative accessory pieces, canisters, kitchen accessories, planters, etc.

IDEAL POTTERY COMPANY. See Trenton Potteries Company for history.

ILLINOIS CHINA COMPANY started in Roodhouse, Illinois, then in 1919 the factory was moved to Lincoln, Illinois, under the direction of James H. Smith, who stayed with the pottery for one year before leaving. Some of the old employees also made the move with the factory which operated successfully until a disastrous fire in 1922 which burned the entire plant. With $50,000 insurance money and $50,000 raised by selling stock, the factory was rebuilt and started again with four upright bisque kilns, two decorating kilns, and six upright glost kilns, all coal-fired (changed to gas in 1935). James Shaw came from the W.S. George Pottery of Canonsburg, Pennsylvania, to the Illinois China Company in 1920, bringing his knowledge of dinnerware manufacture and decorating to the company. On February 1, 1946, the Illinois China Company was sold to Stetson China Company which spent two and one-half million dollars on the plant by 1953, making it one of the most modern plants in America. In the early years Illinois China Company employed between ninety and one-hundred eighty-five people according to the season. After Joseph Stetson took over the plant the number of employees increased to five hundred. (Information from "Stetson China Was Moved Here from Roodhouse," *Lincoln Courier*, August 26, 1953, sec. 8, p. 11.)

IMPERIAL PORCELAIN CORPORATION, Zanesville, Ohio, from 1946 to 1960 became Imperial Pottery until 1967 when the plant burned. The three principal lines made by the company were decorative; the Paul Webb Mountain Boys, Americana Folklore Miniatures, and the Al Capp Dogpatch Series, but shakers and kitchen pieces may be found marked "Imperial Porcelain Corp. Zanesville, Ohio. Handcrafted, U.S.A."

Illinois China Company.

IMPERIAL PORCELAIN WORKS of Trenton, New Jersey, was founded in July, 1891, by Frederick A. Dugan, and their main production was electrical porcelain until 1944. They are mentioned in this book only because there have been many china pieces found with the mark involving "Imperial" which have remained unidentified as to maker. Little by little, I came to realize that any pottery in business making a specific type or composition of pottery may make something from that type of pottery which is completely out of their ordinary run of products. Centennials, birthday celebrations, even Christmas, sometimes call for a special production, thereby creating the collector's nightmare or delight, depending on whether the collector can ever get the product identified. The United States Ceramic Tile Company makes only wall tile and commercial tile, but for Christmas, one year, they made plates from the heavy wall tile type of ceramics. I love the plate; it is hanging in my bathroom which it matches. If Imperial Porcelain did decide to make a run of plates, they would be of the best quality of fine porcelain, and they would be attractive. In 1918 there were nineteen potteries in Trenton making sanitary earthenware (toilet fixtures) and most of them had made dishes at some time or other. After East Liverpool became so prominent in the making of dinnerware, the Trenton potteries switched to other products. (The companies which made sanitary earthenware, as they named it, used the broad definition of earthenware. See page 11. Also see Pioneer Pottery, Wellsville, for "Imperial China."

THE INDIANA POTTERY COMPANY in Troy, Indiana, was incorporated January 7, 1837, by James Clews who came from England. It was thought that whiteware similar to that made in England could be made from the Troy, Indiana, clay, but that soon proved to be false. After about a year the property was leased to a Samuel Casseday of Louisville, who in turn leased it occasionally to be used by workmen who came from England. (Barber, *Pottery and Porcelain of the United States*, p. 159.) One of the potters who came to Troy was Jabez Vodrey, from 1839 to 1947 in the Indiana Pottery building, making Rockingham, brownware, and cream-colored earthenware. (Ramsay, *American Potters and Pottery*, p. 231.) See Vodrey and various associates.

INTERNATIONAL CHINA COMPANY. See Cunningham and Pickett for history. Pictured is a platter in "Gold and Turquoise" with Cavalier shape made by Homer Laughlin China Company for International China Company between 1958 and 1968. Another shipment made to International from Homer Laughlin in 1959 was "Butterfly Pink" in Georgian Eggshell. See picture with Cunningham and Pickett.

INTERNATIONAL D.S. COMPANY. See Cunningham and Pickett for history. Between 1961 and 1968, Homer Laughlin China Company made dishes for International D.S. Company. Pictured is a fruit dish in "Glenwood" pattern which has a wide pink edge with a line of gold trim and flowered center. "Viking" was also made for this company in fifty-one piece sets by Homer Laughlin. See picture with Cunningham and Pickett.

THE INTERNATIONAL POTTERY COMPANY of Trenton, New Jersey, was formed in 1860 by Henry Speeler. In 1868 he admitted his two sons and the business became Henry Speeler and Sons in the International Pottery. Carr and Clark assisted by John and James Moses purchased the Speeler works and named it the **LINCOLN POTTERY OF CARR AND CLARK**. The name was once more returned to the International Pottery at the time of the reorganization of the Lincoln Pottery. (See Lincoln Pottery, Trenton.) In 1879, Burgess and Campbell became the owners of this pottery and called it the International Pottery. The last listing I found for this company in the *Trenton City Directory* was in 1936 making general and sanitary ware. In *China, Glass and Lamps*, June 4, 1923, p. 76, they advertised hotel ware, semiporcelain, and toilet ware. They made "Royal Blue" and "Rugby Flint" ware. Some of their semiporcelain ware had blue decorations beneath the glaze and these had marks printed in the same blue (Barber). In the *1902-1903 Complete Directory*, International Pottery Company was listed as making semiporcelain, white granite dinner sets, toilet sets, and short sets of odd dishes, some decorated. They also made novelties.

80

Barber mentions the forming of the International Pottery in 1879 by Messrs, Carr and Clark assisted by John and James Moses. The double shield was adopted as being an appropriate design for the name of the company. *(Marks of American Potters*, p. 56.) Barber said also that they called it the Lincoln Pottery for a short time at this reorganization. Whatever the name used for the time of Carr and Clark, the mark was the one described, and that mark was also used by the next owners, Burgess and Campbell, by just substituting their name under the double shield. One more point on this confusing mark: John Moses was at least a part owner with Carr and Clark in the International Pottery Company, and James Moses was the head of the Mercer Pottery Company of Trenton, which was organized in 1868. (See Mercer Pottery.) Mercer and International made the same products and used the same mark. According to Barber, we have three Trenton potteries using the double shield mark. Also Mr. Campbell must have sold his interest to Burgess in 1903, because the name became **BURGESS AND COMPANY** at that time, but Mr. Campbell stayed on as treasurer until 1906. (See Glasgow Pottery for more on John Moses as owner of Glasgow Pottery.) The following is a small excerpt on the life of Campbell which tells about his becoming involved with the International Pottery (taken from *Bulletin of the American Ceramic Society*, XXIII, April 15, 1940, p. 128).

> After leaving Princeton in 1876, Mr. Campbell went to New York City to engage in the pottery importing business. He remained there until 1879, when he went to Trenton to become associated with the International Pottery. On October 30, of the same year, he married Fannie Cleveland of Shushan, New York.
>
> In the International Pottery, he was associated with his former classmate at Princeton, the late William Burgess, with whom he had engaged in pottery jobbing in New York. The pair turned their attention to Trenton as a prospective business field when they found it difficult to obtain regular shipment of goods from England. Trenton at that time was known as "the Staffordshire of America."
>
> During a conversation with John Moses, owner of the International Pottery, the latter offered to sell a half interest in the plant to the two young men. The offer was accepted, and later the youthful partners purchased the remainder of the business from English holders.
>
> Mr. Campbell became treasurer of International, retaining that position until 1906, when he was made general manager of the Trenton Potteries Company.

INTERPACE CORPORATION is similar to Jeannette Corporation and Anchor Hocking Corporation in that they have diversified interests but have become a real factor in the dinnerware field. They are defined as a building and construction products company serving the building, construction, specialty mineral, and ceramic markets. A parent company was incorporated in 1914 as Electro-Chemical Engineering and Manufacturing Corporation. In 1962, that company was merged with Lock Joint Pipe Company and Gladding, McBean and Company to form International Pipe and Ceramics Corporation (see Gladding, McBean and Company for history). In 1968, the name was changed to Interpace Corporation. On March 25, 1968, Interpace acquired its second big pottery, Shenango China which was the owner and maker of "Castleton China." Shenango China had purchased Mayer China in 1964, so Interpace acquired both plants. (See Shenango China and Mayer China for history.) In February, 1974, Interpace acquired Alfred Meakin, Tunstall, England. There is a considerable list of companies owned by Interpace that are not related to the field of pottery.

In April, 1979, an agreement was reached whereby Josiah Wedgwood and Sons, Ltd. will acquire the Franciscan Division of the Interpace Corporation. (See Gladding, McBean and Company for more information.)

IRON MOUNTAIN STONEWARE of Laurel Bloomery, Tennessee, might be called the modern version of Southern Potteries, Inc. of Erwin, Tennessee. They make a beautiful line of stoneware dinnerware with the most enticing names. Many of the pieces have hand-painted designs on them. Located at the foot of the Iron Mountains, the pottery has served as an economic development model for the whole area. Sixty workers are employed to hand- and machine-make the dinnerware. Machinery is relied upon to process the clay and to fire it. Fitting the clay into the molds, trimming the dried, unfired pieces, and decorating are all done by hand. Nancy Patterson, a

Los Angeles ceramics designer, and Albert Mock, an architect-businessman, started the pottery in 1965. Their production approach is summed up in the statement by Nancy, "Studio pottery is too small an operation to manufacture items and still keep the unit cost down. A highly mechanized approach is just too expensive. The hand and machine approach is more interesting." Patterns made at Iron Mountain Stoneware are "Pond Mountain," "Roan Mountain," "White Top," "Night," "Solid Cherry," "Blue Ridge," "Whispering Pines," "Lookout Mountain," etc. Many one-of-a-kind pieces are turned out there, and the decorating varies a little from piece to piece within a given set, as is true of most hand-painted china.

THE IROQUOIS CHINA COMPANY of Syracuse, New York, was started in 1905 (McKee date). Between 1905 and 1939, part of that time, the plant was controlled by George H. Bowman who owned Cleveland China, a sales agency (McKee, p. 39). (See Cleveland China Company.) Bowman's mark may be found on some very nice semiporcelain and how much of that was made by Iroquois would be very hard to determine. In 1939, the company was owned by a local bank (probably following a bankruptcy), and at that time the plant was sold to Earl Crane, who manufactured only hotel ware until 1946. In 1946, the Iroquois China Company began production of a line of "Casual China" which had been designed by Russel Wright. There were actually three lines made by Iroquois China that became outstanding and will be quite collectible, "Iroquois Casual China," already mentioned and two lines designed by Ben Seibel, "Impromptu" and "Informal." (See the Russell Wright, p. 171, for a cup and saucer of "Casual China.") According to Frank L. Rudesill of Buffalo China, Inc., Iroquois stopped their commercial or hotel type ware in the late 1950s or early 1960s, continuing only the lines mentioned. Financial difficulties forced them in and out of production in the late 1960s and in 1969 they ceased operations permanently. A liquidation sale was held August 12, 1971, and the plant sold to a woodworking company.

In 1947, Iroquois began the building of a plant in Vega Baja, Puerto Rico, to manufacture under the name **CRANE CHINA COMPANY.** This project was in conjunction with the Puerto Rico Industrial Development Corporation. In the early 1950s the plant in Puerto Rico was acquired by Sterling China Company of Wellsville, Ohio (with offices in East Liverpool). From that time on the factory in Puerto Rico was known as **CARIBE CHINA** and the products were so marked. The Puerto Rico factory was closed in 1977. (Much of the foregoing information was furnished by letter by Stanley Campion of the Syracuse China Corporation, as well as Frank L. Rudesill of Buffalo China, Inc.)

JACKSON VITRIFIED CHINA COMPANY of Falls Creek, Pennsylvania, was founded in 1917 on the site of the old **BOHEMIAN ART POTTERY** which had gone bankrupt during World War I. Jackson Vitrified China was not incorporated until 1920. Then in the mid-1920s the company withstood a severe blow when two of the principals of the corporation were killed by a disgruntled debtor of the old Bohemian Art Pottery. Local support and the bank in DuBois kept the pottery going until it was functioning properly again. In 1946, Philip R. Distillator purchased all shares of stock from local stockholders, doubled the floor space, provided modern equipment, and doubled the work force. A decorating plant was operated in New York until it was destroyed by fire in 1967. Jackson Featherweight China, designed by M.A. Van Nostrand, was made after 1939 until the 1960s and was marketed under the name "Royal Jackson," according to company information. See the picture of an advertisement. Due to the ever-increasing price and competition from foreign countries, particularly Japan, the company was pretty much forced out of the fine home china business in the mid-1960s. At the present time (1978) production is 100 percent institutional china for restaurants and hotels. In September, 1976, Andrew Greystoke purchased the company and the name changed to **JACKSON CHINA, INC.** At present the company employs three-hundred seventy-five people and specializes in

BLUE HEAVEN   WAVERLY   LARCHMONT   MODERNE

custom decorating of specialty design for fine hotels and restaurants across the country. (Company furnished information.) In the "Story of American China" by H.A. Brown, *House and Garden*, October 1942, p. 34, Mr. Brown stated that English, French, and other continental china patterns all influenced the design of "Royal Jackson," which was a fine true thin china.

Jackson China Company "Royal Jackson." Photograph: Bennett Brother's, Inc. 1964 catalog.

JAMES RIVER POTTERIES. Hopewell, Virginia. See Hopewell China.

THE JEANNETTE CORPORATION which had its beginning in 1898 is another corporation like Anchor Hocking Corporation which is known in the field of glass but which now has entered into the pottery industry as well. Jeannette Glass Company was incorporated in Pennsylvania on April 8, 1936, to acquire assets and business of its predecessor company of the same name which had been started in June, 1898. The Jeannette Corporation name was adopted in 1971. In 1961, Jeannette acquired McKee Glass and in 1968, Blefeld and Company – an importing company. Then in 1969 they became involved in pottery as a part of their "Tabletop" concept by acquiring Harker Pottery which was stopped from producing in 1972. (See Harker Pottery.) Also in 1969, they purchased Royal China Company of Sebring, Ohio (see Royal China), which had already purchased French Saxon China of Sebring in 1964 (see French Saxon). Hence, Jeannette acquired both plants. In 1978, vitreous iron-stone dinnerware was still being manufactured in both plants. On November 15, 1976, Jeannette acquired the assets of Walker China, Inc. (See Walker.)

J.E. JEFFORDS AND COMPANY. See Philadelphia City Pottery.

JENSON POTTERY COMPANY was listed in the *1902-1903 Complete Directory* in Brooklyn, New York, making semiporcelain dinner sets, table sets, and odd sets of dishes with some decorated. The name Jenson appeared several times in the study of American potteries. The "Early History of Electrical Porcelain in the United States" by Arthur S. Watts, *American Ceramic Society Bulletin*, XXVIII, October 1939, pp. 404-408, tells that a James L. Jenson purchased the old Empire China Works at Greenpoint, New York, in 1870. In the 1930s and 1940s hand-painted tableware was advertised by Georg Jensen. Through the 1950s until the present, a distributor Svend Jensen of Denmark in Rye, New York, was found advertising glass and china.

THE JERSEY CITY POTTERY was built in Jersey City, New Jersey, in 1825 and incorporated as the *JERSEY PORCELAIN AND EARTHENWARE COMPANY.* (Jervis, also Barber.) Jersey Porcelain and Earthenware Co. won a silver medal at the Franklin Institute in Philadelphia in 1826 and their products were good enough that the company should have lasted more than the two years it did. In 1829 the factory was reopened by David and J. Henderson as the *AMERICAN POTTERY MANUFAC-TURING COMPANY* until 1840 when the name became the *AMERICAN POTTERY COMPANY.* From 1845 to 1854, William Rhodes was the owner and made white granite and cream-colored ware. Jersey City Pottery made eight-sided pitchers decorated with the bust of William Henry Harrison in 1840. (Shull, Thelma, "American Scenes for the China Collector," *Hobbies*, June 1942, p. 66.) In 1855, the owners were Rouse, Turner, Duncan, and Henry, and later the name was just Rouse and Turner, who made white pottery exclusively. The American Pottery Company imported Staffordshire potters from England in 1840 to make dinnerware in the "Canova" pattern. Canova pictures an urn set in a Venetian background and has a border pattern with flowers, leaves, and ships. (Ripley, Katherine B. "Canova Pottery," *Hobbies*, January 1942, p. 58.) Daniel Greatback molded his first hound handled pitcher while working at the American Pottery Company. (Cook, Peter, "Bennington's Hound Handled Pitchers," *Antique Trader*, May 25, 1976, p. 332.) Barber states in *Marks of American Potters*, p. 44, the old buildings were torn down in 1892 to make room for modern improvements. Then in *Pottery and Porcelain of the U.S.*, p. 440, Barber states that the last proprietor of the Jersey City Pottery had died.

JERSEY PORCELAIN AND EARTHENWARE COMPANY. See the Jersey City Pottery.

KASS CHINA COMPANY of East Liverpool, Ohio, started in 1929 and closed around 1973. They were manufacturers of novelty china and kitchenware. They also decorated china made by other potteries as well. In an article, "History of Kass China Company" by June Kass Jackson in the *Glaze*, April 1978, p. 13, the daughter of the founder of the pottery relates that Kass China decorated quite a lot of Hall Pottery and also decorated a line of Homer Laughlin's Eggshell Nautilus for George H. Bowman (Cleveland China Company) who also had a cut glass cutting concern in Salem, Ohio, not too far from East Liverpool. (See Cleveland China for story of Bowman.) Mrs. Jackson said that foreign competition forced Kass China to decorate only through the 1950s; business was worse in the 1960s and her brother's illness in 1971 forced him to retire. Kass China struggled on for a little over another year then closed permanently.

KENWOOD CERAMICS. See Shawnee Pottery Company.

KESWICK (or KISWICK) CHINA COMPANY was listed only twice in the material I had. In the *1900 Factory Inspection Report* for the state of Pennsylvania they were listed as employing eighty to make queensware. Then in 1902 they were listed as making semiporcelain dinner sets, toilet sets, and short sets of odd dishes, some decorated, in the *1902-1903 Complete Directory*. In 1904 they had a float in a parade. The next listing I had was 1916 in the *Industrial Directory for Pennsylvania* and there was no pottery in Fallston at all.

KETTLESPRINGS KILNS are decorators, not manufacturers, in Alliance, Ohio, who have been operating since the 1950s until the present (1978). The designs are created by Gene Cunin, operator of the kilns, then stamped on the plates by Royal China Company, and glazed with Royal's underglazing technique.

KEYSTONE CHINA COMPANY in East Liverpool, Ohio, was found listed only in the *1954 Crockery and Glass Directory* issue with the mark pictured in the back. In the *East Liverpool City Directory* they were listed in 1951 through 1954 and were not listed in 1955-1956. In 1951 Keystone advertised artware and china specialties. They are listed here mainly because they could be confused with the other Keystone potteries.

KEYSTONE POTTERY COMPANY was incorporated in Rochester, Pennsylvania, in 1890, and destroyed by a fire in 1895. (Bausman, Joseph H., *History of Beaver County, Pennsylvania*, Vol. II, p. 743, New York, 1904.) Evidently the Keystone Pottery bought a pottery in New Brighton in 1899. (Bausman, p. 710.) In the *1902-1903 Complete Directory* they were listed in New Brighton making semiporcelain dinner sets, short sets of dishes, and novelties. When the Bausman book was written in 1904, they were still in operation. The next factory listing that I had was 1916 and they were no longer listed. Several potteries used the mark of a keystone. Also there was a Keystone Pottery in Trenton, New Jersey, but they made vitreous sanitary ware.

KEYSTONE POTTERY COMPANY in Trenton, New Jersey, started in 1892 and was listed in the *Trenton City Directory* until 1935. They have been known mainly as the makers of sanitary ware using the mark in the Marks Section which was shown in Barber. They are listed here only because so many of the potteries that were supposed to have been mainly sanitary ware manufacturers did make dishes at one time or another. Examples are Mercer Pottery and the various Maddock potteries.

L.S. KILDOW, Roseville, Ohio. See J.W. McCoy and Associates.

KINGWOOD CERAMICS, East Palestine, Ohio, started in 1939 and will best be known among the dinnerware collectors for their line called "Weeping Gold" on teapots, creamers, sugars, various serving dishes, coffee sets, candy dishes, etc. (See the Marks Section for marks.) Kingwood Ceramics is still operating at present. (1979).

KIRK CHINA COMPANY was listed in New Brighton, Pennsylvania, in the *Industrial Directory for Pennsylvania* for 1953 under pottery and chinaware. I did not find them listed in 1950 or 1956. They were listed in *1954 Crockery and Glass Journal Directory* as making "Brighton China" dinnerware. They may have decorated only.

Edwin M. Knowles China Company.

EDWIN M. KNOWLES CHINA COMPANY. There are two companies by the Knowles name that made very fine dinnerware from East Liverpool. Knowles, Taylor, Knowles was the first, but Edwin M. Knowles was also an old company which made good quality ware from 1900 to 1963. In 1900, Edwin M. Knowles, son of Isaac W. Knowles, founded the Edwin M. Knowles China Company. Their first plant was located in Chester, West Virginia, later occupied by the Harker Pottery Company. In 1913 they put into operation the building now in existence, but no pottery has been made there since 1963. Under the guidance of Mr. Knowles and his successors this developed into one of the most modern and best equipped plants in the industry. Edwin M. Knowles Company kept their offices in East Liverpool until 1931. They manufactured in Chester, West Virginia, and from 1913 to 1963 they had their factory in Newell, West Virginia. The only confusing mark used by Edwin Knowles was the big K with the word Knowles. This might be taken for a mark for Knowles, Taylor, Knowles by a beginning collector. Several of the Edwin M. Knowles marks have the name completely written out. This company made vitreous and semivitreous or semiporcelain. Pictured for E. Knowles is an assortment of plates, a tea or coffeepot, and a very servicable looking pitcher with a little hand-painted trim over the glaze. The Dutch scene plate with flowers all around the couple is "Mayflower" shape. The other Dutch scene where the couple have an umbrella in hand is a very yellow glaze and the plate is marked "Goldina" for color. Another "Goldina" glazed plate with flowers all around the shoulder is shown. The square-like plate with raised edge trim and a decaled garden scene is a favorite. An octagon shape with fluted edges is called "Marion" shape; this was an older shape used by Knowles. Pictured in the *Winter 1925 Catalogue* of the Butler Brothers is the "Golden Wedding" pattern (picture no. 2) which was white semiporcelain in Mayflower shape with a gold coin band decoration and gold coin handles. In the same catalog with the Mayflower shape was "Plaza" with a border of rose and flower spray panels, Oriental medallions, and gold edges, and "Parisian Border" vitreous semiporcelain, extra light weight with a lattice border of black and green, pink rosebuds, and blue forget-me-nots.

HOMER KNOWLES POTTERY COMPANY was listed in the *1924 California Manufacturers' Directory* as making plates and dishes in Santa Clara, California. Homer S. Knowles was the son of Isaac W. Knowles, founder of Knowles, Taylor, Knowles.

KNOWLES, TAYLOR, KNOWLES CHINA COMPANY. The company as we know it today didn't really start until 1870, but the Knowles name had a long history in pottery in East Liverpool dating from 1853 and starting with Isaac Knowles and an Isaac Harvey who operated a store boat selling pottery, glass, and staples along the Ohio and Mississippi rivers. In 1854 they started their first factory. (For early history see Lehner, Lois, *Ohio Pottery and Glass, Marks and Manufacturers*, p. 47.) Isaac W. Knowles in 1870, took John N. Taylor and Homer S. Knowles as partners in his pottery. This company, after much experimenting and many trials and disappointments, drew in 1872 the first kiln of "white granite ware" considered to be of commercial quality. This firm under the name of Knowles, Taylor, and Knowles was one of the best known manufacturers of semivitreous dinnerware of its day. Very few American companies attempted to make what is called "Flow Blue" or "Flown Blue" china, where the blue that makes the design seems to run into the white background. Knowles, Taylor, Knowles came pretty close to this type in one dinnerware pattern seen. Buffalo China made ware even closer to the old blue of the English. There were probably a few other American makers, but this type of china just isn't easily found today. Knowles, Taylor, Knowles greatest single achievement was "Lotus Ware." In the *Sixth Annual Tri State Pottery Festival Booklet*, June, 1973, p. 36, (no author given) is this account of the manufacture of Lotus Ware:

Knowles, Taylor, Knowles "Tea Leaf" pattern cup and saucer.

> The fine bone china which has become a collector's item today, was manufactured by the firm of Knowles, Taylor and Knowles. The men involved included Isaac Knowles, founder of the firm; his two sons, and his son-in-law, Col. John N. Taylor. These men along with Joshua Poole, who came to K.T.K. from the Belleek Pottery in Western Ireland, George and William Morley from England and Henry Schmidt, a German artist originated Lotus Ware, Schmidt, who brought to America talents in decorating unknown to our potters, worked in secrecy in a small work shop where he designed and applied lavish ornaments to the graceful varieties of bowls and vases. He worked with a tool resembling that used by bakery shop decorators to apply the lacy-like patterns to the ware.
> This procedure was the end product. The first step in making the new ware was to calcine bones from a city slaughterhouse. The bones were first cooked in a vat until the meat dropped away and then placed in kilns and burned to powdery ash.
> Lotus Ware was fired in the same kilns as those used for hotel and restaurant ware. The losses from breakage was high as the delicate ware passed through the bisque, gloss and decorating kilns. There were also complaints from residents of the area regarding the odor from the processing of bones.
> The ware Schmidt received was in a hard, green state. From this such elaborate designs were developed that they have never been reproduced in such fine quality.
> Production of Lotus Ware, which began in 1889, had a short life. Operations halted when Col. Taylor turned his attention to politics and other matters. Homer Knowles died and W.A. Knowles moved to California.
> Lotus Ware was exhibited in Chicago World's Fair in 1893 and won many awards. The search for Lotus Ware goes on by many collectors. The Brunner Collection is now on display at the Ohio State Museum in Columbus. The East Liverpool Historical Society also has a display in the Carnegie Library Museum (1973).
> Why the term Lotus Ware? The first tall, graceful vase produced from this process had, at the top petal shapings which resemble the leaves of the Lotus blossom.

Knowles, Taylor, Knowles China Company.

Pictured for Knowles, Taylor, Knowles is a strawberry-decorated plate with a mark found in the Barber book (1904). Another plate with a country cottage scene and delicate decaled flowers is a favorite. The teapot has a pearl lustrelike finish; the old vegetable dish has the decorator's mark inside. There are no pattern names on any of this ware.

KURLBAUM AND SCHWARTZ started experiments in making hard-paste porcelain in 1851 in Philadelphia, Pennsylvania. They were listed for the last time in business in 1855 at Front and Oxford streets as manufacturers of porcelain (Barber, *Marks of American Potters*, p. 27.) Barber showed a tea set and bowls made by them.

LABELLE CHINA. See Wheeling Potteries Company.

LAMBERTON CHINA. See Scammell China Company, also Sterling China Company, Wellsville, Ohio.

LA SOLANA POTTERIES, INC. with the factory located in Mesa, Arizona, had its early beginning in Glendale, California, in 1946 until 1953 as Bergstrom and French, makers of ovenware. By January, 1954, the business was relocated in Scottsdale, Arizona, where the offices are still located with the factory in Mesa. At present, La Solana Potteries, Inc. is listed making earthenware dinnerware, pitchers, tumblers, mugs, cups and saucers, microwave oven-to-table casseroles, serving pieces, bean pots, salad bowls, etc. See the Marks Section for marks.

HOMER LAUGHLIN CHINA COMPANY. As early as 1869 a Laughlin is recorded making pottery, but the story of the Homer Laughlin China Company had its beginning in 1873 when the town of East Liverpool, Ohio, furnished $5,000 to build a whiteware plant to be known as the **LAUGHLIN BROTHERS.** In 1877 Homer Laughlin bought out his brother Shakespear's interest in the company and renamed it **HOMER LAUGHLIN AND COMPANY** until 1897 when the name became **HOMER LAUGHLIN CHINA COMPANY,** as it remains today. Until 1932 three plants were in operation in East Liverpool, Ohio, but between 1905 and 1931, five plants were built and operated in Newell, West Virginia, too. In 1973 the company operated five plants which employed thirteen hundred people. A great variety of trademarks were used by this company as may be seen.

According to the company, the first trademark used was just Homer Laughlin. Secondly, after 1890, came the American Eagle carrying the Lion, until around 1900. From then on the "HLC" monogram with variations was used. In 1900, Homer Laughlin started using a series of numbers which meant the month, a second single numeral identified the year, and a third number identified the plant. Hence 74L would mean July, 1904, factory L on the east end of town. In the years 1910 to 1920, the first figure was the month, the next two numbers were the year and the third figure designated the plant. (East End plant was L, Number 4 Plant was N, and Plant 5 was N5.) From 1921 to 1930, a letter was used first to indicate the month such as an A for January, etc. The next single number was the year, and the last figure was the plant. From 1931 to 1940 the month was the first letter, the year was the next two numbers, and the last letter was the plant. So E-44N5 would be May, 1944, Plant No. 5. (Company information.)

In the 1925 *China and Glassware Catalogue* of the Butler Brothers which is currently being reprinted and sold (see Bibliography), several kinds of wares are described and pictured that were made by Homer Laughlin China Company in 1925. (1) "Vandemere" with "Kwaker" shape is a white lightweight semiporcelain with a border of tan and pale green with ivory and pink rosebuds in a medallion border effect. There is gold on either side of the border. (2) "Century" a lightweight semi-porcelain with scalloped, embossed edges and spray decorations of pink roses, cherry blossoms, green foliage, and gold edges. (3) "Gold Bowknot," a thin white semiporcelain trimmed with gold bowknots in a border decoration. (4) "LaSalle," a white semiporcelain trimmed with blue lines and blue medallions. (5) "Virginia," a white semiporcelain with a green and tan conventional band, green scrolled, blue medallions, and rose festoons. (6) "Presidential," a white semiporcelain with a "Kwaker" shape and a design in blue, green, and yellow. The "Kwaker" shape mentioned had square side handles and lid handles. (7) "Capitol," a lightweight semi-porcelain, highly glazed, new shape, gold band, and gold ornamental handles.

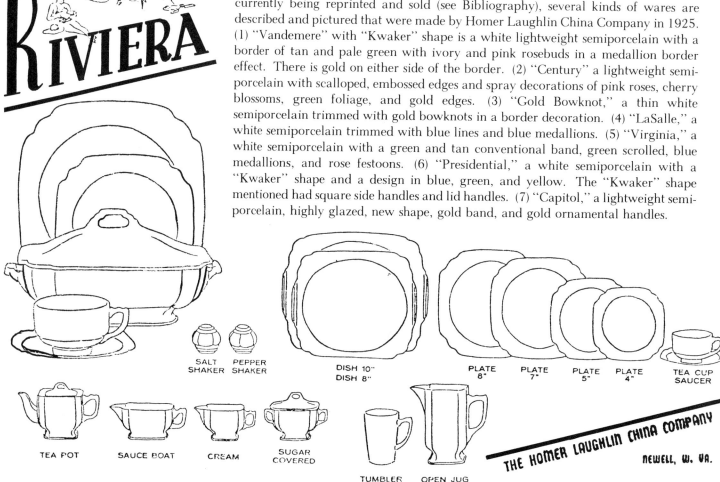

88

The following information furnished by the company is reprinted almost in its entirety because of the interest in Fiesta Dinnerware.

The Story of Genuine Fiesta Dinnerware (1936-1973)

Fiesta comes in four lovely colors; green, blue, yellow, and red, all brilliant, all cheerful, all endowed with a pleasant feeling of good fellowship, informality and gracious living. Whether used for serving breakfast, luncheon, informal supper, or buffet, Fiesta makes the meal a truly gay occasion, it's fun to set a table with Fiesta!

Designed by Fredrick Rhead an English Stoke on Trent potter, working under the direction of M.L. Aaron, President and J.M. Wells, Secretary and General Manager. Design modeled by Arthur Kraft and Bill Berrsford, the distinctive glazes developed by Dr. A.V. Bleininger in association with H.W. Thiemecke. A talc body was introduced for the first time making Fiesta entirely different in body materials and glazes.

Initially 54 items (69 individual pieces) were produced in green, blue, yellow and red. Soon it was apparent that Fiesta was to be the all time leader in the colored dinnerware field. Ivory was added in 1936, turquoise in 1938, blue, rose, grey, chartreuse and olive green colors in 1943 to be followed by several other distinct colors over the years.

The original design, colors and name are registered property of Homer Laughlin. The Fiesta trademark was imprinted from the mould or by a rubber stamp hand operation depending upon the method of producing the individual item. Those without trademarks are merely the result of human error and as many imitations appeared over the years, it would be safe to assume that only those items bearing the trademark are genuine Fiesta.

In an effort to serve all markets, especially the syndicate stores, competitive lines identified as Harlequin and Riviera were produced in a slightly different design in the true Fiesta colors and sold without trademark in tremendous quantities for a number of years. In 1941 the continued success of the Fiesta colors was applied to a "Bake & Serve" line identified as "Fiesta Kitchen Kraft."

A juice set consisting of 30 oz. disc water jug with six 5-oz. juice tumblers was produced merely as a special sales stimulator between 1940 and 1943 and was part of a promotional program involving six special items that included the juice set, covered refrigerator jars, casserole and pie plate, handled chop plate, French casserole and individual sugar, cream and tray. These were initially offered for sale at 98¢ retail.

Records list those colors manufactured as royal blue, yellow, old ivory, red, turquoise, forest green, chartreuse, grey, rose, antique gold, turf green and two additional green colors that were never singularly named.

Fiesta Red was discontinued in 1943 because this color was manufactured from depleted uranium oxide and our government assumed control of uranium oxide at that time. "Fiesta Red went to war."

The color assortment during this period was forest green, chartreuse, grey and rose.

The Atomic Energy Commission licensed The Homer Laughlin China Company to again buy this material and Fiesta Red, the most popular of all colors, returned to the market in May of 1959.

With the return of red, new colors consisting of yellow, turquoise, and medium green, replaced the war year colors to more clearly match the original four colors.

Finally in November 1972, all production of Fiesta Red was discontinued because many of the original technicians who developed this color and maintained control over the complicated manufacturing and firing had retired and modern mass production methods were unsuited to this process.

Silverware and glassware sold in Fiesta ensembles were manufactured by other companies and merely shipped here to our plant and reshipped with the Fiesta and other items included in the ensemble. Records fail to identify the company that may have manufactured these complementary accessories.

The famous old line of Fiesta Ironstone dinnerware was discontinued January 1, 1973 and there will be no further production.

ICE PITCHER

FLOWER VASE 10"

COFFEE POT REG.

CARAFE

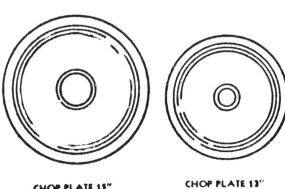

CHOP PLATE 15"

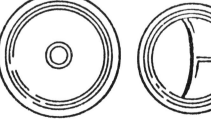

CHOP PLATE 13"

COMPARTMENT PLATE 10½"

For F.W. Woolworth's One-Hundredth Anniversary year in 1979, Homer Laughlin China Company produced "Harlequin" in four colors, three of which matched the original colors. Only the salmon was a little deeper in color. The turquoise, yellow, and green matched the original colors. The only difference in design was a solid handle on the new sugar as opposed to an open handle on the original.

Pictured for Homer Laughlin is an "Indian Tree' design, "Eggshell Georgian" (shape) plate. Eggshell described the weight of the plates, light and more thin than almost all semiporcelain ware. Eggshell was used in the making of many shapes, so we get marks such as "Eggshell Nautilus" and "Eggshell Georgian" and "Eggshell Theme." (See the Marks Section.) Homer Laughlin also used many different decorations or decals with Eggshell. The cream and sugar and plate pictured are "Eggshell Nautilus" made for the Household Institute in a design called "Priscilla."

Also pictured for Homer Laughlin is a set dated 1904 and marked "Majestic" for shape. This same set was given the name "Carnation Beauty" for its design in the 1918 Sears and Roebuck catalog. A "Willow" ware plate dated 1957 is also shown.

Homer Laughlin China Company. **Front row:** *"Eggshell Georgian" plate, "Wells" glazed plate, "Eggshell" cream and sugar with Household Institute mark.* **Back row:** *"Indian Tree Eggshell Georgian" plate, "Willow" pattern plate, 1904 vegetable dish named "Carnation Beauty" in the "Majestic" shape, "Kenilworth" jug.*

LAUGHLIN INTERNATIONAL CHINA COMPANY. See Cunningham and Pickett for history.

LAUREL POTTERIES had several addresses in the few California directories I had. In 1941 and 1958, they were at 354 Pine Street, San Francisco, with either an office or a plant in Stockton, California. By 1954 they were at 322 Hayes Street, San Francisco. In 1957, they were at 1355 Market Street in the same city. In the *Crockery and Glass Journal*, March 15, 1964, p. 32, they had an advertisement for "California Life" dinnerware which looked a lot like Steubenville Pottery's "American Modern." Colors were Sierra Yellow, Peach Blossom, Sea Green, and Desert Brown. This ad showed outlets in several major cities for the ware. They also made "Holiday" pattern.

LEIGH POTTERY COMPANY. See Crescent China in Alliance, Ohio, for picture and history.

LENEIGE CHINA, INC. was listed at 2445 Naomi Street in Burbank, California, in 1934. They were listed in the 1948 and 1951 *California Manufacturers' Register* as making table and hotel semivitreous dinnerware under the chinaware section of the directory. They were not listed in the next directory I had, which was 1955, so they were evidently out of business by then.

LENOX, INC. As was stated in Part One, in a few instances throughout the book, company histories have been presented almost as they were sent by the company because they lend so much to the understanding of the industry as a whole. The Lenox information that follows tells about the fierce struggle required for success, the problems confronted, and also much about Lenox products and the way that really fine china is made.

Walter Scott Lenox was born in Trenton in 1859. As a boy he completed an apprenticeship in how to make pottery. When he was in his 20's he became art director of the Ott and Brewer factory. He saved his money and, in 1889, got together $4,000 and became a partner with Jonathan Coxon, Sr., in the Ceramic Art Company. At that time all fine chinaware was imported from Europe but the idea of making ware comparable to any in the world was in Lenox's mind from the beginning. It was an idea that was far more daring and far more hazardous as a business proposition than might have seemed on the surface. In the first place, the technique of making fine china was difficult to master; secondly, Americans were strongly prejudiced in favor of the famous European china names; and thirdly, it seemed highly probable that a company would go broke trying to produce high-quality ware while paying American scale wages. About 70 percent of the cost of fine chinaware is labor, much of it highly skilled.

In 1894, when he acquired sole ownership of the company, about all he had was debts and a three-story pottery that had been built, on the insistence of financial backers, so that it could easily be converted into a tenement house if the business failed. It didn't fail, but it would have except for Lenox's ability to make friends. There were many times when he dashed from friend to friend to borrow $500 to meet the payroll; or to borrow from one friend to pay back, often without interest, what he had previously borrowed from another. And there were many times when Harry A. Brown, secretary of the company, stood by as china was taken from the kilns and then, if it had turned out well, hurried to New York to collect in advance enough money to buy more materials for the potter.

At first, Lenox concentrated on production of a rich, ivory-tinted ware referred to as Belleek similar in appearance to the china which originated in Belleek, Ireland. He was forced to import two skilled potters in order to learn the methods but even then the next few years brought more disappointments than successes. The ware lacked the durability of the finest foreign product but Lenox slowly developed his own formula and soon after the turn of the century was making dinnerware comparable to the best. But even then the American buying public wouldn't believe this and the majority kept right on buying foreign-made ware.

Furthermore, personal disaster was descending on Lenox. He was a bachelor whose manner of living was graceful, but soon after the turn of the century, his health began to fail. He was becoming both blind and paralyzed. For a man who enjoyed life as Lenox did, such an illness might have been a shattering blow. Actually, it had the opposite effect on him. He continued to go to the pottery daily and his interest in details of manufacture became more intense as his physical condition deteriorated. Even when he could "see" the chinaware only with his sensitive fingers and when his chauffeur had to carry him piggyback to his desk, he supervised each step in production and ran the business with Harry Brown as his assistant and alter ego.

He formed Lenox, Inc., in 1906 and redoubled his efforts to overcome the prejudice against American-made fine china. Almost at once he got a spectacular break. In 1905 the company had received a large order from Shreve and Company of San Francisco, with a request to get the ware there for the opening of their new store. The order was rushed through and shipped to the West Coast just in time to become a casualty of the San Francisco earthquake and fire. Except that it wasn't exactly a casualty, it became proof of Lenox quality. Out of the wreckage was dug a Lenox plate that had been decorated in green and gold. The gold had melted, the green had become streaked with smoke and the design was almost obliterated but the glazed plate was basically as perfect as on the day it was made. With the blackened plate as Exhibit A in his campaign, Lenox concentrated in the next few years on the most expensive market. Tiffany's became the new company's first account.

The encouragement of Tiffany's played an important part in the progress of Lenox and caused other New York and Philadelphia stores to take an interest, but it was not until 1917 that the company received outstanding recognition. Since 1826, Congress had been on record as requiring that, so far as possible, all equipment for the White House should be bought in the United States. No President, however, had been able to find American-made china fit for the White House table and even Theodore Roosevelt, who had scoured the country's potteries, had to admit that "we are dependent upon foreign factories for the very dishes from which the Chief Executive of the United States must eat." Woodrow Wilson, who had served in Trenton as governor of New Jersey, finally broke the precedent with the encouragement of his friend, the late James Kerney, Sr., editor of the *Trenton Times*. Wilson ordered a 1,700 piece dinner set costing $16,000 from Lenox in 1917. Franklin D. Roosevelt and Harry S. Truman followed Wilson's example when they turned to Lenox years later to supplement the White House dinner service. The company has made many dinner sets for state governors, presidents of Latin American countries and dignitaries around the world.

It was introduction of his ware into the White House in Wilson's time, however, that climaxed Lenox's career. He remained in command only two more years.

The real struggle for position in the American market, however, was only begun. Although Lenox had demonstrated that fine china could be made in the United States, foreign firms still dominated the domestic market and produced perhaps eight of every ten pieces sold in this country. European ideas of shape and design were paramount and were followed here just as American dressmakers followed Paris fashions. It took another fifteen years, under the presidency of Harry Brown, to break down this tradition. In the 1930's, when the company was still doing considerably less than $1,000,000 worth of business annually, designer Frank Holmes began introducing a new style in china that was generally called modern, and represented the first real effort to break away from European traditions. It was clean and simple of line in contrast to the elaborate and often rococo style that had been popular for years in Europe. This modern style, particularly Holmes' unencumbered decorative motifs against ivory backgrounds, soon attracted attention. By the late 1930's the Lenox trademark was on perhaps one of every four pieces of chinaware purchased by Americans.

World War II completed the transition, by cutting off practically all imports of fine china. A dozen American firms, some new and some established companies which had not previously made fine chinaware, got into the field. Starting about 1943, the American market went domestic with a bang. For the first time, it attracted big and aggressive capital, put emphasis on modern business methods as well as high artistic standards and flourished because of American manufacturing ingenuity, merchandising and sales methods.

With competition mounting among American firms, the old system of having a few salesmen who packed their trunks and toured around to see important customers perhaps once a year was abandoned. A number of sales regions were set up to keep in regular touch with dealers. Merchandising methods such as exhibits, attractive display ideas and publicity programs were introduced. A long-range program of educating women and girls in the use of American-made china was inaugurated and copies of a full-color motion picture demonstrating the making of Lenox China were put into circulation in schools and clubs all over the country. Special training courses were arranged for the sales forces in large stores and recommended coordinations of china design and style with crystal, silver and other table appointments were created in order to increase the harmony of table settings.

But perhaps the most important change broke away from the old European system of selling china services principally by the set, which in practice had required the purchaser to invest perhaps $600 in a lump sum. This tended to limit the market because the average housewife couldn't afford such an investment. The company, instead, began putting emphasis on buying 5-piece place settings or individual pieces.

Today, Lenox, Inc. is a multi-million dollar enterprise. The company has been expanding rapidly into other product lines over the past two decades. In 1962 Oxford Bone China, now widely known for its pure white color, translucency, delicate appearance and remarkable strength, was introduced to the American market.

1972 was marked by the much heralded introduction of a versatile new line of super-ceramic, casual dinnerware, Temper-ware by Lenox.

In 1965, Lenox acquired the oldest crystal glass blowing company in the United States and thus Lenox Crystal was born.

Between 1968 and 1972, the Lenox family added Lenox Candles, Paragon Products Corporation, a refiner of custom waxes; Kaumagraph Company, a specialty printer; Carolina Soap and Candle Makers Company, a producer of scented candles, soaps and toiletries; Art Carved, Incorporated, a designer and manufacturer of wedding and engagement rings; H. Rosenthal Jewelry Corporation, a distributor of high fashion jewelry. In late 1972 Lenox acquired the Imperial Glass Corporation, a manufacturer of quality cut glassware. In 1973 Lenox added Taunton Silversmiths, Ltd., makers of silver-plated gifts, serving pieces and accessories. In 1975 Lenox acquired ownership of the John Roberts Company, now known as ArtCarved Class Rings, Incorporated; Eisenstadt Manufacturing Company, a wholesale distributor of jewelry and awards, now named Lenox Awards, Inc. In addition Lenox, Inc. operates two Latin American subsidiaries producing melamine dinnerware, stainless steel flatware, sterling silver and silver-plated flatware.

Understanding how various kinds of dinnerware is made is an essential part of dinnerware appreciation and collection. The following is a condensed version of a 1924 thirty-four page booklet published by Lenox giving a wonderful description of how their china has been made. In a letter dated November 7, 1977, from Joseph J. McArdle, sales promotion manager, is the statement, "The basic process (of making Lenox China) has not changed since the inception of the company." The company also furnished the pictures which are shown here.

Transmuting elemental materials into Lenox china is a wonderful process, one of rare refinement and precision. The raw ingredients are passed upon by Lenox experts, who subject them to close inspection in order that they may meet unvarying Lenox standards of quality. They are weighed and tested at every stage of their transition from mine to mixing-room and are closely examined in the laboratories by Lenox chemists and mineralogists, who superintend the intricate task of combining them in their proper proportions. Even the water with which they are mixed is filtered and metered to the last ounce.

The clays are brought from several different deposits, yielding a grade demanded after experimentation with clays from various localities. In the state in which they go into the bins of the Lenox pottery they are creamy white in color and very fine in texture. The feldspar is a

Far left, a member of the Lenox design staff is working on minute pattern detail. Hundreds of such sketches will be made and many hundreds of hours spent before a design concept will become a pattern reality. Photograph: Lenox, Inc.

At left, a Lenox designer is "throwing" or forming the shape of this vase. Later a mold will be made from the model. Starting with a lump of clay, he models it from the bottom up as the wheel spins— just as in the earliest days of pottery making. Photograph: Lenox, Inc.

Far left, with infinite care and control a Lenox craftsman removes excess dried slip with a "trimmer" stick. All marks left by molds are erased with a soft brush dipped in water, giving a satin smoothness to the "green" or unfired ware. Photograph: Lenox, Inc.

At left, a new piece of Lenox China must first be sculptured in clay. From the model, a master mold is made. An artist creates a graceful swan . . . one of the many charming Lenox giftware pieces. Photograph: Lenox, Inc.

Far left, in jiggering, the potter's wheel and experienced hands, at the precise moment, must exert the proper pressure to shape the piece. Each piece of Lenox China goes through more than two hundred pairs of hands before it leaves the pottery. Photograph: Lenox, Inc.

At left, the twenty-four karat gold and gleaming platinum on Lenox China are expertly hand-applied by an artisan using a camel's hair brush brought to an extremely fine point. Photograph: Lenox, Inc.

rock formation, which, when crushed becomes a glistening white powder. When these two ingredients have been assembled with flint, according to the Lenox formula, they are placed in a large revolving cylinder, lined with porcelain blocks with a certain amount of water and flint pebbles. In this device, they are subjected to the process known as "pebble grinding," the flint pebbles grinding the minerals into a mass of uniform density as the huge cylinder slowly revolves.

A meter records each revolution, with the result that absolute uniformity of every charge is assured. "Pebble grinding" is a slow process, consuming fifty hours, after which the contents of the cylinder are found to have attained a thick, cream-like consistency. The mixture is then forced through a fine wire screen by air pressure, this process lasting two hours and eliminating all the larger particles, leaving a fine-textured fluid called "slip."

"Slip," however, a potter's term with which many are familiar, means more at the Lenox pottery than a fluid strained through a wire screen with 200 meshes to the square inch. It must first have all metallic iron particles removed and then undergo "aging" before it is ready for the hand of the potter. The removal of the iron atoms is accomplished by forcing the slip over electro-magnets, while the "aging" is done according to a pottery principle handed down from earliest times. It is not definitely known why "aging" makes clay easier to handle. When this process is completed and the "slip" has reached the correct stage of plasticity, it is ready for "casting," or for the "jiggering machine."

The "jiggering machine" is a potters' wheel greatly improved, but the "jiggering machine" is still a flat, revolving disc, but instead of being operated manually, it is spun by an individual electric motor, the speed being governed by the operator's foot.

The operator of the "jiggering machine" uses a working mould upon the wheel, made of plaster from the designer's original clay model. This plaster working mould is limited to relatively short use, after which time it becomes rough and pitted and has to be replaced by a fresh mould made from the master model.

The working mould is placed upon the wheel and the slip is poured into it, being permitted to thicken until semi-plastic. It requires the judgement of long experience to determine when the clay is exactly ready to "work." It is a matter of seconds: a few too soon and it is unworkable; a few too many and the "slip" has become too hard.

With a tool known as a "profile" the potter shapes the material to the mould. This man is an artisan, with a skilled hand, an accurate sense of proportion and an unerring eye.

Not all pottery is produced upon the wheel. Simple shapes, such as plates, cups, bowls, etc., are turned upon the "jiggering machine." Elaborate or intricate shapes are cast in moulds, the latter being made one-fifth larger than the completed articles, in order to allow for the shrinkage which results from firing later. Handles, spouts, knobs, etc., for such shapes as pitchers, pots and similar products are moulded separately and affixed by hand.

When the shapes have been completed, they are stored in the drying room for twenty-four hours. They are then carefully smoothed with a camel's hair brush to remove every suspicion of roughness from the surface.

Graceful forms are now to be placed in the big ovens. The delicate pieces of clay cannot be exposed to the direct heat of the kilns without being discolored or cracked. They are placed in containers of coarse clay called "saggers," in which they receive their first baptism by fire.

These saggers are packed in the kiln with care, as it is necessary to fill the great cylindrical oven completely. The workmen engaged in this operation pile the saggers accurately one upon another like hat boxes, until every available inch of space has been utilized, after which they are wadded to resist fire gases.

When the kiln is fully loaded, the entrance is tightly cemented with fire bricks and the fires are started. For thirty hours the heat is gradually increased until it reaches 2200 degrees Fahrenheit. To obtain some idea of what a temperature of this intensity means, it is only necessary to realize that but for the steel bands with which the kilns are bound, they would burst under the terrific heat. After the thirty-hour firing period, the temperature is gradually reduced, the cooling process consuming two full days.

When the ware is removed from the saggers it is in an ivory-toned, vitrified state called "biscuit ware." Imperfect specimens are immediately destroyed. The perfect pieces are then placed upon a large revolving table which carries them, one by one, through either a blast of fine sand or vibrating pebble bath, which scours them so completely that not even a trace of a ridge or a bubble remains. The clinging particles of sand and dust are removed by compressed air.

In this marvelously smooth condition the holloware and gift pieces are ready to receive a glaze by being dipped in a solution by a glaze-dipper. He seems barely to touch the piece of biscuit ware as he holds it gently in his fingers, immerses it in the vat of liquid and removes it like a flash. He runs his fingers over the surface to remove excess drops and then sets the piece down, the whole operation having taken but a few seconds of time. It is done so quickly, accurately and delicately that it is hard to realize the glazer has handled the piece at all. Plates and other flat surface pieces are evenly sprayed with glaze.

The neccessity of applying the glaze with absolute uniformity is revealed when the piece is subjected to the next step, that of being fired in the "glost" kiln. If the liquid has been put on unevenly, the fierce heat of the "glost" klin—2100 degrees Fahrenheit—can crack the object. The purpose of the kiln is to fuse the glaze, giving it the deep rich, ivory-cream tint which distinguishes Lenox ware. Owing to the fact that the glaze does not permeate the "body" of the china, as in the case of some varieties, Lenox, after emerging from the "glost" klin, is neither brittle nor easily broken.

94

It is in this condition that the ware is ready for decoration. Lenox designs vary from chaste simplicity to the most elaborate patterns and are applied by three principle methods. Any one of these, or all, may be used upon a single piece of china, depending entirely upon the effect desired.

These methods are known as acid-gold, flat-gold, and color. The Lenox plant employs scores of highly-skilled decorators.

Those familiar with Lenox ware know that it makes a specialty of gold ornamentation. The combination of opulent, glowing metal and lustrous ivory is a thing of rare beauty. A vast amount of gold, worth hundreds of thousands of dollars annually, is required for embellishing the ware, and nothing but 24-carat quality is employed. No so-called commercial gold, an adulterated imitation, is tolerated. In order that loss may be reduced to a minimum, all wiping cloths and utensils used in gold decorating are burned to recover the precious metal that is in them.

When an etched gold design is required, the part to be occupied by the etching is left exposed and the remainder of the object is covered with acid-resisting material. It is from this process that the "acid-gold" method derives its name. The entire piece is dipped in hydro-fluoric acid until the etching is completed. Pure gold is then applied to the design, after which the piece is fired in a special decorating kiln.

Flat-gold work is not so intricate, pure bar gold being reduced to a semi-plastic state and applied by the artist's brush.

Color work is done in three different ways. When objects are to be decorated with birds, flowers, fish, etc., the work is generally done by free-hand. Other pieces have designs outlined upon them for the artist to follow. Yet others have elaborate designs transferred to them, sometimes consisting of from fourteen to sixteen colors, while frequently the transferred design is supplemented by hand work.

All pieces ornamented in gold, platinum or color must be fired in the decorating kiln, where the color is fused with the glaze. Color-firing and gold-firing, however, require different degrees of heat, so that it is often necessary to fire one piece several times for the various parts of the decoration.

Plates are burnished by hand and by machine, and each and every piece must pass the vigilant eyes of many experts. The most microscopic flaw is eventually discovered and immediately, when it is evident that a piece of china falls below the Lenox standards, it is destroyed.

Ever since the founding of the Lenox factory the one rule of perfect quality has remained inflexible and inviolate. It demands that nothing less than the best shall ever bear the Lenox mark. For this reason there are no imperfect specimens or "seconds" of Lenox ware ever sold.

The jewel-like effect on the Rutledge china pattern is created by hand applied raised enamel dots. Not every Lenox pattern is as intricate, but each decoration requires the same craftsmanship. Photograph: Lenox, Inc.

The Standard shape patterns were among the first patterns to be produced. Some of the patterns are still in the open line today, such as:

Standard Shape	Introduced
Tuxedo	1912
Westchester	1915
Lowell	1917
Autumn	1919
Blue Tree	1927
Coupe Shape	
Wheat	1940
Temple Shape	
Cretan	1938
Rutledge	1939

The Dimension shape was introduced in 1965 and Lenox's most recent shape, Innovation, was introduced in the early 1970s. Blue Tree at one time was a custom order pattern. When President Nixon's daughter, Tricia, married, she chose this pattern and it was put back into open stock.

Golden Gate

Fountain

Trellis

Coronado

Festival

Tremont

Peking

Blue Tree

Mystic

Lenox China

Mystic

Harwood

Trent

Orchard

Floralia

Colonial

Madison

Florida

Springfield

LEPERE POTTERY was listed in business in Zanesville, Ohio, the 1933-1934 directory at 1470 Greenwood Street. The owner and president was Albert E. Lepper who later became the technical director of Shawnee Pottery in Zanesville. Lepere Pottery went out of business early in the 1950s. Some hand-painted or hand-decorated kitchenware items were made by them. See Marks Section for mark.

LEWIS BROTHERS CERAMICS in Trenton, New Jersey, are decorators of glass and china who started in business in 1946 and are still operating in 1978, creating a nice line of decorated mugs, souvenir plates, glasses, lamps, etc.

LEWIS POTTERY COMPANY in Louisville, Kentucky, was a very early pottery started in 1829 to make queensware and china. The plant was taken over by Vodrey and Lewis and run until 1836. (Barber, E.A., *Pottery and Porcelain of the United States*, p. 157.)

LIBERTY CHINA. From 1910 to 1913, a pottery operated in New Lexington, Ohio, called the **VIRGINIA POTTERY**, when it became the Consumer Insulator Company which in turn consolidated with insulator companies from New Jersey. The Consumer Insulator Company only operated in the building a few short years before it was torn down. (Todd Jack, *Porcelain Insulators, Guide Book for Collectors*, p. 172.) From what I can find out from residents, there was only the one pottery in New Lexington, Ohio. Whether that company ever used the name Liberty China as a company name or whether that was just the trade name used on hotel ware made in New Lexington, I haven't found out. Very heavy hotel ware marked "Liberty China" may be found made by what was apparently the only pottery in the town, and that one operated for a very short time. Several companies will be found in this listing that made a very heavy type hotel ware and electrical insulators. Some manufactured both at the same time, some switched back and forth between the two products. For examples see Thomas China Company, Lisbon, and Trenton China Company, Trenton.

LIFETIME CHINA COMPANY. See Cunningham and Pickett for history. The Lifetime China Company was one of the names used by Alfred Cunningham in his distributing business. Homer Laughlin China Company made a great many dishes in various patterns for the Lifetime China Company. Pattern names in the various shapes included: "Jaderose," "Burgundy," "Imperial," "Pink Rose," "Gray Dawn," "Cameo," all in the Brittany, Nautical, and Cavalier shapes, made between 1953 and 1968. Pictured with "Gold Crown" in the Brittany shape, is a little plate. See page 51 for picture of plate.

LIMOGES CHINA COMPANY was established in Sebring, Ohio, in 1900, and operated until shortly before 1955, at which time the building was sold in a bankruptcy sale. By 1920, Limoges had a daily output of 45,000 pieces of semiporcelain dinnerware. What I am finding of their ware is just beautiful, and it is destined to become a great collectible because there is enough of it around to complete sets. The plant was first called **STERLING CHINA**, then the name was quickly changed to **SEBRING CHINA COMPANY**, but that didn't work because the E.H. Sebring China Company was also called the Sebring China Company; so the name was very shortly made Limoges China Company.

The five Sebring brothers, who founded the town of Sebring, Ohio, to have a place for their potteries, changed ownership and names of the potteries very frequently. **LINCOLN CHINA** was a name used by Limoges China Company on some dishes. See the Marks Section under Limoges China Company. At one time Limoges China was threatened with a lawsuit by the Haviland interests in France. They incorporated the use of "American" with their Limoges. The Lincoln China name may have been part of this sham.

Helen Stiles in *Pottery in the United States*, p. 78 had a great deal to say about dinnerware made by Limoges in the 1940 era.

The Manhattan shape as designed by Mr. Schreckengost for the American Limoges China Company has been decorated in a number of interesting patterns. The "Meerschaum" pattern is the color of a mellowed meerschaum pipe with deeper brown flecks. There is a streaked band of darker sepia brown which gives strength and beauty to this pattern. A design called "Red Sails" is printed in brilliant red and black with red band and handle treatment on a soft ivory-toned body. The "Animal Kingdom" consists of eight different characters which are gay and humorous designs in bright red. This design is used for children's sets, and has been very successful for bridge sets. The bridge plate, with well for cup, is one of the new pieces which has been added to the Manhattan shape. Another gay little design is "Ship Ahoy" with nautical flags spelling good luck. Mr. Schreckengost's "Jiffy Ware" is also made by the American Limoges China Company.

Limoges China Company produced some of the most attractive of the old semiporcelain ware. They stayed in business long enough to produce ware that had a lasting quality. The company existed through the 1940s when the emphasis on design became so important to our American potteries. Consequently this company produced some really beautiful ware. "Triumph" shape by Limoges had many rings clear around the shoulder of the plate in a recessed design. The rings were around the bottom of the cups, which had square handles. The handles on the creamer and sugar stuck out like little wings. Decoration names for this shape were "Tahiti" which had a mass of flowers in the center of the plate, "Karen" which had fernlike leaves and flowers in small design in the middle of the plate, "Posey Shop" which had pots of flowers on steps, "Waldorf" which had a wide border of flowers all around the shoulder of the plate, to name only a few decorations used with Triumph shape. Pictured is a small plate in Triumph shape and "Vermillion Rose" decoration. "Joan of Arc" in the "Diana" shape made a beautiful set of dishes. The Diana shape involved an edge with large scallops and the Joan of Arc decoration consisted of little crosses in red all over the dishes. Viktor Schreckengost, a well-known sculpter and designer, designed dishes for Limoges, for example, "Regency (shape) "Bouquet" (decoration). Around 1940, Limoges China, Salem China, and the Sebring Pottery Company were all under the same management. Sebring Pottery called the fluted shape pictured, "Corinthian" so this was probably the same shape by Limoges. See the picture of the plate marked "Blue Willow" with this shape. The Dutch scene with a blue raised border pictured is a favorite. The little jug is "Jiffy Ware" with the "Posey Shop" decoration. The cup with saucer that has a more square design is marked "Rose Marie." The other cup with saucer is "Wheatfield" with the fluted edges. In the 1930s the three companies mentioned above used a glaze that made some of their ware very yellow in color. One plate, almost square with the older flowered decals in orange, purple, and some black, made an attractive piece of china which was marked "Golden Glow" for the yellow glaze color.

Limoges China Company. **Front row:** *"Blue Willow" plate, "Rose Marie" cup and saucer, plate with Dutch decal and raised edge design, "Wheatfield" cup and saucer, "Vermillion Rose" in "Triumph" shape plate.* **Back row:** *"Jiffy Ware" jug, older vegetable or serving dish.*

LINCOLN CHINA COMPANY, Lincoln Illinois. See Stetson China Company.

LINCOLN CHINA COMPANY, Sebring, Ohio. See Limoges China Company.

THE LINCOLN POTTERY in Trenton, New Jersey, was started by James Carr and Edward Clark in 1879 at which time they purchased the Old Speeler Pottery of Trenton and organized it as the Lincoln Pottery. Mr. Carr only stayed with the Lincoln Pottery for a very few months. The same mark he used at the Lincoln Pottery may be found on his wares in the New York City Pottery which he helped to operate and owned with various partners. (See New York City Pottery for more on Carr.) Barber didn't say if the International Pottery owned by Burgess and Campbell bought the Lincoln Pottery from Carr, but he did say they were the next ones to reorganize the Lincoln Pottery, so we assume they bought it. Then they used some marks similar to the ones Carr had used changing only the initials or adding the names Burgess and Campbell. (See Marks Section.)

LION'S VALLEY STONEWARE, Lemon Grove, California, started in 1974. In 1976 Mr. Sam M. Aron was president and general manager. They were makers of stoneware dinnerware and accessories, including such pieces as soup tureens, accessories, and coffee services and serving pieces. The company went out of operation in December, 1977. (Information by letter from Mr. Sam Aron.)

THE LOS ANGELES POTTERIES were listed in 1948 and 1951 and 1954 as makers of artware and dinnerware at 11700 Alameda in Lynwood, California. They were not listed in 1955. Pattern names listed for them in the *1954 Crockery and Glass Directory* were "Cabana," "Santa Rosa," and "Plum."

LOUISIANA PORCELAIN WORKS. See New Orleans Porcelain Company.

LOUISVILLE POTTERY in Louisville, Kentucky, was incorporated in 1906, succeeding a similar business established in 1898. Keith P. Snyder operated the Louisville Pottery until his death in 1941, at which time his son-in-law took over the business until it sold in 1970. The pottery made a wide assortment of shapes, sizes and purposes of typical stoneware items such as: pitchers, pots, bowls, jars, mugs, cruets, feeders, chambers, casseroles, urns, vases, planters, cups, saucers, etc. (Information furnished by George Hadley of Hadley Pottery.)

LOWRY BROTHERS POTTERY. Lyman Lowry started a business in Roseville, Ohio, in 1882, followed by W.B. Lowry and Lowry Brothers. In 1888 they were listed by Henry Howe as employing eight to make stoneware cooking ware. But by 1920 they were operating two plants with the capacity of about three thousand pieces per day according to W. Stout *(History of Clay Industry in Ohio,* p. 61). Stout mentions an interview around 1920 with an F.S. Lowry who gave the following information about the cooking ware:

> The product known as asbestos fire clay cooking ware is made of refined fire clay and crushed asbestos and by an improved process, the results of many years experimenting. The firm is able to furnish ware of a superior character at a small portion of the cost of vessels made of other materials. All danger of acid or metal poisoning is avoided and food can be allowed to remain in the vessels without deleterious effect. The products of this firm consist of about everything that is needed for roasting, boiling, or baking.

JOHN MADDOCK AND SONS. See Thomas Maddock and Sons.

MADDOCK POTTERY. (See Thomas Maddock and Sons and also see the Scammell China Company.) There were three separate potteries operating in Trenton at the same time operated by members of the same family. The Maddock Pottery operated from 1893 to about 1923 in the old Lamberton Works that was eventually to become the home of Scammell China Company. "Lamberton China" was the name given to the hotel china made by Maddock Pottery Company. The name Lamberton came from the location of the pottery at the port of Lamberton on the old Delaware and Raritan Canal, which became part of the city of Trenton. Tolls were collected and traffic was heavy in the early days. (Also see Scammell China and Sterling China for makers of Lamberton China.) Pictured is a hotel platter with Maddock Pottery and Albert Pick (distributor) marks.

Maddock Pottery.

THOMAS MADDOCK AND SONS followed a long line of owners of a pottery on Carroll Street in Trenton, New Jersey. The pottery was first established by **MILLINGTON AND ASTBURY** in 1853 to 1859. The owners were **MILLINGTON, ASTBURY AND POULSON,** 1859 to 1870, who used the mark "M.A.P. Trenton" in an oval. They were making whiteware goods in 1861 (Barber). In that same year, Mr. Poulson died, and a Mr. Coughley bought his interests, but he died in 1869. Then Thomas Maddock entered the company buying Coughley's share and also that of Millington. (Millington left to start the Eagle Pottery.) From 1875 to 1882 (Ramsay) the firm was Astbury and Maddock. In 1882, Mr. Maddock became sole owner and took his sons as partners. The last listing for Thomas Maddock and Sons in the *Trenton City Directory* was in 1929. The products of the firm went from Rockingham, brownware, and yellowware, under Millington and Astbury, to white granite between 1859 and 1975. Then 1875 to 1882, only sanitary ware was listed by Ramsay. Thomas Maddock and Sons made white earthenware in addition to sanitary wares. (Marcia Ray in *Collectible Ceramics*, p. 95, gives "Indian Tree" as a pattern made by Maddock and Sons.) Ramsay gives their mark as "T.M. & S" with an anchor. In the *1902-1903 Complete Directory* **MADDOCK POTTERY COMPANY,** which was owned by Thomas Maddock and Sons and operated in the old Lamberton Works, was listed as making white granite dinner sets, toilet sets, and short sets of odd dishes, some decorated. (See Scammell China for the history of Maddock Pottery Company 1893 to 1922 in the old Lamberton Works.) In the same directory for 1902, Thomas Maddock and Sons in their original pottery on Carroll Street were making only sanitary ware at that factory. John Maddock was a son of Thomas Maddock who started a business of his own and took his own sons as partners from 1894 to 1929. As far as I can determine **JOHN MADDOCK AND SONS** made only sanitary ware, sanitary specialties, and plumbers' ware. They are mentioned here only to emphasize the fact that the Maddocks had three factories operating at once in Trenton and to help to keep them straight as to which made what products.

MADDUX OF CALIFORNIA is located in Los Angeles, California. One of the main objectives of this book is to give background and understanding of an industry which has produced and is producing our American dinnerware and also the accessory pieces used by housewives and collected by collectors. Toward this end, a few company histories which so well exemplify the problems faced by the industry have been presented just as they were sent by the companies and almost in their entirety. The following history of Maddux of California tells us a great deal about the problems, organization, marketing, attempts at success, etc.

Maddux of California was founded in 1938 by Bill Maddux. In 1948 it was incorporated and purchased shortly thereafter, by Lou and Dave Warsaw. During those early years and proceeding through the mid 50's, the bulk of their volume was sold through the variety chains. Their line consisted mainly of novelty and figurine planters.

In 1956 Dave Warsaw sold his 50% interest to Morris D. Bogdanow and went into the import business. At about the same time, the variety chains began to import low-priced ceramic products from the Orient. During the next five or six years, however, Maddux showed satisfactory increases in volume so that they purchased houses around their location at 3030 Fletcher Drive and expanded their production facilities. This culminated in 1959 when they completed their 25,000 sq. ft. factory, employing approximately seventy-five people. With no tariffs to protect them, the import of foreign ceramics continued unabated. This was and is a labor intensive industry unable to compete, at that time, with low-priced foreign labor. Hence, volume began to fall off during the early 60's. Lou Warsaw sold out his share and retired. Maddux began floundering around searching out a new market. For a few years they found solace in the Department Stores aided by their introduction of the Shell Line of Pearltone Serving Accessories. This hot new line gained them entry into almost every major department store nationwide. However, they were never successfully able to follow up this line. They also started doing business with the Stamp Companies, which were entering their prime during this period. By the mid 60's they had items listed in every major stamp catalog. This fact, has continued to date.

During the late 60's Maddux changed its emphasis to the mass market. This included Discount Stores, Drug Chains, Hardware-Houseware Jobbers, etc. They put their emphasis in

Basic Stock Programs. They were able to list such chains as Zody's, Caldor, Rinks Bargain City, and Community Discount among the accounts they serviced. Community Discount is still being serviced today, some ten years later. The nation's two largest hardware distributors, Cotter (True Value) and Ace, have also been steady customers for well over fifteen years.

In the Fall of 1968 Norman Bogdanow joined his father. Utilizing his degree in Marketing from U.C.L.A., he began to revitalize the marketing department. While Maddux had always sold through Manufacturers Representatives, in 1968 they had only five reps doing over $10,000. in annual volume, with two doing over $20,000. Over half of their volume was from stamp companies. By the end of 1974, (their last full year as a manufacturer) they had nine reps over $10,000 eight over $20,000, five over $50,000 and two over $100,000. Only 20% of their volume was from stamp companies.

During the mid 70's Maddux led the way into the planter boom, having its most profitable year ever in 1974. However, the boom was not without its dark side: imports from Brazil, Italy and the Orient began to increase and an economic recession of unknown size and duration was getting into full swing. With all of this in sight, Mr. Bogdanow received and accepted a substantial offer for his factory facilities from Grandinetti Products, Inc.

So in early 1975, Maddux suddenly found itself with molds, designs and accounts, but no factory. All of this in a year that, while ceramic pots were still in high demand, prices were rapidly falling, as more and more people entered the field. As Maddux shifted from factory to factory seeking out satisfactory quality and delivery, its own deliveries to its customers went from bad to worse. To remain competitive, with all of the new entries to the market place, margins were cut. The result was a small loss in dollar volume and a large loss in profit.

In March of 1976, after three months of difficult negotiations, Norman Bogdanow bought the assets of Maddux of California and *Hollywood Ceramics*, Los Angeles, (the former manufacturing corp. for Maddux) from his father. His aims for the first year of operation were to rid himself of unprofitable accounts; to seek out more profitable lines of merchandise; to break-even or show a small profit. Toward these ends, he took on the national representation of Valley Wholesale Supply, a medium-sized manufacturer and distributor of quality picture frames. He also began distributing the *Y.D. Designs* line of stoneware. The end result of these moves was a turn-around. Even after writing off the majority of the high organization expenses, his new corporation, *Rinor Marketing Corporation* showed a small profit.

In August, 1977 Carol Lee Tirre, former owner of the Pottery Shack, became the new owner of Maddux which is strictly a selling organization now. (Company furnished information.)

MARSHALL BURNS, Division of Technicolor, a sales agency that operated in Chicago, Illinois, and is now out of business, very widely distributed its products, including complete table settings with the mark "Marcrest." The products were probably made by many factories.

MARSH INDUSTRIES was started by Arthur Marpet and Mike Shein in 1950, in Glendale, California. In 1959, the company moved from Glendale to Los Angeles where they are still in business at present making California giftware and "French Chef" cookware. In 1969, Mike Shein retired and the business is owned by Arthur Marpet and his son, Richard A. Marpet, in 1978. In 1969 the line of "Gourmet Cookware" was introduced. Some of the products are hand-painted.

MARYLAND POTTERY COMPANY, Baltimore, Maryland. See Maryland Queensware Company.

THE MARYLAND QUEENSWARE COMPANY was built in Baltimore in 1879 by Hamill and Bullock. In 1880 they were followed by Hamill, Brown and Company. In 1888 the **MARYLAND POTTERY COMPANY** was incorporated. The Maryland Pottery made a variety of dinnerware in white granite, opaque porcelain, and stone china with the marks that are shown in Marks Section. Barber says that Maryland Pottery also used the word 'Etruscan" on a black and white granite toilet set. They may have used it on other products they made not knowing that the Griffen, Smith, and Hill Company of Phoenixville, Pennsylvania, were using the mark on Majolica. There would be no similarity in the ware, so this should not cause trouble for collectors. W.P. Jervis in "A Dictionary of Pottery Terms," *Pottery, Glass and Brass Salesman*, May 16, 1918, p. 11, said the Maryland Pottery made decorated earthenware and later, semiporcelain. The works were afterward controlled by Edwin Bennett Pottery Co. In *Pottery, Glass, and Brass Salesman*, July 2, 1914, p. 15, Jervis stated that the Maryland Pottery Company was closed at that time after a checkered existence.

MAYER CHINA COMPANY. In 1880, Joseph Mayer came to New York from England to engage in a pottery importing business with his brother, Arthur Mayer. He moved on to Beaver County, Pennsylvania in 1881 with another brother, Ernest, to organize the **MAYER POTTERIES COMPANY, LTD.** on the banks of the Beaver Falls. The pottery was later incorporated as the Mayer China Company. ("Necrology–Joseph Mayer," *American Ceramic Society Bulletin*, vol. 13, December 1930, p. 336.) The present product of Mayer China is a fine grade of very attractive hotel ware. But in their long history, Mayer made a great variety of products. Mayer Brothers of Beaver Falls, Pennsylvania, advertised white ironstone underglaze "Lustre Band and Sprig" (Tea Leaf) in 1881. Also an 1893 advertisement of Mayer's said "Lustre Band and Sprig already over ten years on the market will not wear off." (Hutchinson, Jeanette Ray, "Story of Tea Leaf Ironstone," *Antique Reporter*, November 1973, p. 16.) Marcia Ray called Mayer China a leading producer of the Tea Leaf pattern. ("A.B.C.'s of Ceramics," *Spinning Wheel*, June 1968, p. 21.) In 1896 the old buildings were destroyed by fire and a new building erected. Listed in the *1902-1903 Complete Directory* Mayer China was manufacturing white granite, semiporcelain dinner sets, toilet sets, and odd sets of dishes. In the *1900 Factory Inspection Report*, Mayer was listed as employing one-hundred forty-five to make white granite.

From *The Heritage of a Century* published around 1915 and copyrighted by Mayer China, is a list of the various kinds of clay used by Mayer. Ball clay from Tennessee, feldspar from Canada, Connecticut, and New York, kaolin from England and Florida, and flint from Illinois. These materials mixed in proper proportions achieved the quality of the Mayer's products. Around 1915, 75 percent of Mayer China's output was whiteware and 25 percent was decorated before it was dipped and glazed. Company information said that about this time (1914 to 1915) the Mayer China Company entered the hotel ware field almost exclusively and gradually discontinued tableware for home use. Shenango China Company of New Castle, Pennsylvania, purchased Mayer China in 1964. (See Shenango.) Then in 1968 both companies were purchased by Interpace (see Interpace.) Pictured for Mayer China Company is one of their very early thin plates with transfer stenciling or printing on semiporcelain; it is very porous pottery and the glaze is checked considerably. The mark is J. & E. Mayer as shown and "Columbia" pattern. There is a little raised design around the border. Also pictured is an old Tea Leaf pattern hotel ware saucer marked Mayer. Mayer's version of an old favorite, "Indian Tree," is shown. No matter how many companies made this pattern, no two are ever quite alike, yet they are easily recognized for the pattern that they are. The "Indian Tree" plate is a thick hotel type plate that has seen a lot of use but is still in fine shape, except for a little dulling of the glaze.

103

Nelson McCoy Pottery.

NELSON McCOY SANITARY AND STONEWARE COMPANY was started in 1910 by Nelson McCoy, Sr. who retained control until 1954 when Nelson McCoy, Jr. became president at age twenty-nine. Under his leadership the company prospered greatly. The products are so well established that the name McCoy is known universally. Household products of fine quality, so very nice to use and sold at a reasonable price, make McCoy a winner. Originality, attractiveness, and ingenuity have made McCoy products collectibles. McCoy makes many different items in pottery, but our concern for this book is kitchenware.

There were two McCoy potteries, J.W. McCoy Pottery and the Nelson McCoy Pottery. The old J.W. McCoy Pottery Company was listed in 1902 as making dinner sets and jardinieres, but I have no more information on that dinnerware. (See J.W. McCoy and Associates for history.)

There have been detailed histories of the two potteries published in several books such as *Ohio Pottery and Glass Marks and Manufacturers* or the *Collector's Catalog of Brush-McCoy Pottery*. Since March, 4, 1974, McCoy Pottery has been owned by the Lancaster Colony group. Nelson McCoy Pottery was formerly associated with the D.T. Chase (see Mount Clemens). For a period of time the mark used on cups made by Mount Clemens can be found on flowerpots made by McCoy, because the "MCP" mark was used by both companies during their affiliation. (Information from Mrs. Nelson McCoy.)

The following information on McCoy Pottery was furnished by Douglas Butler, Roseville, Ohio. In 1954, a "Cook & Serve Line" was introduced for outdoor or casual service which came in a two-tone, brown or birchwood color (highly glazed). The pieces offered were: no. 2—24 oz. long-handled pitchers; no. 7—6″ salad bowls; no. 105—36 oz. teapots; no. 10—10″ salad or spaghetti bowls; no. 5—1-pint French covered casseroles; no. 6—2-pint covered casseroles; and no. 9—3 pint covered casseroles. In 1955, the "Cook & Serve Line" added no. 4—16-oz. mugs and no. 3—2-quart beanpots with covers. Also introduced were a 7- and 9-piece salad set which consisted of 11½″ pedestal salad bowls and 5″ bowls. These came in three color combinations which were yellow, amethyst, or white inside with matching small bowls with wooden spoons and forks.

Beer steins were introduced in 1959. They were BM-5, which was a 15-oz. stein; BM-3, a 20-oz. stein; and BM-2, a 12-oz. stein in sham-bottom in white or brown.

In 1959, a coffee server (no. 266F) 40-oz. size was introduced. It came in turquoise, yellow, and pink, and had a flecked finish with a matching covered sugar and creamer.

Soup and sandwich sets were offered for the first time in 1963. They came in eight piece settings, containing four cups and four plates, in gloss green or gloss brown. One set contained square plates and the other set contained somewhat heart-shaped plates.

The McCoy tea sets came in four types. "Pine Cone," introduced in 1945 came in green and brown (high gloss). "Ivy" came in a cream color with green and brown accents and was introduced in 1949. Then in 1943, "Daisy" was introduced in green and brown colors with a high gloss, and also in pink and green matt or a white matt finish. "Moderne" was introduced in 1954 in green, high gloss glaze with dark shadings. The tea sets contained six cups, a teapot, and a creamer and open sugar (no. 108). Pictured here is a plate from a discontinued set that had cups, saucers etc., the Pine Cone tea set, and a casserole with a swigged on decoration on top, which was made in 1945 according to Butler.

J.W. McCOY AND ASSOCIATES. In 1886, *WILLIAMS AND McCOY* were established to make cooking ware in Roseville, Ohio. In 1890 the name was changed to *KILDOW, WILLIAMS AND McCOY* in the Midland Pottery and later to just *L.S. KILDOW.* This plant according to Wilbur Stout in *History of the Clay Industry in Ohio*, p. 61, was one of the most extensive in the valley producing a variety of culinary articles and stoneware. In 1890 they employed thirty people. From 1899 to 1911, the *J.W. McCOY POTTERY* operated in Roseville, making a corn line, yellow "Dandyline" ware, butter jars, etc. in the culinary line. From 1911 to 1925, J.W. McCoy joined with George S. Brush to form *BRUSH McCOY POTTERY.* (See that listing for history.)

MC FARLAND, WILLIAM. In Kentucky 1789 to 1799. Moved to Cincinnati 1799 to 1801. Made earthenware.

MC NICOL POTTERIES: THE D.E. MC NICOL POTTERY and *THE STANDARD POTTERY OF PATRICK MC NICOL* and *T.A. MC NICOL POTTERY CO.* There were three McNicol potteries in East Liverpool around the turn of the century. *D.E. MC NICOL POTTERY* operated from 1892 to 1920 in Ohio, then this pottery went to Clarksburg, West Virginia, where they were still operating in the 1960s under the ownership of New York interests. Before 1920, D.E. McNicol made whiteware and after moving to West Virginia they made mostly hotel ware but they did make some other products. In the *1902-1903 Complete Directory* (these very early directories listed both glassmakers and potters), D.E. McNicol was listed as making common china and semiporcelain dinner sets, toilet sets, and short sets of odd dishes, some decorated. The second McNicol pottery was the *PATRICK MC NICOL STANDARD POTTERY* in East Liverpool, Ohio from 1886 until the early 1920s. In 1919 or 1920 they lacked room to expand. He had evidently been inoperable for a while because at that time he filed with the secretary of state to be reinstated in business, but very quickly quit for good. The third McNicol was *T.A. MC NICOL POTTERY COMPANY* which operated from 1913 to 1926 in what had been the old Globe Pottery Co. building in East Liverpool. Some of the McNicol marks are easily identified as to one or other of the companies; "The Standard," found on plain white semiporcelain soup bowls, was for Patrick, and the initials D.E. tells which McNicol, but some of them I found I really didn't know which company the mark represented. Standard Pottery or Patrick McNicol was listed in 1902 as making white granite and Rockingham ware in dinner sets, toilet sets, and short sets of odd dishes, some decorated. One of the McNicols made a calendar plate which is marked "Carnation McNicol." Restaurant ware is easily attributed to D.E. McNicol for that is what he made in West Virginia. The "Roloc" mark is on hotel china. The two pieces of dinnerware that are pictured are both marked D.E. McNicol. The deep dish has a nice decal of flowers in the center and some sort of a fired on, lustre-colored design around the rim. The plate which has overglaze decal of cherries is rather thick and

D.E. McNicol Pottery.

Mellor and Company.

Mercer Pottery.

the glaze is checked which would indicate a porous clay body. The plate doesn't ring at all. The bowl is much thinner, more vitrified, of better quality in glaze and body. (See Novelty Pottery for early history of D.E. McNicol.) In *China Glass and Lamps Magazine*, July 23, 1923, p. 19, in the article "American Pottery Trade Marks," it tells that D.E. McNicol Potteries were operating solely in the making of yellowware. (The only plant left making it at that time.) D.E. McNicol also made specialties like colored tea sets, children's ware, baby plates, etc. See the children's dish pictured.

DR. MEAD in New York, New York, in 1816 is important because of his contribution toward the development of a fine porcelain made from American materials very early in the century.

MELLOR AND COMPANY. See Cook Pottery.

MERCER POTTERY was organized in 1868 with James Moses as head of the company. (See International Pottery, Trenton, and the Glasgow Pottery, for more on the Moses family.) Barber lists this company as making ironstone or white granite, semivitreous and semiporcelain products. The *1902-1903 Complete Directory* listed them as making porcelain and white granite, in dinner sets, toilet sets, short sets of odd dishes, druggists' supplies (such as mortars and pestles, etc.), and sanitary ware. Mercer Pottery was listed in the *Trenton City Directory* until 1937. I found no listing for them in 1937 or after that. But in the listings there were two Mercer factories after 1924. Mercer Porcelain, the second factory, lasted until 1938; there was no listing that year. In the 1931 *Industrial Directory for the State of New Jersey*, Mercer Porcelain was listed as making electrical supplies and hardware and bathroom fixtures, located at Penn Avenue and Mulberry. Mercer Pottery was still listed as making general pottery in 1931 at 39 Muirheid Avenue. A Mercer Pottery advertisement in the *Crockery and Glass Journal*, September 9, 1875, showed white granite ware typical of the 1870s. The advertisement mentioned above was reprinted in *Antiques Magazine*, July 1976, p. 156. Pictured is a little saucer made by Mercer Pottery with the design all in deep blue and an attractive plate with only a border decal on the shoulder and one gold trim line beyond that.

METLOX POTTERIES at Manhattan Beach, California, was founded in 1927 by T.C. Prouty to make the ceramic part of neon signs. The name Metlox (Manufacturing Company) was derived from the metal oxide used in the signs. In 1934, Prouty bought out Mallinite to produce some solid-colored ware for the May Company. In 1938 the first tunnel kiln was built at Metlox. But the pottery hadn't really gotten heavily into dinnerware yet because World War II came along and Metlox produced machine parts for the duration. During 1946 and 1947 Prouty made some ware for National Silver. The list of discontinued patterns sent by the company started with the year 1941 and listed both Vernonware and Poppy Trail lines. However, the real beginning of the Metlox Potteries fabulous dinnerware manufacture began when the plant was purchased by Evan K. Shaw in 1947; from that reorganization the success was determined. In 1958 Metlox bought the patterns and equipment from Vernon Kilns. (See Vernon Kilns.) In 1978 Evan Shaw is still the owner of Metlox, and working with Evan are his son and daughter, Ken and Melinda, also Melinda's husband, Kenneth Avery. (Company furnished information.)

The "Poppytrail" line is made from original designs reproduced by American craftsman from the finest raw materials, then either cast or molded and fired at 2100 degrees for forty hours to make a clean, high-fired bisque. The decorations are then applied by hand and a signature number of the artist is added. A spray glaze is added and the piece refired at 1875 degrees to seal the pattern under glaze which preserves the decoration for the life of the article. The glaze is hard and beautiful. The designs are timeless and will fit with any style of living. The colors used are gorgeous. The ingenuity and imagination that goes into the Metlox Potteries products have only been rivaled in a very few instances by another American pottery.

"Vernon Ware" is made by much the same careful process as "Poppy Trail." The glaze is porcelain strong, the styles cover a wide spectrum, including modern coupe shapes, luxuriously carved borders, and fluted edges with scalloped rims for the traditional, provincial, or Mediterranean-style home. (Information furnished by company.)

In the wide scope of the history of American dinnerware, Metlox Potteries would be considered a relative newcomer to the scene. But very soon they will be recognized as one of our most outstanding potteries and their products will be one of the most collected of the future because their products will be chosen and widely used now. And because their products are so durable, they will still be around to be collected. Pictured for Metlox are two plates. The plate with three big leaves is "Poppytrail, Woodland Gold." The other plate is "Vernon Ware, Vineyard." A list of discontinued patterns follows.

Metlox Potteries.

Metlox Potteries
Discontinued Patterns, 1941-1976

Poppytrail		Vernonware	
Apple	P160	Accents	V611-614
Aztec	P330	Anytime	V830
Blueberry Provincial	P350	Blue Fascination	V981
Blue Dahlia	P562	Blue Zinnia	V640
Blue Provincial	P120	Butterscotch	V710
California Fruit	P180	Caprice	V982
California Geranium	P450	Castile	V910
California Palm	P540	Classic Antique	V680
California Rose	P570	Classic Flower	V670
California Tempo	P441-447	Fancy Free	V860
Cape Cod	P370	Golden Amber	V621
Capistrano	P360	Heavenly Days	V820
Central Park	P270	La Jolla	V622
Colonial Heritage	P380	Patrician White	V960
Confetti	P430	Petalburst	V620
Contempora	P340	Pink Lady	V940
Country Side	P280	Rose-A-Day	V870
Del Rey	P420	Sherwood	V850
Flamenco Red Sc.	P577	Sierra Flower	V620
Fleur De Lis	P150	Springtime	V760
Free Form	P310	Sun and Sand	V630
Golden Fruit	P510	Tickled Pink	V810
Golden Scroll	P430	Tisket-A-Tasket	V840
Happy Time	P290	Town & Country	V720-750
Impressions	P320-323	Vernon Calypso	V626
Indian Summer	P260	Vernon Pacific Blue	V628
Indigo	P570	Vernon Pueblo	V631
Jamestown	P480	Year Round	V880
La Casa Brown	P573		
Luau	P460		
Mardi Gras	P370		
Mayan Necklace	P130		
Mission Verde	P580		
Mobile	P320		
Monte Carlo	P210		
Navajo	P470		
Painted Desert	P530		
Palm Springs	P410		
Peach Blossom	P220		
Peppertree	P520		
Provincial Flower	P360		
Provincial Rose	P550		
Rooster Bleu	P380		
Rooster Premium	P410		
Shoreline	P230		
Solid Colors	P360		
Street Scene	P350		
Tradition White	P164		
Tropicana	P580		
Yorkshire	P500		

MIDLAND POTTERY. See J.W. McCoy and Associates.

MILLER, ABRAHAM. See W.E. Tucker.

MILLINGTON (RICHARD) ASTBURY (JOHN) started on 1853 in Carroll Street in Trenton, New Jersey. By 1859 the firm was **MILLINGTON, ASTBURY, AND POULSON.** By 1861 they were making whiteware goods. Barber shows a pitcher with a Civil War scene modeled by Josiah Jones and made at this factory, then decorated by Edward Lycett who had a decorating shop on Greene Street. (Barber, *Pottery and Porcelain of the U.S.*, p. 452.) Barber does not give an ending date for this factory, but the fact that he was writing to people who had been at one time connected with the factory for information tells us the factory was gone for some time before Barber wrote his book. My *Trenton City Directories* began with 1900 and there was no listing of any of the names mentioned above.

MITCHELL, JAMES. See Caleb Farrar, Middlebury, Vermont.

MONMOUTH POTTERY. See Western Stoneware, Monmouth, Illinois.

MORGAN BELLEEK CHINA COMPANY started in 1923 as the **REA CHINA COMPANY** and in 1924 the name was changed to the Morgan Belleek Company. In 1929 the company merged with the American China Corporation with sales offices in Chicago, which dissolved in 1934 due to the depression. The name Morgan came from William Morgan of Trenton, New Jersey, who had worked for Lenox and was the production man at Canton who started the production of the Belleek. There were three firing kilns and three decorating kilns at the factory. The company made a complete dinnerware line, an 83-piece set retailed for $295 and a more expensive Victorian set cost $425. Sets were decorated in maroon or green. A set of cobalt blue cost $1,200 in 1930. So one could see how precious a set would be today. There were about one hundred accounts that sold the Morgan Belleek including Wanamaker's of Philadelphia, B. Altman and Sterns of New York, Barr of St. Louis, and Sterling and Welch of Cleveland. Coxon Belleek China was made at the Coxon Pottery in Wooster, Ohio, from 1926 to 1930, and offered great competition to Morgan Belleek. Both companies went under with the depression. There is a picture of Morgan Belleek China plates in a book which was printed by the Stark County Historical Society, four volumes (seven books) of *The Stark County Story*, by Edward Thorton Heald in 1959.

MORLEY AND COMPANY made majolica and white granite in Wellsville, Ohio, from 1879 to 1885. They were followed by the Pioneer Pottery Company and Wellsville China Company. (See these companies for more history.) Pictured is a semigranite plate made by Morley and Company. Attractively stenciled with fruits and nuts overglaze, the plate has a yellow iridescent border with a line of gold inside the yellow. The glaze is not crazed with age and the clay body has a fine ring.

Morley and Company.

MORRIS AND WILLMORE. See the Columbian Art Pottery, Trenton, New Jersey.

MORRISON AND CARR. See the New York City Pottery.

MOSES, JOHN & SONS. See Glasgow Pottery, Trenton, New Jersey.

MOUNT CLEMENS POTTERY. Ground breaking for the building of Mount Clemens Pottery of Mount Clemens, Michigan, took place in May, 1914, and by January, 1915, the pottery was making its first shipments. Charles Doll served as general manager of the company from the time it started until 1962, when he retired. He was succeeded by one of his sons, Charles E. Doll, Jr., with another of his sons, J. Randolph Doll as assistant manager. By 1964, the company was turning out 240,000 pieces of dinnerware per day. Although the plant was doing well, by 1920 they were needing capital to expand. Doll succeeded in selling all of the outstanding shares of stock to the S.S. Kresge Company, and Mount Clemens Pottery became a wholly owned subsidiary of that company. They always continued to operate completely independently of Kresge, except to furnish them with dishes. Mount Clemens made semiporcelain dinnerware of the type shown in the pictures. The solid color ware which came in a dark green, blue, and pink was probably Mount

Mount Clemens Pottery.

Clemens's answer to Fiesta Ware. Mrs. W.J. Eschenburg, a former employee of the pottery who helped secure the information gave us names for cups; "Cosmos," "Montell," and "Kolemont" and one other cup with a high rounded handle called "St. Dennis" shape. The pottery also made thick, coffee-type mugs. Pictured in the group of five plates is a small plate marked "Toulon." None of the rest of the ware pictured has a name in the mark. The plain colored ware came with the "MCP" mark and much of it was unmarked. (See McCoy in Marks Section for use of this same mark.) The Robin decal with wreath and flowers is one of my favorites. There are figures and letters in the marks which look like a dating system when we find out what it was. The plate with a large center decal of flowers is "Kolemont" shape. The plate with flowers all around the shoulder is "Mildred" shape. In the green room, the sets or shapes went by one name. Then when they were decorated they were given a second name. At this point a few basic shape names might be assigned a lot of new pattern names before leaving the factory. No employee, from any factory that I have corresponded with, can remember the names, because they say there were always so very many of them.

In 1963, David T. Chase and Chase Enterprise purchased the Mount Clemens Pottery and later they also purchased Sabin Industries of McKeesport, Pennsylvania. Sabin Industries is a primary decorator of ceramics and glass. (See Sabin Industries, Inc. for more. Information furnished by Sabin Industries.) In the 1967, *Crooksville-Roseville Pottery Festival* booklet is an article on Nelson McCoy Pottery (no author given) which tells that McCoy Pottery at Roseville was sold to Mount Clemens earlier that year. (See McCoy for more on that pottery.) The article went on to say that Charles L. Meteer, who was president of Mount Clemens at that time, considered the purchase of McCoy potteries as one more step toward the company's policy of building a complete manufacturing and sales capability in dinnerware, giftware, housewares, novelties, souvenirs, and advertising specialties. The article called Mount Clemens Pottery one of the largest producers of semivitreous dinnerware in the world, which may or may not have been exaggerating a little, but at least we know they were big.

By 1978 the companies had undergone another reorganization. By this time McCoy Potteries had been purchased by the Lancaster Colony group. Mount Clemens has been formed into a new company called Jamestown China and is being operated by new company owners of which are David Chase, C. Ikuta, and the Neachimen Corporation. Sabin Industries is being run as a separate company too. (See Sabin.) (Early history of Mount Clemens Pottery from *The Daily Leader*, Mount Clemens, Michigan, May 22, 1939, 25th anniversary issue, pp.1, 4, 8.)

MURPHY POTTERY COMPANY was in East Liverpool from 1900 to 1903. Shortly after organization the pottery became a member of East Liverpool Potteries Company which was dissolved in 1903. A variety of marks for semiporcelain and porcelain dinnerware is shown in the Marks Section for Murphy Pottery Company. A handsome vegetable bowl made by Murphy is pictured on page 54 with the East Liverpool Potteries Company history.

MUTUAL CHINA COMPANY of Indianapolis, Indiana, was a retail institution that was started in May, 1861, by Louis Hollweg. In 1915, the business was incorporated as Mutual China Company. On January 29, 1972, the doors were closed following a public auction (Rogers, JoAnn, "Mutual China Closes," *Collectors Weekly*, February, 1972, p. 4). See Marks Section for mark they used on china made in this country and abroad. Sometimes the mark is found alone; sometimes it is accompanied by the maker's mark.

NATIONAL CHINA COMPANY was incorporated June 15, 1899, in East Liverpool, Ohio, and moved to Salineville quite awhile before 1923, then operated there until the American China Corporation, which the company had joined in 1929, went under due to the depression in 1934. In East Liverpool the National China Company made tableware and hotel ware and a fancy shaped dinner service, vases, jugs, etc. In Salineville efforts were concentrated more on an exclusive line of dinnerware. Around 1923 the company was making only one dinner service called "La Rosa" which had become very popular in the trade. ("American Pottery Trade Marks," *China, Glass, and Lamps*, September 10, 1923, p. 15.) There are several marks shown that were used by this company. They were still in East Liverpool in 1908, because they made a 1908 calendar plate marked "N.C. Co. E.L.P." Pictured for National China are some attractive dishes.

National China Company.

NATIONAL POTTERIES CORPORATION, 1938 to present, is mentioned here only for purposes of identification, because so many collectors have inquired about the company. They are distributors of pottery and glass in operation in Bedford, Ohio, near Cleveland. They partially manufacture. They used the trademark "Napco."

NATIONAL SILVER COMPANY, New York, New York, is a selling agency of glass, pottery, etc. They used the mark "Nasco" on their ware. Southern Potteries, Glanding, McBean and Company, Santa Anita Pottery and probably many other potteries made products with National Silver's mark.

NEW CASTLE POTTERY (or CHINA COMPANY) was organized in 1901 and they built a six kiln plant on the present site of Shenango China in New Castle, Pennsylvania. The company only operated around four years until around 1905 when it was closed. (Information from Shenango China Company.) In 1912 the

Shenango Pottery purchased the New Castle Pottery buildings and moved the machinery and equipment to the Shenango plant on Emery Street which had also been started in 1901. (See Shenango.) New Castle Pottery was organized to make vitreous hotel and dinnerware. In 1903 they were listed as making semiporcelain dinner sets, toilet sets, and short sets of odd dishes. The only piece I have found from this company was a little oval, hotel ware vitreous or semivitreous dish which had an impressed mark, "New Castle China, New Castle, Pennsylvania."

NEW ENGLAND POTTERY COMPANY in East Boston was founded by Frederick Meagher to make Rockingham and yellowware in 1854. The next owner was William H. Homer who in turn sold to Thomas Gray in 1875. Dinnerware as we are concerned with it in this book became the product in this period, namely white granite and cream-colored table service. After 1888 this company made "Rieti" ware, a semiporcelain decorated product with a colored body. They also made a porcelain with a mazarine blue and old ivory finish. Besides tableware this company made vases, a two-handled cracker jar, jardinieres, chocolate jugs of stone porcelain, and many other products, even cups for electrical purposes. (Barber, *Pottery and Porcelain of the United States*, p. 245.) In 1902 this factory was listed in the directory as manufacturers of common china dinner sets, toilet sets, and short sets of odd dishes. The ending date for this factory according to Ketchum is 1914.

THE NEW JERSEY POTTERY COMPANY, Trenton, New Jersey, was organized in 1869 and in 1883 became the Union Pottery Company according to Barber in *Marks of American Potters*, p. 58. They made cream-colored and white graniteware. During the presidential campaign of 1880 they issued a series of plates with overglaze printed portraits of the candidates. I found no mention of a Union Pottery listed in the *Trenton City Directory* in 1900 or after, except a Union Electrical Porcelain Works which stayed in business until 1946.

NEW MILFORD POTTERY COMPANY. According to Barber, the New Milford Pottery Company of New Milford, Connecticut, was founded in 1886 as a stock company. According to Evans, the pottery had a kiln in operation by September 1887. The products of the New Milford Pottery Company were the ordinary grades of whiteware and cream-colored ware which was marked with a square and the initials of the company. They also made semiopaque china marked with an eagle mark. In 1892 the pottery was sold to W.D. Black, L.F. Curtis, C.M. and Merritt Beach (Evans). In the *1902-1903 Complete Directory* the company was listed as *BLACK AND BEACH POTTERY COMPANY* making common china dinner sets, toilet sets, and short sets of odd dishes. The name was changed in 1890 (W.P. Jervis's date in "Dictionary of Pottery Terms," *Pottery, Glass, and Brass Salesman*, September 26, 1918, p. 11) to the *WANNOPEE POTTERY* and the ware was of a fancy decorative type or art pottery type. (For a description of the artware, see Evans' book.) In 1903, the pottery stopped operating and was liquidated in 1904. Jervis said they made a lettuce ware of good quality in addition to a general line of colored glazes that entitled them to a longer life-span than they achieved.

Advertisement from New Orleans City Directory, 1887.

THE NEW ORLEANS PORCELAIN MANUFACTURING COMPANY of Saloy and Hernandez made hard porcelain or china. They were listed in the *New Orleans City Directory* only for the years 1887-1888-1889. Barber refers to this company as the *LOUISIANA PORCELAIN WORKS* and said that they started around 1880. Their importance is that they made a Frenchlike china from French materials with French workmen. The china was sold in solid white colors because the plant closed before a decorating department could be added.

There were twenty-three potteries listed at different times in the city of New Orleans from 1880 to 1900 in the city directories. From as many as nine at one time in 1884, the potteries finally dwindled to two in number in 1900. One was a very short-lived art pottery; the rest seemed to have made stoneware, etc. (Barber, E.A. *Pottery and Porcelain of the United States*, p. 313.)

NEW YORK CITY POTTERY in New York City was started by James Carr in October, 1853 (Barber's date) under the firm name **CARR AND MORRISON.** In 1852, for one year, Carr had operated a little pottery of his own in South Amboy, New Jersey. (Stradling, J., "American Ceramics at the Philadelphia Centennial," *Antiques Magazine*, July, 1976, p. 146.) The firm name stayed Morrison and Carr until 1871. Carr continued to operate the New York Pottery until 1888 when the pottery closed. Carr died January 31, 1904, at the age of eighty-four. Carr, an English potter, had worked for Ridgeway and James Clews in England. Carr was a remarkable person who managed in a lifetime to have affiliations with several potteries. (See Carr and Clark in Lincoln Pottery and Carr and Clark at the International Pottery.) According to Ramsay, Carr made a cauliflower majolica teapot, and according to Jervis he made a wide variety of articles in majolica. Carr, in his long career also manufactured Parian, cream-colored ware, and white granite; and his very early products included Rockingham and yellowware. From *The Ceramic Art, the History and Manufacture of Pottery and Porcelain*, by Jennie J. Young, New York, 1878, Harper & Brothers, p. 458, it is found that Carr made six or seven different bodies all composed of American materials. Young also stated that the dinner services were decorated with the same care usually reserved for porcelain. Carr's "semi-china" was nearly as translucent as porcelain, made of American kaolin clay with a large admixture of feldspar and decorated in styles similar to those found on ironstone china, according to Ms. Young.

JAMES E. NORRIS was listed only twice, in the 1901 *Trenton City Directory*, then again in 1902 in the *Complete Directory of Glass Factories and Potteries of the United States and Canada*. In 1902 he was listed as manufacturing porcelain, semi-porcelain, and white granite dinner sets, toilet sets, and short sets of odd dishes, some decorated. I was fortunate to have copies of the *Trenton City Directory* from 1900 to 1971. So this must have been a very short-lived company.

NORTH CAMBRIDGE CHINA around 1769 advertised in the *Boston Evening Post* of May 15, 1769, for samples of white clay. Then on October 16, 1769, they advertised for four boys to learn the art of making tortoiseshell, cream and green colored plates, coffeepots, teapots, cups, saucers. (Eberlain and Ramsdell, *The Practical Book of Chinaware*, New York: J.B. Lippincott Co., 1948, p. 293.) Another company in North Cambridge, more than a hundred years later, was mentioned by Arthur G. Peterson who found an advertisement in the *American Pottery and Glassware Reporter* of September 2, 1880. The advertisement is for **A.H. HEWS AND COMPANY** which the ad says started in 1765 in North Cambridge. In 1880, A.H. Hews and Company claimed to be the oldest pottery in America and that year they showed a line of fourteen items in fancy earthenware and flowerpots. This particular advertisement consisted of flowerpots and vases.

NORTON AND FENTON. See the United States Pottery at Bennington, Vermont.

NOVELTY POTTERY in East Liverpool, Ohio, from 1863 to 1892 became the D.E. McNicol Pottery Company in 1892. See D.E. McNicol under McNicol Potteries. The Novelty Pottery had a succession of owners from John Goodwin in 1863, Manly and Riley from 1865 to 1869, A.H. Marks from 1869 to 1870, then McNicol, Burton and Company from 1870 to 1892. "McN, B. & Co. Semi Granite" was found on a plate made by the last company mentioned. Early products for this pottery would be Rockingham and yellowware; then later, semiporcelain.

ODELL AND BOOTH BROTHERS in Tarrytown, New York, made faience and majolica from 1878 until around 1890. (Barber, *Pottery and Porcelain of the United States*, p. 308.)

OHIO CHINA COMPANY operated in East Palestine from around 1886 until it failed in 1912. This was another of the potteries built under the direction of the

Ohio China Company.

Sebring brothers. Pictured is a fancy, footed semiporcelain dish made by Ohio China. (See Marks Section for marks.) In 1902 the company was listed as making porcelain dinner sets, toilet sets, and short sets of odd dishes, some decorated. However, I wonder if the person compiling the directory did not really mean semiporcelain instead of porcelain. The piece pictured is definitely semiporcelain. Perhaps the porcelain is yet to be found.

THE OHIO POTTERY of Zanesville, Ohio, began around 1900 and in 1923 became the **FRAUNFELTER CHINA COMPANY** which was in business until 1939. According to W. Stout in *Clay Industries in Ohio*, p. 62, the Ohio Pottery began to manufacture restaurant and cookware around 1918. Before that time they made chemical laboratory articles. In 1920 they introduced a thinner brand of ware suitable for hotels and restaurants and also made china pieces for decoration. The cookware produced by this company was a true hard-paste porcelain and known as the "Pestroscan" brand. (See picture.) The ware, made in a large variety of articles, was glazed on the outside with a rich brown coating and was white inside. The same quality of ware was maintained under the Fraunfelter administration. Charles Fraunfelter took over the Ohio Pottery in 1915 as director, but the name was not changed to Fraunfelter China Company until October, 1923, when Fraunfelter purchased the plant. Also at that time, he bought the **AMERICAN CHINA PRODUCTS COMPANY** of Chesterton, Indiana, to make dinnerware in both plants.

Front row: "Petroscan French Metallic Lustre Ware" baking dish (lid missing), Ohio Pottery. Back row: Various beverage servers all matching in decoration, Fraunfelter China Company.

114

John Herold came to the pottery as plant manager in 1915 (see Herold China for more on Herold) and was a great asset to the company because of his exceptional talent for making fine china. In 1925, Fraunfelter died of pneumonia and the Chesterton plant was closed. Fraunfelter China failed due to the depression, reorganized, opened again, then closed for the last time in 1939. The article, "In Memorium, Charles Fraunfelter," *American Ceramic Society Bulletin*, VIII, February 1925, p. 185, 186, states that Fraunfelter developed the first and only hard true porcelain that had been produced in this country at that time. (Evans, Paul, "Artware of the Ohio Pottery, *Spinning Wheel*, December 1976, p. 15; W. Stout, *History of Clay Industry in Ohio*, p. 62.) The baking dish that is pictured has the Petroscan brand mark and was called "French Metallic Lustre Ware" as advertised in *China, Glass, and Lamps*, June 25, 1923, p. 5. The coffeepot, teapot, and cup pictured are marked with the Fraunfelter mark.

OHIO VALLEY CHINA COMPANY. The **WEST VIRGINIA CHINA COMPANY** was organized in Wheeling in 1887 or 1888 according to Barber and two years later was reorganized as the Ohio Valley China Company. The plant was operative until after 1893, then idle and became known as their Riverside Plant. ("Charles W. Franzheim," *Bulletin of American Ceramic Society*, XX, May 1941, p. 185.) At the Riverside Plant only sanitary goods were made. The Ohio Valley China Company manufactured porcelain in striking shapes and decoration, some of which were exhibited at the Columbian Exposition in 1893. This company produced a fine grade of true hard porcelain in tableware with overglaze colors. They also made a heavy hotel ware and artistic wares already mentioned. (Barber, *Pottery and Porcelain of the United States*, pp. 335, 497.) See Wheeling Potteries Company, p. 168.

OLIVER CHINA COMPANY operated in Sebring, Ohio, from 1899 to 1909. This is another of the companies founded by the Sebring brothers. This company was supposed to have made porcelain according to their marks, but again I believe it is a loose usage of the term. All the other Sebring wares I have seen are definitely semi-porcelain. (See Marks Section.) In the *1902-1903 Complete Directory* Oliver China is listed as making semiporcelain dinner sets, toilet sets, and short sets of odd dishes, some decorated.

ONONDAGA POTTERY COMPANY. See Syracuse China for history.

OTT AND BREWER. See the Etruria Pottery.

OVERBECK POTTERY was established in a cottage around 1911 and operated in Cambridge City, Indiana, until 1955. Art pottery is the term used to distinguish creative work from the strictly commercial type of pottery. All of the work of the four Overbeck sisters would have to be considered art pottery, but they did make a kind of dinnerware including plates, tea sets, cups, saucers, tumblers, etc. For lengthy discussions on this pottery see the various fine books now available on American art pottery. The Overbecks made beautiful vases, bowls, and a great assortment of figurines. ("The Overbeck Pottery," *American Ceramic Society Bulletin*, XXVIII, May 1944, p. 156.) By the time the 1944 article was written they were doing mostly, or almost completely, art-type pieces. The more functional pieces were early wares.

THE EDWARD J. OWEN CHINA COMPANY in Minerva, Ohio, operated from 1902 to 1933, and was another one of our potteries that succumbed to the depression. As early as 1904 the company won a gold medal for the best domestic semiporcelain at the Louisiana Purchase Exposition in St. Louis. The mark shown in the Marks Section commemorates this success. In 1923 the company operated eleven kilns and planned to add eleven more to double their capacity. ("American Pottery Trade Marks," *China, Glass and Lamps*, August 6, 1923, p. 15.) The company made dinnerware, calendar plates, and some nice hand-decorated pottery under the direction of John I. Bahl who worked at Minerva from 1907 to 1912. Pictured are two very pretty plates made by Owen. One has decals of bluebirds. The one with rose decal has a nice raised design.

Edward J. Owen China Company.

THE J.B. OWENS POTTERY in Zanesville, Ohio, from 1885 to 1907, has much more interest for the art pottery collectors because of the beautiful art pottery made there. After 1907 the plant became the Empire Floor and Tile Company until Owens lost his business in the depression. But of interest to the dinnerware collectors is the fact that in the *1902-1903 Complete Directory*, Owens was listed as making dinner sets, jardinieres, and novelties.

OXFORD POTTERY was started in 1914 by Charles Gross in Cambridge, Ohio. (I had reported around 1913 in *Ohio Pottery and Glass Marks and Manufacturers*, but Wilbur Stout in *History of the Clay Industry in Ohio*, Columbus, Ohio; Reis and Leighton, 1923, p. 62, gives us an exact date. Stout's book also furnishes us with more information on the ware made at Oxford Pottery. "Its ware is of the highest quality, staple, practical, and artistic. The raw materials are obtained largely from near-by sources as is also the necessary fuel. Both body and glaze are well matured. The exterior color is largely deep brown or jet and the interior pure white. This firm produces about every article needed for baking, roasting, or boiling." In 1925, the plant became Globe China Company. (See Various Cambridge Potteries listing for the succession within this building. Also with the Various Cambridge Potteries on page 37 is a picture of a job made by Oxford Pottery, along with products made by other Cambridge factories.

OXFORD TILE COMPANY. See Universal Potteries, Inc.

PACE BROTHERS, founded in Roseville, Ohio, in 1875 (Stout, *History of the Clay Industry in Ohio*, p. 61), made stoneware articles for cooking and baking for awhile between 1890 and 1900. In the *1906 Factory Inspection Report* for the state of Ohio they still employed eight to make pottery, but the type of pottery was not listed.

Pacific Clay Products Company.

PACIFIC CLAY PRODUCTS COMPANY was established in 1881 according to McKee (p. 49). There was a Pacific Porcelain Ware Company listed in 1924 in Richmond and San Francisco, making sanitary-type products. Around 1930, for a short time they made dinnerware, but went back to technical or commercial products. A little plate made by this company is pictured. A book was released in 1975, called *Pacific Pottery Notebook* by Barbara Jean Hayes in which she says by the late 1800s Pacific Clay Manufacturing Company had several plants in Southern California. Elsinore, Alberhill, and Riverside were all locations for the very early plants that made yellowware and red clay products. Hayes states that 1931 was the year Pacific Clay began to experiment with bowls, etc., and by 1937 they were in full swing making pottery products such as dinnerware and vases as opposed to the early products of brick and tile. At the beginning of World War II the pottery went to the production of Steatite high frequency insulators for radio equipment and that was the end of the dinnerware production. The dinnerware they made, as described by Hayes, was a pastel-colored ware with low-fired glazes. *American Home*, 1937, had an ad for "Coralitos," a thin dinnerware in chartreuse, ivory, yellow and turquoise.

PADEN CITY POTTERY near Sisterville, West Virginia, was chartered September 15, 1914, with principal offices in Paden City, West Virginia, with a capital stock of $75,000 which was increased to $225,000 in 1921. The company was dissolved on November 12, 1963. The foregoing information was furnished by the secretary of state's office of West Virginia. The Paden City Pottery was a large manufacturer of a good grade of semiporcelain dinnerware. The one thing a collector will notice right away about the Paden City ware is that some of their decals looked as if they were hand-painted china. Sears sold the "Nasturtium' pattern made by Paden City Pottery around 1940. Jerry Barnett, in the article "Paden City Pottery Company," *Glaze*, November 1977, p. 8, give us some more decoration names such as "Jonquil," "Terry's Tulips," "Rose Arbor," "Crazy Flower," "Diane," "English Ivy," etc. McKee tells us that Paden City Pottery devised a method for applying the decal underglaze, but went back to decals overglaze because the colors that could be used underglaze with their method was too limited. In single colors of glazed ware, Paden City made some very dark green, dark maroon, etc. as well as the light pastel sets. They had a "Princess shape," a very plain round plate, and simple but very tasteful shapes in creamer and sugar. The "Patio" decorated "Caliente" shaped small plate shown in the picture is sometimes referred to incorrectly as handled. These were not handles, but simply part of the Caliente shape which came with different decorations. See the picture of sugar and shakers and cereal bowl in Caliente shape. Paden City made a "Bakserv" line. Jo Cunningham of *The Glaze* found an "Autumn Leaf" plate with the Paden Bakserv mark. Jerry Barnett in an article, "Paden City Pottery Company's Shenandoah Ware," in the *National Glass, Pottery and Collectables Journal*, April 6, 1979, p. 38, tells us that there were six different decorations used on the Shenandoah line made by the Paden City Pottery; Morning Glory, Nasturtium, Cosmos, Strawberry, Poppy, and Jonquil. This ware was sold in abundance during the 1940s according to Barnett. These were made in full sets, including coffeepots, teapots, demitasse cups, etc. There was also a line of plain colored "Shenandoah Ware" in pastel colors. Pictured are two pieces of Shenandoah Ware. The platter is decorated "Cosmos" and the dessert plate is "Morning Glory." The small, squarelike plate in the picture is marked "Regina, P.C.P. CO." The large plate with roses and tulips is marked "La Rosa."

Paden City Pottery. **Front row:** *"Caliente" shaped saucer and small plate, "Regina" plate, "Morning Glory" Shenandoah Ware small plate.* **Back row:** *"Caliente" salt and pepper and sugar, "Cosmos" Shenandoah Ware platter, "La Rosa" plate.*

Pennsbury Pottery.

PEARL CHINA COMPANY is now known as a selling operation, but they did have a direct connection with a pottery in the middle 1930s to 1958 in East Liverpool, Ohio. In a plant formerly owned by Hall China Company, Mr. George Singer, wanting products to expand his jobbing business, made art and novelty ware until 1958 when he sold to Craft Master of Toledo. Pearl China Company still exists in East Liverpool today as a huge outlet for pottery. Many pieces of pottery ware may be found with Pearl China marks, ranging from decorative to very functional kitchenware and heavy brown dinnerware. (See the Marks Section.) They have used no mark at all for a long time due to the cost of backstamping.

PENN CHINA COMPANY, Phoenixville, Pennsylvania. See Phoenixville Pottery.

PENNSBURY POTTERY started in 1951 or 1952. They were listed as making pottery and chinaware at Tyburn Road near Morrisville, Pennsylvania. In 1971 the pottery closed for economic reasons. They made some items for the table and kitchen use, but mostly their production was a decorative type pottery.

PENNSYLVANIA CHINA COMPANY had plants in Kittanning and Ford City, Pennsylvania, as advertised in the *Pottery, Glass and Brass Salesman* in December, 1912, p. 14. By 1916 there was no plant making pottery listed in Ford City and only W.S. George was in Kittanning. Their predecessor company was probably Ford China Company (see Ford China) in Ford City, and they followed Wick China Company in Wicksboro or Kittanning. In the *History of Armstrong County, Pennsylvania*, by J.H. Beers published 1914, p. 128, is this history of the Kittanning plant.

> The china works were first organized as the Wick Chinaware Company in 1889. The plant, until closed down at a recent date, was operated by the Pennsylvania China Company. The plant employed several hundred workmen of the highest skill, producing the finest grades of tableware, plain and decorated jardinieres, and ornamental vases. Seven different materials were used, two of the clays being imported from England and one coming from Florida. Another clay, as well as the feldspar and flint, are procured in Pennsylvania.
>
> In the latter part of 1913 the pottery closed down indefinitely, all of the workmen being laid off without warning. This was a heavy blow to the men, as most of them had bought homes and made investments in Wickboro, and were compelled to sacrifice their property in order to leave for other cities where employment could be had. At this date the works were on the market for sale, with several buyers in sight. The W.H. George Pottery Company, of East Palestine, Ohio, was one of the bidders.

The Kittanning plant was purchased by W.H. George and continued to operate under the name of George China Company until shortly after World War I. George continued to operate in Pennsylvania and Ohio in other plants. (See W.S. George.) The buildings were very shortly torn down after George closed the plant.

PEORIA POTTERY COMPANY operated from 1873 to 1904. The American Pottery Company in Peoria, Illinois, was organized in 1859 and started making pottery in 1860. When Christopher Webber Fenton's United States Pottery in Vermont failed because of the high cost of production, he came to Peoria to start the American Pottery Company. The American Pottery made glazed yellowware and whiteware of excellent quality. The pottery closed because of the Civil War. In 1873 when it was opened again it was known as the Peoria Pottery Company which operated until 1904. In 1881 the Peoria Pottery had five kilns to make heavy buff stoneware in all kinds of utilitarian pottery trimmed with blotches, bands, stains, and dribbles, in red, green, cream, smoky, or brown slipware. In 1893 they were making cream-colored and decorated wares, white granite, or ironstone (Barber). They exhibited fine dinnerware in delicate pastel colors at the Columbian Exposition in 1893. The colors included a pale green and a salmon. In 1902, the Peoria Pottery was taken over by Crown Pottery of Evansville, Indiana, to form the Crown Potteries Company. In 1904, the doors were closed completely. (Rosenow, Jane, "Peoria Pottery and How It Grew," *Antiques Journal*, December, 1969, p. 30; Barber, *Pottery and Porcelain of the U.S.*, p. 244.)

PERLEE INCORPORATED was listed in the *Trenton City Directories* from 1926 through 1930. According to the *Encyclopedia of Collectibles*, vol. B, p. 36, they made Belleek.

PETERS AND REED. W. Stout records in *History of Clay Industry in Ohio* that the Peters and Reed Pottery Company in Zanesville, Ohio, from 1901 to 1920, started making brownware cookware with a white lining around 1903. He said the body was composed of weathered shale and the white lining was largely of clay. This ware was discontinued around 1906. Peters and Reed made a line marked "Pereco" with a semi-matt finish in plain green, orange, and blue. The pieces were mostly artistic such as vases, etc., but they did make bowls in this line. Bowls, covered jars, and trays were made in the "Landsun" line as well as artistic pieces. Some have referred to this line as a "drip" or "sheenware effect." For more on Peters and Reed, see Evans's book or "Peters and Reed, Zane Pottery," by Deb and Gini Johnson in *The Antiques Journal*, April, 1975, p. 12.

PFALTZGRAFF POTTERY started around 1811 in York, Pennsylvania and employed twenty-eight under the name J.K. Pfaltzgraff in the *1900 Factory*

118

Inspection Report for the state of Pennsylvania. Company information gave the early 1800s as a starting date. A German immigrant, George Pfaltzgraff began by making redware and stoneware with a "Pfaltzgraff Pottery" impressed mark. The company has remained a family business until the present time (1979). In the lengthy history of the pottery they have expanded their production from that originally made primarily for agricultural, industrial, and domestic purposes (storage crocks and jugs) to include a wide range of dinnerware and serving pieces which became the main product since W.W. II, plus kitchenware and decorative accessories.

By 1931 the company was employing one-hundred thirteen people. In 1947, "Brownie" beanpots were displayed at the Museum of Modern Art, New York City, and chosen as one of the hundred useful objects of fine design for 1947. ("Company News," *American Ceramic Society Bulletin*, XXVI, December 1947, p. 415.) The Gourmet Brown Drip pattern of Pfaltzgraff following W.W. II was the pottery's first big success in dinnerware and is much copied according to the article "Pfaltzgraff Not a Dirty Word," *American Art Pottery News*, July, 1976, p. 4. The trademark of Pfaltzgraff shows the outline of a castle still standing in the German Rhineland which bears the Pfaltzgraff name. A variety of marks involving the Pfaltzgraff name have been used over the years; Pfaltzgraff Stoneware Company, Ltd.; B. Pfaltzgraff; H.B. & G.B. Pfaltzgraff; Pfaltzgraff Company; The P.S. Company; and J.K. Pfaltzgraff and currently, The Pfaltzgraff Company, a division of the Susquehanna Broadcasting Company. In 1974 at an exhibition of regional folk pottery held in York County, Pennsylvania, a plate was shown marked "H.B. Pflatzgraff, York, Pa." The piece was identified by the catalog of the exhibition as a late nineteenth century plate with a brushed slip decoration. This same mark was found on a mid-nineteenth century crock. The company has now expanded to include handcrafted pewter, glass, copper, tin, and Buenilum products as well as pottery pieces. Pfaltzgraff Pottery purchased Stangl Pottery in Trenton, New Jersey, on July 31, 1978.

PHILADELPHIA CITY POTTERY in Philadelphia was started in 1868 by J.E. Jeffords and Company as the **PORT RICHMOND POTTERY COMPANY** and was out of business by 1915. Somehow this company displeased the old master writers on pottery. W.P. Jervis in "A Dictionary of Pottery Terms" in *The Pottery, Glass, and Brass Salesmen*, March 28, 1915, p. 13, said they made a "cheap grade" of earthenware around 1904, and were out of business at the time the article was written. E.A. Barber in *Marks of American Potters*, p. 32, written in 1904, said "they manufacture cow creamers in brown glaze after the old shapes, and while not intended to deceive, these are such excellent reproductions of early patterns that examples frequently find their way into the shops of secondhand dealers and are sold as genuine antiques at high prices." He also said "much of the ware of this firm is unmarked." Other products made by Jeffords were teapots, table and toilet white-wares, jardinieres, Rockingham, yellowware, and blue glazed ware. They also exhibited majolica at the Philadelphia Exhibition in 1876.

PHOENIXVILLE POTTERY, KAOLIN AND FIRE BRICK COMPANY operated from 1867 to 1872 making yellowware, Rockingham, and fire brick in Phoenixville, Pennsylvania. In 1872 when the works were leased to **SCHREIBER AND BETZ**, animal heads in terra-cotta and Parian were added to the production. Lithophanes and transparencies for windows and lampshades were made and some of these were marked "Phoenix Pottery." (Barber, *Marks of American Potters*, p. 28.) In 1877 the pottery was leased by **L.B. BEERBOWER AND HENRY B. GRIFFEN** at which time manufacture of white granite was started at Phoenixville. (See L.B. Beerbower and Co.) During 1878 the name was Griffen, Smith and Company for a short time. In 1879 the name was changed to **GRIFFEN, SMITH, AND HILL**. In 1880 they began to manufacture their "Etruscan Majolica" (Barber). They also made a good grade of white and decorated tableware. The company name was changed when Hill resigned. Then around 1882 according to Barber in *Pottery and Porcelain of the United States*, p. 267, **GRIFFEN, SMITH AND COMPANY** started making porcelain. In 1890 a fire destroyed a large portion of the works and majolica was discontinued (Barber). In 1889, Smith withdrew and the firm became *GRIFFEN, LOVE AND COMPANY*. In 1891 it was called the *GRIFFEN CHINA COMPANY*, which for just one year manufactured a translucent French-type of china in plain white table service according to Barber. In 1892 the works closed. Apparently the buildings were not used until 1894 when several different owners used the buildings after that time. From 1894 to 1897 it was called *CHESTER POTTERY* making cream-colored and semigranite dinnerware. From 1899 to 1902 it became *PENN CHINA COMPANY* making blue mottled dinnerware. Then for less than one year after January, 1902, they were the *TUXEDO POTTERY COMPANY*.

The Etruscan Majolica made under Griffen, Smith, and Hill was chiefly in designs taken from nature. Tablewares was made in the form of leaves, etc. (La Grange, Marie J. and Goldman, J.D., "More About Makers of Majolica," *Hobbies*, June 1939, p. 54.) In the *Antiques Journal*, September 1964, p. 24, "Etruscan Majolica," by Bernice M. Ball a table setting is shown in the beautiful seaweed pattern, with cups, bowls, pitchers, plates, a platter, compote sugar, etc. According to this article, David Smith was the manager, William Hill the potter, and an Englishman named Bourne was the designer. The majolica was made from Chester County, Pennsylvania clay. The Chester Pottery made semigranite ware bearing the mark of the state of Pennsylvania. (Barber, *Marks of American Potters*, p. 31.) They also used a keystone mark with "C.P. Co." and sometimes "C.P. Co." alone. (Jervis, "A Dictionary of Pottery Terms," *The Pottery, Glass & Brass Salesman*, June 27, 1918, p. 11. Also Smith, Clarissa, "Etruscan Majolica," *Antiques Journal*, June, 1957, p. 8.)

ALBERT PICK was a sales organization that operated out of Chicago, Illinois, for a number of years. His mark with or without the mark of the manufacturer may be found on a great variety of wares. He was mentioned as operating in 1904 when the *Marks of American Potters* was written by Barber. His mark may be found on dishes made by companies in business through the 1930s. See the hotel ware platter pictured for the Maddock Company on page 100 which also had an Albert Pick mark.

PICKARD CHINA founded by Wilder Pickard in Chicago in 1894 as a decorating establishment, existed for a period of more than forty years, and achieved a high reputation for painted and gold decorations on fine table china obtained in white form from other china factories.

At the turn of the century, Wilder's china decorating studio in Chicago specialized in hand-painted art pieces and dessert and tea sets. Most of the original artists were from Chicago's famous Art Institute. Business mounted swiftly and soon the staff was swelled by renowned ceramic artists from all the countries of Europe. Since most china was manufactured abroad at that time, the Pickard studios imported blank ware to be decorated. These early hand-painted pieces are now sought by collectors.

When Wilder's son, Austin, entered the business, he longed for the day that Pickard no longer would be dependent upon outside sources. In 1930 they decided to make china as well as to decorate it. An addition was added to their plant in Chicago and five years of experimentation in manufacture followed. After two more years of test production, a new plant was built in Antioch. Finally in 1938, chinaware made by Pickard appeared on the market. (Eberlein and Ramsdell, *The Practical Book of Chinaware*, Philadelphia: J.B. Lippincott Company, 1948, p. 302.) Pickard China makes wares that are completely vitrified, translucent, with an excellent glaze. The Pickard mark consists of a lion supporting a shield with a fleur-de-lis above a scroll bearing the name "Pickard" with "China" below and "Made in U.S.A." In the period of time when Pickard merely decorated and did not manufacture, two marks may be found, one for Pickard and one for the company that made the china. For instance the Pickard mark and a Haviland mark may be found on the same plate. Before Pickard started making their own china they used mostly French china to decorate. While the output of the company was virtually confined to tableware,

Pickard's early china has become a valuable and desirable collectors' item because of the artists and their signatures on the china. In a staff-written article, "The Marks and Signatures of Pickard," *Collector's Weekly*, June, 1977, p. 13, was an assortment of Pickard marks and the dates the marks were used. Pickard still manufactures a line of decorative accessories introduced by Wilder A. Pickard in 1915, with 23-karat gold hand-painted over an intricate rose and daisy design in etched relief. In 1976, Pickard began manufacturing an annual series of limited edition Christmas plates. Pickard, Incorporated was proud to be selected in 1977 by the U.S. Department of State to manufacture the official service of china used by our embassies and other diplomatic missions around the world. The special decoration has an embossed gold border of stars and stripes and an embossed gold reproduction of the Great Seal of the United States. (Company furnished information.)

PIONEER POTTERY COMPANY of East Liverpool, Ohio. See Pearl China Company.

PIONEER POTTERY of Wellsville was preceded by Morley and Company from 1879 to 1885, then became Pioneer Pottery from 1885 to 1896, and then became the Wellsville China Company. (See Morley and Wellsville potteries for more.) There is a variety of marks recorded for this company shown in the Marks Section. For a very short time Barber said the company was called the Wellsville Pioneer Pottery and then became Wellsville China Company. It was listed in a 1902 directory as Wellsville China Company. Pioneer made white graniteware, porcelain, and some ware that Barber called "Imperial China." In Ramsay's *American Potters and Pottery* is shown a mark as pictured in the Marks Section with the words "Aurora China." This mark was not given in Barber's book. Barber does show a very similar mark with the words "Aurora China" being used by Wick China Company of Kittanning, Pennsylvania. (See Wick for picture of Wick Aurora china.) The Pioneer Pottery mark had "P.P. Co." in the center and Wick had "W.C. Co."; that was about the only difference in the mark.

*Pisgah Forest Pottery Cameo pitcher. Photograph: Duke Coleman, **American Art Pottery News**.*

PISGAH FOREST POTTERY near Mount Pisgah in North Carolina started around 1926 according to Ralph and Terry Kovel, *Collector's Guide to American Art Pottery*, New York: Crown Publishers, 1974, p. 177. There was an extensive family background in pottery making before that time in Tennessee and in North Carolina. Although the products of this pottery are more in the class of art pottery, they did make a lot of products for table use such as teapots, mugs, jugs, tea sets, and cream and sugar sets, etc. Walter B. Stephen, operator of the pottery died in 1961, but the firm continued under other direction and was still operating when the Kovel book was written in 1974. Pictured is a cameo pitcher dated 1939 and signed "W.B. Stephen" furnished by the courtesy of Duke Coleman, owner of Nothing New Antiques in Baltimore, Maryland and editor of *American Art Pottery News*, a monthly newspaper.

POPE-GOSSER CHINA COMPANY was organized in Coshocton, Ohio, in 1902, by C.F. Gosser, and the company started in 1903 to produce a high-grade translucent china body for vases, etc. (Stout p. 83.) Finding this unprofitable, the company changed to dinnerware which was described by Stout as "not truly vitrified but much harder than semiporcelain." He said the product was light in weight, decidedly translucent, and quite hard, comparing well with any foreign ware. In 1929, Pope-Gosser joined the American China Corporation, a merger of eight companies. (See American China Corporation.) After the A.M.C. was dissolved, Pope-Gosser was reorganized in 1932 by Frank Judge. They still made beautiful semiporcelain ware until 1958, but it was not as thin or translucent or quite the quality of the earlier ware. However, Pope-Gosser's late ware was as good or better than most Ohio ware; it was of that good a quality.

In 1904, Pope-Gosser China won the silver medal for superior semiporcelain at the St. Louis Louisiana Purchase Exposition. In 1907, Pope-Gosser received the gold medal for plain and decorated china and semiporcelain at the Jamestown Tercentennial Exposition.

Because Pope-Gosser made artware in the very early years, a basic body had to be developed that was good enough for hand decorating. The clay body was made almost entirely from American kaolin. Pope-Gosser was not able to compete with foreign artware and turned to dinnerware. Pictured are parts of two matched sets by Pope-Gosser made in their later years of production. Also pictured is some earlier ware. The cup in the picture is a thin, fine china and the pitcher is almost that thin. Pope-Gosser's early ware was translucent when it was cast thin. Rose Point is a favorite shape with a raised border design which comes with many different decal decorations.

PORCELIER MANUFACTURING COMPANY was started in East Liverpool, Ohio, in 1927 by Harry and Hymie Tauber in a pottery they rented on Dresden Avenue. (Information from a reader whose family worked there and who also moved to Pennsylvania with the company.) In the Spring of 1930, the Porcelier Company moved to South Greenburg, Pennsylvania, taking about a dozen workers with them. Jack and Emanual Dim and Hymie and Harry Tauber were the founders of the pottery in Greenburg. During the depression the workers received twenty-five cents an hour and the bosses got twenty-five dollars a week. But even though starting during the depression and in a new location, the Porcelier Manufacturing Company was successful until June, 1954, when the business ended and the equipment was sold and shipped to several states. By 1931, Porcelier was listed in the *Industrial Directory* as employing three-hundred two people. The vitrified china they made consisted of teapots, electric coffee makers, sugars, creamers, cups, bowls, etc. These products are now being collected and are found in fine condition because of the quality of china. A very pretty electric grill with a porcelain top (looked like a waffle maker) with raised ridges and flowers was found. The grill was marked with the same mark found in small variations on most of the ware, which always involved Porcelier Manufacturing Company in script. Pictured are a teapot and three coffeepots made by Porcelier. All are marked with the Porcelier mark. See the Marks Section for the marks used by this company. (Much of the early history as given here was supplied by a former employee of Porcelier.) In 1954 the building was taken over by the Pittsburgh Plate Glass Company.

Porcelier Manufacturing Company.

123

PORT RICHMOND POTTERY COMPANY. See Philadelphia City Pottery.

POTTER'S COOPERATIVE, East Liverpool. See Dresden Pottery, East Liverpool for history and picture.

PROSPECT HILL POTTERY was operated by Dale and Davis in Trenton, New Jersey, from 1880 until 1894 or 1895 making decorated semiporcelain and white granite dinnerware according to Barber. After that time the pottery was sold to Charles H. Cook of Cook Pottery. There were no listings for the Prospect Hill Pottery in Trenton in 1901, 1902, 1903, or 1904. Then from 1905 until 1920, the pottery was listed every year, so I assume this was the period it was operated by Cook. It was not listed in the *Industrial Directory*, only the *City Directory* so I couldn't tell what products it made that year. After 1920 the Prospect Hill Pottery was not listed until it was listed again in 1925 and 1926. That was the final mention of the pottery. The early marks in Barber for the Prospect Hill Pottery involve the names Dale and Davis. Dale and Davis had exhibited white granite and decorated crockery in Philadelphia in 1876 (Barber, p. 305).

PURINTON POTTERY COMPANY was in operation in Shippenville, Pennsylvania, from 1941 to 1959. The mark was the trademark logo plus, sometimes, "Hand-Painted." The concept and processes were developed by Bernard S. Purinton in a pilot operation in Wellsville, Ohio, beginning in 1936. Purinton Pottery Company was formed and production begun in 1941 in a plant designed and built for the purpose in Shippenville, Pennsylvania. Originally all the slipware was cast. (Later on, some was pressed, with the introduction of the Ram Press process.) The strictly free-brush decoration was made of the same slip as the body, with colored minerals added. The decorations were painted on the leather-hard body of the greenware. The decorators were local people trained at the factory. Glaze was applied by dipping the decorated ware, and the ware was one-fired. The body was formulated to stand the handling necessary for this process. Manufacture was ended and the company liquidated for economic reasons in 1959. The building was sold for other use. Competition from foreign imports was one of the underlying factors. Pictured for Purinton Pottery is a beautiful, hand-decorated slipware plate and other hand-painted pieces.

Purinton Pottery Company.

124

QUEEN CITY POTTERY. See Robinson Ransbottom.

RAVENSCROFT, LTD. is the sales agency in Lancaster, Ohio, belonging to Anchor Hocking which markets American-made glass and dinnerware. (Dinnerware made by Taylor, Smith, and Taylor.)

RED CLIFF COMPANY is a decorating and distributing company which started in business in 1950 in Chicago, Illinios. They decorate very beautiful ironstone pieces which are patterned after the old patterns and shapes.

RED WING STONEWARE COMPANY, the forerunner of *RED WING POTTERIES, INC.* was founded in 1878 in Red Wing, Minnesota, according to Darlene Dommel in an article in *Spinning Wheel,* December, 1972, p. 22, entitled "Red Wing and Rum Rill Pottery." She based that starting date on papers found in the Minnesota Historical Society. From 1878 to 1892 the name was Red Wing Stoneware Company which became Red Wing Union Stoneware from 1892 to 1936, and was then called Red Wing Potteries, Inc. from 1936 to 1967. Red Wing produced the Rum Rill pottery that was made there from 1930 to 1933, according to Ms. Dommel. All stoneware production ceased in 1947. In the 1930s the dinnerware manufacture was started on a large scale. Solid color dinnerware became a popular selling item. Later the hand-painting of dinnerware and artware was added, which was to grow until the process required ninety workers. The following quote from Ms. Dommel's article tells us about the ending struggle of Red Wing and is reprinted here with permission of *Spinning Wheel*'s Editor, Albert Christian Revi.

The 1920's and 1940's were prosperous years and Red Wing became an established leader in the dinnerware fields. Red Wing pottery was sold in department stores, gift shops, floral shops, small-town hardware stores, even roadside stands. Then, around 1950, department stores, the major market for dinnerware, began importing increasing quantities. In 1950 about 10 per cent of all dinnerware sold by department stores was imported and, by 1967, imports had increased to 90 per cent. It was difficult to compete with imports since foreign potteries were as modern and efficient but paid wages only a fraction of the United States scale.

Red Wing Potteries showed its first year of loss in 1955 and continued with greater losses until 1958. R.A. Gilmer became president and general manager in that year and the company started making marginal profits again. As foreign import dinnerware sales continued to wreck havoc, the company sought new markets. Dinnerware was made specifically for trading stamp companies. Supermarkets were also large volume customers but carried lines only a limited time and were not a consistent sales source. As well as facing marketing problems, the antiquated physical plant prevented fluid production flow.

Further diversification was needed. Red Wing Potteries began producing a line of casual dinnerware in 1959 and started making restaurant and hotel china in 1964. Both casual and restaurant dinnerware showed promise of success as well as dinnerware manufactured for Sears, Roebuck and Company . . . .

Nationally recognized as a tourist attraction, the retail store was located across the street from the factory. Annually, thousands of tourists from throughout the country came to purchase second-quality Red Wing wares and tour the plant. In 1966, a gift shop and candy store were added and the retail store accounted for nearly one-fourth of total company sales.

The fatal blow to Red Wing Potteries came on June 1, 1967, when factory workers went on strike for higher wages. Unable to meet the workers' demands, Red Wing Potteries, which gained world-wide fame and stature during 90 years of pottery production, closed on August 24, 1967.

Red Wing Potteries, Inc.

Thanks to an article released just as this book is being completed enabled me to name more of the pieces shown in the picture for the readers. David A. Newkirk, well known among pottery collectors, authored "Red Wing Dinnerware" *Antique Trader,* March 12, 1980, p. 58. He is co-author of a book soon to be released on Red Wing Pottery. Left to right in the back row is "Capistrano," Anniversary line; "Lotus," Concord line or shape; "Lexington," also Concord shape. In the middle row the cup is "Pepe." The saucer in the front row is "Roundup," Casual shape. The other two pieces are still unknown to this author, but we may know soon when Mr. Newkirk's book is out.

PAUL REVERE POTTERY operated in and around Boston in several locations from 1906 to 1942 according to *Collector's Guide to American Art Pottery* by Ralph and Terry Kovel, New York: Crown Publishers, 1974, p. 189. Dishes made by this pottery are pictured in the Kovels' book. The Paul Revere Pottery was mainly an art pottery producer but they did make children's dishes and plates, cups, bowls, etc. for table use. They even made bisque doll heads and decorative tile. Full luncheon and dinner sets were sold in stock patterns and to special order according to the Kovels. See the Kovel book for several pages of information on the factory and many pictures.

RHODES AND YATES. See City Pottery, Trenton, New Jersey.

RIDGEWOOD INDUSTRIES, INC. started in business in Southampton, Pennsylvania, in the 1970s. Prior to 1977 they manufactured just one line of translucent fine china with exclusive shapes and hand-decorating. They made a complete dinnerware set with a hard glaze and durable pattern which was sold through franchised dealers. After 1977, Ridgewood discontinued the manufacturing of all fine china and became exclusively a decorating facility. In 1978 they were decorating commemorative pieces only, such as the "Game Bird" series which includes "Ring-necked Pheasant," "Bobwhite," "Woodcock," etc. Sets of Ridgewood China have now entered the realm of collectors' items. Ridgewood Industries went out of business in 1978, according to a former employee.

RINOR MARKETING CORPORATION, Los Angeles, California. See Maddux of California.

RITTENHOUSE, EVANS AND COMPANY. See American Art China, Trenton, New Jersey.

ROBINSON CLAY PRODUCTS in Akron, Ohio, formed in 1902 from a combination of Whitmore, Robinson, and Company and the E.H. Merrill Company, combined with Robinson Ransbottom of Roseville in 1920. The emphasis has been placed on the brick and tile and similar products made by this company. I didn't realize until reading the *Crockery and Glass Journal* directory issue of March, 1954, that Robinson Clay Products made as many housewares as they did. They were listed for several brand names, "Crown Stoneware" (probably the same as produced by Robinson Ransbottom, their affiliate), "La Pomma," "Pinehurst," and "King O Dell." (See Robinson Ransbottom.)

ROBINSON RANSBOTTOM POTTERY COMPANY in Roseville, Ohio, started as the **RANSBOTTOM BROTHERS POTTERY** Company in 1900. In 1920 the name was changed to its present form when they merged with Robinson Clay Products Company of Akron. The very early products were a utilitarian type of pottery—jugs, churns, chicken waterers, salt jars, chamber pots, milk pans, bowls, etc. By 1916 the company was one of the leading producers of stoneware jars. From the mid-thirties to 1940, the company produced the "Old Colony" line under the brand name "Crown Pottery." Each piece was hand-decorated under glaze with its own individual decoration and color combination. This line consisted of vases, flowerpots, etc. The "Rustic" line which was produced through the sixties under the Crown Brand name was a kitchenware line including a "Sheriff" cookie jar, "Hootie" cookie jar, a hand-decorated cookie jar, No. 313, an apple cookie jar (similar to the complete "Apple Ware" line being produced in 1978 and 1979), a condiment jar and cover, three pitchers in 12-, 32-, and 48-ounce sizes, 5-, 7-, 10-, 12-, 14-inch shallow bowls, a 12-inch deep bowl, an "Oscar" cookie jar, and No. 311-15 cookie jar. This whole line had freehand decoration under the glaze in flashing colors.

Because of the quality of the product made by this company, and because the company used the word Roseville in so many of Robinson Ransbottom's marks, dealers are constantly selling the products of this company as old Roseville Pottery's products. The best defense for beginning collectors is to study the marks for Robinson Ransbottom in the Marks Section. Robinson Ransbottom's products should be collected because they are made by Robinson Ransbottom, not because they are thought to be some other company's work. The variety, quality, careful workmanship, attractiveness, and availability make Robinson Ransbottom's wares a great collectible.

The Queen City Pottery in Cincinnati was originally a wholesale outlet which was purchased by Robinson Ransbottom and used as a warehouse and wholesale outlet for the Cincinnati and Kentucky areas.

ROOKWOOD POTTERY COMPANY. As if it were only to prove the statement by Paul Evans, found elsewhere in this book, that every major pottery made dinnerware at some time or other, I have included Rookwood Pottery, considered by many to be the most outstanding art pottery of all. Rookwood Pottery was in business from 1880 until 1967 in Cincinnati, Ohio. In Herbert Peck's book, *The Book of Rookwood Pottery,* New York: Crown Publishers, 1968, p. 174, it is stated that if an article could be produced in clay, Rookwood made it. In addition to many other articles Peck lists mugs, chocolate pots, teapots, pitchers, compotes, cups and saucers, dinnerware, etc. On page 26 is a photograph of a salad bowl by Rookwood which was dated 1883 and decorated by Louise McLaughlin. A piece like that could make a kitchenware collector out of anyone! In the *Pottery Collectors' Newsletter,* May 1976, p. 43, is a staff-written article that tells about "Blue Ship" dinnerware that seems to have been a complete set.

Roseville Pottery Company pitcher with hand-painted tulips. Photograph: Martha Brisker's Antiques, Richwood, Ohio.

ROSEVILLE POTTERY COMPANY started in 1892 and operated until 1954. They opened the first plant in Roseville, Ohio, in 1892 and opened the Zanesville branch in 1898. A third plant in Putnam, Ohio, was destroyed by fire in 1917. After 1917 all Roseville pottery was made in Zanesville. In the *1902 Glass Factory Directory,* the Roseville Pottery is listed as operating in Zanesville to make dinner sets, jardinieres, and novelties. Roseville Pottery Company was an art pottery for the duration of its existence and could in no way be considered a maker of dinnerware as are most of the other factories in this book. However, they made dinnerware at the start, and again very late in the life of the pottery, a line called "Raymor" was manufactured. The plates are oval with a raised place on the ends for handling. The cups are also oval, as are the saucers and salad plates. The colors included a mixture of earth colors of brown, beige, gray, deep green, and medium tan. They are marked "Raymor by Roseville." Pictured is one of the dinner plates. Also some time between 1912 and 1931, Roseville Pottery made juvenile dinnerware with a plate, a child's bowl (about like an adult soup bowl) and a pitcher, with bands of green and yellow around the shoulder and little chickens at intervals around the plate, which was cream-colored ware. According to Douglas Butler they also made a pitcher with a dog in brown and green colors on cream-colored ware. A rabbit design was used on plates and pitchers with brown and green colors. Ducks were used on plates, pitchers, egg cups, etc. All were made for use by children.

An article by Eloise M. Fruge tells about a fourth plant acquired by Roseville Pottery in 1901—the old Mosaic Tile Company where cookware was made in four kilns with fifty men working.

Also pictured for Roseville is a black bowl which could have been used for serving salads or possibly as a bottom for a flower holder; I couldn't decide which. The pitcher with the hand-painted tulips is a delight to behold. The three-piece tea set did have lids. They shade from a light blue at the top to a dark blue at the bottom and have an R mark just a little different from those I have found. (See the Marks Section.) (Fruge, Eloise, "McCoy Pottery Still Being Produced," *Tri State Trader,* February 3, 1973, p. 20.)

Roseville Pottery Company.

ROUSE AND TURNER. See Jersey City Pottery.

ROYAL CHINA COMPANY in Sebring, Ohio, has undoubtedly produced so many different kinds of dishes from its beginning in 1934 to the present that the pattern information alone would fill a book. Three old favorite patterns which Royal did in a single color are the Willow pattern in bright blue, Indian Tree in green, and a Currier and Ives scene in a grayish blue. To show how confusing marks on china can be, Royal made, using a single orchid decal in the center, two different shaped plates with two different gold-trimmed shoulders. One plate is called "Gold Orchid," named for the gold edge and single orchid decal. The other plate has the single orchid decal in the center, but it is named "Delmar Lace" for the wide lacy border all around the shoulder with no mention of the decal in the name. "Camelot" is a heavy semivitreous, restaurant-type plate with a brownish yellow design about an inch wide around the shoulder. "Platinum Exotic" is an attractive plate with a thin line of platinum trim around the edge and a purple flower with long leaves and stems. The design covers most of the plate on this one. In ironstone Royal made many beautiful plates, but one that appeals to me looks like an effect that might be used in a stained glass church window done in blue and green. A single large rose is found in the center of a semiporcelain, handled, cake or serving plate with a painted, maroon-colored edge line. "Aliber" had a swirled shoulder and a decal with all kinds of flowers in the center. "Enchantment" had two pink and gold tulips in the center and an edge of gold tulips circling the shoulder. "Twilight" underglaze was an overall cover of interrupted streaks or lines in gray and pink probably meant to represent the last rays of the sun. "Royal Maytime" was a modern, servicable plate in a very plain shape, but overglaze was a bouquet of spring flowers that really looked like an old design from the transfer printing days.

Names for shapes, lines, and decorations are a selling device, but it will help to remember that their main function was to give a means to identify the ware for ordering Royal China issued in what they termed "series." These were composed of the various patterns in a given line for that particular year. The patterns in the series varied from year to year. The shapes within a given series were not identical, so the series cannot be considered to be a shape. The same decoration was sometimes used in two different series or shapes such as "Queen's Rose." Some of the series and the patterns they include are as follows: The Royal Hostess Series styled by Joan Luntz, an underglaze decorated ironstone in "It's a Daisy," "Leaf Song," "May Queen," and "Overture." The Florentine Series of Royalstone (Royal's name for ironstone) in "Monaco," "La Scala," and "Persian Gold," which has a deep, rich gold color and freezer-to-oven use. Regal Series by Joan Luntz included "Sunshine," "Enchantress," "Angelina," "Pandora," "Clear Day," "Terrace," and "Barcelona." Futura Series included "Tangier," "Sleepy Lagoon," "Flower Dance," "Break of Day," "Surrey," "Devon," "Young Love," "Frolic," "Amhurst," "Baghdad," "Queen's Rose," "Santa Fe," "Fantasia," "Caprice," and "Lily." New for 1968 was the Cavalier Series, which included "Lucky Charm," "Mozambique," "Leaf Spirit," "Sweet and Lo," "Midnight Melody," "Camelot," "Trellis," and "Cortez." A later Cavalier Series lists "Casablanca," "Damsel," "Long Ago," "Country Garden," "Casa del Sol," "Currier and Ives," and "Blue Willow." The Imperial Series had a "Queen's Rose" with a different shape than the Futura "Queen's Rose" but the same decoration. Both lines had underglaze decoration. Other patterns or decorations in the Imperial Series were "Triple Treat," "Overture," "Clear Day," "Carousel," "Zinnia," "Mum's the Word," "Ceylon," "Snowdrops," "Boutonniere," "Morocco," "Love Me, Love Me Not," "Acapulco," and "Sierra Madre." The Royal Phoenix Series included "Recollections," "Normandy," "Ionia," "Majorca," "Night," and one other that had a huge rose that reached across the plate, complete with stem and leaves. Royal Renaissance Series included "Fernwood," "Trinidad," "Strawberries Blue," and "York." My favorite series was Heritage Series which included old favorites such as "Blue Willow," "English Ivy," "Currier and Ives" in pink and blue, "Doorn," "Colonial Homestead," and "English Legend." The Uptown Series included "Day and Night," "Pebble Beach," "Sahara," "Sonoma," "Patio," and "Central Park." This last series was described as "a contrast of shimmering white and rich color (in deep bands around the shoulder) with gracefully sculptured cups." Actually the handles on the cups are square with a completely round fingerhole, very different in appearance.

128

It was a difficult task to choose the pieces to picture for Royal China. In the photograph a few of the old favorite patterns are shown so the reader may see Royal's version of these patterns: "Blue Willow," a version of "Indian Tree" in solid green; "Ming Tree" so marked; a "Currier and Ives" winter scene; and a wheat pattern marked "Red Wheat."

RUM RILL was a sales organization in Little Rock, Arkansas, from 1933 or before to 1942. Ending date furnished by the Little Rock Public Library. From 1933 to 1938 pottery was made for Rum Rill at Red Wing Potteries, Inc. From 1938 to 1941, Florence Pottery in Mt. Gilead, Ohio, made the Rum Rill pieces. From 1941, when the Florence Pottery burned until Rum Rill went out of business, the ware was made for the company at Shawnee Pottery in Zanesville, Ohio. Rum Rill owned their own molds and ordered their pieces made to certain specifications. They sent representatives to the potteries to make sure the products were what they wanted and various attempts were made until the product suited them. Undoubtedly other potteries will come to light that made products for Rum Rill. A former employee of the pottery gave kitchenware items in the Rum Rill line as mixing bowl sets, cookie jars, salt and pepper sets, coffee pitcher and mugs sets, sugar and creamers, water pitchers, etc. For a good article with many pictures of Rum Rill decorative products see Rena London, "Rum Rill Pottery, A Different Collectable Pottery," *National Glass, Pottery and Collectables* Journal, December 1979, p. 6. Recently a Red Wing Potteries catalog titled "Manufacturers of Rum Rill Art Pottery," with a June, 1933, date was reprinted and is being sold. We can assume Rum Rill was in business 1933 or before.

SABIN INDUSTRIES, INC. was founded in McKeesport, Pennsylvania, in 1946 by Samuel Sabin to decorate ceramics. Later a technique was developed to decorate and bend glassware also. Today they are a decorating company for both ceramics and glassware in the giftware and advertising specialty fields, but this doesn't begin to tell the story of the beautiful pottery kitchenware finished from blanks by Sabin.

The "Microcks" line was so named because the stoneware is safe for microwave ovens. The pieces are so beautifully designed that they could be taken for pottery of the early American era.

In 1963, Sabin Industries was purchased by Mount Clemens Pottery of Mount Clemens, Michigan. McCoy Pottery of Roseville was purchased by Mount Clemens Pottery in 1967 to develop a complete line of manufacturing and marketing. (See Mount Clemens for more on this.) At the present time, Sabin Industries is being run as a separate company owned by David Chase. See a photograph of a plate made by Sabin Industries on page 14.

SALEM CHINA COMPANY, incorporated in 1898, is still operating as a distributing concern, but they have not made dinnerware since 1967. Following a very short period of financial difficulty early in the history of the company, Salem has been very successful and has made a great quantity of chinaware. In the *Salem City Directory of 1906*, p. 28, first articles manufactured were "Excelsior" porcelain and ironstone. They also made earthenware. Then they developed a fine line of dinnerware and an active decorating business. See the bird decorated plate and the "Indian Tree" plate by Salem China. Salem China Company used a great variety of marks. Since 1967, Salem China Company has had dinnerware made in Japan and England over their backstamp. Pictured are two of the Godey's Ladies plates. The one with the blue border was made around the 1940s. The older plate was made around 1910; the clay body is soft and discolored. The newer plate is highly vitrified. (See another plate made by Salem on page 14.) A favorite shape made by Salem China Company was "Victory" which was highly advertised in the 1940s. A plate is pictured named "Sun Valley" for decoration in the "Victory" shape. The stencil of three big flowers, some buds, and leaves, looks as if it were hand-painted but it was not. The decoration is underglaze and covers most of the plate in a colorful fashion. "Main Street" was a plain colored semiporcelain in a kind of square shape which came in four colors, as advertised in Sears catalog in 1951 and 1952. Many different decorations came on the Victory shape, "Doily Petit Point" which looked like a doily was resting on the plate, "Jane Adams" colorful flowers like a corsage at one side of the plate, also "Garden," "Vienna," and the "Godey Prints." One other decoration on the Victory shape that was especially appealing was Salem's "Colonial Fireside" which pictured four different subjects or fireside scenes in early Colonial times in shades of mellow brown, tan, and green.

SALOY AND HERNANDEZ. See the New Orleans Porcelain Company.

SANTA ANITA POTTERY was in business at 3025 Fletcher Drive in Los Angeles, California, in 1948, and by 1951 they were at 3117 San Fernando Road in Los Angeles. All that Floyd McKee, in *A Century of American Dinnerware Manufacture*, 1963, p. 48, had to say about Santa Anita Pottery was that it was controlled by National Silver of New York and managed by Gertrude Gilkey. He noted it had ceased operations several years back (before 1963). Barbara Jean Hayes, author of

Santa Anita Pottery. "California Modern" plate and saucer on the ends, "Flowers of Hawaii" plate in the center.

Bauer-The California Pottery Rainbow stated in a letter that in the late forties, Santa Anita Pottery shipped their molds to Japan (probably when the address changed), and after that the products were really Japanese. The pottery was still listed in business in 1957, but must have ended very close to that time. Santa Anita Pottery made very desirable lines of dinnerware. Bud Shields, a former employee of the Santa Anita Pottery, said they made lines called "California Modern" and "Flowers of Hawaii." Pictured is a plate and saucer of "California Modern." Santa Anita Pottery made decorative ware, lazy susans, pepper mills, etc., along with full lines of dishes.

SAXON CHINA COMPANY. See French China, Sebring, Ohio.

SCAMMELL CHINA COMPANY was formed around 1924 in Trenton, New Jersey (first listing in *Trenton City Directory* was 1924) but its roots go back much further than that. The establishment or location which was to become Scammell China has always been informally known as the **LAMBERTON WORKS** which dates its foundation to 1869. In 1869 three Quakers, George Comfort, Thomas Bell, and Jonathan Stewart, started a pottery of two kilns in the part of Trenton called Port of Lamberton where the canal joins the Delaware River. They named the pottery the Lamberton Works.

In 1892, there was a fire in one of the Maddock potteries. At that time the newly formed Maddock Pottery Company purchased the old Lamberton Works. At first the old plant was used to make sanitary ware until a new building could be built by the Maddocks for that purpose. (There were three Maddock potteries. See Maddock Pottery history.) When the new building was ready to manufacture the sanitary ware, the old Lamberton Works began producing hotel ware called "Trenton China." Barber said that fine grades of semiporcelain were made at the Lamberton Works under the Maddocks. (See Maddock in Marks Section for marks.) In 1901, D. William Scammell joined the Maddocks, and little by little bought out the Maddocks' interest in the Lamberton Works. (Last listing for Maddock Pottery was 1923.) Around 1923, Scammel and his five brothers purchased the remaining stock and formed the Scammell China Company which was then primarily involved in making hotel china. In 1938, Scammell China Company agreed to produce a well designed, thin, hard, translucent china of excellent quality for the Philadelphia firm of Fisher Bruce and Company. The new Lamberton china appeared in January, 1939, with a fine porcelain body of delicate ivory tone. The Lamberton china output was all varieties of tableware. (Eberlein, Harold and Ramsdell, Roger, *The Practical Book of Chinaware*, Philadelphia: J.B. Lippincott, 1948, pp. 303–304; *Trenton City Directory*, 1923-1924.) Decorations were molded, modeled, painted, transfer

Scammell China Company "Lamberton" china as shown in **House Beautiful**, *November, 1942.*

printed, and gilded types. Scammell was one of the very few American potteries that made their own decalcomania for transfer-printing. The Lamberton mark is "Lamberton/Ivory/China/Made in America," in a square. Scammell China Company went out of business in 1954. Scammell China made the Baltimore and Ohio blue railroad china for around twenty-five years according to an article by Meredith Havens. Scenes included the "Cumberland Narrows," "Indian Creek," "Thomas Viaduct," "Potomac Valley," "Harper's Ferry," etc. (Havens, Meredith, "B. & O. Blue Railroad China," *Antique Trader Annual of Articles* for 1973, pp. 84-85.)

VIKTOR SCHRECKENGOST was born in Sebring, Ohio, in 1906 and was the son of a potter. He studied at the Cleveland Institute of Art from 1924 to 1929 and did postgraduate work in Vienna, studying ceramics and sculpture. He accepted a teaching position at the Cleveland School of Art and also worked as a designer for R. Guy Cowan at the Cowan Pottery where the production was mainly art pottery. Cowan Pottery closed in 1931. In 1933, Schreckengost reorganized production of Limoges China in Sebring, and also began to design dinnerware for them. Production increased from 30 percent to more than full capacity in one year's time under his direction. He also worked in the same capacity for Sebring Pottery, Leigh Potters, and Salem China. (For a full discussion of Schreckengost's life and work, see *A Century of Ceramics in the United States, 1878-1978*, by Garth Clark and Margie Hughto, New York: E.P. Dutton, 1979, p. 325.)

SCHREIBER & BETZ. See Phoenix Pottery, Phoenixville, Pennsylvania.

SCIO POTTERY COMPANY in Scio, Ohio, since 1932, is a remarkable company in many ways. For one thing they began operations right in the middle of the depression and have been successful from the start. Lew Reese had the idea that a really mechanized pottery operation could enable an American pottery to compete with the Japanese ware that was flooding our markets at that time and putting pottery after pottery out of business. He bought the property at sheriff's sale, recruited townspeople to help make building repairs, even lived in one corner of the plant for a while. The townspeople cut away a woods and rebuilt a road only on the hope that the plant would provide them with jobs. Reese managed to get his first loads of clay on credit, and twenty people from Scio put in $100 each to meet the first payroll. There were various improvements and kiln after kiln followed. With such a fine business head and the terrific town support the Scio Pottery was able to meet its share of setbacks and continue to prosper right up to the present (1979). In the winter of 1947 a fire destroyed three-fourths of the plant, but in just sixty-two days of winter weather the local people had a new steel building erected.

The second way in which Scio Pottery is a little different is that they have never used a mark on the huge quantity of fine ware that they have made in the last forty-five years. The one exception was the mark "Golden Wheat" on a line made for a grocery store promotion, but that mark did not include Scio's name. They produce a reasonably priced good grade of dinnerware which sells because of price as well as quality and without any particular name or advertisement such as marks. Scio pays top wages and has been able to keep prices down by constantly installing the very latest equipment available to the pottery industry. Mechanization has made it possible to cut the production time of cups from fourteen days to nineteen hours. In the present plant, the ware constantly moves; the workers stand still.

From 1933 to 1950, Scio Pottery made plain white dinnerware. From 1950 to the present the ware has been attractively decorated and will one day make fine collectible sets, but it will have to be identified by pattern and shape, not by marks.

SCOTT POTTERY COMPANY of Cincinnati, Ohio, had its beginning around 1853 with George Scott manufacturing Rockingham and yellowware. Around 1889 the firm became George Scott and Sons, then in 1901 the name was Scott Pottery Company. In the *1902-1903 Complete Directory* they were listed as making white granite and common china dinner sets, toilet sets, and short sets of odd dishes some decorated. Wilbur Stout, p. 82, described the company's products as white granite, cream-colored, decorated, printed table and toilet wares. George Scott died in 1889, and in 1901 the factory belonged to Sarah A. Waite.

SEBRING BROTHERS POTTERY. See American Pottery Works, East Liverpool, Ohio.

SEBRING CHINA COMPANY was a name used by the E.H. Sebring China Company. (See E.H. Sebring.) Sebring China Company was also a name used for the Limoges China Company for a short while. See Limoges China Company.

E.H. SEBRING CHINA COMPANY operated from around 1909 (Stout said 1911, p. 83) to 1934. This was formerly the Oliver China Company. In 1934 this company was purchased by the founders of the Royal China Company. This company used a confusing mark with the word "Art" on semiporcelain dinnerware as is pictured (see the soup bowl, trimmed in deep blue with a Dutch scene), leaving the researchers on art pottery hunting for an art pottery that didn't exist. See the Marks Section.

E.H. Sebring China Company.

SEBRING MANUFACTURING COMPANY was formed out of the consolidation of French China, Saxon China, and Strong Manufacturing Company in 1916. They in turn became a part of the American China Corporation which failed in 1934. (See the American China Corporation.) Sebring Manufacturing Corporation made semiporcelain dinner sets.

SEBRING POTTERY COMPANY operated from 1887 and into the depression around 1934. This company was started in East Liverpool and moved to the town of Sebring after the town was founded in 1898 by F.A. Sebring. This company used a great variety of marks on the semiporcelain that they made. See the Marks Section. In 1923, after two years of working to perfect it, Sebring Pottery Company introduced "Ivory Porcelain" ware at an exhibit in Pittsburgh. See the picture of the plate marked "Ivory Porcelain." This particular plate has the same decoration as the dishes sold by Sears and Roebuck in the early 1940s which were named "Heirloom" for that promotion. The plate pictured and the ones shown in Sears were not the same shape. The smallest platter in the picture is the shape of the dishes sold by Sears and being collected today. The small platter is marked "Trojan" for shape. Now comes the confusing part, at least confusing to this author. The big platter in the picture is marked "Corinthian" for shape and I can't see one bit of difference in the shape of the two platters except for size and that doesn't enter into it. I am almost ready to think someone stamped one of the platters with the wrong mark at the pottery, but until I find some more dishes with these shape marks, I will have to settle for describing these as they are. In 1923, Sebring Pottery

Sebring Pottery Company. **Front row:** *deep dish with raised design.* **Back row:** *"Trojan" platter (which is oblong but came out looking round in picture), "Corinthian" platter, "Heirloom" plate, marked "Ivory Porcelain."*

Company was operating eleven kilns. Charles L. Sebring, son of Frank A. Sebring was president. All of the Sebring potteries were hard hit by the depression. Sebring Pottery Company was combined with the Limoges China Company after the depression. The Limoges China Company didn't go clear out of business until around 1955. If pottery were still being made in both plants after the consolidation, some of the pattern name confusion could have resulted from this fact.

SEIXAS, DAVID G. made cream-colored ware in Philadelphia from 1817-1822.

SEVRES CHINA COMPANY existed in East Liverpool for a few short years around 1900. Perhaps in this case it would be better to tell the succession that took place in a given building. Around 1862, Agner, Fouts, and Company started a pottery in East Liverpool to make Rockingham and yellowware. The firm became Agner and Gaston, then the Sebring brothers arrived on the scene. The plant became the Sebring Pottery in 1887 and in 1900 the building housed Sevres China. Stout said the plant was sold to Sevres China as if it were a company that existed prior to 1900, but Barber said Sevres started in 1900. In 1910 the building belonged to Warner-Keffer China Company until 1912 when it ceased operations. The Sebring brothers left the building around 1900 to go to the town of Sebring. In the 1908 *East Liverpool Directory*, p. 524, the name was still listed as Sevres China Company. They manufactured semiporcelain and hotel ware dinner sets, toilet sets, and short sets of odd dishes, some decorated. Pictured is a very beautiful bowl and plate made by Sevres.

Sevres China Company.

SHAWNEE POTTERY COMPANY of Zanesville, Ohio, was incorporated under Delaware laws, December 9, 1936, with an authorized stock of $500,000. The **KENWOOD CERAMICS DIVISION** was a trade style used in connection with the manufacture of certain products by the company. The products were plain and decorated art pottery, novelties, kitchen pottery and allied items, ceramic bathroom accessories, ashtrays, and ceramic giftware. One of the most popular items manufactured by Shawnee was their corn line consisting of "Corn Queen," and "Corn King" in the various dishes pictured. Some very well known persons in the field of pottery were at one time associated with Shawnee. The son of the founder of Hull Pottery Company of Crooksville, Addis E. Hull, Jr. was an early manager of Shawnee. John F. Bonistall was president and general manager of Shawnee from 1954 until 1961. Shawnee was liquidated in 1961 after paying the first dividend in their corporate history. Bonistall was vice-president and general manager of Stangl Pottery in Trenton, New Jersey, and he started Terrace Ceramics and was president and general manager of the American Pottery Company at Marietta. See each of

134

these company histories for more. The footed bowl in the picture is marked "Kenwood Oven Proof." John F. Bonistall said that the bulk of Shawnee Pottery's volume trade was with Kresge, Woolworths, and other mass marketers. The Kenwood Ceramics line was developed for fine department stores and produced a line of beautiful household giftwares, some for serving and some decorative. This line did include a few casseroles.

Shawnee Pottery Company.

*Shenango China Company "Theodore Haviland, Made in America" china as shown in **Better Homes & Gardens**, October, 1947.*

SHENANDOAH POTTERY. See Paden City Pottery.

SHENANGO CHINA COMPANY. In 1901 two companies were started in New Castle, Pennsylvania. The **NEW CASTLE POTTERY COMPANY** (1901 to 1905) built a six-kiln plant at the present location of Shenango China on West Grant Street. Also in 1901, Shenango China was incorporated in New Castle on the north side of Emery Street. Shenango China Company and New Castle Pottery Company were both listed in 1902 as making semiporcelain dinner sets, toilet sets, and short sets of odd dishes, some decorated. Shenango employed approximately one-hundred fifty people. Very quickly Shenango China got into financial difficulty and a receiver was appointed, the company reorganized and a new charter taken under the name **SHENANGO POTTERY COMPANY.** More financial trouble followed until in 1909 an entire new group took over the property headed by James MacMath Smith as president and treasurer. Under his direction the company began to get established in the industry after nine hard years of struggle. The plant of the New Castle Pottery Company was purchased in 1912 and Shenango moved to Grant Street. In 1913, just as all of the machinery was in place and the plant ready to go, a flood put three feet of water in the entire plant. But under the direction of Smith the plant prospered slowly but surely, because Smith was a man who would just not quit trying. If a machine didn't do what he wanted it to, he built his own. He started having raw feldspar shipped directly to the plant and ground there as one of his innovations. Actually James M. Smith was a novice to the pottery business when he started, but he came to be regarded as the real founder of Shenango China Company. There were some distinct advantages for the potteries in New Castle, such as soft coal which burned clean, and money from the men of the steel industry for capital. All that was needed was real leadership, and Shenango gained that in James M. Smith. ("James MacMath Smith, President of Shenango Pottery," *Bulletin of the American Ceramic Society*, XX, June 1941, p. 163.) Shenango was described as employing twelve hundred people and covering twelve acres. In 1977, a highly mechanized Shenango still employed one thousand and now covers seventeen acres under one roof. (*Complete Directory of Glass Factories and Potteries of the United States and Canada*, Pittsburg: Commoner Publishing Company, 1902-1903.)

In 1928 the Shenango Pottery Company ran porcelain trials researching a vitrified fine china dinnerware product. The depression and its aftermath kept Shenango manufacturing the same very durable type of hotel ware that they had made since 1909. Then in 1936 a great change came. William Haviland, representing the Theodore Haviland Company of Limoges, France, came to America looking for a company to make Haviland China in America. I found several reasons for this change. McKee suggested that the Havilands may have sensed the coming war with Hitler. The *American Ceramic Society Bulletin*, said the high duties on Haviland china coming to America and mounting costs made it impossible to continue manufacturing in France for American markets. From 1936 to 1958, Shenango Pottery Company made china for the Theodore Haviland Company of France using their formula, blocks, cases, decals, etc. which the Havilands brought over here. This ware was marketed with the trademark, "Haviland, New York."

In 1939, Mr. Louis E. Hellman, American representative for the famous Rosenthal China of Germany, came to Shenango and arranged to have Rosenthal's shapes and patterns made at Shenango. In 1940 another great collectible was born when the first Castleton China entered the market manufactured by **CASTLETON CHINA, INC.** Shenango Pottery had $25,000 invested in this new company, Castleton China, Inc., but not until 1951 did Shenango purchase all of the stock from Louis E. Hellman. At that time Shenango took over the sales as well as the manufacture of Castleton China, a very fine dinnerware line, which they made until just a few years ago. The aim in creating Castleton China was to create a fine china by combining the age-old craftsmanship of Europe with the technological superiority of America. Louis E.

Hellman, an expert in European porcelains, wanted contemporary design in fine tableware, both in shape and decoration, and he hired the world's outstanding artists to create new designs. (McKee, Floyd W., *A Century of American Dinnerware Manufacture*, privately printed, 1966, p. 38)

Shenango China Company "Castleton" china as pictured in **House and Garden,** *November, 1940.*

One of the most notable achievements in ceramic art is Castleton "Museum" shape, the first freeform modern shape in fine china. Designed by Eva Zeisel, it was created by Castleton under the auspices of the Museum of Modern Art. It has been hailed in Europe and America as marking a new epoch in ceramic history and is on display in many American collections as well as in museums in France, Belgium, Portugal, Spain, Italy, and England. Castleton studio patterns were entirely hand-crafted and executed to order by skilled craftsmen.

In 1955, Castleton was commissioned by Mamie Eisenhower to create a formal design for gold service plates for the state dining room in the White House. Another design was created to commemorate President Eisenhower's "first birthday" in the White House and was presented to those attending a birthday party given for him by the Pennsylvania Republican Party at Hershey, Pennsylvania, in 1953. The plates are decorated with intertwined doves in a Pennsylvania Dutch symbol signifying love and peace.

In 1968 a set of Castleton china was manufactured by Shenango for the Johnson administration to present to the White House as a state service. This consisted of two-hundred sixteen place settings of ten pieces each plus large and small centerpiece bowls. Castleton dinnerware also graces the tables of many foreign heads of state.

As was stated in the opening pages of this book, our American potteries have fought to exist against the greatest difficulties. Shenango was no exception. Even though their growth has been steady and determined, it was never easy. The following is an exerpt taken directly from the histroy sent by the company and is included here for the purpose of giving understanding to the American dinnerware industry which is one of the two stated purposes of this book.

By 1949 Shenango had grown ten times in ten years, but the growth was in sales it did not control; i.e. government ware and dinnerware. Through a number of circumstances, the Company was again in financial straits, one of which was that the very expensive expansion program had been made without any long term financing; second, Haviland and Rosenthal of Europe were back in business; third, huge badklogs were being produced at fixed prices when the final blow was struck. The winter of 1948-49 was an extremely cold one over extended periods of time and the company had been forced to get standby oil to keep operating. Suddenly, the sulphur content in the oil went above normal and every piece of glost ware came out of the kilns with matteglaze and had to be thrown out.

Application was made to Reconstruction Finance Corporation for a long term loan. This was approved with the backing of the Pittsburg First National Bank and short term loans were paid off. A loan of $648,000 was paid off in five years.

In the Fall of 1950, contract negotiations with the C.I.O. — USWA broke off and the union called a strike which lasted 11 days. This marked the first serious labor problems with the C.I.O. Added to the other financial problems which had been encountered even this comparatively short strike hurt the company.

In 1951 Shenango China purchased all the stock of Castleton China, Inc. from Mr. Louis E. Hellman and took over the sales as well as the manufacture of the Castleton fine china dinnerware line.

In the Fall of 1953, once again contract negotiations with the Union were broken off with a strike that lasted for 43 days and had a drastic effect on the company fortunes. Let it be noted that the Union finally settled for the offer made by the Company just prior to the strike.

The name of the Company was changed to SHENANGO CHINA, INC. on August 1, 1954, bringing it back to the same name of September 3, 1901, the date of the bankrupt Shenango China.

In 1956, Shenango's efforts to mechanize were culminated by the development of the first "Fast-Fire" kiln which revolutionized the vitrified china industry. For the first time we had a kiln that would fire glost ware that normally took from 36 to 40 hours as fast as one hour and ten minutes.

Settlement of the Minority Stockholders suit caused the Trustees of the Smith Estate to sell the controlling interest of Shenango to Sobiloff Brothers, who also offered the same opportunity to other stockholders. Early in 1959, all of the shares were finally purchased by Sobiloff.

In Jan., 1959, Shenango bought Wallace China in California. Operated as a wholly owned subsidiary, adding $1 million in sales, principally on the West Coast.

After Shenango was purchased by Sobiloffs the working capital of the company was pledged for loans to finance other Sobilogg interests.

In 1961, all of the assets of Shenango China, Inc. were transferred to a newly formed, totally held subsidiary, SHENANGO CERAMICS, INC. held by the Sobiloffs.

In Sept., 1964, Mayer China Company, Beaver Falls, Pennsylvania purchased by the Sobiloffs, rounding out $1 million of prestige, quality sales in the Hotelware field.

Following a serious loss in inventory at Wallace China Co. during an outside audit, in 1963, which was the result of figuring the inventory incorrectly over a period of years, Wallace China was liquidated late in 1964.

In 1968, the assets of Shenango Ceramics, Inc., including its two wholly owned subsidiaries, Castleton China, Inc. and Mayer China Company, were sold by Sobiloffs to Interpace Corporation, who already manufactured Franciscan earthenware and fine china on the West Coast.

Today Shenango manufacturers a very fine line of hotel, restaurant, and institutional dinnerware. Castleton China had a body of high quality porcelain with a soft ivory tone. Besides tableware, there were bowls, trays, plaques, vases, etc. made with the name Castleton China. The decorations ranged from the unusual flower types to ultramodern shapes and decorations like the square shape called "Green Thumb," a salad service that looked like the salad was already on the plate with all different types of vegetable pictured. "Sunnyvale" was charming sprays of garden flowers on pearl edged shape plate. "Lace" was decorated with white and pink blossoms, similar to the flower Queen Anne's Lace, on a dove gray shoulder crowned by two platinum bands. A line of everyday china made at Shenango for a very short time

was marked, "Peter Terris" (information from Marion Church, collector and dealer in Castleton China). Castleton China made a series of game plates, all 10¾″ in diameter, with the following game: California Quail, Mountain Quail, Woodcock, Prairie Chicken, Dog and Birds, Ring-necked Pheasant. Pictured for Shenango is a game plate marked "Castleton China," Shenango's version of the old "Indian Tree" pattern, and a sugar container with a hand-painted design. *China, Glass and Tableware,* February 1979, p. 28, states that there are recent reports that Anchor Hocking officials have been negotiating with Interpace Corporation to purchase Shenango China, now called Shenango Division of Interpace Corporation.

SMITH, FIFE & COMPANY in Philadelphia, Pennsylvania, made porcelain around 1830. The porcelain made by them had a yellowish tone but was true hard porcelain although inferior to that of Tucker according to Barber. He mentions pickle dishes and pitchers that were found made by this company and marked with their name. (Barber, *Marks of American Potters,* p. 22.)

SMITH PHILLIPS CHINA COMPANY was in business from 1901 to 1934 in East Liverpool, Ohio. It was started by Josiah T. Smith and W.H. Phillips. In the *1902-1903 Complete Directory* they were listed as making semiporcelain dinner sets, toilet sets, and short sets of odd dishes, some decorated. In the article "Smith Phillips China Company" in the *Pottery, Glass, and Brass, Salesman,* December 27, 1917, p. 16, is the announcement of a pattern made by Smith Phillips called the "Cuckoo" design which was described as an overall tropical design in bright colors with a cuckoo as a feature in the design surrounded by wildflowers. See accompanying picture. Also the pattern had a double hairline border in green with a brown fanciful effect inside the border. Smith Phillips merged with seven other companies in 1929 to form the American China Corporation (see that listing) and at that time they made hotel ware as well as semiporcelain dinnerware. Several marks are shown in the Marks Section. In "American Pottery Trade Marks" in *China, Glass and Lamps,* September 3, 1923, p. 19, was the statement that Smith Phillips confined themselves to one distinctive shape which at that time, was known as the "Princess" shape.

Smith Phillips China Company.

SOUTHERN CALIFORNIA CERAMICS. See B.J. Brock Company.

SOUTHERN CALIFORNIA POTTERY at 4513 West 153rd Street in Lawndale, California, was listed in the 1948 *California Manufacturers' Directory* under chinaware. In an article "Daring Dishes," no author, *Fortnight Magazine,* August 4,

1950, p. 23, Southern California Pottery is mentioned as one of the largest of the dinnerware makers in California at that time.

SOUTHERN PORCELAIN MANUFACTURING COMPANY operated in Kaolin, South Carolina, from 1856 to 1876 (Barber and Ramsay). In Aiken County where the pottery was located Barber tells that the clay was so white that it was used for whitewashing fences and buildings. William H. Farrar who had been a stockholder of the U.S. Pottery in Bennington started Southern Porcelain after he got the support of some wealthy people in Augusta and some planters in the area to become stockholders. During the first year an English potter was hired and much ware was destroyed in the firing. During the second year, Josiah Jones, a skillful designer and competent potter took over management and made some very fair porcelain, a good white granite, and some cream-colored ware, according to Barber. The business was doomed to failure as Barber tells it because Farrar could not see the need for mixing other imported clay with the South Carolina clay to make a sturdy product. Farrar arranged for other management to come from Vermont in 1857 and the pottery was only reasonably successful until the Civil War. They then started making tableware, toilet ware, and a general line of whiteware. During the Civil War potters were exempt from service according to Ramsay. Southern Porcelain Manufacturing Company made brown insulators and earthenware water pipe for their war effort. In 1863 or 1864 the works were destroyed by fire, but in 1865 a new porcelain company was organized under R.B. Bullock as president. (He later became governor of Georgia.) Under his direction the pottery had varying success as Barber expressed it, and in 1875 or 1876 the pottery was sold to McNamee and Company of New York. By the time Barber wrote the book in 1893 he said the old kilns and buildings had long since disappeared. (Barber, *Pottery and Porcelain of the U.S.*, p. 187; Ramsay, *American Potters and Pottery*, p. 89.) See the picture of the semiporcelain bowl made by this company.

Southern Porcelain Manufacturing Company.

SOUTHERN POTTERIES, INC. had its origin much earlier than the 1920 date given in the Tennessee directories. In 1910, E.J. Owen, commonly called Ted, went to Erwin to start a pottery. The *Pottery, Glass and Brass Salesman*, June 13, 1918, p. 14, listed Owen as manager of Southern Potteries, Inc. Owen had been one of the organizers of the East End Pottery in East Liverpool, Ohio; he founded Owen China Company of Minerva, Ohio; he was later manager at the Paden City Pottery for a while, leaving there to go to Erwin, Tennessee.

From the book, *A Century of American Dinnerware Manufacture* by Floyd W. McKee, p. 35, we gain a great insight into the inner workings of many of the American potteries, because McKee worked forty-five years of his life in them. He had an understanding of the whole trade that this author will never reach if I read about potteries for the rest of my life. His little book is a tribute to the man, now deceased. He tells us that the Southern Potteries, Inc. was born out of the idea that the Carolina, Clinchfield and Ohio Railroad should get some industries going that would help to bring traffic through the Johnson City area. The pottery was first called **CLINCHFIELD POTTERY** before it became known as the Southern Pottery around 1917 or 1918. The name became Southern Potteries, Inc. with the incorporation in 1920. McKee tells us that the task of keeping the experienced potters down there while training boys from the hills was a difficult task. He said the pottery had to be reorganized a couple of times. Finally, "Charles Foreman from Minerva, happened along and took a try at it," (in 1922). Foreman was the man who would probably be credited with the success of the pottery. He introduced hand-painting on the bisque using girls from up in the hills in a production line method. Colors were put on old hand-painted prints, with each person filling in a part, then the next adding their part. McKee said, "the mode of operation permitted the withdrawal of one pattern and the issuance of a new one with a minimum of time and trouble." The ease in changing patterns, the small wages accepted by the hill people, the growth of the use of

Southern Potteries, Inc. **Front row:** "Mountain Ivy" plate, "Sunny Spray" plate in "Skyline" shape, plate in "Pie Crust" shape, "Ridge Daisy" plate in "Colonial" shape, "Autumn Apple" plate in "Colonial" shape. **Back row:** "Ridge Daisy" coffeepot in "Colonial" shape, cream pitcher made by Clinchfield Pottery (almost lost in picture), "Poinsettia" plate in "Colonial" shape.

dinnerware for theatre premiums, all helped the pottery to succeed. Foreman had a sales agency in Canton, Ohio, which handled a great part of the production. In the 1940s and 1950s Sears and Montgomery Ward sold a great deal of Southern Potteries products. Foreman died in 1953. According to McKee the decision to liquidate came in January, 1957. The plant was sold to the National Casket Company and no more pottery was made there. Pictured is an assortment of hand-painted plates made by Southern Potteries, Inc. There will be hundreds of the various patterns of this company documented in time. Many of the patterns will never have names assigned to them; they probably were known only by numbers at the time they were sold. Many names will be discovered, though, through study of the various sales promotions and catalog advertisements.

SPAULDING CHINA COMPANY was located in Sebring, Ohio, from 1939 to 1960, with offices in the Empire State Building in New York City. They were the makers of the decorative type pottery marked "Royal Copley." Some of the articles marked "Royal Copley" such as little pitchers, etc. could be used in serving. Some pieces are being found marked with Spaulding China Company's name. No doubt kitchenware and serving pieces made by them will be found and documented.

SPEELER AND TAYLOR. See Trenton Pottery Company for history.

STANDARD POTTERY COMPANY of East Liverpool, Ohio. See Patrick McNicol for history. They were makers of table, toilet, and decorated ware.

STANFORD POTTERY in Sebring, Ohio, from 1945 to 1961 made a great deal of decorative pieces and florists' ware, but more and more kitchenware made by them is being found. They made an attractive "Corn" line with products similar to Shawnee's various items in their "Corn" line. John F. Bonistall, recently with Stangl Pottery and previously at Shawnee Pottery, said Stanford's corn line was not earlier than that of Shawnee. Only a few of the Stanford pieces seemed to be marked in the corn line. The leaves are very sculptured and outstanding and the corn is realistic looking; the product is very attractive. Pictured on page 18 is a corn cookie jar made by Standford Pottery.

STANGL POTTERY COMPANY on New York Avenue, Trenton, New Jersey, was an outgrowth of the Fulper Pottery Company, Flemington, New Jersey. (See Fulper for preceding history.) In 1930, Stangl acquired the Fulper firm. Not until late 1955 was the corporate title changed to Stangl Pottery, according to Evans; however, he adds that the Stangl name had been in use for ten years then. So this is one of the cases where it is difficult to tell where one pottery ends and another starts. The same people, the same products to a great extent, and then one day a name change! After 1935 all manufacturing operations were transferred to the Trenton plant, and the emphasis was changed from artware to dinnerware. In 1940 Stangl began to manufacture a finer grade of dinnerware. In 1941 the Stangl Fruit pattern was designed and became a best seller in American dinnerware. Stangl initiated hand-decorated dinnerware during World War II. From the beginning a distinctive red clay body was used with white clay applied to the front of the red clay body. Sometimes the body was carved to let the red clay show through on the surface. Cheerful and bright underglaze colored decorations were also applied by hand. Stangl made Kiddieware sets for children with gay, colorful nursery characters. Apple Delight is an attractive dinnerware pattern by Stangl with a single, hand-painted apple design on smaller pieces such as cups and a group of apples in the center of the plates. (Company history, *Stangl: A Portrait of Progress in Pottery*, privately printed, 1965.) In 1973, Frank H. Wheaton, Jr. acquired the operation. According to John F. Bonistall, recent vice-president and general manager of Stangl Pottery, the Stangl Pottery was purchased by Pfaltzgraff Pottery on July 31, 1978.

The following is a list of pattern names furnished by Stangl Pottery showing the dates of introduction and discontinuation of the various patterns.

Introduced	Pattern	Discontinued	Introduced	Pattern	Discontinued
1942	Fruit		1958	Florentine	
1942	Blue-Yellow Tulip	1955	1959	Garland	1963
1947	Garden Flower	1955	1959	Fairlawn	1961
1947	Mountain Laurel	1955	1960	Bella Rose	1961
1947	Flora	1955	1960	Chicory	1963
1949	Prelude	1955	1961	Florette	1963
1949	Water Lily	1955	1961	Festival	1964
1950	Blueberry	1965	1962	Bittersweet	1969
1950	Kumquat		1962	Orchard Song	1975
1950	Lime		1963	Golden Grape	1968
1951	Thistle	1965	1963	Paisley	1965
1952	Star Flower	1955	1963	Blue Daisy	
1952	Magnolia	1956	1964	Golden Blossom	1975
1953	Pink Lily	1955	1965	Maple Whirl	1971
1953	Golden Harvest	1964	1965	Spun Gold	1971
1954	Lyric	1957	1965	Rustic	1971
1954	Carnival	1957	1965	Dogwood	
1954	Amber Glo	1960	1965	Apple Delight	1975
1955	Wild Rose	1963	1965	Mediterranean	1975
1955	Windfall	1957	1965	Bachelor's Button	1968
1956	Country Garden		1966	Pink Cosmos	1970
1956	Country Life	1959	1966	Sculptured Fruit	
1957	Tiger Lily	1959	1967	White Grape	
1957	Provincial	1962	1967	Holly	
1957	Frosted Fruit		1968	Star Dust	
1957	Concord		1968	First Love	1970
1958	Fruit & Flowers	1975	1968	Treasured	
			1965	Inspiration	

Stangl Pottery Company. **Front row:** *"Dogwood" plate, bowl marked "Terra Rose" and "Tulip," "Wild Rose" plate.* **Back row:** *"Blueberry" coffee pot.*

Stangl's attractive, hand-painted ware will be one of the greatest collectibles in American dinnerware. Pictured for Stangl is a coffeepot marked "Blueberry," a bowl marked "Terra Rose," and "Tulip." The small plate with a single flower is "Wild Rose," and the small plate with flowers and leaves around the edges is "Dogwood."

STARKEY AND HOWARD. See Hampshire Pottery.

STEPHENS, TAMS AND COMPANY. See Greenwood Pottery.

STERLING CHINA COMPANY, today a large modern maker of hotel and restaurant dinnerware, was started by B.E. Allen in 1917 in Wellsville, Ohio. The very early years' products were cups, mugs, bowls, etc. Gradually new items were added to the line; body color and decorations were added and varied. Additional buildings were built and the latest equipment installed. Sterling had the first dipping machine in the hotel china industry, according to the company history. Prior to the machine all items were dipped by hand in a tub of glaze. Sterling started "Inlay" patterns in the hotel ware industry. (Colored clay was applied to a piece of clayware and a bond created between the two pieces.) Sterling made a tremendous amount of china for the armed services during World War II. After the war they brought out a new shape designed by Russel Wright and called the Russel Wright line. In the 1950s some of the older hotel china plants went out of business but Sterling continued to grow. In 1954 they took over the Scammell lines of china which had been the leaders in the industry for eighty years (see Scammell). Today Sterling produces the famous Lamberton China along with the large line of Sterling china. Pictured are two "Willow" restaurant plates made by Sterling. The divided plate is blue, the other is pink. An adorable mug of the same heavy vitrified china has this verse, "As you ramble on thru Life Brother, Whatever be your goal, Keep your eye upon the dough-nut. And not upon the hole.". See p. 82 for Sterling's "Caribe China."

Sterling China Company. Two different "Willow" plates, the first is blue, the second is pink, and an Irish coffee mug.

STETSON CHINA COMPANY started as a decorator and distributing company in Chicago, Illinois. McKee, p. 30, said that they installed Ladd-Cronin kilns for firing decorated ware. Stetson obtained their blanks in the very early years from Mount Clemens. To secure a steady source of supply, Joseph W. Stetson and others took over the Illinois China Company in Lincoln, Illinois, on February 1, 1946. The name was changed shortly to the Stetson China Company. In the 1963 *Polk's Lincoln City Directory*, p. 197, the listing was the **STETSON CORPORATION** with J.W. Stetson as chairman of the board, Phillip R. Stetson as president, and Burt Chudacoff as executive vice-president. They advertised themselves as "America's foremost dinnerware manufacturer of small oven-proof semi-porcelain and break resistant Melmac." The Stetson China Company stopped manufacturing in 1966, but a retail outlet was maintained for a period of time in Lincoln, Illinois. In the 1966 *Polk's Lincoln City Directory* the pottery was called the **LINCOLN CHINA COMPANY** with the same executives and same products listed as in the 1963 directory. So unless the compiler of the directory made a mistake, the pottery must have had a new name for a year; perhaps there was an attempt at a reorganization of some sort before closing. The Lincoln China Retail Store was also listed that year. In 1955 Stetson China Company claimed in their advertisement to be the largest manufacturer of individual hand-painted ceramic dinnerware in the U.S., and since Southern Potteries, Inc. was about to reach its time of closing, this may have been a very true claim. There are pieces of Stetson's hand-painted ware that are very easily confused

with that made by Southern Potteries, Inc. Stetson made a great deal of ware without marks. Southern Potteries seems to have very seldom used a mark on large platters and some accessory pieces and cups. There is room for error in confusing the products of these two companies. Pictured is an assortment of hand-painted patterns all marked Stetson that might be mistaken for dishes made by Southern Potteries, Inc. Stetson's ware will be very hard to identify as to patterns, lines, or shape. Few pieces are marked. In the front row the first plate on the right is marked "Rio." The last plate, on the left side, in the front row is "Heritage" ware. In the top row the first plate on the left is "American Heritage" ware. I have found no advertisements so far that help to identify Stetson's China's wares.

Steubenville Pottery Company. Dishes in the "Woodfield Leaf" pattern.

STEUBENVILLE POTTERY COMPANY was in business from 1879 through 1960 in Steubenville, Ohio. See the picture shown with the Russel Wright listing for some pieces of American Modern which was first made in 1939 and was designed by Russel Wright, a New York City designer. The ware came in a variety of colors: Granite Grey, Curry (chartreuse), Bean Brown, and Sea Blue. Another pattern, "Woodfield Leaf" by Steubenville is a favorite. Advertised in *American Home*, 1952, the snack set (one big plate with recessed place to fit a cup plus one cup) cost $2.50. At that time $1 would buy a set of four cups and plates from Indiana glass, or $3 bought a plate of this type and a cup from Red Wing Pottery, so "Woodfield Leaf" was not exactly cheap. Pictured in "Woodfield Leaf" are a pitcher, beverage mug, snack trays and a beautiful teapot. The snack trays have a place indented for the cup. Colors are a tannish orange, a greenish yellow, gray, and a very dark green. According to McKee, the Steubenville Pottery had very rough going in the 1950s because sales had always been slanted toward retail distribution under the direction of Harry D. Wintwringer, who died in 1955. The Steubenville Pottery made pieces marked "Final Kiln" on December 15, 1959. A Cleveland Chemical Company bought the plant. "Adam Antique" is a pattern with raised design that is proving to be popular with collectors. The design appears to be a two-handled covered dish and leafy vines. This shape and raised design may be found in plates with no decoration, or sometimes trimlines or other decorations were added. In 1900, Steubenville Pottery employed three-hundred fifty people to make dinner and toilet sets in semivitreous and "Canton China." In 1902, they were listed as making semiporcelain, porcelain, and white granite, dinner sets, toilet sets, and short sets of

odd dishes, some decorated. They used a great variety of marks as shown in the Marks Section. Canton China, according to Barber, was semivitreous, lightweight, of a rich cream color, and was used more for decorative pieces than dinnerware. See the picture of the two very old plates with the "Empire" china mark.

STOCKTON TERRA-COTTA of Stockton, California, from 1890 to 1895 became the Stockton Art Pottery from 1895 to 1902 (Evans, p. 273). This company made many things ranging from bricks to fine art pottery during its existence. (For detailed history see Evan's *Art Pottery of the U.S.*) But according to Evans they made some cast bowls, teapots, creamers, sugars, mostly decorated with in-mold-entwined ivy pattern. In a letter to this author (January 26, 1978), Paul Evans said, "Seems like about every major pottery tackled dinnerware at some time or other; if not dinnerware, than some sort of kitchenware." This has proved to be true as I have progressed through the research, making the choice of companies to have a place in this book so very difficult.

SUMMIT CHINA COMPANY was located in Akron, Ohio, from 1901 to 1915. In 1905 they employed ninety-five people to make semiporcelain or white decorated earthenware and granite. (Blair, The Summit County Historical Association, and *Factory Inspection Report for Ohio*, 1905.) In the 1902 annual *1902-1903 Complete Directory*, Summit China Company was listed as manufacturers of semiporcelain dinner sets, toilet sets, and short sets of odd dishes.

SWAN HILL POTTERY, South Amboy, New Jersey. See New York City Pottery.

SYRACUSE CHINA COMPANY. After ninety-nine years of manufacturing a fine grade of tableware, Syracuse China discontinued their line of china for home use in 1970. In 1971 they became one of the country's largest producers of beautiful hotel, restaurant, airline, and commercial types of tableware. In *A Century of Fine Services*, a booklet from Syracuse China Company, is this explanation: "Stepped-up competition from foreign imports, most notably from Japan, forced closing of fine and casual dinnerware production in 1970. With the closing of the Fayette Street plant, household dinnerware production became a thing of the past. After 99 years of dinnerware production, phasing out procedures began at Fayette, allowing the full energies of Syracuse China to be devoted to continued excellence in commercial ware production."

In 1841, in Syracuse, New York, W.H. Farrar operated a pottery to make Rockingham in whiskey jugs, butter crocks, mixing bowls, clay animals, etc., from local clay covered with a brown glaze in his little plant on Genesee Street. From 1855 until 1871, the plant was called **EMPIRE POTTERY** after being moved to Fayette Steet to a building built along the Erie Canal. The Empire Pottery added a line of whiteware to the products. In 1871 the plant was again reorganized when businessmen pooled resources and bought out Empire, and the name was changed to **ONONDAGA POTTERY COMPANY** until 1966, when the name became **SYRACUSE CHINA COMPANY** in order to incorporate the trade name "Syracuse China" into the official name of the company. This is confusing to collectors because the Syracuse China mark was used since 1879 on a particular type of china, and the name of the company didn't change until 1966. Onondaga was organized in 1871 to manufacture white graniteware with the coat of arms of New York as the mark. A high-fired semivitreous ware was originated in 1885, the very first of its kind to carry any kind of a guarantee against crackling and crazing. This was the real beginning of success for the company. In 1888, under the direction of James Pass, the beautiful "Imperial Geddo" was created. This was a true vitrified china, thin and translucent, which won an award at the Columbian Exposition in 1893. By 1891 the company had developed a full line of fine china. In 1893 white granite, cream-colored wares in plain and decorated, dinner and toilet services were introduced (Barber). In 1897 the Syracuse China mark was first used, also according to Barber. Semiporcelain was made from 1886 to 1898. The *1902-1903 Complete Directory* listed Onondago as making china dinner sets, toilet sets, and short sets of odd dishes. In 1921, a new plant was added to the business called the Court Street plant, which was to be used solely for commercial ware production. In 1979 that plant covered fourteen acres under one roof and is the seat of all the company's production. Syracuse China is no longer a privately owned enterprise and stocks may be purchased by the public. The company has been under the same management since 1971.

In 1959, Syracuse China acquired a subsidiary, Vandesca-Syracuse, Ltd., of Joliette, Quebec, Canada, which is also a large producer of vitrified hotel china.

The shapes of fine china produced by Onondago, and later Syracuse, and the year they were begun includes: Juno, Oneida, and Imperial Geddo, in 1888; Doris, 1889; Marmora, 1891; Plymouth, 1896; Puritan, 1903; Mayflower, 1927; Winchester, 1929; Federal, 1931; Shelledge, 1935; Virginia, 1936; Berkely, 1951; Carolina, 1953; Coupe, 1954; California, 1955; Silhouette, 1961; Empire, 1966; Wellington, 1969; (Information by company.) The casual lines included: Carefree, 1957; Carefree XL (Syralite), 1967; Calypso, 1969. The innovations in the commercial line are numerous, but to mention just a few: Ivory Hotel China, 1928; Adobeware, 1932; Econorim, 1933; Shadowtone, 1933; Vitritone, 1933, Airlite (featherlight china for airplanes), 1945. This is just a partial list and not meant to be complete. (Company information.)

A suggestive list of patterns includes "Plum" with a blue band and gold trim, made before World War I, and "Baroque" with a swirl design. "Debutante" with a wide border that covered the whole shoulder, was very plain and simple.

Pictured is a plate for home use with a "Bird of Paradise" decal marked "Somerset" made in 1932 according to the dating system shown. The large beautiful plate with the big flower decal is a hotel plate of medium weight marked "Old Ivory" for shape and "Nature Study" for design. In the picture is a gold-trimmed service plate in light-weight hotel ware. The handled plate is thin, fine Syracuse China marked "Canterbury." Note: There was a Syracuse Stoneware Company operating with eleven factories around 1900, but that had no connection with Onondaga Pottery.)

Syracuse China Company. **Front row:** *thin handled plate marked "Syracuse China," "Bird of Paradise" plate marked "Somerset."* **Back row:** *"Nature Study" in "Old Ivory" shape, and gold-trimmed service plate.*

146

The following dating system is reprinted by permission of Syracuse China for the benefit of China collectors.

Syracuse Date Coding

For many years Syracuse China has followed the policy of showing the year and month of chinaware manufacture by one "code" technique or another which appears as a portion of the chinaware back stamp.

This code system enables you to determine how old the ware is and can be related into benefits for your customer. Savings = benefits! Your understanding of the code system may at some future time enable you to change a "negative" customer into a positive one. When the need for replacement of china is apparent, there are some customers who may feel their ware did not hold up long enough. By determining the manufacturing date, you are able in most cases to show the customer the long service life he obtained from his Syracuse China.

Any salesman who can relate benefits in terms of profitability . . . has a lot going for both the customer and himself. (Your Syracuse China Area Manager will be glad to help you in any situations involving date coding.)

The number (s) in the first column represent the year the ware was manufactured. Date coding has been used by Syracuse China for over seventy-five years.

Today, only one digit is used to denote the year.

6	1977
5	1976
4	1976

In earlier years more digits or initials were used.

103	1974
102	1973
101	1972
100	1971
99	1970
98	1969
97	1968
96	1967
95	1966
94	1965
93	1964
92	1963
91	1962
90	1961
89	1960
00	1959
NN	1958
MM	1957

Reaching back into history, china that was manufactured from October, 1903 through December, 1911 was marked with a numeral enclosed in a circle. For example: China produced in January through December, 1905 would be marked 16 through 27, the latter, denoting it was manufactured December, 1905.

The code marking was changed in January, 1912 with the numberal enclosed in a diamond. China made between and during the dates of January, 1912 through June, 1919 was marked in the following manner.

January to December 1912 -	◇1 thru 12*
January to December 1913 -	13 thru 24
January to December 1914 -	25 thru 36
January to December 1915 -	37 thru 48
January to December 1916 -	49 thru 60
January to December 1917 -	61 thru 72
January to December 1918 -	73 thru 84
January thru June 1919 -	84 thru 90
January to December 1919 -	1 thru ◇6

*Manufactured during January of 1912.

The Month the ware was produced is indicated by a letter, e.g.: **

A = January
B = February
C = March
D = April
E = May
F = June
G = July
H = August
I = September
J = October
K = November
L = December

EXAMPLE:

Ware manufactured during May, 1977 would carry the code number 6—E. The 6 denotes the year 1977. E refers to the month of May.

Shapes Introduced:

Econorim	1933
Winthrop	1949
Essex	1953
Trend	1955
Signet	1976

**The exception would be:

1930-K	1938-S	1946-AA	1954-II
1931-L	1939-T	1947-BB	1955-JJ
1932-M	1940-U	1948-CC	1956-KK
1933-N	1941-V	1949-DD	1957-LL
1934-O	1942-W	1950-EE	1958-MM
1935-P	1942-X	1951-FF	1959-NN
1936-Q	1944-Y	1952-GG	1960-OO**
1937-R	1945-Z	1953-HH	

The backstamp changed February, 1960 from OO for 1960 to 89, indicating the 89th year of the Company, founded in 1871. For a short period the month was indicated by a series of dots.

1961—	90 (Dots for the months)
1962—	91 (Dots for the months until July then letters A, B, C, Etc.)
1963—	92 (A, B, C, Etc.)
1964—	93 (A, B, C, Etc.)
1965—	94 (A, B, C, Etc.)
1966—	95 (A, B, C, Etc.)
1967—	96 (A, B, C, Etc.)
1968—	97 (A, B, C, Etc.)
1969—	98 (A, B, C, Etc.)
1970—	99 (A, B, C, Etc.)
1971—	100 (A, B, C, Etc.)
1972—	101 (A, B, C, Etc.)
1973—	102 (A, B, C, Etc.)

TAFT, J.S. & COMPANY. See Hampshire Pottery.

TAMS AND STEPHENS. See Greenwood Pottery.

THE TATLER DECORATING COMPANY of Trenton, New Jersey, was listed in the 1904 book, *Marks of American Potters*, by Barber as china decorators. In the *Trenton City Directories TATLER, INC.* was listed from the years 1930 to 1941 as makers of art pottery. Barber said the names of the early decorators were frequently found on their work. He mentioned Jesse Dean and George Tunnicliffe.

TAYLOR AND COMPANY. See Trenton Pottery Company for history.

TAYLOR, GOODWIN AND COMPANY, Trenton, New Jersey, see the Trenton Pottery Company for history.

TAYLOR, LEE AND SMITH. See Taylor, Smith, and Taylor for history.

TAYLOR, SMITH, AND TAYLOR was started in 1899, or early 1900, by W.L. Smith, John N. Taylor, W.L. Taylor, Homer J. Taylor, and Joseph G. Lee. In 1903, the Taylors bought Lee's interests in the factory, and in 1906, the Taylor interests were purchased by the Smiths. In the *1902-1903 Complete Directory,* the company was listed as Taylor, Smith, and Taylor. In 1907 the company was incorporated in West Virginia with the factory in Newell and offices in East Liverpool. Then in 1973, Anchor Hocking Glass Company purchased Taylor, Smith, and Taylor, and the name Taylor, Smith, and Taylor, has now been phased out in preference to the Ceramic Division of Anchor Hocking.

A reference to a dating system in information furnished by Emil Rohrer, who has been with the company since 1937, is reprinted here:

> There was a dating system used on some of our earlier patterns, but that was discontinued in the fifties. The Taylor, Smith, and Taylor name was encircled in a Laurel wreath then under it, as an example, 11-49-3 indicating November 1949, and I believe the 3 indicated the crew that worked on it. Another backstamp did not spell out the name but used T. S. & T. Co. I am enclosing reproductions of this backstamp showing 5-33-7, obviously May of 1933, also, the pattern on the reverse side. Lu-Ray Pastels, as I recall, were introduced in the late 1930s.

No exact record has been kept over the many years of the long list of patterns, shapes, and designs used by Taylor, Smith, and Taylor. Numerous marks used by the company are in the Marks Section. Many different types of ware have been produced over the years. In the *1902-1903 Complete Directory,* Taylor, Smith, and Taylor were listed as producing porcelain and white granite dinner sets, toilet sets, and short sets of odd dishes, some decorated. Semiporcelain and ironstone are their later, and still current, products. The pieces in the "Lu-Ray Pastels" included cups, saucers, six/seven/eight/nine/and ten-inch plates, coupe soups, lug soups, five-inch fruits, bowls, ten-inch oval bowls, covered sugar, cream pitcher, salt and pepper shakers, teapots, fifteen-inch chop plates, gravy boat with attached plate, sauceboats, utility tray, and covered butter in solid colors of Windsor Blue, Surf Green, Persian Cream, Sharon Pink and Gray.

There were three big lines by Taylor, Smith, and Taylor that this author thinks will be the most collectible of their ware. "LuRay" just described is one of them. "Pebbleford" and "Vistosa" are the other two. Pebbleford is a plain colored ware with specks like sand sprinkled over the color. I have found pieces of this in dark blue green, yellow, light blue green, gray, and light tan. Vistosa has a small scalloped edging and lines a little over one-half inch wide leading into the scallops.

In choosing the dishes to be pictured in this book, I would have quite a time deciding whether to show what I considered the prettiest or the most helpful to the collector for purposes of identification. An old plate named "Heather Bloom" for its decoration was shown in Sears and Roebuck, 1936. This plate had an octogan center. Thompson Pottery also made a plate in this shape. Many plates with octogan centers and different decal decorations are shown in the catalogs in the 1930s. But the picture of this plate lost to two plates in a series called "Classic Heritage." Shown here are two of these plates, one with a decal of birds, the other a Christmas tree. The big casserole or vegetable dish pictured was called "Golden Jubilee" in the 1936

Taylor, Smith, and Taylor. **Front row:** *"Classic Heritage" plate with a birds decal, "Blue Castle" platter, Pennsylvania Dutch type decal on plate.* **Back row:** *"Golden Jubilee" compote, "Classic Heritage" plate with Christmas tree decal.*

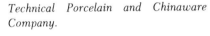

Technical Porcelain and Chinaware Company.

catalog for Sears. The platter was marked "Blue Castle" by Sears in 1934. This decoration came on a full service for eight. Shown in a 1942 *House Beautiful* advertisement was "Pink Castle" with the same design in pink. The ad said, "Derived from an 18th century design in 1933, this gadrooned earthenware has been a leading light for nine years." So there should be a set or two of this left to be gathered up by collectors. In the 1967 Sears catalog may be found pictures of "Honey Hen" and "Wayside Inn." 1964 Sears featured "Wheat," "Break-O-Day," and "Eastwind." The other plate pictured has a Pennsylvania Dutch type of decal that is appealing.

TECHNICAL PORCELAIN AND CHINAWARE COMPANY in El Cerrito, California, started in 1922 and was listed in the *California Manufacturers' Directory* in 1948 and 1951 as making hotel and institutional dinnerware and also technical or sanitary porcelain. Pictured is a semiporcelain plate made by them.

TERRACE CERAMICS, INCORPORATED was founded in Marietta, Ohio, on October 12, 1960, with John F. Bonistall as sole owner of all corporate shares. It closed January 1, 1975. Terrace Ceramics did not make pottery; they were a sales agency which until 1965 acted as sole distributor for the products of the American Pottery Company of Marietta, Ohio. In 1964 the offices of the Terrace Ceramics were moved to Zanesville, Ohio. The first line marketed by Terrace Ceramics was manufactured by Haeger Potteries of Dundee, Illinois. The line consisted of horticulture artware named "Patrician-Ware" which was designed by John F. Bonistall. In fact, all or almost all, of the ware sold by Terrace Ceramics was designed by Bonistall, and then made at different factories. McNicol China Company of Clarksburg, West Virginia, made a line of porcelain cookie jars for Terrace Ceramics to sell. They marketed a line of cornware colored from tan to brown instead of the usual yellow to green colors. (Information from Mr. Bonistall.)

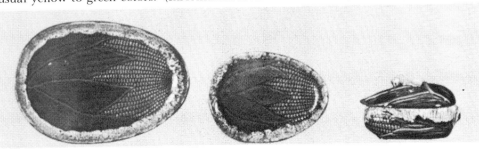

THOMAS CHINA COMPANY was founded as **R. THOMAS AND SONS** in East Liverpool, Ohio, in 1873. This plant continued in East Liverpool until 1927. A second plant started by R. Thomas and Sons in Lisbon, Ohio, in 1900, and operated there until 1963. The company was founded to make doorknobs and specialties of clay, which after 1885 were primarilly insulators. But from 1902, for a short span of one and a half years, the company made a complete line of whiteware in the Lisbon factory. At that time the Lisbon factory's name was changed to Thomas China Company. In 1904 when dinnerware was discontinued, both factories were referred to again as R. Thomas and Sons Company. (Information from R.F. Mason grandson of founder, Richard Thomas, by letter, 1973.) In the *1902 Glass Factory Directory* the Thomas China Company was listed as producing semiporcelain and hotel ware, dinner sets, toilet sets, short sets of odd dishes and jardinieres, some decorated. These would have to be very hard dishes to find. They would undoubtedly be of a good quality coming from a factory capable of making porcelain products.

C.C. THOMPSON POTTERY COMPANY was started as Thompson and Herbert in 1868 (Stout, p. 69). Their first products were Rockingham and yellowware. By 1878 the plant had five kilns and was very progressive with fine equipment, etc. The name style from 1870 to 1889 was C.C. Thompson and Company. In 1889 it was incorporated as C.C. Thompson Pottery Company and was in business until 1938. Around 1884 the plant began to make cream-colored ware and then semiporcelain, some decorated. A variety of ware is found for this company. Pictured is a plate marked "Thompson's Old Liverpool Ware 1868," which was really made in 1938. The Sears catalog in a 1938 advertisement describes the flowers as being applied on ivory-toned semiporcelain in old Liverpool shape, with borders of richly embossed scroll design. The price was $2.98 for thirty-two pieces! Also pictured is a colorful decaled semiporcelain plate by Thompson Pottery.

C.C. Thompson Pottery Company. "Old Liverpool Ware" plate with raised edge design. Notice the octogan-shaped centers on next two plates.

THROPP AND BREWER. See Trenton Pottery Company for history.

TREASURE CRAFT in Compton, California, is a pottery manufacturing business that was started by Alfred A. Levin after he was discharged from the Navy in 1945. They are located in Southern California and manufacture a product line of earthenware products including gourmet cooking accessories and serving items, cookie jars, canister sets, ashtrays, planters, etc. In their thirty-second year of operation the business is still solely owned by the family.

TRENLE CHINA COMPANY. The predecessor company of Trenle China Company was the **EAST END CHINA COMPANY** which started in 1894 and became Trenle China Company when the factory was taken over by Gus Trenle in January, 1909. At that time Trenle filed to change the name of the East End China Company to Trenle

China Company. (Secretary of State Report for 1910.) Trenle China Company operated in East Liverpool from 1909 to 1934 when they moved to Ravenswood, West Virginia, to become *TRENLE BLAKE CHINA COMPANY* which was still listed in business in 1967. Pictured are two very pretty little seven-inch plates made by Trenle China. They are souvenir plates with place names and attractive decals in a very good grade of semiporcelain. Trenle also made heavy hotel ware.

Trenle China Company.

TRENTON CHINA COMPANY started in 1859 and operated until 1891 (Barber). Their specialty became vitrified china, white and decorated for table use. In 1888, Trenton China Company added the manufacture of electrical porcelain to their regular line of hotel china and vitrified dinnerware. (Watts, Arthur, "Early History of Electrical Porcelain Industry," *American Ceramic Society Bulletin*, XVIII, November 1939, p. 401.)

TRENTON POTTERY COMPANY. Two of the owners of the Trenton Pottery from 1852 to 1865 were Taylor and Speeler (Ramsay), and part of that time between 1853 and 1863, John Goodwin was with Taylor and Speeler. A third man, William Bloor was owner from 1856 to 1859. Bloor later went to East Liverpool to form Brunt, Bloor, and Martin. The Trenton Pottery Company was incorporated in New Jersey in the old Taylor and Speeler building in 1865 by *TAYLOR & COMPANY.* In 1870, John Goodwin went to Trenton and purchased interest in the pottery and it was called *TAYLOR, GOODWIN, AND COMPANY.* (Barber, *Pottery and Porcelain of the U.S.*, p. 200.) They were manufacturers of ironstone china, cream-colored ware, sanitary and plumbers' earthenware. In 1872, Goodwin sold his interest and went back to East Liverpool. From 1872 to 1879, Ramsay lists *ISAAC DAVIS* as owner. According to Barber, p. 239, *FELL AND THROPP COMPANY* were the owners of the Trenton Pottery before 1901, and in 1901 it became *THROPP AND BREWER* with the addition of J. Hart Brewer. In the *1902-1903 Complete Directory* is a listing for the *HART BREWER POTTERY COMPANY* making semiporcelain, hotel ware, white granite dinner and toilet sets, and short sets of odd dishes, decorated. Also see Brewer Pottery Company of Tiffin.

TRENTON POTTERIES COMPANY. There were five potteries that went together in 1892 to form the Trenton Potteries Company. They were Crescent, Delaware, Empire, Enterprise, and Equitable. Ideal was built later. The five potteries were all makers of sanitary ware such as bathtubs, etc., but they made just enough general pottery that they need to be included in this book. Some of them continued to operate under their original name as a part of the Trenton Potteries Company. From this I was able to establish ending dates for them from the *Trenton City Directories.* *CRESCENT POTTERY* was organized in 1881 and was listed until 1907, then was not in the directories from 1908 through 1910, then was again listed until 1924. (This is not at all unusual for potteries to be busy, then idle, then back again.) Crescent made white granite and cream-colored ware as well as sanitary ware. Patterns such as "Dainty," "Melloria," "Severn," "Utopia," "Paris White," and "Alpha," were described in Barber's book. See Crescent listing in Marks Section for marks. The **DELAWARE POTTERY** started in 1884 and was a sanitary ware and druggists' ware type of factory, but at one time, according to Barber, they made a limited amount of Belleek porcelain. He doesn't say whether it was made into dinnerware or decorative pieces. I found the Delaware Pottery listed through 1918. A pottery was established in 1863 by **COXON AND COMPANY** to make white granite and cream-colored ware. Coxon died in 1868 but his widow and sons continued the business with various people. In 1875 the owners were **COXON AND THOMPSON** until 1884 when they sold to **ALPAUGH AND McGOWAN** who had operated another pottery from 1863 to 1883 or 1884 at which time they merged with the **EMPIRE POTTERY.** (Jervis, *Pottery, Glass and Brass Salesman*, October 4, 1917, p. 13.) They made thin china dinner sets, tea and toilet wares, and also sanitary ware. Then in 1892, Empire became part of Trenton Potteries Company. Empire was listed in business until 1918 in the *Trenton City Directories.* (See Empire Pottery listing, Marks Section, for marks.) The **ENTERPRISE,** founded in 1879, and the **EQUIT-ABLE,** founded 1888, were the only two of the five that made sanitary ware before and after the consolidation, and seemed to make nothing else. The Enterprise was listed until 1916 and the Equitable until after 1941. **IDEAL POTTERY** was first listed in 1902 and continued until 1918. Barber said the Ideal was built after the initial consolidation of the first five companies and made only sanitary ware. The *Trenton Directories*, for one year only listed Equitable and Mutual Potteries as part of Trenton Potteries Company in operation. **MUTUAL POTTERY** was listed as Mutual for the first time in 1922. They were sanitary pottery manufacturers, but they are a part of Trenton Potteries Company story and so are included here. The Trenton Potteries Company was listed in business through 1960 in the directories.

TRENTON POTTERY WORKS is listed in the Barber book, *Marks of the American Potter*, p. 66, as if it were a separate company in 1904 when the book was written. I had a complete run of the *Trenton City Directory* from 1900 to 1975, and there was no listing for such a company. Whether or not it was a member of the Trenton Potteries Company, I had no way to determine. The Barber book gave us the marks shown in the Marks Section and stated that the company made semigranite, white granite, and opaque porcelain.

TRITT CHINA COMPANY. See Bradshaw China Company, Niles, Ohio, for history.

TROPICO POTTERY. See Gladding, McBean and Co. for history.

TROTTER, ALEXANDER. See Columbian Pottery, Philadelphia, Pennsylvania.

TUCKER AND HULME. See William Ellis Tucker.

WILLIAM ELLIS TUCKER began in a very small way in his American China Manufactory by decorating china and firing it in a kiln built by his father, Benjamin Tucker, on Market Street in Philadelphia. He began experimenting with the manufacture of china and succeeded in making an opaque queensware (white earthenware). By 1825 he was manufacturing a hard-paste, true porcelain. Tucker's wares were described by Elsie Walker Butterworth in an article, "Tucker China," in *Spinning Wheel*, June 1949, p. 3: "The first article produced by Tucker were yellowish in cast and were lacking in finish and artistry. The decorations were done by hand, mostly with landscapes applied by a few strokes of the brush. The models were mostly after the fashion of the English potters of the day." In 1828, William's brother, Thomas Tucker, and Thomas Hulme of Philadelphia became his partners. The product was improved; the decorations became sprays of flowers, roses, birds, some bold decorations, etc. These pieces were sometimes marked "Tucker and Hulme." The partnership lasted only about one year. Sometime before 1832, Joseph Hemphill became a partner. William Ellis Tucker died in 1832 leaving the business to Hemphill. Hemphill had made a trip to Europe to the great porcelain factories and he brought back workers who were able to produce a more elaborate china which was purchased by the more wealthy American families. In 1837, Hemphill retired and Thomas Tucker leased the building and continued making china for about a year before he closed the business and sold the equipment to Abraham Miller. Charles J. Boulter worked for Abraham Miller in Philadelphia.

TUXEDO POTTERY COMPANY, Phoenixville, Pennsylvania. See Phoenixville Pottery.

W.I. TYCER POTTERY occupied some five acres in the middle of Roseville, Ohio. In 1954, they were listed with offices in Zanesville, and ten outlets were given for their products. The trade name "Cook-Rite" was listed for cookware and bakeware made by this company. In 1959 the Tycer plant was purchased by Melick Pottery, which is still in operation making vases, planters, garden dishes, etc.

UNGEMACH POTTERY COMPANY in Roseville, Ohio, from 1938 to present, has made a mostly floral and decorative pottery but more and more cookie jars are showing up that were made by this company. Their products are hand cast in plastic molds. Bowls with the marks of this company are also found.

UHL POTTERY COMPANY. See Crown Pottery, Evansville, Indiana.

UNION PORCELAIN WORKS of Greenpoint, New York, was established by German potters before the Civil War according to Barber. Jervis gives the starting date as 1854. ("A Dictionary of Pottery Terms," *Pottery, Glass, and Brass Salesman*, October 24, 1912, p. 33.) Jervis said they were still in business at the time the article was written (1912) and that they made a true hard porcelain. There are several marks in the Marks Section shown from Barber's book. Just before the war broke out the works were purchased by C.H.L. Smith and Thomas C. Smith who introduced the kaolinic body to make translucent bone china. In 1865 they perfected plain whiteware and in 1866 started to decorate. They made a lot of art pieces, and a table service decorated in overglaze colors and white enameled designs. (Barber, *Pottery and Porcelain of the United States*, pp. 252-259.) Arthur Watts listed the Union Porcelain Works as being at 156 Greene Street, Brooklyn, New York. He said they turned to the manufacture of electrical porcelain insulators around 1900. (Watts, Arthur, "Early History of Electrical Porcelain Industry in the United States," *Bulletin of the American Ceramic Society*, XVIII, November 1939, p. 404.)

UNION POTTERIES COMPANY had plants in East Liverpool and Pittsburgh according to Barber. In the *1902 Glass Factory Directory* they were listed in both places making semiporcelain dinner sets, toilet sets, and short sets of odd dishes, some decorated. Vodrey, William H., "Record of the Pottery Industry in East Liverpool," *Bulletin of the American Ceramic Society*, XXIV, August 1945, p. 282 has the company listed as being in business from 1891 to 1904 in East Liverpool. Barber stated that they made fine china and he showed a variety of marks used by them. (See Marks Section.) (In "Ohio Ironstone," staff-written, *Spinning Wheel*, June, 1954, p. 25, it is said the Wyllies sold their plant to the Union Potteries Company in 1891.) In the *1896 East Liverpool Business Directory*, they were listed as the Union Co-operative Pottery Company making fine decorated ware and white granite at Walnut and Kossuth streets. A plate made by this company is pictured.

Union Potteries Company.

UNION POTTERY was listed in the *1902–1903 Complete Directory* in Brooklyn, New York, as making semiporcelain dinner sets, toilet sets, and short sets of odd dishes, some decorated. I did not establish a connection between this listing and the Union Porcelain Works, or the Union Pottery in Trenton, or Union Potteries in East Liverpool and Pittsburgh. Union was a popular name.

UNION POTTERY COMPANY of Trenton, New Jersey. See New Jersey Pottery.

UNITED STATES POTTERY COMPANY started in Wellsville, Ohio, in 1898 making semiporcelain, some of which was decorated. John J. Purinton, Robert Hall, and Silas M. Ferguson were the first owners. Then around 1900 this pottery joined the East Liverpool Potteries Company, a group of six potteries that banded together in an attempt to stay in business. The East Liverpool Potteries Company disbanded in 1903. A list of the East Liverpool potters and potteries compiled by William H. Vodrey mentions nothing in the building at the southwest corner of Main and Twentieth streets after 1903 until the building was taken over by the Purinton Pottery Company in 1936. But Wilbur Stout in *History of the Clay Industry in Ohio*, p. 73, lists the United States Pottery Company of Wellsville, Ohio, in operation in 1921 when Stout's book was written. Evidently this pottery continued operating under its own name after leaving the East Liverpool Potteries Company group. See the photograph of the large platter made by the United States Pottery at Wellsville, which is pictured with the East Liverpool Potteries Company history.

THE UNITED STATES POTTERY in Bennington, Vermont, had a long history before it became known by this name. In 1793 three generations of Nortons, including Julius Norton, operated a pottery in Bennington making earthenware and stoneware. (The following is a composite of the material found in Spargo, pp. 256-264, and from Barber's books. See Bibliography.) About 1839, Christopher Webber Fenton joined Julius Norton to form **FENTON AND NORTON** and experiments in porcelain making were conducted. In 1845, Spargo tells us there was a disastrous fire which destroyed the pottery buildings and the attempt to make porcelain was postponed. Spargo stated that in June, 1847, the partnership was dissolved, although Barber said Fenton was apparently working alone as early as 1845 based on a marked piece of Parian that was found. From September, 1848, to November, 1849, the firm was Lyman, Fenton and Park. New buildings were built and Barber gave 1849 as the date for the name change to the United States Pottery (Spargo gives 1852). In 1849, according to Spargo, the name was Lyman, Fenton & Company after Calvin Park withdrew in November. This name was found on Rockingham and other wares. But Lyman, Fenton, and Park was found only in advertisements. In 1852 when the pottery was called the United States Pottery the firm name was O.A. Gager and Company. The company failed and the works were shut down in May, 1858, according to Spargo. A great quantity of wares of all sorts was made at Bennington. The pottery employed two-hundred fifty people. The porcelain made at the United States Pottery was nearly all of the hard-paste type or bone china, but Spargo said it was not marked. (Spargo, p. 264.)

The following was of great interest to this author because I had spent a lot of time wondering just how this very early porcelain was made. The excerpt is from *Early American Pottery and China* by John Spargo, p. 273.

> All ware of this type was made by the "casting" process. That means that the materials of which the body is composed were ground very fine and mixed to the consistency of liquid paint. This "slip" was poured into plaster molds, the porousness of which insured the absorption of the water and the settling of the solid content of the slip in the mold. As the water was absorbed and evaporated more slip had to be poured into the mold. When the proper condition was reached, the mold was opened, and the article was ready for the next stage, the addition of handles, applied ornaments, and so on. Now if it was desired to have blue groundwork, let us say this was done in the casting. Some of the same slip used for the body of the ware was placed in a small vessel and the necessary color added to it. Of course the only difference between the colored slip and the slip used for the body was the color. What may be termed the fictile quality was the same in both cases. With a camel's-hair brush the parts of the mold where blue was wanted were covered with the blue slip, the mold at once closed, and the uncolored slip poured in. Being of the same substance, the white slip united with the blue, and, as the color did not affect it at all, the whole fired alike. The blue on a genuine Bennington vase, therefore, not only appears to be and in fact is — in a thicker layer than paint would be, but it has the appearance, and the quality, of the rest of the body.

Universal Potteries, Inc. **Front row:** shakers, platter, cup and saucer, all in "Ballerina" line, salt and pepper and plate in "Laurella" line. **Back row:** pitcher, water jug, and platter in "Cat-tail" decoration.

UNIVERSAL POTTERIES, INC. in Cambridge, Ohio, made semiporcelain and earthenware type dishes from 1934 until 1956 when they started making tile. (See Bradshaw Pottery for previous history.) Universal produced both heavy and a finer type of dinnerware and kitchenware. Their Ballerina dinnerware in Jonquil yellow, Forest green, Chartreuse, Dove gray, Burgundy, and Sierra rust is of a fine quality. Pictured in this ware is a plate, platter, cup and saucer, and shakers. They also made this Ballerina shape decorated with a moss rose and a pine cone decal among others. In kitchen items, the "Cat-tail" is a great favorite. There was a full line of "Cat-tail" decorated dinnerware as well. See the water bottle, platter, and pitcher which are pictured. "Laurella" was a shape of dinnerware with an edging very similar to some made by Harker Pottery. See the plate in the photograph with the raised vines and bows around the edge. Also pictured for Universal is an assortment of plates and a bowl. The plate with the pioneer kitchen and the plate with flowers are "Camwood Ivory" which refers to shape and basic color. The Dutch windmill scene is marked "Netherlands." The leaf-shaped plate by Universal is very similar to the leaf plate made by Steubenville Pottery. The bowl in the picture came in a dark brown and ivory and also in a vivid blue and ivory, and is marked "Oxford Stoneware." It is just impossible to begin to cover the vast amount of products produced by Universal Potteries, Inc. in the short space that must be allotted in this book. There is no doubt that Universal will be one of the most collected of our American potteries, because not only are their lines numerous, but they sold well and can be found with comparable ease.

Universal Potteries, Inc. **Front row:** "Camwood Ivory" plate with flowered decal, leaflike plate similar to those made by Steubenville Pottery. **Back row:** "Camwood Ivory" plate with country kitchen scene decal, bowl marked "Oxford Stoneware," plate with raised design and Dutch scene.

155

VANDESCA SYRACUSE LTD. See Syracuse China Company.

VERNON KILNS was located in Vernon, California, which is southwest of Los Angeles. According to McKee the pottery started in 1916, and until 1928 it was called Poxon China, Ltd. (McKee, Floyd, *A Century of Dinnerware*, p. 48.) From 1928 to 1948 the name was **VERNON POTTERIES**. Vernon Kilns was taken over by Metlox Potteries in 1958 and ceased production in 1960. (Information furnished by Metlox Potteries.)

There were two artists who designed ware for Vernon Kilns, Don Blanding, a wandering poet and artist, and Rockwell Kent. Their designs on the shapes created by Gale Turnbull brought into existence some of the most beautiful American dishes made. Two lines designed by Blanding were "Hawaiian Flowers" and "Coral Reef." Rockwell Kent adapted his illustrations for the books *Moby Dick* and *Salamina* to decorations for dinnerware patterns for Vernon Kilns. He also designed the "Our America" series which included over thirty scenes; among them was "Power," a picture of a big dam; "Progress," a skyscraper; "Food," a field at harvest; "History," Mesa Indians herding sheep; "Romance," a mansion looking out over cotton fields, etc. Others were "Florida," "Maple Sugaring in Vermont," "Newport Yacht Races," "The Everglades," "A New England College," "Horse Racing in Kentucky," "New York City," "New Orleans Wharves," "An Indian Herding Sheep," etc. All together Vernon Kilns issued several plate series including forty-eight states plates, forty-four city plates, and thirty-seven "Bits" plates such as "Bits of the Southwest," "Bits of the Old West," "Bits of the Northwest," "Bits of old England," etc. (Sources: Stiles, Helen, *Pottery of the United States*, New York: E.P. Dutton and Company, Inc., 1941, p. 143. Scott, Virginia, "China Ad Search and Research," *Depression Glass Daze*, August 1977, p. 40. Also Hunter, Bess, "Vernon Kilns," *Glaze*, July-August 1977, p. 16.)

Stiles mentions an artware created by two sisters, Vieve Hamilton and May Hamilton De Causse. Vernon Kilns made flower vases colored and glazed to match the dinnerware, so that it was possible to have a flower container to match the dishes on the table. "Native American" had ten designs by Gale Turnbull, including full sets with coffee servers with wooden handles and muffin dishes showing people in dress native to the Southwest, views of missions, and three different scenes depicting life in old California.

A series of plaid designs stamped "Vernonware" (see photograph) included "Tam O' Shanter," in cinnamon, green, and yellow green with a green trim; "Homespun" which was green, cinnamon, and yellow with a cinnamon trim; "Gingham," a yellow green with yellow bands and green trim; "Organdie" with brown and yellow bands and brown trim; "Calico" with bands of pink and blue, etc. (Fridley, Al, "West Coast Pottery," *The Glaze*, November, 1977, p. 7.)

Vernon Kilns. Left to right: "Organdie" plate, "Brown Eyed Susan" teapot and plate, "Tam O' Shanter" cup and cake plate.

Another Vernon Kilns dinnerware pattern was "Brown Eyed Susan." (See photograph of teapot and plate.) Described in *Good Housekeeping* magazine advertisements are the following lines: "Early California," a bright glazed ware in orange, turquoise, green, brown, blue, and yellow, which could be purchased to make a set in solid colors or mixed like a rainbow. "Modern California" was in delicate pastel colors in azure blue, sand, straw yellow, orchid, pistachio green, and mist gray. "Casa California" had a gay, bold design of big, Mexican-type flowers in several designs. "Ultra California" was described as having rich halftones in carnation, aster, gardenia, and buttercup. "Vernon Ware" was made by both Vernon Kilns and Metlox Potteries. (See Metlox Potteries.)

VICKERS, THOMAS AND JOHN in Downingtown, Pennsylvania, made a variety of products in queensware (cream-colored ware) between 1806 and 1813 including jugs, pitchers, bowls, mugs, cups, coffeepots and teapots, sugar bowls, salt cups, dishes, plates and much more, glazed and unglazed. (Barber, *Pottery and Porcelain of the U.S.*, p. 15.)

VIRGINIA POTTERY. See Liberty China, New Lexington, Ohio.

VODREY AND VARIOUS ASSOCIATIONS. Before going to the Indiana Pottery, Vodrey had a history in several potteries. He came to this country from England in 1827 and built a pottery in East Liberties, Pennsylvania, near Pittsburgh, Pennsylvania. From there, *VODREY AND FROST* moved to Louisville, Kentucky, in 1829 where they made a good grade of creamware. From 1832 to 1836 the firm in Louisville was *VODREY AND LEWIS* after Frost retired. In 1836 the Louisville firm was dissolved, and in 1839 Vodrey came to the Indiana Pottery. In 1846, Stout says Vodrey was "forced to abandon" the Indiana Pottery Company and at that time went to East Liverpool and established *WOODWARD AND VODREY* which began operation in 1848 and which burned out in 1849. After reorganization the firm opened again as *WOODWARD, BLAKELY, AND COMPANY* until 1857 when a financial panic hit. After the panic in 1857, three sons of Jabez, William, James, and John, took one of the Woodward, Blakely, and Company buildings and operated as Vodrey Brothers until around 1885, when the title was *VODREY AND BROTHERS.* In 1896 it was Vodrey Pottery Company and remained so until after 1920. There is a great variety of marks shown for this company. The products of the various companies progressed through the usual stages, starting with Rockingham, yellowware, and cream-colored ware in the earliest years, then on to white granite and to semiporcelain. See photograph of plate made by Vodrey Pottery Company. In the *1902-1903 Complete Directory*, Vodrey Pottery Company made semiporcelain and white granite dinner sets. (W. Stout, p. 66.) (Also, see Lewis Pottery history.)

VOGUE CERAMICS INDUSTRY was a jobbing agency in New York City for which Homer Laughlin China Company and others made exclusive patterns which Vogue in turn sold to Montgomery Ward and other customers. (Information from E.S. Carson, Homer Laughlin China Company.) Such advertisements were in the Montgomery Wards Catalog, 1949-1950.

VOHANN OF CALIFORNIA was founded at Capistrano Beach, California, in December 1950, and they are operating at present (1979). Included in many of the products which they manufacture is a nice line of kitchen accessories marked Vohann.

WALKER CHINA COMPANY in Bedford, Ohio (near Cleveland), had its early start as the *BEDFORD CHINA COMPANY,* was reorganized in 1923 to become *BAILEY-WALKER CHINA COMPANY* for the purpose of making hotel china. In the late 1920s Albert Walker bought out Harry Bailey and the plant became known as *WALKER CHINA.* The Walker China Company became a division of the Alco Standard Corporation and is listed as making vitreous china and tableware. The really collectible china from this company was made by Albert Walker in the late

Vodrey Pottery Company.

1920s when he bought out a fine line of thin, vitrified china in addition to making the thick hotel ware. According to Annise Heaivilin, some Tea Leaf pattern was custom-made by this company for institutions. The Walker China Company was purchased by the Jeannette Corporation from the Alco Standard Corporation on November 15, 1976 (see Jeannette Corp.). (Annise Heaivilin is a leading authority on the Tea Leaf pattern.)

WALLACE AND CHETWYND started in the **COLONIAL POTTERY** in East Liverpool around 1881 or 1882 making a high grade of opaque china, stone china, and decorated goods. In 1900, they joined the East Liverpool Potteries Company which was dissolved in 1903. From 1903 to 1929 this building was operated as the **COLONIAL COMPANY.** Chetwynd had learned the pottery business working for his father in England. The two plates pictured are marked "Iron Stone," and they are decorated with the transfer designs which are similar but not quite alike. (Also see Colonial Company, East Liverpool, Ohio.)

Wallace and Chetwynd.

WALLACE CHINA COMPANY in Vernon, California, was established in 1931. McKee termed this company a small hotel ware plant but it grossed a tremendous sales record under Shenango. In January, 1959, the Wallace China Company was purchased by Shenango China Company of New Castle, Pennsylvania, and operated as a wholly owned subsidiary adding one million dollars in sales principally on the West Coast (Shenango China Company information). In 1964 the Wallace China Company was completely liquidated by Shenango China Company. Shenango joined Interpace in 1968, so Wallace China Company was never actually a part of Interpace.

WALRICH POTTERY in Berkeley, California, was an art pottery, but Paul Evans said they made some dinner sets on a special order basis. The pottery was in business from 1922 until around 1929, at the onset of the depression. (Evans, Paul, *Art Pottery of the United States*, New York: Charles Scribner's Sons, 1974, p. 319.) Evans has done such extensive study in the field of American art pottery that he is considered by many to be the living authority on the subject today. Since I don't know which of the marks were used on dinnerware or which ones were used on artware, the impressed marks shown in his book are reprinted in the Marks Section with Mr. Evans's permission.

WANNOPEE POTTERY COMPANY. See New Milford Pottery Company.

WARWICK CHINA COMPANY in Wheeling, West Virginia, started in 1884 (Hoffman), incorporated in 1887, and closed in 1951. In an article in *The Glaze*, July-August, 1977, p. 9, by Donald C. Hoffman, Sr., entitled "Introduction to American Made Warwick China," Hoffman states that Warwick produced over ten thousand sets of dinnerware per month at the height of their production. Warwick made beautiful dinner sets of high quality porcelain. They also made semiporcelain and hotel ware over the years, as may be seen in the photograph. Warwick's many lines included florals, fraternal order pieces, Indians, monks, nudes, etc. They used decals, hand-painting, and tintype decoration (Hoffman) at various times. According to Barber the first stamp to be used was a helmet and crossed swords. From 1893 to 1898 the "Warwick Semi-Porcelain" mark was in use (Barber, *Marks of American Potters*, p. 152). Different sources state that different marks came first at Warwick. Warwick made hotel china after 1912 and some bone china after 1940. The last few years the company was in business they made mostly hotel ware, according to one source. Some of the products described by various people seeking information on Warwick and also in various articles written by collectors are fascinating and beautiful pieces. One was a beautiful set of vitrified china named "Regency" with a wide gold band made of coin gold on each piece. Warwick used the mark "IOGA" on some of their earliest and finest ware, including some tankard pitchers, flow blue (one of the few American companies to attempt flow blue) vases, plates, umbrella holders, etc. From a for sale ad: "Warwick China chocolate pot 9 inches to top, white back ground, sprays of pink flowers and pale green leaves, pot trimmed in gold." (Schmitt, Agnus, "Ohio Valley Pottery and China Gain Popularity" *Collectors Weekly*, July 14, 1970, p. 3.)

Warwick China Company.

Included in the photograph is a little oval dish marked semiporcelain which is decorated with a delicate purple pink flowers with yellow to brown leaves and a gold trim around the edge. The big platter is very heavy semiporcelain, heavy in weight with a porous clay body, but it is beautiful, anyway. The glaze is bright and not crazed and the little pink flowers and green leaves are dainty. The gold decoration makes an added touch of taste and beauty. Pictured for Warwick is a garden scene plate marked "Tudor Rose." This plate has a wide border trim which covers the whole shoulder of the plate with flowers and branches in a rose background. The Tudor Rose plate has only the white and rose for coloring, but its brightness is very effective. Also pictured is Warwick's version of the old "Indian Tree" pattern in semiporcelain.

C 9295

C 9294

AB 9501

A 9417

C 9296-105-152

D 9340 Bright

AB 9490 Ivory Center

C 9293-110

B 9451

B 9289 Coin

C 9385

C 9433 Blue

D 9309 Coin

AB 9427

C 9393 Coin

AB 9487

9306

AB 9010 Bright

9303

B 9367

C 9388

C 9291

C 9386

9301 Butcher S 2880

O 9288

A 9210

161

Warwick China Company

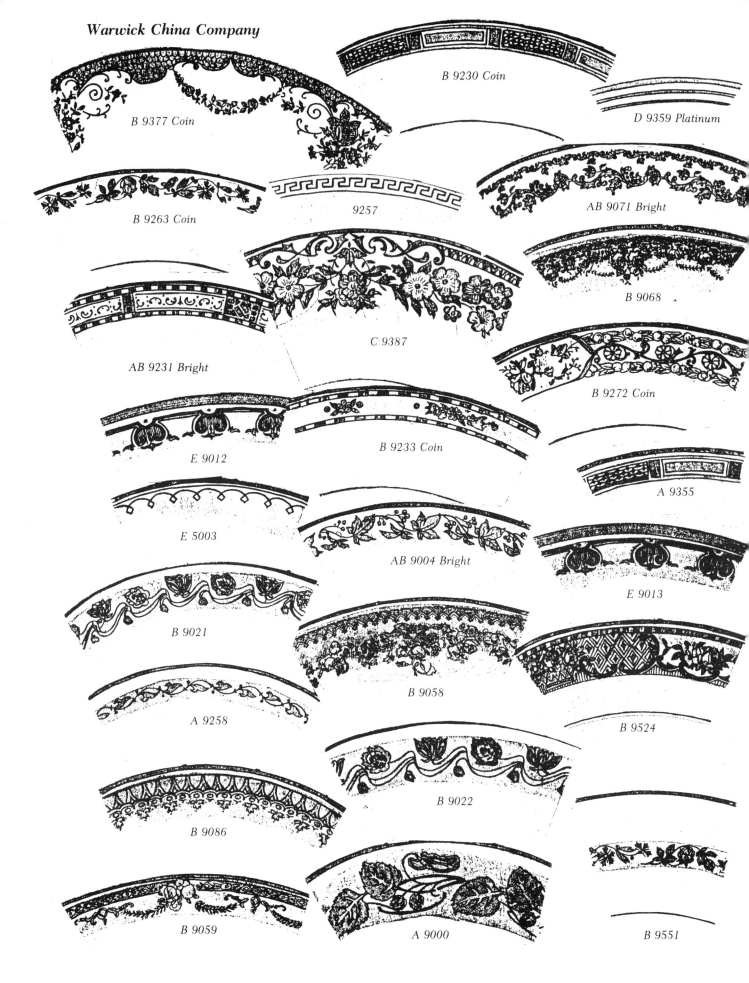

B 9377 Coin

B 9230 Coin

D 9359 Platinum

B 9263 Coin

9257

AB 9071 Bright

AB 9231 Bright

C 9387

B 9068

B 9272 Coin

E 9012

B 9233 Coin

A 9355

E 5003

AB 9004 Bright

E 9013

B 9021

B 9058

A 9258

B 9524

B 9086

B 9022

B 9059

A 9000

B 9551

C 9208

C 9234

AB 9265 Bright

AB 9265 Bright

A 9354

C 9099

B 9721 Coin

A 9083

AB 9021 Bright

9270

AB 9361 Bright

D 9360 Coin

9279

C 9368 Coin

AB 9362 Bright

C 9406 Coin

AB 9009 Bright

E 9450

B 9274 Coin

A 900B

9319

B 9273 Coin

Watt Pottery.

WATT POTTERY in Crooksville, Ohio, was in business from 1922 until the pottery burned in 1965. The pottery was located at the site of the old Globe Stoneware Company which in turn became the Z.W. Burley pottery and which was followed by Watt Pottery. "Watt Pottery," *Antique Trader*, September 13, 1978, p. 66, is a fine article by Marv and Bev Tyacke. The Watt pieces of the type shown in the photograph were made of local Crooksville clay and were clear glazed and hand-painted according to the Tyackes. In an interview with Mr. and Mrs. W.I. Watt, the Tyackes were able to secure some names and dates for Watt's ware. In 1940, "Kitch-N-Queen," a series of kitchenware banded in turquoise and pink was introduced. In 1950 the "Red Apple," was first offered. In 1955 the "Cherry" design was introduced, and in 1956 the "Star Flower." In 1957, a rooster outlined in black with red and green feathers was brought out. In 1958, the "Dutch" style with tulips was introduced. Most of the pieces pictured are "Red Apple." One pitcher has merely leaves in red and green. The large "spaghetti" bowl in the picture is an authentic Watt piece. The mark on this bowl is shown in the Marks Section. According to the Tyackes, the Japanese copied and made these bowls too, but they marked theirs with just "U.S.A." for a mark. The old, plain cookie jar or container is marked with "Peedeeco" and "U.S.A." In the 1954 *Crockery and Glass Journal Directory* was listed "Wild Rose" serving dishes and a cookie jar, "Kolar Kraft" and "Flav-R-Bake" kitchenware, "Peasant Ware" serving plates with cups and saucers, and "Even-Bake" kitchenware.

WEBSTER, CAMPBELL AND COMPANY of Wellsville, Ohio, made white granite for a couple of years after 1886 before selling the plant to James H. Baum. The plant was called the School House Pottery according to Stout, page, 80.

WEIL CERAMIC COMPANY was listed as Max Weil of California at 3160 San Fernando Road, Los Angeles, in the 1948 and 1951 *California Manufacturers' Directories*. In the March 15, 1954, *Crockery and Glass Journal* Directory Issue, Weil of California, Inc. was still listed at the same address. The company was no longer listed in the 1955 *California Manufacturers' Directory*. At one time this factory was managed by Fred Grant. In the magazine, *Fortnight*, "Daring Dishes," August 4, 1950, p. 23 (staff-written), Max Weil was mentioned as one of the six biggest dinnerware makers in California at that time. Pictured for Weil Ceramic Company is an assortment of hand-painted china.

Weil Ceramic Company.

WELLER POTTERY, so well known for its beautiful art pottery, also made a great deal of kitchen products such as bowls, casseroles, pitchers, etc. Samuel Weller arrived in Zanesville, Ohio, in 1882 (Stout said he came from Fultonham, Ohio, in

1888, p. 96) and founded a small pottery business. In 1890 he moved from his Pierce Street plant to a three-story building which he built between Pierce Street and Cemetery Drive (Stout, p. 96). In 1895, in addition to the Zanesville plant, he purchased the Lonhuda Pottery in Steubenville. In 1948, the Weller Pottery was dissolved and sold to the Essex Wire Corporation. (For a more detailed history of the moves and growth of Weller, see Lehner, Lois *Ohio Pottery and Glass, Marks and Manufacturers*, and *Zanesville Art Pottery*, by Norris F. Schneider, both listed in the Bibliography.) Weller made a line of baby dishes in the 1920s. In 1920, the Zanesville Art Pottery Company was purchased by Weller according to Stout, p. 61. For years, Zanesville Art Pottery had been making culinary articles along with other kinds of ware. (See Zanesville Art Pottery.) Weller continued to make cookware in that plant. Stout said Weller had also made such ware in his other plants for a number of years (p. 61). Pictured for Weller is a pitcher with a basketweave type of decoration, a mixing bowl with circles and red trim, and creamer, sugar, and teapot in Weller's apple ware with raised design and hand-painted flowers.

Weller Pottery.

WELLSVILLE CHINA COMPANY had two predecessor companies in Wellsville, Ohio. In 1879 to 1885, **MORLEY AND COMPANY** made white granite and Majolica. (See Morley and Company, Marks Section, for marks.) Then Morley and Company became **PIONEER POTTERY** from 1885 to 1896 making white granite. (See Pioneer Pottery, Marks Section, for marks.) From 1896 to 1959, the factory was operated as the Wellsville China Company, makers of vitreous china tableware and kitchenware. There is a variety of marks for these companies shown in the Marks Section. See individual companies for marks. In 1902 the Wellsville China Company was listed as making semiporcelain and white granite (ironstone) dinner sets, toilet sets, and short sets of odd dishes, some decorated. The celery dish shown is the best quality of the china pictured here. It has the ring of porcelain but is very opaque. The shape is nice with a decaled rose overglaze and a thin gold trimline around the edge. Three plates in semiporcelain are shown. Very few American potteries ever made any flow blue wares. The one plate pictured with a ring of flowers to the outside and a ring of flowers in the center is about as close as a collector can come to flow blue in American dishes except for examples from a very few companies. (See Buffalo

Wellsville China Company.

West End Pottery.

China.) The decoration on this little plate is underglaze and spills over a little into the white portion of the plate. There are no pattern names involved in the marks on the Wellsville China that is pictured. The graniteware pitcher is an old piece, very plain with only two gold trimlines, relying on shape for its attractiveness. In 1959, the Wellsville China Company was acquired by Sterling China Company, and in 1969 the plant was closed because the equipment was outdated. The plant was later under lease to Rival Manufacturing to make crockpots. The "Willow ware" plate is restaurant ware marked Wellsville, made after the Sterling acquisition.

WELLSVILLE PIONEER POTTERY. See Pioneer Pottery.

WENCZEL COMPANY was listed as the **WENCZEL TILE COMPANY** on Klagg Avenue in Trenton, New Jersey, in the city directories for the years 1940 through 1944. These were the only listings I found. In *Better Homes & Gardens* in the 1940s, the Wenczel Company advertised some very attractive teapots. The pattern names for the teapots were "Victoria" and "Sandra." The tile that this company made must have been decorative tile. Any kitchen pieces made by them would have a fine, hard quality. Their colors for the teapots were dogwood pink, periwinkle blue, canton green and lotus white.

WEST END POTTERY COMPANY operated from 1893 to 1934 in East Liverpool, Ohio. They made ironstone and a very fine decorated china. The plate shown, which has stenciled birds and a lovely border decoration, is thin and highly vitrified, much better than most of the Ohio pottery of this era. In 1929, West End Pottery became a member of the American Chinaware Corporation which dissolved in 1934 following the depression.

WESTERN STONEWARE COMPANY. Ramsay lists a Western Stoneware Company operating in Monmouth, Illinois, from 1870 to 1890. He indicated that at that time it became the Monmouth Pottery making stoneware and Rockingham. Company furnished information states that the Monmouth Pottery was incorporated in October, 1892. These very early potteries were family potteries, of which there were ten in the 1800s within a hundred miles of Monmouth. In April, 1906, seven of these small potteries went together under the name of Western Stoneware Company, which may have been an early name used by the Monmouth Pottery if Ramsay is correct. The following we know for sure. The seven potteries that formed Western Stoneware in 1906 were: **WEIR POTTERY** at South Third and East Fifth Avenue, Monmouth, Illinois; **MONMOUTH POTTERY COMPANY** at 521 West Sixth Avenue, also in Monmouth; **MACOMB STONEWARE COMPANY** at Campbell and

166

Western Stoneware Company. "Mojavi" dishes.

Dudly streets and **MACOMB POTTERY COMPANY** at the junction of Piper Street and the CB&Q RR tracks, both in Macomb, Illinois; the **D. CULBERTSON STONE-WARE COMPANY** in Whitehall, Illinois (sometimes referred to as Whitehall Pottery); **CLINTON STONEWARE COMPANY** in Clinton, Missouri; and **FORT DODGE STONEWARE** Company of Fort Dodge, Iowa. Barber listed the products of Western Stoneware Company as all kinds of stoneware, and around 1900 they used the mark of two men in a huge stoneware container that looked like a barrel. In 1929 and 1941, Western Stoneware suffered major fires which destroyed many records of the company. The company is well known for the premiums made for the Sleepy Eye Milling Company early in the Sleepy Eye Company's history. The "Flaming Blue" bowl is one of the first stoneware premiums made by Western Stoneware for Sleepy Eye. (Company information.)

Sleepy Eye Milling Company started in 1893 and in 1917 was owned by the Kansas Flour Mills but was kept in operation until 1921. The cobalt blue and white pitchers and steins were used as premiums for Sleepy Eye Flour before and after the change of ownership in 1917. Isobel Hellender states in "One Hundred Years of Sleepy Eye," *Western Collector*, May 1972, pp. 4-9, that none of these Indian Head items were produced by Western Stoneware for the milling company after 1937. However, in 1952, the 22-ounce and 40-ounce steins were redesigned (gave the Indian a larger nose) and produced in an overall chestnut brown glaze. Then in 1968 the same 40-ounce design was used to make a few steins to be presented to the company's board of directors and as V.I.P. gifts. These steins were hand-decorated in blue and white with the maple leaf mark of the company and date added to the bottom of the stein. (Hellender, pp. 4-9.) In 1969, 1970, 1971, 1972, and a very limited quantity in 1973, mugs were made for the same purpose with none available to the public. Another excellent article on "Old Sleepy Eye" (no author) is in *Spinning Wheel*, January-February, 1965, p. 18, for those who are interested mainly in this one aspect of the pottery's production. However to limit one's self to collecting only Western Stoneware's Old Sleepy Eye would be a shame, because they have produced and are producing some really fine, beautiful ware.

In 1906 Western Stoneware issued no catalog in their first year of production, but they made items in a whiteware clay body with relief trim in Delft blue according to the *Spinning Wheel* article already mentioned. The success of the Western Stoneware Company is due in large part to the high quality clay available in Colchester, Illinois (south of Monmouth). Stoneware made from this unusual clay is conventional and radar oven heat-resistant, provides superior retention of either heat or cold, and is lead-free, making it completely safe for use with all foods and drinks.

Pictured is part of a set of dishes including a plate, saucedish, and small bowl, made by Western Stoneware Company bearing the maple leaf mark as shown in the Marks Section. The glaze has a beautiful appearance on the pieces because each piece is hand-dipped and the glaze is heavily applied. The company supplied the name "Mojavi" for these dishes and added that all dinnerware manufacture was discontinued by Western Stoneware January 1, 1975. (Company furnished information.)

WEST VIRGINIA CHINA COMPANY. See Ohio Valley China Company.

WHEELING DECORATING COMPANY on Market Street in Wheeling, West Virginia, used several marks that might be taken for marks used by the Wheeling Pottery which was out of business before 1910. Wheeling Decorating Company listed in business as late as 1962 decorating china and glassware. In the 1954 Directory Issue of the *Crockery and Glass Journal*, six different sales outlets were listed for products of the company. The point to remember is that the old Wheeling Pottery products are very old and Wheeling Decorating products are late.

WHEELING POTTERIES COMPANY and ASSOCIATED COMPANIES: "The Wheeling Pottery Company of Wheeling, West Virginia, made plain and decorated white granite and was organized in November, 1879. In 1887, a second company was formed under the same management and called LaBelle Pottery Company which made "Adamantine china, plain and decorated, and in 1889 . . . the two companies were consolidated." (Barber, *Marks of American Potters*, p. 149; also *Pottery and Porcelain of the U.S.*, p. 308.) Barber also stated that "on January 1, 1903, the Wheeling Potteries Company was organized by combining the Wheeling, La Belle, Riverside, and Avon Potteries, each of which is now a department of the former." At this time, he stated, the potteries were making utilitarian pottery, semiporcelain, sanitary wares and artware in the various factories, with each designated to make certain products. Then in 1909 or 1910, the name of the Wheeling Potteries Company was changed to the *WHEELING SANITARY MANUFACTURING COMPANY*. From the *American Ceramic Society Bulletin*, XX, "Notes for Ceramists," (on Charles Franzheim), May 1941, p. 186 is the following quote:

> When the Wheeling Pottery Company was organized in 1879 in what is known as the "old Wheeling Pottery," it was operated with five kilns and employed about 150 men. At first, only white granite ware or "Queensware," as it is more commonly known, was manufactured. Three or four years later, however, it began to decorate the ware, and in 1904, the plant was making everything from common sanitary ware to the finest china and was employing about 1200 persons. Although the plant was not the largest in number of kilns, the decorating departments employed a greater number of persons than any similar institution in the country.
>
> There were four plants, with twenty-seven biscuit and glost kilns and twenty decorating kilns. Their production covered a wide range of ware, semi-granite (or "C.C."), white granite, semi-porcelain, and a line of highly decorated faience ware and sanitary goods.
>
> The building, known as the LaBelle Pottery, on the South Side, was built in 1889, and the Ohio Valley China Company plant in North Wheeling, now known as the Riverside, was acquired in 1900. A little later, the Tiltonsville, Ohio, plant was added to the Company.
>
> C. Merts Franzheim, the eldest son of Charles Franzheim, was assistant general manager in 1904, with direct supervision over the Wheeling and LaBelle plants. He spent two years at the ceramic school of the Ohio State University and one year in Germany at one of the celebrated pottery schools in that country.
>
> In the early nineties, Anton Reymann of Wheeling established a chinaware plant in North Wheeling and brought Hermann Zimmer to this country from Germany. It was soon discovered that even though beautiful products were being made, the cost was so high that the Company could not compete with imported articles. The plant was closed about 1896, and Mr. Franzheim employed the services of Dr. Zimmer for the Wheeling Pottery Company to develop a better grade of earthenware art objects and china. Dr. Zimmer thus became one of the first ceramic engineers in this country.
>
> Dr. Zimmer developed the Cameo chinaware, but that too was unprofitable owing to the high cost of production as compared with the imported articles of the same nature and also to the lack of real artists at reasonable cost.
>
> In the nineties, Mr. Franzheim became president of the Warwick China Company for two years, but he then returned to the Wheeling Pottery Company. He served as president of the United States Potters' Association for one year. With Frank Sebring and Fred Gosser, he developed and used Texas clay at their plants.
>
> The Wheeling Pottery Company was the first to make extensive use of the casting process in this country, which was directly due to the continental experience and the assistance given by Rudolph Gaertner."

The *History of West Virginia, Old and New*, published by the American Historical Society, Inc., 1923, p. 465, stated that the Wheeling Potteries Company went into receivership in 1910 with a Mr. Wright, who had been the president of the company, appointed as receiver. He reorganized the company and put them on a profitable basis making sanitary ware under the name of The Wheeling Sanitary Manufacturing

168

Company. In 1923 when the history already mentioned was written, The Wheeling Sanitary Manufacturing Company was still operating three of the four plants which had made up the Wheeling Potteries Company. Two were in Wheeling and the other plant was in Tiltonsville.

According to an article in the *Antique Trader Annual of Articles*, by Pamela Coates entitled "Wheeling Potteries Company," vol. IV, 1975, p. 228, she states that the LaBelle and Wheeling Pottery plants were operating at capacity right up to the time of reorganization, but that they had been loosing money for some years. "Flow Blue" ware was made at Wheeling, as well as tankards, "Virginia Girl" plates, jardinieres, cracker jars, children's items, and full lines of dinnerware. Cracker jars are a favorite with collectors. In the *1902-1903 Complete Directory* the Wheeling Potteries Company was listed as operating the following plants making the good listed: Avon Faience Company making high grade artware; the Riverside Pottery making sanitary ware; the Wheeling Pottery Company making semiporcelain, white granite and common china dinner sets, toilet sets, short sets of odd dishes, jardinieres, and decorated novelties. Pictured is a semiporcelain creamer and sugar marked "LaBelle" china. The fancy oval semiporcelain platter is also marked "LaBelle." The old ironstone rectangular platter is marked "Wheeling Pottery Company."

Wheeling Potteries Company. **Front row:** *"LaBelle" cream and sugar, square platter marked "Wheeling Pottery Company."* **Back row:** *"LaBelle" platter.*

WHEELOCK POTTERY began in 1888 in Peoria, Illinois. The state of Illinois had so many potteries that they ranked second in the nation, with Ohio being the only state with more, according to Betty Madden in "Jug Towns," *The Living Museum,* Illinois State Museum Booklet, p. 164. The business was begun by C.E. Wheelock and Son in 1888 and at first made all of their own pottery, which was a utilitarian type typical of Illinois' early potteries, in the form of jugs, mugs, crocks, etc. They got into retailing as much as pottery making as the years went along, and they began to import china which was sold under the Wheelock name. In 1971, Fred C. Bodtke, who owned the business at that time, closed it and went into the investment business. A pitcher with a lid and nicely decorated with a basket of flowers was found bearing the mark shown in the Marks Section.

WHITMORE, ROBINSON, AND COMPANY was located in Akron, Ohio, from 1862 to about 1900. They followed **JOHNSON, WHITMORE AND COMPANY** which had operated from 1856 to 1862. This company made a white granite with a buff body, according to Ramsay, that had an opaque glaze. They employed one-hundred twenty-nine in 1888. They also made stoneware, Rockingham, and yellowware.

WICK CHINA COMPANY was first organized as the **WICK CHINAWARE COMPANY** in 1889, and it was purchased by W.S. George in 1913, then operated as one of his plants under his name. (See W.S. George.) In J.H. Beer and Company's *History of Armstrong County, Pennsylvania*, Philadelphia; 1914, p. 128, is stated that Wick China produced the finest grades of tableware, plain and decorated jardinieres, and ornamental vases. They used clay from England and Florida and a little from Pennsylvania. Actually Wick China was located in the town of Wickboro which was very close to Kittanning. In the 1895 *Factory Inspection Report for Pennsylvania*, Wick China was listed as employing one-hundred sixty people to make ironstone and decorated ware. By 1900, they employed two-hundred sixty-three people. They were a leading producer of Tea Leaf china. They used an English mark and the words "Wick China" as the mark on Tea Leaf (Annise Heaivilin). Pictured is a plate with raised design and flowered transfer prints marked "Aurora China," on the right side of picture. The plate on the left in the same picture is by Wick China Company. (See Pioneer Pottery in Marks Section for similar marks.)

Left to right: Wick China Company plate, Willets Manufacturing Company plate.

WILLETS MANUFACTURING COMPANY of Trenton, New Jersey, started in 1879 and was last listed in the *Trenton City Directory* in 1909. They made white granite, semiporcelain and porcelain toilet sets, and short sets of odd dishes and novelties, as was recorded in the *1902-1903 Complete Directory*. This company used a great variety of marks. On the left of the picture with the Wick plate is a plate made by Willets, with roses for design and a small amount of raised trim around the edge.

WINFIELD POTTERY was listed as operating in Pasadena, California, in the few California directories which I secured for years 1937 through 1960, at 150 West Union Street. They made the "Bamboo" and "Primitive Pony" patterns along with a "Grape" ovenware. In the 1954 *Crockery and Glass Journal* Directory Issue, the Winfield mark was shown as belonging to American Ceramics Products, Inc. Since Winfield Pottery was still listed as operating, American Ceramics Products must have purchased Winfield Pottery rather than just continuing the line. The listing for Winfield China in that directory said merely to see American Ceramic Products, Inc. An advertisement in *House Beautiful*, November, 1942, for Winfield's "Bamboo" pattern, described it as "brilliantly glazed semiporcelain silhouettes, gray-green bamboo leaves against ivory. After five years, it's still making popularity records." (This also tells us that Winfield Pottery was well established before 1937.)

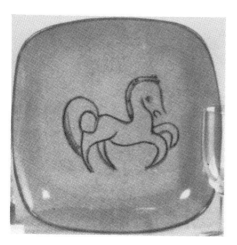

Winfield Pottery. "Primitive Pony" plate as shown in **Better Homes & Gardens,** *March, 1947.*

RUSSEL WRIGHT appears so often in the discussion of American dinnerware, kitchenware, and accessory pieces, that he must have a listing of his own. Russel Wright was a designer from New York City. Steubenville Pottery, Iroquois China,

Sterling China Company, Harker Pottery, Paden City Pottery and Bauer Pottery, all employed him at one time or another to design dishes for them. (See the histories of these companies.) Sometimes his name is included in the mark. Helen E. Stiles, in *Pottery in the United States*, p. 179, said "the lamps with a new and modern feeling (1941) are designed by Russel Wright and manufactured by Wright Accessories Incorporated of New York City." So he must have had a type of business of his own also. In *Better Homes & Gardens*, September, 1946, is an ad for a "graceful center-piece in terra cotta, jonquil yellow, or figurex white" called a "Flower Boat," designed by Russel Wright for Bauer Pottery Company, 1800 Murphy Avenue, S.W., Atlanta, Georgia. The *1954 Crockery and Glass Journal Directory* tells the story of Russel Wright in the listings it contained for him: "(1) Russel Wright—American Modern dinnerware, Steubenville Pottery Co. & dist. by Richard Morgenthau & Co.; (2) Russel Wright China by Iroquois-Iroquois China Co.; (3) Russel Wright Flame-tumblers, Imperial Glass Corp.; (4) Russel Wright Flare-tumblers, Imperial Glass Corp.; (5) Russel Wright Highlight-pottery dinnerware, Justin Tharaud & Son, Inc. (author's note: Tharaud was a distributor); (6) Russel Wright Pressed Pinch-tumblers, Imperial Glass Corp."

*Winfield Pottery. "Bamboo" pieces as shown in **House Beautiful**, November, 1942.*

Pictured are products designed by Russel Wright showing a handled cake tray by Harker Pottery, an oval hotel platter designed for Sterling China, and a cup and saucer of Iroquois China's "Casual China." The cup and saucer on the right in the picture were supposed to both be "American Modern" by Steubenville Pottery. However, we ended up with a Laurel Potteries saucer and an American Modern cup. I have several pieces of this ware by Laurel Potteries, not pictured in this book. I haven't found proof that Russel Wright designed this ware but it is so similar to his other products.

*Russel Wright designs for various potteries. **Front row:** cup and saucer, Iroquois China; hotel platter, Sterling China; cup and saucer on the right were supposed to be both "American Modern" by Steubenville Pottery, but the cup is "American Modern" and the saucer was made by Laurel Potteries. (See text.) **Back row:** handled cake tray, Harker Pottery; "American Modern" pitcher, Steubenville Pottery.*

According to Betsy Brown in "Readers Say," *Depression Glass Daze*, June 1979, p. 5, Russel Wright was born in Lebanon, Ohio, in April 1905. (He died in 1976.) She goes on to tell us that he attended Columbia and Princeton universities and studied design under Kenneth Hayes Miller, but was most indebted to Norman Bel Geddes who worked with Wright on his early designs for the theatre. Wright's designs were smooth, clear, sweeping, and very utilitarian as opposed to Art Deco. He designed furniture, household appliances, cameras, radios, etc. as well as glassware and ceramic dinnerware. Some of his original works are housed at Syracuse University.

Helen Sprackling's article, "The Glory of Glass," *Country Life*, September 1933, p. 33, speaks of Wright as not having abandoned his designing in metal, but having broadened his scope at that time to include glass. She describes the crystal clear stemmed glasses with a fish design by Wright. She praises his "quick sense of the strategy of line and the play of texture" as being characteristic of his designing.

In a staff-written article, "Russel Wright's Genius Is Largely Unrecognized," *Tri State Trader*, October 6, 1979, p. 43, the author tells us that Wright designed one of the first stove to tableware lines, the first Wurlitzer piano to be mass-produced, and the first three-piece sectional sofa which was for Heywood-Wakefield. From 1939 to 1946, this article tells us, fourteen million pieces of his dinnerware were sold.

JOHN WYLLIE AND SON operated 1874 to 1891 (not listed in *1891 East Liverpool Directory*) in the old *GREAT WESTERN POTTERY* in East Liverpool, Ohio, which had been started by the Brunts in 1867. Before 1874, the pottery had made yellow-ware and Rockingham. Wyllie and Son re-equipped the pottery to make whiteware or ironstone. Some of the patterns made by Wyllie were Octogan Pattern Dinnerware with five specific forms of decoration: "Blackberry," "Verbena," "Pine cone," "Daisy," and "Cornflower." Plain, all white ironstone was made in the following patterns: "Silver," "Great Western," "Grand," "St. Dennis," "St. Louis," "Minton," "Florence," "Normandy," "Tulip," "Mystic," "Stella," "Ninevah," and "Southern." (See "Ohio Ironstone," *Spinning Wheel*, June 1954, p. 26, staff-written, for pictures of Wyllie's ironstone.) According to Ramsay in *American Potters and Pottery*, pp. 215-218, the Wyllie Brothers were in East Liverpool from 1848 to 1854, at which time they moved to Pittsburgh. Then in 1874, John Wyllie came back to East Liverpool from Pittsburgh.

THE H.R. WYLLIE CHINA COMPANY operated in Huntington, West Virginia, from around 1910 until the late 1920s according to Floyd McKee in *A Century of American Dinnerware*. This Wyllie's father had been one of the partners to build a plant in East Liverpool which McKee termed unsuccessful. Perhaps this is a reference to John Wyllie and Son. (See John Wyllie and Son for history.) "Colonel" H.R. Wyllie had been traveling on the road selling dinnerware when he was induced to come to Huntington by free gas, free taxes, and a free site to build the pottery which the townspeople collected money to help construct. The H.R. Wyllie China Company made a nice grade of semiporcelain dinnerware. Pictured is a plate made by the H.R. Wyllie China Company.

YATES, BENNETT AND ALLEN. See City Pottery, Trenton, New Jersey.

WILLIAM YOUNG AND SONS, Trenton, New Jersey, from 1853 to 1857, operated in the old Hattersley Pottery. Then in 1857, they started a new pottery called the *EXCELSIOR POTTERY WORKS* which was operated by the family until 1879. They made crockery, hardware trimmings, pitchers, and a few dishes according to Barber in *Marks of American Potters*, p. 44.

ZANESVILLE ART POTTERY in Zanesville, Ohio, which was founded in 1900 and purchased by Weller in 1920, was mainly a maker of art pottery. But according to Stout in *History of the Clay Industry in Ohio*, p. 61, they also made culinary articles designed for cooking and baking purposes which consisted of bowls, nappies, casseroles, coffeepots, teapots, etc., described as having brown exterior with white linings.

ZANESVILLE STONEWARE COMPANY was organized in 1887, incorporated in 1889, and is still in business producing stoneware items in Zanesville, Ohio. Their very first production included cooking vessels among other items. Although they make stoneware flower planters, jardinieres, etc., today, they still produce such items as the frontier-type kitchenware in the hand thrown tradition in casseroles, mixing bowls, pitchers, and the like.

H. R. Wyllie China Company.

PART THREE

Introduction to Marks Section

SOLID LINES BETWEEN THE MARKS DIVIDE THE COMPANIES; BROKEN LINES DIVIDE THE MARKS OF A SINGLE COMPANY.

A wealth of information about a company and the types of ware they made may be gained from the study of a company's marks. Semiporcelain, porcelain, and ironstone are often marked as such. Decorators' names, designers' names, shape names, etc. may be found in marks. Modern day marks used by Shenango, Mayer, and others tell where they sell their products! Read the company's history in conjunction with the study of its marks. Sometimes the company had one name and became known for its mark name. Onondaga Pottery became so well known for Syracuse China that the company finally changed its name to the kind of china it made.

Unless a company intended that the dish they manufactured was supposed to be able to be dated by the mark, there is **no** way to date exactly by marks as some authors and collectors try to do. One will hear discussions about old marks and later marks, etc. If a company wanted to reissue a mark at any time they could do it. They did reissue marks at times because the mark stood for a type of ware that was being made again, etc. If the company had a dating system for their own use, and they issued information to collectors about their system, then, and only then, can we be sure which mark is old and which is new. When the company went out of business is generally a good time limit, but all someone has to do is to buy the rights to the mark or name and the ware can be right back on the market with the original factory still dismantled. Several companies furnished dating systems: Homer Laughlin, Syracuse China, and Taylor, Smith, and Taylor, for example. A company may tell us at what time they stopped making a particular type of ware, such as Homer Laughlin's Fiesta, and then we have an ending date. Advertisements in magazines and catalogs are good for giving us a date or at least a general idea of time. Types of ware like Belleek, Majolica, etc. had periods of time for which they were made. (For information on Belleek and Majolica, turn to the pattern or shape list, find the makers, then read the history of the company.)

Try to understand marks in terms of company practices, rights, and the reasons for the company's use of marks. Marks were a way to identify dishes so that a company could fill orders. The factory owned their own trademarks (as well as shapes, patterns, molds, etc.). If a company decided to go back to make something, it had made anytime in the past, they were perfectly within their legal rights. They could also sell the rights to someone else to make something they had made, but they seldom did. They may sell the use of their name, their trademarks, etc., if they choose, but again this seldom happens. Sometimes potteries quit making their own pottery; they may have products made somewhere else from their own molds with their own marks and become a selling organization. (See Salem China.)

Harvey Duke and the *Depression Glass Daze* allowed me to reprint marks. Franciscan Interpace (formerly Gladding, McBean and Company) was wonderful to furnish us with such a wealth of information on their marks. Many of the companies, such as Shenango China and Mayer China, sent marks, and I'm sure you can tell which they have sent, from the ones I have found on dishes and attempted to draw for you.

This is a very important point to the collector. Not only the companies who made the dishes used marks, but decorating companies, and retailers or distributors also used marks of their own. For the purposes of this book, I have concentrated mainly on the marks of the manufacturers, but a few decorator and distributor marks are shown. Sometimes a dish will have more than one mark, such as the manufacturer's mark and the distributor's mark. (See the photograph with Maddock Pottery.)

Index of Hard-to-Identify Marks

FRANCISCAN, Gladding, McBean and Co.
FRENCH CHEF, Marsh Industries
F.S. CO., French Saxon China Co.
F.&T. CO., Fell & Thorp Co.

G.C.M. & CO., George C. Murphy Pottery Co.
GENEVA, Sevres China Co.
G.H.B. CLEVELAND, George H. Bowman
G.P. CO. E.L.O., Globe Pottery
G.P. CO., Globe Pottery
G.P. CO., Greenwood Pottery Co.
GREEK, French China

H in a circle, Hull
H in a diamond, Carrollton China Co.
HARMONY HOUSE, Sears and Roebuck Co.
HAVILAND MADE IN AMERICA, Shenango China
HELEN, Crown Pottery
H.L. monogram, Homer Laughlin China Co.
H.L.C., Homer Laughlin China Co.
HOBSON, Crown Pottery
H.P. CO., Harker Pottery
H.P. CO., Hull Pottery

IMPERIAL CHINA, Empire Pottery
IMPERIAL CHINA P.P., Pioneer Pottery
IMPERIAL GEDDO, Onondago Pottery
IMPERIAL PORCELAIN, Wheeling Pottery
INDEPENDENCE IRONSTONE, Shenango China
IVORY FRANKLINWARE, Sebring Pottery Co.
I.V.W., American Pottery Co.

J.C., New York City Pottery
J & E.M., Mayer China
J.M. & S. CO., Glasgow Pottery
J.W. & SON, John Wyllie and Son

K in a crown, Kingwood Ceramics
KAOLENA CHINA, Gladding, McBean and Co.
KENILWORTH, Homer Laughlin China Co.
KENNETH, French China Co.
KENWOOD, Shawnee Pottery
KEYSTONE, Vodrey Pottery
KOSMO, Smith Phillips China Co.
K.T.K., Knowles, Taylor, Knowles

L.A. POTTERIES, Los Angeles Potteries
LABELLE, Wheeling Potteries Co.
LA FRANCAISE, French China Co.
LAMBERTON, Maddock Pottery and Sterling China Co.
LELAND, C.C. Thompson Co.
LIBERTY CHINA, Virginia Pottery
LIMOGES, Limoges China Co.
LUZERNE, Mercer Pottery
LYGIA, French China

MADRID, Dresden Pottery
MANHATTAN, George C. Murphy Pottery Co.
MARY LOUISE, Gladding, McBean and Co.
M & CO., Morley and Co.
M.C.P., Mount Clemens Pottery, also McCoy P.
McCY U.S.A., McCoy Pottery
MELLOR AND CO., Cook Pottery
MELLORIA, Crescent Pottery
MELLOTONE, Coors Porcelain
MELROSE, C.C. Thompson Pottery Co.
MELTON, Sevres China Co.
MITUSA, Brush Pottery
M & S, Glasgow Pottery
M.T., Mercer Pottery

NASCO, National Silver Co.
NASSAU, Mercer Pottery
N.C. CO. E.L.O., National China Co.
N.J. POTTERY CO., New Jersey Pottery Co.
N.M., Nelson McCoy Pottery Co.
N.M. P. CO., New Milford Pottery Co.
N.Y.C.P., New York City Pottery

O & B, Ott and Brewer in Eturia Pottery
O.C. CO., Ohio China Co.
O.P. CO., Onondaga Pottery (later Syracuse C.)
O.V.C. CO., Ohio Valley China Co.
OVEN PROOF, Shawnee Pottery Co.
OVENWARE, Watt Pottery
OXFORD-WARE, Oxford Pottery
OXFORD STONEWARE, Universal Potteries

P, Bonnin and Morris
PARMA, Gladding, McBean and Co.
P.C.P. CO., Paden City Pottery
PEEDEECO, Watt Pottery
PETROSCAN, Ohio Pottery Co.
PLUTO, French China Co.
P P (back to back) Pioneer Pottery Co.
P.P.CO., Peoria Pottery
PUEBLO, Gladding, McBean and Co.

RAINBOW, Gladding, McBean and Co.
RAVENSCROFT, Taylor, Smith, and Taylor
RAVENSWOOD, Pickard, Inc.
RAYMOR, Roseville Pottery
RAYMOR, Universal Potteries Inc.
R.C., Royal China
R.E. & CO., American Art China Co.
RENA, Crown Pottery
REVERE CHINA, Akron China Co.
R.H. HANDCRAFT, Hoffman China
RIETI, New England Pottery
ROCKET, Bennett Pottery
ROSEVILLE, Robinson-Ransbottom Pottery
R.P. CO. Roseville Pottery Co.

R.R.P.CO. Robinson-Ransbottom Pottery
R.&T., American Pottery Co.
RUM RILL, Florence Pottery also Red Wing P.
   and Shawnee Pottery
RUSTIC WARE, Robinson-Ransbottom Pottery

SABINA LINE, Sabin Industries Inc.
SALAD BOWL, Gladding, McBean and Co.
SANTONE, Warwick China Co.
S.C.C., Summit China Co.
SEQUOIA, American Bisque Co.
SEVERN, Crescent Pottery
SHAW, Bradshaw China Co.
SHENANDOAH, Paden City Pottery
SIDNEY, C.C. Thompson Co.
SIGSBEE, Union Potteries Co.
SIRUS, Globe Pottery
S.P., Glasgow Pottery
S.P., Southern Porcelain
S.P. CO., Steubenville Pottery Co.
S.P. INC., Southern Potteries
States names, Knowles, Taylor, Knowles
STINTHALL, Crooksville China Co.
STUPELL, CAROLE, Gladding, McBean and Co.

TAYLORTON, Taylor, Smith, and Taylor
T.B. CO. Brockman Pottery Co.
TEPECO, Trenton Potteries Co.
TEXAS, Cartwright Brothers
THOMAS, Thomas China Co.
TIGER, French China
T.M. & S., Thomas Maddock and Sons
T.P. C.O. CO., Technical Porcelain and Chinaware Co.
T.P. CO., Gladding, McBean and Co.
T.P.Co. Trenton Pottery Co.
T.P.W., Trenton Pottery Works
TROPICO, Tropico Pottery and Gladding,
   McBean and Co.
T.S.T., Taylor, Smith, and Taylor

UNION CHINA, Union Potteries Co.
U.P.C., Union Potteries Co.
U.P.CO., Ungemach Pottery

VESTA, Steubenville Pottery
VERNON, Vernon Kilns
VERNONWARE, Vernon Kilns
VERUS PORCELAIN, Oliver China Co.
V.P. CO., Vodrey Pottery Co.

W in a diamond, Wheeling Pottery
WACO CHINA, E. Liverpool P. Co.
W.B.P. CO., Brunt Pottery
W.B.S. & CO., Brunt Pottery

W.C.CO., Wellsville China Co.
WEILWARE, Weil Ceramics
W.E.P. CO., West End Pottery Co.
WHEELING GOLD CHINA, Wheeling Decorating Co.
WILSHIRE, Gladding, McBean and Co.
W.M. CO., Willits Mfg. Co.
W.P. CO., Wheeling Pottery Co.
W.P.P.CO., Wellsville Pioneer Pottery
W.S. CO., Western Stoneware Co.
W.S.G., W.S. George Pottery
W.Y.S., William Young and Son

YALE, Dresden Pottery
YORK, Pfaltzgraff Pottery

Marks Section from A to Z

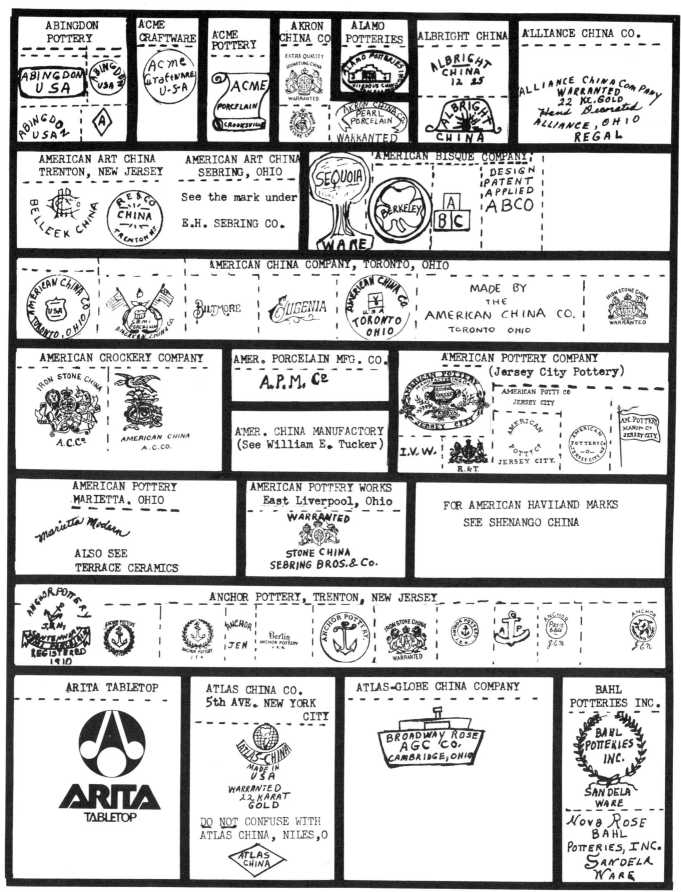

BAUER POTTERY, LOS ANGELES, CALIFORNIA

J.H. BAUM

L.B. BEERBOWER & COMPANY

BEERBOWER & GRIFFEN

BELL POTTERY
FINDLAY, OHIO

THE BELL POTTERY CO
FINDLAY OHIO

BELL CHINA
B.P Co.
Findlay, Ohio

B P Co
F O

BENNETT POTTERY

E & W BENNETT
CANTON AVE.
BALTIMORE, MARYLAND

BENNETT POTTERY

BONNIN & MORRIS

GEORGE H. BOWMAN—CLEVELAND CHINA COMPANY

WILLIAM BLOOR

BRADSHAW CHINA

BRIGHTON, ZANESVILLE, O.

B.J. BROCK AND CO.
LAWNDALE, CALIFORNIA

BRUNT POTTERY COMPANY

BROCKMAN POTTERY COMPANY

BRUSCHE CERAMICS

The
Brush
Pottery
Co.,
Zanesville,
Ohio

IN USE
1927-29

REVISED 1958-68

BRUSH POTTERY

BRUSH—McCOY

used 1915-1925

1930-1933

1965-72

BRUSH POTTERY CO.
FURNISHED DATES

179

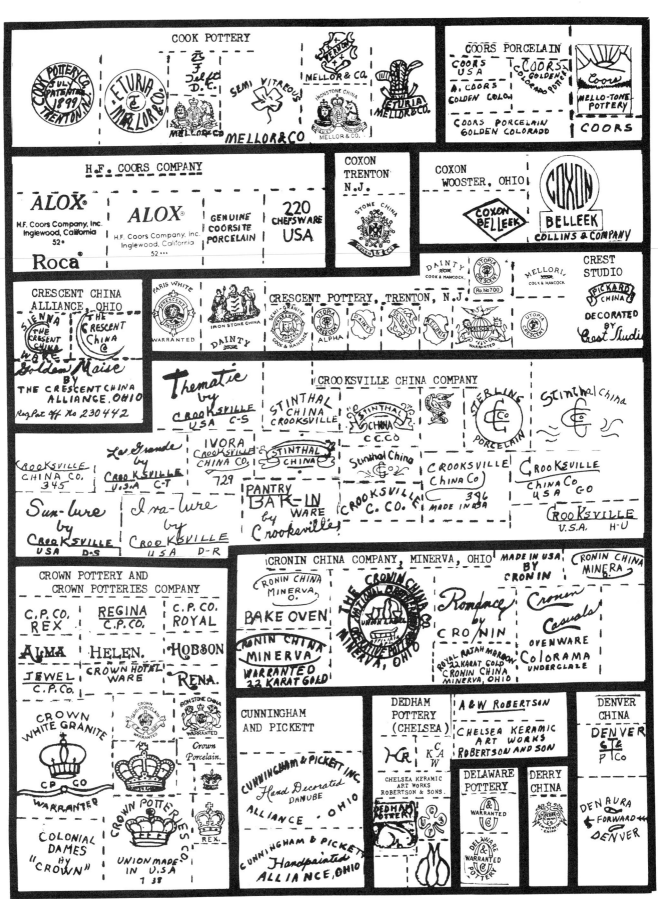

DRYDEN POTTERY

Marks by Deb and Gini Johnson.

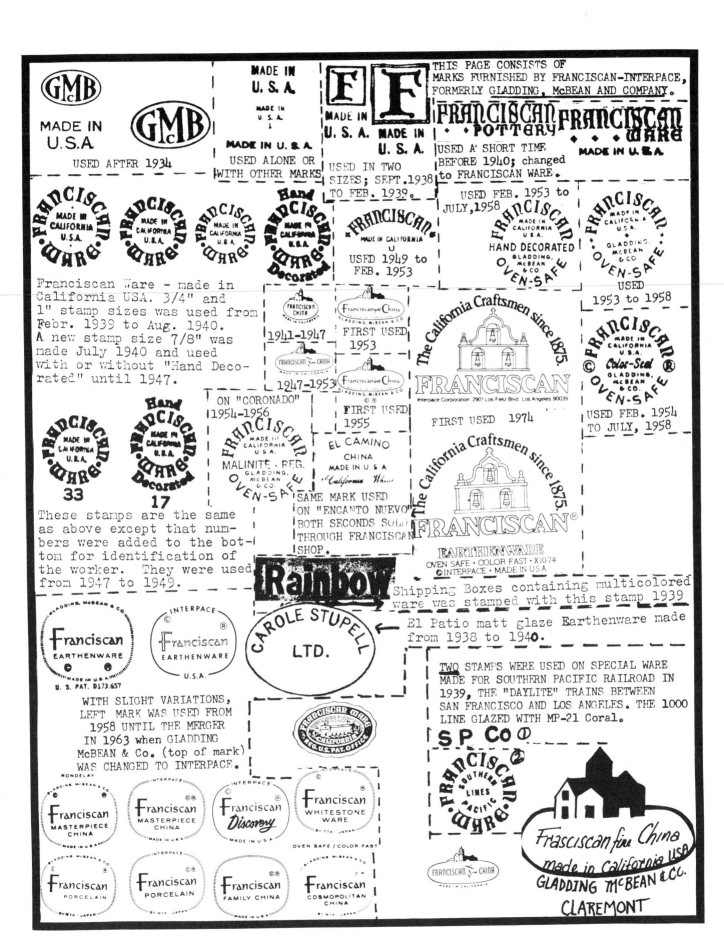

GMB — MADE IN U.S.A. USED AFTER 1934

MADE IN U.S.A. USED ALONE OR WITH OTHER MARKS

MADE IN U.S.A. USED IN TWO SIZES; SEPT. 1938 TO FEB. 1939.

FRANCISCAN POTTERY / FRANCISCAN WARE USED A SHORT TIME BEFORE 1940; changed to FRANCISCAN WARE.

USED FEB. 1953 to JULY, 1958

Franciscan Ware - made in California USA. 3/4" and 1" stamp sizes was used from Febr. 1939 to Aug. 1940. A new stamp size 7/8" was made July 1940 and used with or without "Hand Decorated" until 1947.

FRANCISCAN MADE IN CALIFORNIA — USED 1949 to FEB. 1953

HAND DECORATED OVEN-SAFE

USED 1953 to 1958

FRANCISCAN CHINA 1941-1947

FRANCISCAN CHINA 1947-1953

Franciscan China GLADDING, McBEAN & CO. FIRST USED 1953

Franciscan China GLADDING, McBEAN & CO. FIRST USED 1955

33   17

These stamps are the same as above except that numbers were added to the bottom for identification of the worker. They were used from 1947 to 1949.

ON "CORONADO" 1954-1956

FRANCISCAN MADE IN CALIFORNIA U.S.A. MALINITE - REG. GLADDING, McBEAN & CO. OVEN-SAFE

EL CAMINO CHINA MADE IN U.S.A. California Wheat — SAME MARK USED ON "ENCANTO NUEVO" BOTH SECONDS SOLD THROUGH FRANCISCAN SHOP.

The California Craftsmen since 1875. FRANCISCAN — Interpace Corporation 2901 Los Feliz Blvd Los Angeles 90039 — FIRST USED 1974

The California Craftsmen since 1875. FRANCISCAN EARTHENWARE — OVEN SAFE • COLOR FAST • X10-74 © INTERPACE • MADE IN USA

FRANCISCAN Color-Seal OVEN-SAFE GLADDING, McBEAN & CO. USED FEB. 1954 TO JULY, 1958

Rainbow — Shipping Boxes containing multicolored ware was stamped with this stamp 1939

Franciscan EARTHENWARE — MADE IN U.S.A. — U.S. PAT. D173.657

© INTERPACE ® Franciscan EARTHENWARE U.S.A.

WITH SLIGHT VARIATIONS, LEFT MARK WAS USED FROM 1958 UNTIL THE MERGER IN 1963 when GLADDING McBEAN & Co. (top of mark) WAS CHANGED TO INTERPACE.

CAROLE STUPELL LTD.

El Patio matt glaze Earthenware made from 1938 to 1940.

TWO STAMPS WERE USED ON SPECIAL WARE MADE FOR SOUTHERN PACIFIC RAILROAD IN 1939, THE "DAYLITE" TRAINS BETWEEN SAN FRANCISCO AND LOS ANGELES. THE 1000 LINE GLAZED WITH MP-21 Coral.

S P CO ① ②

FRANCISCAN WARE SOUTHERN PACIFIC LINES

FRANCISCAN CHINA MADE IN CALIFORNIA

Franciscan fine China made in California USA GLADDING McBEAN & CO. CLAREMONT

RONDELAY — GLADDING McBEAN & CO. Franciscan MASTERPIECE CHINA MADE IN U.S.A.

INTERPACE Franciscan MASTERPIECE CHINA MADE IN U.S.A.

INTERPACE Franciscan Discovery MADE IN U.S.A.

INTERPACE Franciscan WHITESTONE WARE BY TTK JAPAN — OVEN SAFE / COLOR FAST

GLADDING McBEAN & CO. Franciscan PORCELAIN BY NTK JAPAN

INTERPACE Franciscan PORCELAIN BY NTK JAPAN

Franciscan FAMILY CHINA MADE IN U.S.A.

GLADDING McBEAN & CO. Franciscan COSMOPOLITAN CHINA BY NTK JAPAN

OVEN
Nasco
PROOF

THIS PAGE
GLADDING MCBEAN, NOW
FRANCISCAN INTERPACE

Records found in the Mold Shop list ware made for National Silver Co. from 1934 to 1940. The ware was stamped as illustrated. In addition to this stamp sales records show that Casseroles S-1 and S-2 also were stamped "California Pottery Nasco", and that a Pie Plate S-43 had an imprint in the mold reading "California Pottery Nasco".

This paste-on sticker was used as additional identification on all ware marked "Catalina" from 1937 to 1941. (blue on silver)

This past-on sticker was used as additional identification on Earthenware from 1937 to 1941. (red on gold)

PULLMAN
CO,

Possibly used on a special vitrious hotel line, the 1100 series, sold in 1938.

FRANCISCAN
MADE IN CALIFORNIA
BARKERTONE

Two-tone Montecito Table Ware made exclusively for Barker Brothers in 1939 with special glazes to be sold at the Golden Gate International Exposition. Also a plate C-3 with following series: California Missions, Winning of the West, California Wild Flowers.

WILSHIRE
EL CAMINO CHINA
MADE IN U. S. A.

This stamp is used on gold banded china made for the Franciscan shop only. Stamped in gold.

T. P. Co.

Special Florist ware 1935 tp 1939

MARKS ON SPECIAL DINNERWARE FOR ETERNAL STAINLESS STEEL CO. 1962

PARMA

Par Soup (cup, lug soup and ramekin) made for Gordon-Allen in 1937 as premium only. Impressed in the ware.

"SUNKIST"

S-37 Bowl with the imprint "Sunkist" made for California Fruit Growers Exchange in 1937. (sample not available)

Salad Bowl

This stamp was used on S-37 Bowls made for Arden Creamery 1938.

MARY LOUISE

A two-tone Earthenware, coral and white, sold to Barker Brothers 1940 to 1945.

PUEBLO
MADE IN U.S.A.
POTTERY

The Pueblo Pottery stamp was used on ware sold as premium only in 1940. The stamp is similar to the Catalina stamp.

Pottery and China made for Max Schonfeld was shipped without identification marks, although one Earthenware sample (B-27) found in the archive suggest that some ware may have been stamped with his trade mark "MS" in script as illustrated. China decorated by Max Schonfeld appeared on the market with a paste-on sticker labeled "Kaolena China", 1939 to 1951.

KAOLENA CHINA

"California Manor"

Special China backstamp in script, approx. 3 inches long. It was used on a special pattern made for a local designer

TIFFANY
Arcadia Gold

Decal backstamp used on China made for Abbey Rents, Los Angeles, 1947. (sample not available)

Regal
FINE CHINA
Made in U.S.A.

MADE IN CALIF. U.S.A.

GONDER CERAMIC ART CO.

Gonder Original   Gonder
902   USA
ON DINNER PLATE

crafted by
Gonder
factory & studio - ZANESVILLE, OHIO

GONDER
USA

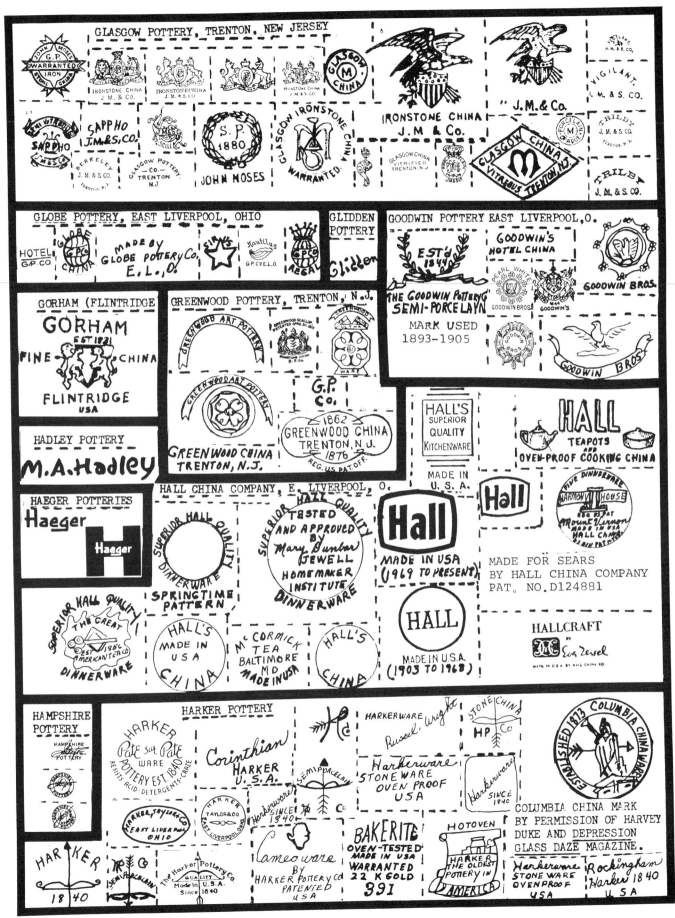

GLASGOW POTTERY, TRENTON, NEW JERSEY

GLOBE POTTERY, EAST LIVERPOOL, OHIO

GLIDDEN POTTERY

GOODWIN POTTERY EAST LIVERPOOL, O.

GORHAM (FLINTRIDGE

GREENWOOD POTTERY, TRENTON, N.J.

HADLEY POTTERY

M.A.Hadley

HAEGER POTTERIES

HALL CHINA COMPANY, E. LIVERPOOL, O.

HAMPSHIRE POTTERY

HARKER POTTERY

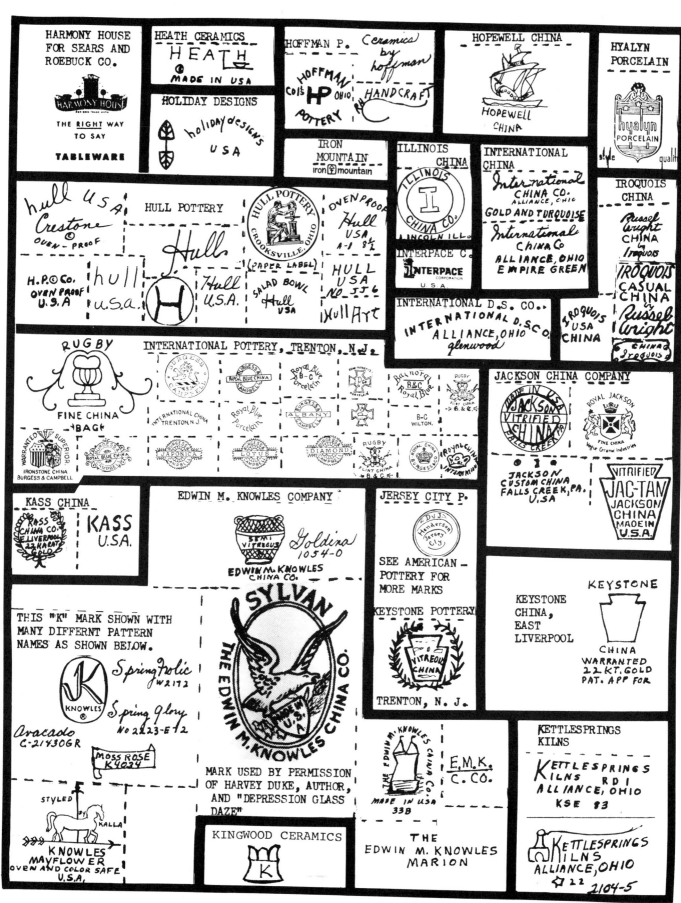

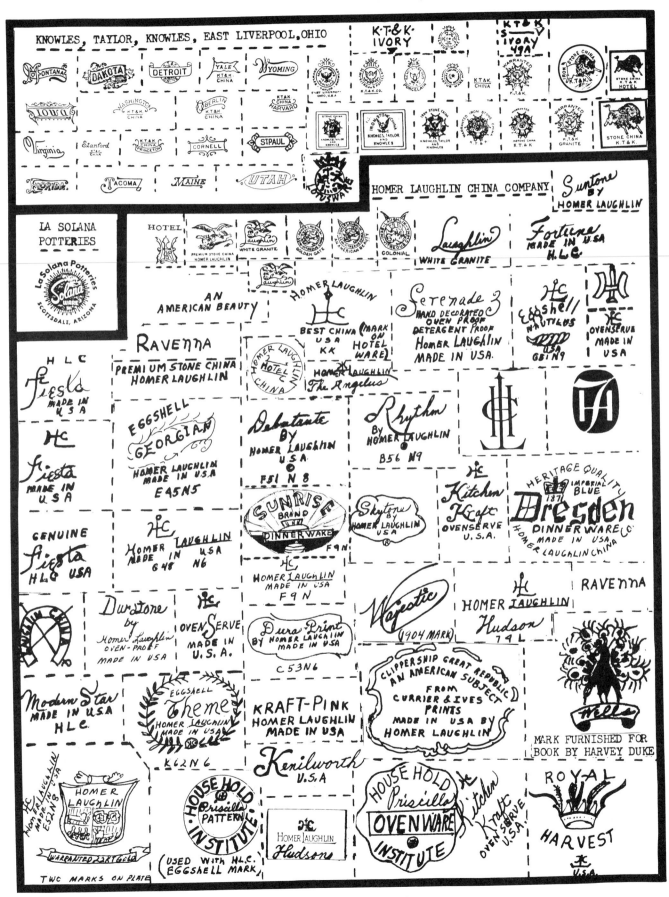

KNOWLES, TAYLOR, KNOWLES, EAST LIVERPOOL, OHIO

KT & K IVORY

KT & K S V IVORY 49A

HOMER LAUGHLIN CHINA COMPANY

LA SOLANA POTTERIES

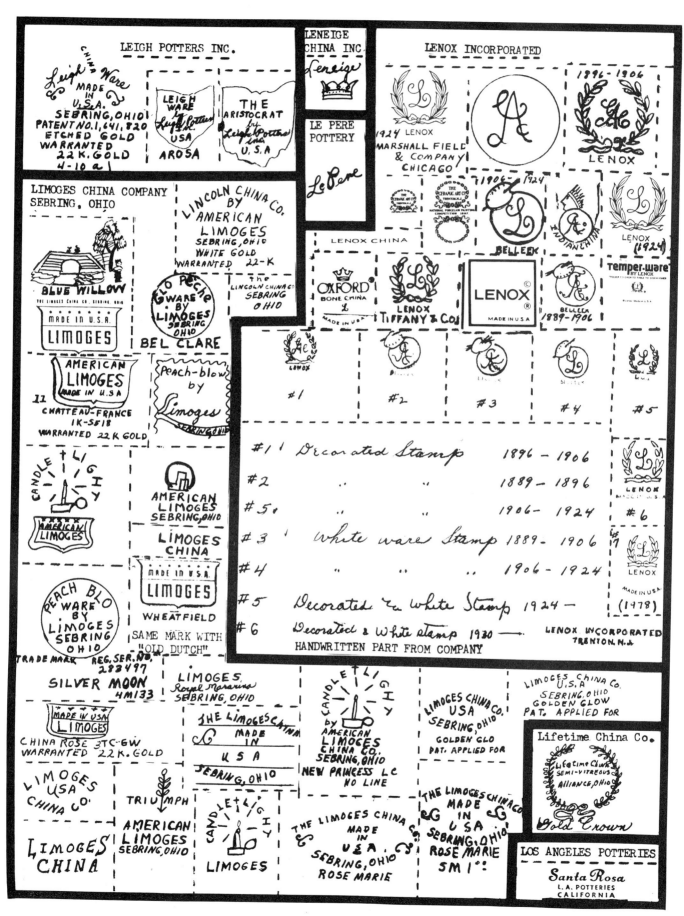

LEIGH POTTERS INC.

China Ware MADE IN U.S.A. SEBRING, OHIO PATENT NO. 1,641,820 ETCHED GOLD WARRANTED 22 K. GOLD 4-10 a|

Leigh Ware

LEIGH WARE *by Leigh Potters* USA AROSA

THE ARISTOCRAT *by Leigh Potters Inc.* U.S.A.

LENEIGE CHINA INC.

Leneige

LE PERE POTTERY

Le Pere

LENOX INCORPORATED

1924 LENOX

MARSHALL FIELD & COMPANY CHICAGO

1896 - 1906 LENOX

LENOX CHINA

1906 - 1924

BELLEEK

INDIAN CHINA

LENOX (1924)

OXFORD BONE CHINA L MADE IN U.S.A.

LENOX TIFFANY & Co.

LENOX MADE IN U.S.A.

BELLEEK 1889 - 1906

Temper-ware BY LENOX

#1 LENOX

#2

#3

#4

#5

LENOX MADE IN U.S.A. #6

LL LENOX MADE IN U.S.A. (1978)

#1   Decorated Stamp   1896 - 1906
#2   ..   ..   1889 - 1896
#5   ..   ..   1906 - 1924
#3   White ware Stamp 1889 - 1906
#4   ..   ..   ..   1906 - 1924
#5   Decorated in white Stamp 1924 —
#6   Decorated & White stamp 1930 —
HANDWRITTEN PART FROM COMPANY

LENOX INCORPORATED TRENTON N.J.

LIMOGES CHINA COMPANY SEBRING, OHIO

BLUE WILLOW THE LIMOGES CHINA CO. SEBRING, OHIO

MADE IN U.S.A. LIMOGES

AMERICAN LIMOGES MADE IN U.S.A. 11 CHATTEAU-FRANCE 1K-5518 WARRANTED 22 K GOLD

CANDLE LIGHT AMERICAN LIMOGES

PEACH BLO WARE BY LIMOGES SEBRING OHIO

TRADE MARK REG. SER. NO. 283497

SILVER MOON HM133

MADE IN USA LIMOGES CHINA ROSE 3TC-GW WARRANTED 22 K. GOLD

LIMOGES USA CHINA CO.

LIMOGES CHINA

LINCOLN CHINA Co. BY AMERICAN LIMOGES SEBRING, OHIO WHITE GOLD WARRANTED 22-K

Glo Peche WARE BY LIMOGES SEBRING OHIO BEL CLARE

The LINCOLN CHINA CO SEBRING OHIO

Peach-blow by Limoges SEBRING OHIO

AMERICAN LIMOGES SEBRING, OHIO

LIMOGES CHINA MADE IN U.S.A. LIMOGES WHEATFIELD

SAME MARK WITH "OLD DUTCH"

LIMOGES Royal Maroons SEBRING, OHIO

THE LIMOGES CHINA MADE IN U S A SEBRING, OHIO

TRIUMPH

AMERICAN LIMOGES SEBRING, OHIO

CANDLE LIGHT LIMOGES

CANDLE LIGHT by AMERICAN LIMOGES CHINA CO. SEBRING, OHIO NEW PRINCESS L.C. NO LINE

THE LIMOGES CHINA CO. MADE IN U.S.A. SEBRING, OHIO ROSE MARIE

LIMOGES CHINA CO. USA SEBRING, OHIO GOLDEN GLO PAT. APPLIED FOR

THE LIMOGES CHINA CO. MADE IN U S A SEBRING, OHIO ROSE MARIE SM 1°°

LIMOGES CHINA Co. U.S.A SEBRING, OHIO GOLDEN GLOW PAT. APPLIED FOR

Lifetime China Co.

Lifetime China SEMI-VITREOUS ALLIANCE, OHIO Gold Crown

LOS ANGELES POTTERIES

Santa Rosa L.A. POTTERIES CALIFORNIA

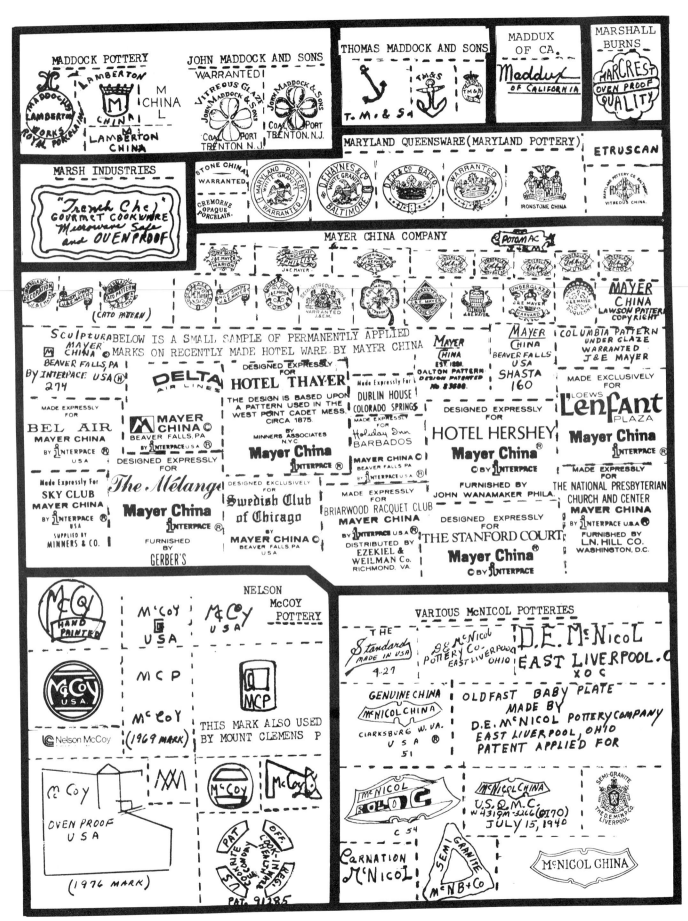

MADDOCK POTTERY

JOHN MADDOCK AND SONS
WARRANTED

THOMAS MADDOCK AND SONS

MADDUX OF CA.
Maddux OF CALIFORNIA

MARSHALL BURNS
HARCREST OVEN PROOF QUALITY

MARYLAND QUEENSWARE (MARYLAND POTTERY)

ETRUSCAN

MARSH INDUSTRIES
"French Chef" GOURMET COOKWARE Microwave Safe and OVENPROOF

MAYER CHINA COMPANY

Sculptura BELOW IS A SMALL SAMPLE OF PERMANENTLY APPLIED MAYER CHINA © MARKS ON RECENTLY MADE HOTEL WARE BY MAYER CHINA

MAYER CHINA BY INTERPACE USA 274 BEAVER FALLS, PA

COLUMBIA PATTERN UNDER GLAZE WARRANTED J & E MAYER

DELTA AIR LINES

DESIGNED EXPRESSLY FOR HOTEL THAYER
THE DESIGN IS BASED UPON A PATTERN USED IN THE WEST POINT CADET MESS CIRCA 1875.

Made Expressly For DUBLIN HOUSE COLORADO SPRINGS

MAYER CHINA EST. 1881. DALTON PATTERN DESIGN PATENTED NO. 83608.

MAYER CHINA BEAVER FALLS USA SHASTA 160

MADE EXCLUSIVELY FOR LOEWS L'enfant PLAZA Mayer China INTERPACE ®

MADE EXPRESSLY FOR BEL AIR MAYER CHINA BY INTERPACE USA

MAYER CHINA © BEAVER FALLS, PA BY INTERPACE USA ®

DESIGNED EXPRESSLY FOR

BY MINNERS ASSOCIATES N.Y.C. Mayer China INTERPACE ®

Made Expressly FOR Holiday Inn BARBADOS

MAYER CHINA © BEAVER FALLS PA BY INTERPACE USA ®

DESIGNED EXPRESSLY FOR HOTEL HERSHEY Mayer China® © BY INTERPACE

Mayer China

Made Expressly For SKY CLUB MAYER CHINA BY INTERPACE USA SUPPLIED BY MINNERS & CO.

The Mélange Mayer China INTERPACE ® FURNISHED BY GERBER'S

DESIGNED EXCLUSIVELY FOR Swedish Club of Chicago BY MAYER CHINA © BEAVER FALLS PA USA

MADE EXPRESSLY FOR BRIARWOOD RACQUET CLUB MAYER CHINA BY INTERPACE USA ® DISTRIBUTED BY EZEKIEL & WEILMAN Co. RICHMOND, VA.

DESIGNED EXPRESSLY FOR THE STANFORD COURT Mayer China® © BY INTERPACE

MADE EXPRESSLY FOR THE NATIONAL PRESBYTERIAN CHURCH AND CENTER MAYER CHINA BY INTERPACE USA ® FURNISHED BY L.N. HILL CO. WASHINGTON, D.C.

NELSON McCOY POTTERY

McCoy USA
McCoy USA

MCP

McCoy (1969 MARK)

Nelson McCoy

THIS MARK ALSO USED BY MOUNT CLEMENS P

McCoy OVEN PROOF USA (1976 MARK)

McCoy

McCoy

PAT. 91285

VARIOUS McNICOL POTTERIES

THE Standard MADE IN USA 4-21

D.E. McNICOL POTTERY CO. EAST LIVERPOOL OHIO

D.E. McNICOL EAST LIVERPOOL.O XOC

GENUINE CHINA McNICOL CHINA CLARKSBURG W.VA. USA ® 51

OLDFAST BABY PLATE MADE BY D.E. McNICOL POTTERY COMPANY EAST LIVERPOOL, OHIO PATENT APPLIED FOR

McNICOL C 54

McNICOL CHINA U.S.Q.M.C. W4319M-3JC6 (0170) JULY/15, 1940

SEMI-GRANITE THE D.E.McN.P.CO. LIVERPOOL

CARNATION McNICOL

SEMI GRANITE McNB+Co

McNICOL CHINA

189

MERCER POTTERY, TRENTON, NEW JERSEY

MERCER WARRANTED CHINA

TACOMA M T

IRONSTONE CHINA

MERCER SEMI VITREOUS

MERCER

SEMI VITREOUS WALDORF MERCERCHINA

SEMI VITREOUS TRINIDAD MERCERCHINA

SEMI VITREOUS MYRNA MERCERCHINA

SEMI VITREOUS ARDMORE MERCERCHINA

MERCER POTTERY TRENTON, N.J.

WARRANTED SUPERIOR IRONSTONE CHINA MERCER POTTERY CO.

TRADE MARK STONE CHINA MERCER POTTERY CO.

Nassau

LUZERNE MC

METLOX POTTERY ALSO SEE VERNON KILNS

POPPY TRAIL BY METLOX MADE IN CALIFORNIA 975 (1977 MARK)

Poppytrail METLOX

WOODLAND GOLD by Poppytrail SAFE IN OVEN AND DISHWASHER DURABLE HAND DECORATED MADE IN CALIF. U.S.A.

Vernon ware

Vernon ware U.S.A MADE FOR OVEN AND DISH USE

Poppytrail

MILLINGTON, ASTBURY, AND POULSON

M.A.P. TRENTON.

M.A.P. TRENTON N.J.

MORGAN BELLEEK CO.

MORGAN BELLEEK

SEMI M&Co PORCELAIN

MORLEY & CO.

M&Co IRONSTONE CHINA

MORLEY & CO. MAJOLLICA WELLSVILLE, O.

MT. CLEMENS P.

MOUNT CLEMENS NMCO TOULON

KPM

MADE IN USA

MCP ALSO USED BY McCOY

C.C. MURPHY COMPANY

J&LCO.

Paris J.C.M.&Co.

Manhattan

MURPHY & CO. VITREOUS HOTEL PORCELAIN

NATIONAL CHINA COMPANY

THE NATIONAL CHINA Co. E.L.O.

N.C.Co. E.L.O.

WESTERN GEM NATIONAL CHINA CO. E.L.O.

NATIONAL CHINA COMPANY

PERFECTION WHITE GRANITE TRADE MARK

NATIONAL CHINA CO SALINEVILLE, O.

NATIONAL POTTERIES

Napco Creation

MUTUAL CHINA

MUTUAL CHINA CO. INDIANAPOLIS HAND PAINTED

NEW CASTLE CHINA

NEW CASTLE CHINA NEW CASTLE PA.

NCPCO CHINA NEW CASTLE

NEW JERSEY POTTERY COMPANY

POTTERY N.J.

NEW ENGLAND POTTERY COMPANY

STONE CHINA

WARRANTED

IRONSTONE CHINA PETIT GRACIUM SUB LIBERTATE

N.E.P.Co.

RIETI

RIETI

N.E.P.C

PARIS WHITE BOSTON, 1854

OWEN CHINA MINERVA, O.

OWEN CHINA MINERVA 10 27 A

ST. LOUIS OWEN CHINA 5 27 ROYAL IVORY

NEW YORK CITY P.

MORRISON & CARR

JAMES M. SHAW & CO. HARTFORD PAT. SEPT. 19. 1871

STONE CHINA JAMES CARR N Y C POTTERY

NYCP

STONE PORCELAIN J.C.

TRADE MARK J.C.

STONE CHINA

TRADE MARK

J C STONE CHINA

NEW MILFORD

N.M.P.CO.

W N.M.P.CO

SEMI OPAQUE N.M.P.Co.

C.F. W N.M.P.Co

L&S

OHIO POTTERY

139 C OHIO POTTERY CO. OHIO ZANESVILLE.O

OHIO ZANESVILLE O

PETROSCAN ZANESVILLE O 62

OHIO CHINA

O C Co. LIMOGES PORCELAIN

O C Co

OHIO VALLEY C.

O.V.

O.V.

O.V. C.Co.

OLIVER CHINA COMPANY

THE OLIVER CHINA CO. SEBRING, OHIO

VERUS PORCELAIN

FOR ONONDAGA P. MARKS SEE SYRACUSE CHINA

OXFORD POTTERY

OXFORD-WARE MADE IN USA

FOR OXFORD STONEWARE SEE UNIVERSAL POTTERIES

PACIFIC CLAY PRODUCTS COMPANY
(MARKS THROUGH COURTESY OF BARBARA JEAN HAYES)

DURA RIM BY PACIFIC MADE IN CALIF-USA

PACIFIC 205 MADE IN USA

ARCADIA BY PACIFIC MADE IN CALIF-U.S.A.

PACIFIC CHINA FINE QUALITY WARRANTED 22k

Preview BY PADEN BONE ASH GLAZE

PADEN CITY POTTERY

SHENANDOAH PADEN CITY POTTERY MADE IN U.S.A. UNDERGLAZE

La Rosa 2SP.3C

PADEN CITY POTTERY MADE IN U.S.A. D-48

PEARL CHINA COMPANY

Pearl CHINA CO. HAND DECORATED 22 kT GOLD

Pearl China Co. EAST LIVERPOOL, OHIO

Quaker Maid COOK WARE PEARL CHINA Co. EAST LIVERPOOL OHIO

PENNSBURY POTTERY Pennsbury Pottery

Pennsbury Pottery Morrisville, Pa.

Grecian Ivory BY PADEN CITY A 31

Regina P.C.P.Co. C 33

Shenandoah PASTELS MADE IN U.S.A. H 53

PERLEE INC.

P PERLEE INC.

PEORIA POTTERY COMPANY

IRONSTONE CHINA WARRANTED

PEORIA ILLINOIS

HOTEL P.P.Co.

WARRANTED BEST IRONSTONE CHINA

SEMI PORCELAIN

PFALTZGRAFF YORK, PA. PFALTZGRAFF POTTERY

YORK P

P PFALTZGRAFF®

PFALTZGRAFF OVEN PROOF U.S.A

THE PFALTZGRAFF POTTERY USA 80

JERRY THE JERK "Muggsey" THE PFALTZGRAFF POTTERY YORK, PENN DESIGNED BY JESSOP

PHILADELPHIA CITY POTTERY

WARRANTED 1868 FIRE PROOF

PHOENIX POTTERY

Phoenix POttery ETRUSCAN MAJOLICA ETRUSCAN

ETRUSCAN IVORY

ETRUSCAN MAJOLICA

ALBERT PICK (DIS.)

ALBERT PICK CO INC. CHICAGO VITRIFIED CHINA L F

ALBERT PICK & CO. CHICAGO.

PICKARD CHINA COMPANY

EDGERTON FINE CHINA MADE IN USA

PICKARD CHINA MADE IN USA

PICKARD CHINA MADE IN USA MOSAIC

HAND PAINTED PICKARD CHINA

EDGERTON HAND PAINTED PICKARD

PICKARD

PICKARD

RAVENS WOOD.

PICKARD

PICKARD CHINA MADE IN U.S.A Established 1898

PP WORKS CHINA PORCELAIN

IMPERIAL CHINA

PIONEER POTTERY WELLSVILLE, O.

AURORA PPCo CHINA W P P Co SEMI-PORCELAIN

SEMI PORCELAIN W.P.P.CO

P P WCo

POPE GOSSER CHINA MADE IN USA

POPE-GOSSER CHINA MADE IN USA LABELLE

POPEGOSSER CHINA MADE IN USA Carrol

POPEGOSSER CHINA MADE IN USA ROSE POINT 42

POPE-GOSSER CHINA MADE IN USA

POPE GOSSER CHINA MADE IN USA MADRID

PORCELIER CO.

Porcelier TRADE MARK VITRIFIED HEAT-PROOF COOKING CHINA

Porcelier TRADE MARK VITREOUS CHINA MADE IN U.S.A.

Porcelier TRADE MARK VITREOUS HAND DEC. CHINA MADE IN USA

POTTERS CO-OPERATIVE

SEMI-VITREOUS THE POTTERS CO-OPERATIVE EAST LIVERPOOL OHIO U.S.A. 6 5 26 4

POTTERS CO-OPERATIVE CO. SEMI VITREOUS

POPE GOSSER CHINA COMPANY

THE POPE-GOSSER CHINA CO SEMI VITREOUS

POPE GOSSER CHINA MADE IN U S A

POPE GOSSER CHINA MADE IN USA STERLING

FLORENCE

PG CO

POPE GOSSER CHINA MADE IN USA

POPE-GOSSER CHINA

ROSEPOINT

POPE-GOSSER U.S.A.

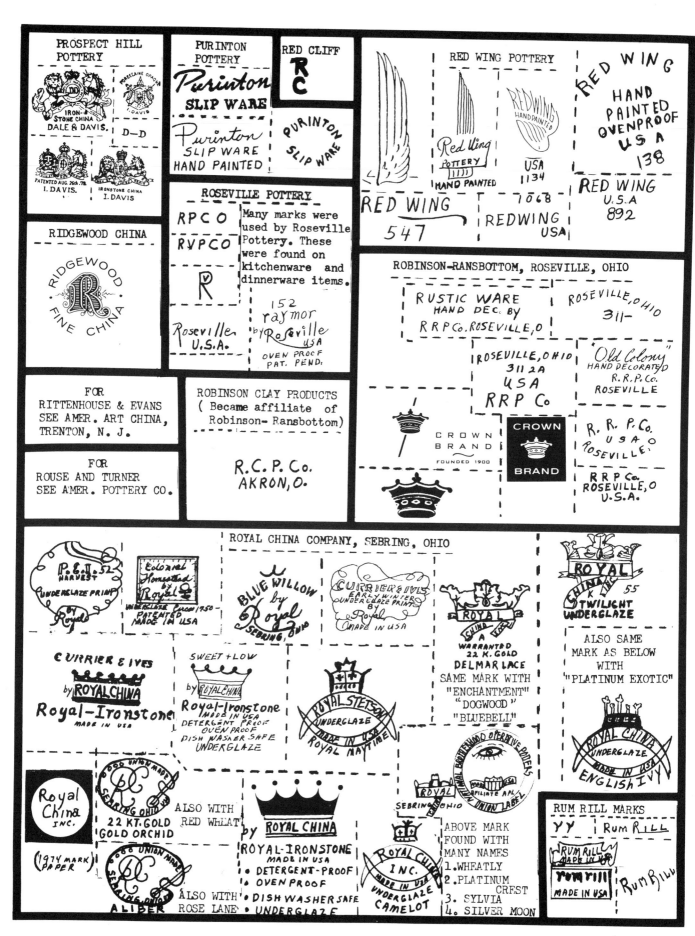

PROSPECT HILL POTTERY

IRON-STONE CHINA
DALE & DAVIS

D-D

PATENTED AUG. 26th .78.
I. DAVIS.

IRONSTONE CHINA
I. DAVIS

RIDGEWOOD CHINA

RIDGEWOOD FINE CHINA

FOR
RITTENHOUSE & EVANS
SEE AMER. ART CHINA,
TRENTON, N. J.

FOR
ROUSE AND TURNER
SEE AMER. POTTERY CO.

PURINTON POTTERY

Purinton
SLIP WARE

Purinton
SLIP WARE
HAND PAINTED

PURINTON
SLIP WARE

RED CLIFF
R C

ROSEVILLE POTTERY

RPCO

RVPCO

R

Roseville
U.S.A.

Many marks were
used by Roseville
Pottery. These
were found on
kitchenware and
dinnerware items.

152
raymor
by Roseville
USA
OVEN PROOF
PAT. PEND.

ROBINSON CLAY PRODUCTS
(Became affiliate of
Robinson- Ransbottom)

R.C.P.Co.
AKRON, O.

RED WING POTTERY

Red Wing
POTTERY
HAND PAINTED

RED WING
HAND
PAINTED

RED
WING
HAND
PAINTED

USA
1134

RED WING
547

7068

REDWING
USA

RED WING
HAND
PAINTED
OVENPROOF
USA
138

RED WING
U.S.A
892

ROBINSON-RANSBOTTOM, ROSEVILLE, OHIO

RUSTIC WARE
HAND DEC. BY
R R P Co. ROSEVILLE, O

ROSEVILLE, OHIO
311-

ROSEVILLE, OHIO
311 2A
USA
RRP Co

"Old Colony"
HAND DECORATED
R. R. P. Co.
ROSEVILLE

CROWN
BRAND
FOUNDED 1900

CROWN
BRAND

R. R. P. Co.
USA
ROSEVILLE, O

R R P Co.
ROSEVILLE, O
U.S.A.

ROYAL CHINA COMPANY, SEBRING, OHIO

P. & I. 52
HARVEST
UNDERGLAZE PRINT
By Royal

Colonial
Homestead
By Royal
UNDERGLAZE PRINT 1950-
PATENTED
MADE IN USA

BLUE WILLOW
by Royal
SEBRING, OHIO

CURRIER & IVES
EARLY WINTER
UNDERGLAZE PRINT
BY Royal
MADE IN USA

ROYAL
CHINA
A
WARRANTED
22 K. GOLD
DELMAR LACE
SAME MARK WITH
"ENCHANTMENT"
"DOGWOOD"
"BLUEBELL"

ROYAL
CHINA
K 55
TWILIGHT
UNDERGLAZE

ALSO SAME
MARK AS BELOW
WITH
"PLATINUM EXOTIC"

ROYAL CHINA
UNDERGLAZE
MADE IN USA
ENGLISH IVY

CURRIER & IVES
by ROYAL CHINA
Royal-Ironstone
MADE IN USA

SWEET + LOW
by ROYAL CHINA
Royal-Ironstone
MADE IN USA
DETERGENT PROOF
OVEN PROOF
DISH WASHER SAFE
UNDERGLAZE

ROYAL STETSON
UNDERGLAZE
MADE IN USA
ROYAL MAYTIME

Royal
China
INC.

(1974 MARK)
PAPER

SEBRING OHIO
22 KT. GOLD
GOLD ORCHID

SEBRING OHIO
ALIBER

ALSO WITH
RED WHEAT

ROYAL CHINA
by ROYAL CHINA
ROYAL-IRONSTONE
MADE IN USA
• DETERGENT-PROOF
• OVEN PROOF
• DISH WASHER SAFE
• UNDERGLAZE

ALSO WITH
ROSE LANE

ROYAL
SEBRING OHIO

NATIONAL BROTHERHOOD OPERATIVE POTTERS
AFFILIATE APL
UNION LABEL

Royal
CHINA
INC.
MADE IN USA
UNDERGLAZE
CAMELOT

ABOVE MARK
FOUND WITH
MANY NAMES
1. WHEATLY
2. PLATINUM
CREST
3. SYLVIA
4. SILVER MOON

RUM RILL MARKS

YY

RUM RILL

RUM RILL
MADE IN USA

rum rill
MADE IN USA

Rum Rill

192

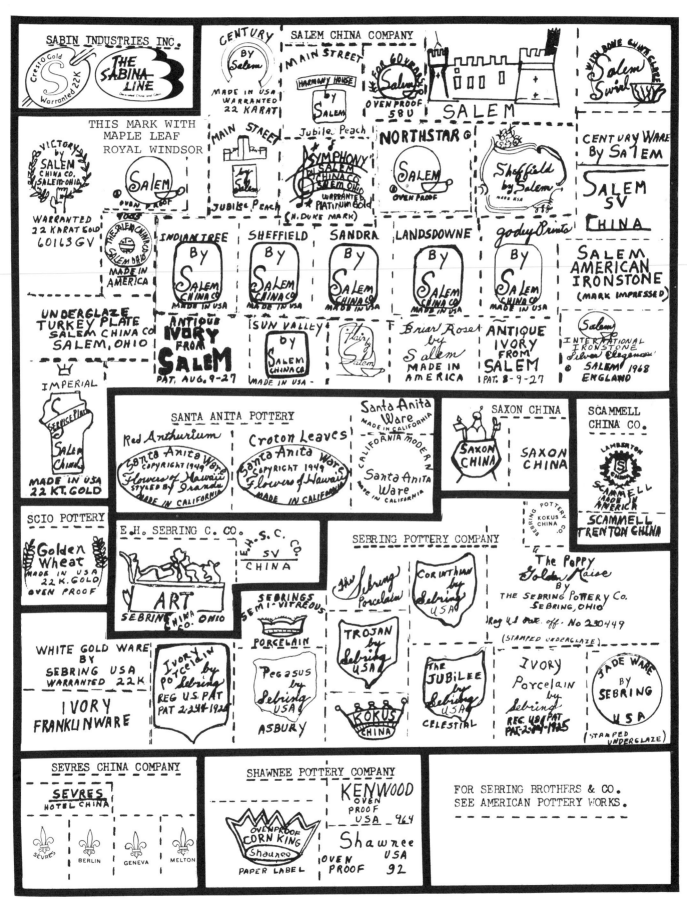

SABIN INDUSTRIES INC.

Cresto Gold S Warranted 22K

THE SABINA LINE

CENTURY BY Salem
MADE IN USA WARRANTED 22 KARAT

SALEM CHINA COMPANY

MAIN STREET
HARMONY HOUSE BY SALEM

FOR 60 YEARS Salem OVEN PROOF 58U

SALEM

WITH BONE CHINA GLAZE Salem Swirl

THIS MARK WITH MAPLE LEAF ROYAL WINDSOR

VICTORY by SALEM CHINA CO. SALEM OHIO
WARRANTED 22 KARAT GOLD 60163 GV

Salem OVEN PROOF

THE SALEM CHINA CO. SALEM OHIO MADE IN AMERICA

MAIN STREET BY Salem
Jubilee Peach

Jubilee Peach

SYMPHONY BY SALEM CHINA CO. SALEM OHIO WARRANTED PLATINUM GOLD
(N. DUKE MARK)

NORTHSTAR
SALEM OVEN PROOF

Sheffield by Salem MADE USA

CENTURY WARE BY SALEM
SALEM SV
CHINA

INDIAN TREE BY SALEM CHINA CO MADE IN USA

SHEFFIELD BY SALEM CHINA CO MADE IN USA

SANDRA BY SALEM CHINA CO MADE IN USA

LANDSDOWNE BY SALEM CHINA CO MADE IN USA

Godey Prints BY SALEM CHINA CO MADE IN USA

SALEM AMERICAN IRONSTONE (MARK IMPRESSED)

UNDERGLAZE TURKEY PLATE SALEM CHINA CO SALEM, OHIO

IMPERIAL S SERVICE PLATE Salem China
MADE IN USA 22 KT. GOLD

ANTIQUE IVORY FROM SALEM PAT. AUG. 9-27

SUN VALLEY BY SALEM CHINA CO MADE IN USA

Fairy by Salem

Briar Rose by Salem MADE IN AMERICA

ANTIQUE IVORY FROM SALEM PAT. 8-9-27

Salem INTERNATIONAL IRONSTONE Silver Elegance SALEM 1968 ENGLAND

SANTA ANITA POTTERY

Red Anthurium
Santa Anita Ware COPYRIGHT 1949 Flowers of Hawaii STYLED BY Irande MADE IN CALIFORNIA

Croton Leaves
Santa Anita Ware COPYRIGHT 1949 Flowers of Hawaii MADE IN CALIFORNIA

Santa Anita Ware MADE IN CALIFORNIA
CALIFORNIA MODERN Santa Anita Ware MADE IN CALIFORNIA

SAXON CHINA
SAXON CHINA
SAXON CHINA

SCAMMELL CHINA CO.
LAMBERTON S SCAMMELL MADE IN AMERICA
SCAMMELL TRENTON CHINA

SCIO POTTERY
Golden Wheat MADE IN USA 22 K. GOLD OVEN PROOF

E.H. SEBRING C. CO.
ART SEBRING CHINA CO. OHIO
E.H.S.C. CO. SV CHINA

SEBRING POTTERY COMPANY

The Sebring Porcelain

CORINTHIAN by Sebring USA

POTTERY KOKUS CHINA

The Poppy Golden Maise BY THE SEBRING POTTERY CO. SEBRING, OHIO
Reg U.S. Pat. off. No 230449
(STAMPED UNDERGLAZE)

WHITE GOLD WARE BY SEBRING USA WARRANTED 22K
IVORY FRANKLINWARE

IVORY PORCELAIN by Sebring REG U.S. PAT PAT 2.274-1924

SEBRINGS SEMI-VITREOUS PORCELAIN

Pegasus by Sebring USA
ASBURY

TROJAN by Sebring USA
KOKUS CHINA

THE JUBILEE by Sebring USA CELESTIAL

IVORY Porcelain by Sebring REC USA PAT PAT-2.74-1925

JADE WARE BY SEBRING USA
(STAMPED UNDERGLAZE)

SEVRES CHINA COMPANY
SEVRES HOTEL CHINA
SEVRES | BERLIN | GENEVA | MELTON

SHAWNEE POTTERY COMPANY
KENWOOD OVEN PROOF USA 964
OVENPROOF CORN KING Shawnee PAPER LABEL
Shawnee USA 92
OVEN PROOF 92

FOR SEBRING BROTHERS & CO. SEE AMERICAN POTTERY WORKS.

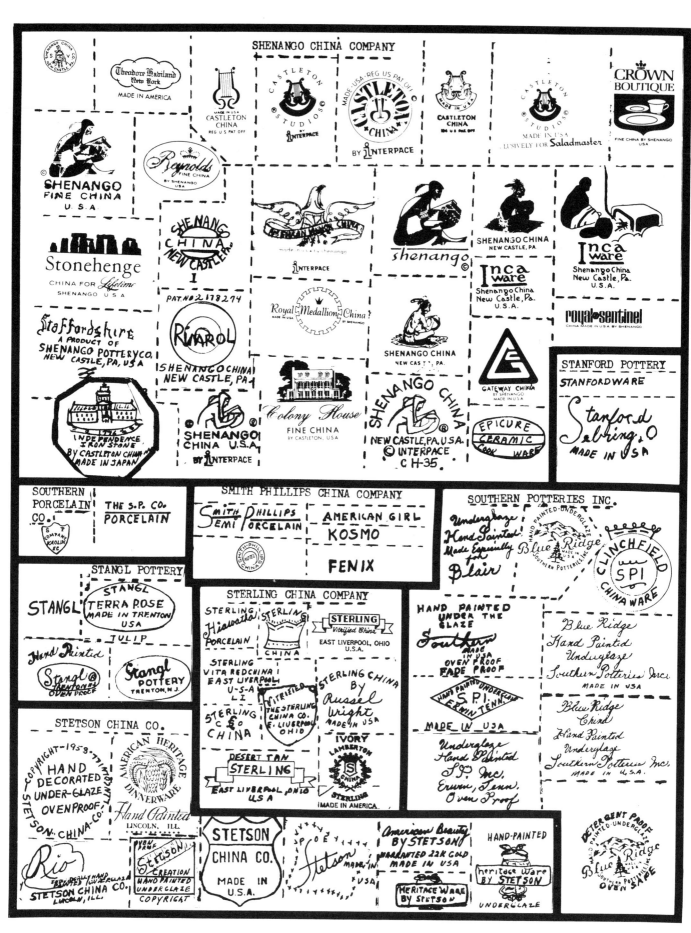

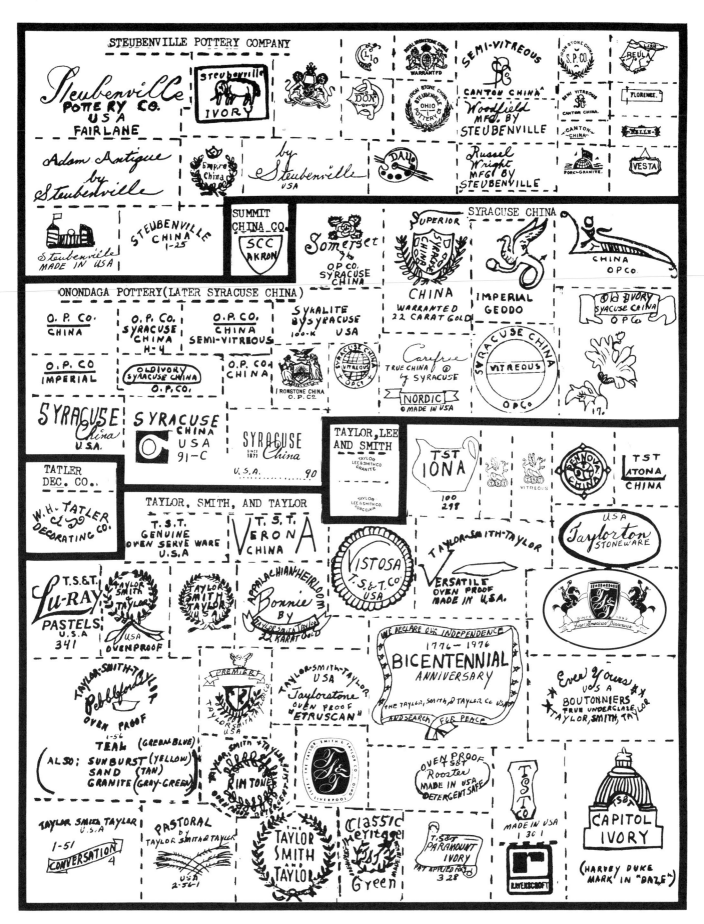

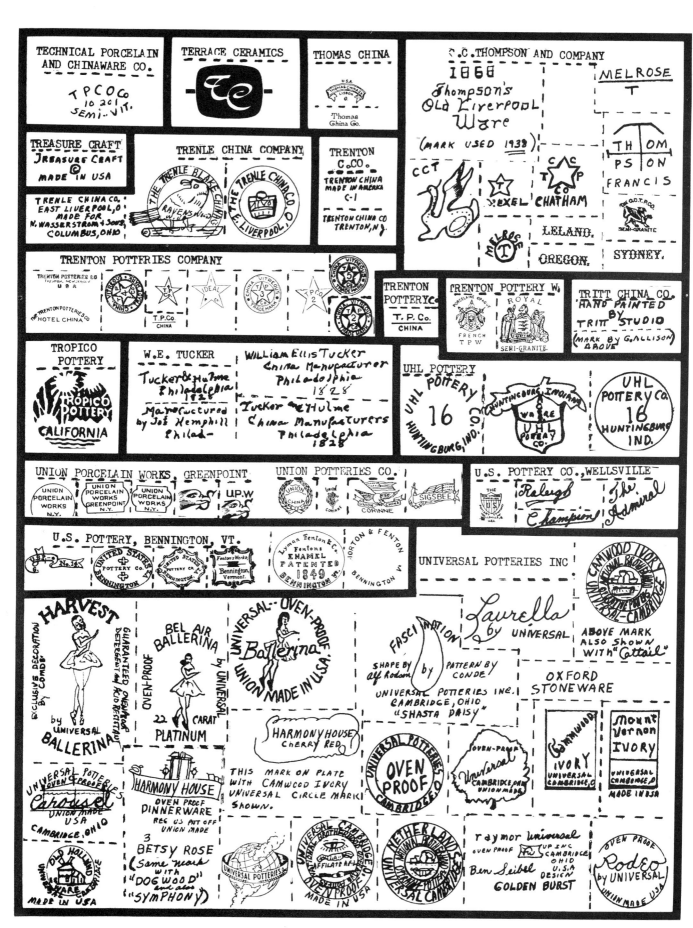

196

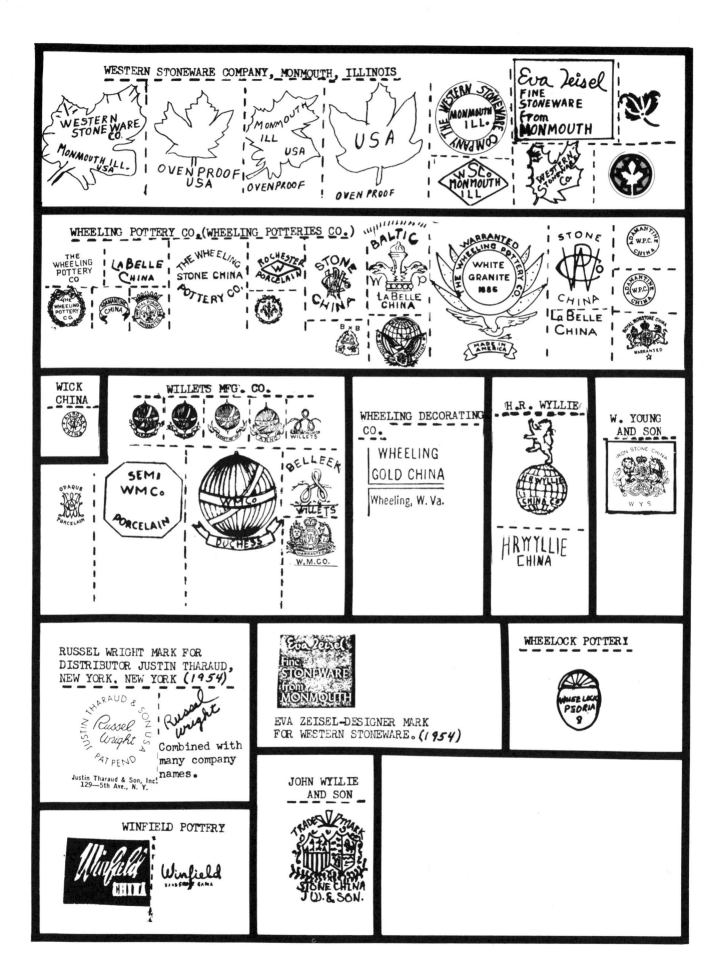

WESTERN STONEWARE COMPANY, MONMOUTH, ILLINOIS

WESTERN STONEWARE CO. MONMOUTH ILL. USA.

OVEN PROOF USA

MONMOUTH ILL USA OVENPROOF

USA OVEN PROOF

THE WESTERN STONEWARE COMPANY MONMOUTH ILL.

WSCo MONMOUTH ILL

Eva Zeisel FINE STONEWARE From MONMOUTH

WESTERN STONEWARE CO

WHEELING POTTERY CO. (WHEELING POTTERIES CO.)

THE WHEELING POTTERY CO

THE WHEELING POTTERY CO.

LaBELLE China

THE WHEELING STONE CHINA POTTERY CO.

ROCHESTER PORCELAIN

STONE CHINA

ADAMANTINE CHINA

BxB

BALTIC WP LaBELLE CHINA

GONE CHINA

THE WHEELING POTTERY CO. WARRANTED WHITE GRANITE 1886 MADE IN AMERICA

STONE CHINA WPO LaBELLE CHINA

ADAMANTINE W.P.C. CHINA

ADAMANTINE W.P.C. CHINA

ROYAL IRONSTONE CHINA WARRANTED

WICK CHINA

WILLETS MFG. CO.

W.M.CO. ARNO

WILLETS

OPAQUE PORCELAIN

SEMI WMCo PORCELAIN

WMCO DUCHESS

BELLEEK WILLETS

W.M.CO. WARRANTED W.M.CO.

WHEELING DECORATING CO.

WHEELING GOLD CHINA

Wheeling, W. Va.

H.R. WYLLIE

HRWYLLIE CHINA Co.

HRWYLLIE CHINA

W. YOUNG AND SON

IRON STONE CHINA WYS

RUSSEL WRIGHT MARK FOR DISTRIBUTOR JUSTIN THARAUD, NEW YORK. NEW YORK (1954)

JUSTIN THARAUD & SON USA Russel Wright PAT PEND

Justin Tharaud & Son, Inc! 129—5th Ave., N. Y.

Russel Wright

Combined with many company names.

Eva Zeisel Fine STONEWARE from MONMOUTH

EVA ZEISEL—DESIGNER MARK FOR WESTERN STONEWARE. (1954)

WHEELOCK POTTERY

WHEELOCK PEORIA 9

JOHN WYLLIE AND SON

TRADE MARK STONE CHINA J.W. & SON.

WINFIELD POTTERY

Winfield CHINA

Winfield HANDCRAFT CHINA

PART FOUR

Introduction to Products List

The following is a list of brand names, shapes, decoration names, types of china as to body composition and form such as eggshell, hotel ware, etc., line names, and all of the miscellaneous names that we throw into one broad category in our attempt to give our favorite dishes a name. The number of names attached to dishes made in this country would reach an unbelievable number. Companies which had shape and decoration names listed with their history material in this book, are mostly *not* listed here. See *STANGL, ROYAL CHINA, GLADDING, McBEAN AND COMPANY, BUFFALO CHINA, METLOX, and ARITA TABLETOP* histories for names assigned to their dishes. Also to keep the size of this list from being prohibitive to the book, Homer Laughlin China is listed as H.L.C.; Taylor, Smith, and Taylor is T.S.T.; Knowles, Taylor Knowles is K.T.K.; Gladding, McBean and Co. is G.M.B.; P. is for Pottery, and C. is for China, etc. The names of all of the companies are a shortened version, but I don't believe the list will give anyone a problem in this respect.

Similar names do not mean that the two companies' version of the same name will necessarily look anything alike. If this were the case, the pattern name was repeated. If the pattern name was listed just once (for instance "Tea Leaf" and the companies listed without repeating the name "Tea Leaf") then this was one of the old favorites that may have varied a little, but for the most part the different versions are similar. On the other hand, four companies made different "Apple Blossom" patterns, Onondaga Pottery, H.L.C., Sterling C., and Shenango China, and none of these were similar. **THIS LIST IS SUGGESTIVE ONLY; it is not meant to be a complete listing of every company that made a given pattern or shape, or used a certain decoration.** There just wasn't room to list more here. There is so much good to be derived from the study of this list that I thought it was better to put in a suggestive list than no list at all. A full list will mean another new book someday.

Cautions and Comments on the Use of This List of Shapes, Decorations, Lines, and Types of Ware

A. Decorations and shape must be the same before you have a name for your china.
B. Many companies used the same name for entirely different types of plates.
C. Sometimes the same plate had more than one name. For instance the maker gave it one name when he sold the plate himself; Sears or some other retailer assigned another name to the same plate.
D. The name found on the back of a plate could be a shape name, a decoration name, or a company name. Sometimes it was the name of a kind of line, such as "Casual China." The name might refer to the weight, such as "Eggshell."
E. Not all of the names in this list can be positively identified by the pictures and histories in this book. Sometimes all I found was a mention that a certain company made a pattern. But I listed them as a lead to someone, a place to start.
F. Patterns like Tea Leaf, Willow, Indian Tree, Onion, Autumn Leaf, etc., were made by several companies. This is not a complete list of the makers of any of these old favorites.

G. Sometimes it just happened that a pattern name used was the same word that happened also to be the name of some company that existed. For example, Steubenville marked a ware, "Empire China" with no mention of the name Steubenville Pottery. There were four companies actually named "Empire Pottery," In fact, Onondaga Pottery, Scammell China, Shenango China which made Castleton China, and Homer Laughlin China, all used "Empire," too. And as far as I know none of this "Empire" marked china was alike.

H. Within one given set of dishes, several shape names may be used. One shape name for the cups, one for the plates, one for the sugar and creamer, etc. For instance for a Homer Laughlin set, you could have Rhythm plates and Vogue cups in a single decoration making a set.

I. Collectors would be better off if the word "pattern" had never started to be used. But as you see this author has used it frequently too. A pattern name is really a shape, decoration, or line name, and when writers or collectors don't know which it is, we call it a pattern (present author included).

The comments at the beginning of the Marks Section will also help to understand the following list.

List of Shapes, Decorations, Lines, and Types of Ware

Accent, E. Knowles Co.
Adam shape, Warwick C. Co.
Adam shape, Steubenville P.
Adam Antique, Steubenville P.
Admantine, Wheeling P.
Admiral, Pope Gosser C. Co.
Admiral, Vodrey P.
Adobeware, Onondaga P.
Alaris, Lenox, Inc.
Alaska, E. End P.
Alba, E. Bennett P.Co.
Albany, International P. (Trenton)
Albion, E. Bennett, P.Co.
Al Fresco Ware, Bauer P.
Allegheny, Canonsburg P.
Allendale shape, Royal C.
Alliance, Brunt P.
Alma, Crown P.
Aloha, French Saxon Co.
Alox, H.F. Coors Co.
Alpha, Crescent (Trenton)
Alpha, Trenton Potteries
Alpine, Brunt P.
Alpine (Syracuse C.) Onondaga P.
Amazon, Mayer C.
Ambassador shape, Sterling C.
Amber Mist, T.S.T.
Amberton (ironstone) H.L.C.
American Beauty, H.L.C.
American Girl, Smith Phillips C. Co.
American Heritage, Stetson C.
American Modern, Steubenville P.
American Series, Vernon Kilns
American Traditional shape, Canonsburg P.
American Traditional shape, Lenox, Inc.
Americana, Canonsburg P.
Andover, Lenox, Inc.
Angus Plaid, W.S. George P.
Animal Kingdom, Limoges C.
Anniversary, Salem C.
Anthony, Chatham Potters
Apollo, Vodrey P. Co.
Apple Blossom (Amer. Haviland), Shenango C.

Apple Blossom Gold, H.L.C.
Apple Blossom (Syracuse C.), Onondaga P.
April, Pickard C.
April Showers, Gorham Co.
April, Southern Potteries
Arbor (Amer. Haviland)
Arbutus, H.L.C.
Arcadia, E. Knowles P.
Arcadia (Franciscan), G.M.B.
Arcadia, H.L.C.
Arcadia (Syracuse C.), Onondaga P.
Arcadia, Vernon Kilns
Ardmore, Mercer P.
Argosy shape, W.S. George P.
Argosy Pink, W.S. George P.
Aria (Castleton C.) Shenango C. Co.
Aristocrat (Eggshell) H.L.C.
Aristocrat, Lenox, Inc.
Aristocrat shape, Leigh Potters
Arizona (Hall Craft) Hall C. Co.
Arlington, H.L.C.
Arlington, Mayer C. Co.
Arno, Willets Mfg. Co.
Arosa, Leigh Potters
Arrowhead, Lenox, Inc.
Artistic, Burford Bros.
Artistic shape, K.T.K.
Arundel, Chesapeake P.
Asbury, Sebring P.
Astor, W.S. George P.
Athena, Lenox, Inc.
Audrey, Pope-Gosser C. Co.
Aurora, Lenox
Aurora Mist, T.S.T.
Aurora, Pioneer P. (Wellsville, Ohio)
Aurora, Wick C. Co.
Autumn, Lenox, Inc.
Autumn Apple, Southern Potteries
Autumn Ballet, Vernon Kilns
Autumn Bouquet, T.S.T.
Autumn Flower, W.S. George
Autumn Gold, H.L.C.
Autumn Harvest, T.S.T.

Autumn Leaf:
This list by Jo Cunningham, *Glaze*, June, 1977:
   Crooksville C.
   Crown Potteries
   Hall C. Co.
   Harker P.
   Limoges C. Co.
   Paden City P.
   Universal Potteries
Avalon (Amer. Haviland) Shenango C. Co.
Avalon, Cartwright Bros.
Avalon, Chesapeake P.
Avalon, Flintridge C.
Avocado (Chesterton Series) Harker P.
Avocado (Concord Series) Harker P.
Avocado Edwin Knowles
Avon, H.L.C.
Avon, Lenox
Avon, Scio P.
Avon Rose, Warwick C. Co.
Aztec, T.S.T.
Azura, T.S.T.

Bake-in-ware (Pantry) Crooksville C. Co.
Bake-oven, Cronin C.
Bakerite, Harker P.
Bak-serve, Hull P.
Bakserve, Paden City P.
Bali-Hai, Santa Anita P.
Ballerina, Universal P.
Bal Moral, International (Trenton)
Baltimore, Hall China Co.
Bamboo, American Ceramic Prdts. Co.
Bamboo, Winfield P.
Barcelona, Pickard, Inc.
Barclay, H.L.C.
Barclay, Lenox
Baroque Scroll (Castleton) Shenango C.
Baroque (Syracuse C.) Onondaga P.
Batik, T.S.T.
Bay Berry, H.L.C.
Beacon Hill, Lenox, Inc.
Beauty, Burford Bros.
Bel Air (Amer. Haviland) Shenango
Bel Air, Universal Potteries
Bella Rose, Stangl P.
Belle, Steubenville P.
Belleek:
   American Art China Works of Rittenhouse and Evans
   Amer. Beleek Co. (one L spelling)
   Ceramic Arts Co. (Lenox)
   Columbian P.
   Cook P.
   Coxon P.
   Eturia P.
   Knowles, Taylor, Knowles

Belleek (cont.)
   Morgan Belleek C. Co.
   Morris and Willmore
   Ott and Brewer
   Perlee Inc.
   Willets Mfg. Co.
Bellefonte, Lenox, Inc.
Bellmere, Flintridge C.
Bellvue, Lenox, Inc.
Bellwood (Castleton) Shenango C.
Belmont (Eggshell) H.L.C.
Belmont, Wellsville C.
Belvidere, Lenox, Inc.
Bennington, Lenox, Inc.
Berkeley, American Bisque Co.
Berkeley, Glasgow P.
Berkshire (Eggshell) H.L.C.
Berkshire, T.S.T.
Berlin, Anchor P.
Berlin, Sevres C. Co.
Bermuda, Harker P.
Bermuda (Ironstone) H.L.C.
Bermuda, Limoges C. Co.
Bermuda Rose, Canonsburg P.
Best China, H.L.C.
Beuhla, Steubenville P.
Beverly, Buffalo C. Co.
Big Sur, Metlox Potteries
Biltmore, American China (Toronto, Ohio)
Bimini (Ironstone) H.L.C.
Birchwood, Weil of Calif.
Bird of Paradise, Chatham P.
Bit of Norway, T.S.T.
Bits-Americana Plates, Vernon Kilns
Bits of Southwest, Vernon Kilns
Bits of Northwest, Vernon Kilns
Bits of Old English, Vernon Kilns
Bits of Old West, Vernon Kilns
Bittersweet, Southern Potteries
Blacksburg, Iron Mountain Stoneware
Blossom Time, H.L.C.
Blossom Time, Red Wing
Blue Belle, Hall China
Blue Bird type decoration:
   George H. Bowman C. Co.
   Buffalo C.
   Clinchfield P.
   W.S. George P.
   H.L.C.
   K.T.K.
   Mount Clemens P. (Robin)
   Owen China Co.
Blueberry, Fulper (Stangl)
Blue Bouquet, Gorham Co.
Blue Bouquet, Steubenville P.

Blue Castle, T.S.T.
Blue Chrysanthemum, Salem China Co.
Blue Dawn (Amer. Haviland) Shenango
Blue Dawn, E. Knowles China Co.
Blue Delft, T.S.T.
Blue Dresden, H.L.C.
Blue Heaven (Royal Jackson) Jackson C. Co.
Blue Horse, Hadley P.
Blue Lace Center, Warwick C. Co.
Blue Lily, Crown P.
Blue Medallion (Castleton) Shenango C.
Blue Mist (Carefree) Syracuse C.
Blue Onion: H.L.C.
Blue Onion, Scio P.
Blue Ribbon, Hull P.
Blue Ridge, Iron Mountain Stoneware
Blue Ridge, Lenox, Inc.
Blue Ridge, Southern Potteries
Blue Spruce, American Ceramic Products
Blue Symphony, H.L.C.
Blue Tree, Lenox, Inc.
Blue Willow:
    (Almost every major company made this pattern.)
    Examples are:
        Buffalo C.
        H.L.C.
        Royal C.
        Scio P.
        Sterling C.
Blue Wreath, Warwick C.
Bob White, Red Wing P.
Bockman's, Bauer P.
Bolero, (ironstone) H.L.C.
Bolero, (Castleton) Shenango C.
Bolero (shape) W.S. George
Bombay, H.L.C.
Botany, Pickard, Inc.
Bordeaux, Mercer P.
Bountiful, Royal C.
Bountiful, Salem C. Co.
Bouquet (Castleton) Shenango
Bouquet, Chatham Potters
Bouquet, W.S. George
Bouquet, (Vernonware) Metlox
Boutonnieres, T.S.T.
Bouquet, W.S. George
Bradford, Lenox, Inc.
Bravado, H.L.C.
Brazilia, Mayer C.
Breakfast Nook, W.S. George P.
Break O Day, Royal C.
Break O Day, T.S.T.
Breeze, French Saxon C. Co.
Brentwood, Weil of Calif.
Briar Rose, H.L.C.

Briar Rose, Salem, C. Co.
Bridal Bouquet, Gorham Co.
Bridal Rose (Syracuse C.) Onondaga P.
Bristol (Castleton) Shenango C.
Bristol, Ford C.
Bristol, H.L.C.
Brittany, H.L.C.
Broadway Rose, Atlas-Globe
Brocade, Pickard, Inc.
Brookdale, Lenox, Inc.
Brooklyn, Cartwright Bros.
Brookmere, Flintridge C. Co.
Brown Betty, Guernsey Earthenware (There was
    a more recent company that used this as
    a mark, unidentified to this author.)
Brown Drip Ware, N. McCoy P.
Brown Eyed Susan, T.S.T.
Brown Eyed Susan, Vernon Kilns
Brown Fleck, Hadley P.
Brown Rose, Pickard, Inc.
Brownieware, Universal Potteries
Bryn Maur, Lenox, Inc.
Buckingham (Hallcraft) Hall C. Co.
Bucks County, Royal C. Co.
Buddha, Sebring P.
Burgundy, E. Knowles C.
Burgundy, H.L.C.
Buttercup, Hall C. Co.
Butterfly Pink, H.L.C.
Buttons and Bows, T.S.T.

Cable shape, Amer. C. Co. (Toronto, Ohio)
Calico, W.S. George P.
Calico (cookware) Marsh Industries
Calico Fruits, Universal Potteries
Caliente, Paden City P.
California, Dresden P. (E. Liverpool, Ohio)
California Fantasy, Santa Anita P.
California Farmhouse, B.J. Brock Co.
California Festival, Santa Anita P.
California Life, Laurel P.
California Living, Laurel P.
California Modern, Santa Anita P.
California Rancho, Santa Anita P.
California Series. See Metlox history.
California (Syracuse C.) Onondaga P.
Calirose, H.L.C.
Calypso, Royal C.
Calypso, Syracuse C.
Cambria, Flintridge C. Co.
Cambridge (Amer. Haviland) Shenango C.
Cambridge shape (cups) Warwick C.
Camellia, Southern Potteries
Cameo, G.M.B.
Cameo, H.L.C.

Cameo, Pickard, Inc.
Cameo Rose (Jewell Tea) Hall C. Co.
Cameo Shellware, Harker P.
Cameoware, Harker P.
Camette shape, W.S. George P.
Campbell Kids, Buffalo C.
Camwood Ivory, Universal Potteries
Canarytone, W.S. George P.
Candlelight, Limoges C.
Cane, Chatham Potters
Canova, American P. Co.
Canova, Jersey City P.
Canterbury (Syracuse C.) Onondaga P.
Canton, G.M.B.
Canton, (hotel) Syracuse C. Co.
Canton, Steubenville P.
Canyon, McCoy P.
Capistrano, Red Wing P.
Capitol, H.L.C.
Capitol Ivory, T.S.T.
Capri, G.M.B.
Capri, H.L.C.
Capri, Lenox, Inc.
Caprice (Hallcraft) Hall C. Co.
Caprice, Red Wing P.
Caprice, Royal C.
Caprice, Santa Anita P.
Caprice (Vernonware) Metlox Potteries
Captiva (Castleton) Shenango C.
Cardinal, H.L.C.
Carefree True China, Syracuse C.
Caribee, Lenox, Inc.
Carlton (Castleton) Shenango C.
Carlysle, H.L.C.
Carmelo, Mayer C.
Carnation, McNicol P.
Carnation Beauty, H.L.C.
Carnival, W.S. George P.
Carnival (hotel) Syracuse C.
Carnival (hotel) Walker C. Co.
Carnival, Stangl
Carousel, Royal C.
Carousel, Universal Potteries
Carroll, Pope-Gosser C. Co.
Casa California, Vernon Kilns
Cascade, Lenox, Inc.
Cashmere, H.L.C.
Castilian, H.L.C.
Castle Garden, Lenox, Inc.
Castleton Rose (Castleton) Shenango C.
Casual Brown, Scio P.
Casual China, Iroquois C. Co.
Casual Living China, Hall C.
Cato, Mayer C.
Cattail, Lenox, Inc.

Cattail, Universal Potteries
Cattails, Pickard, Inc.
Cavalier Eggshell, H.L.C.
Cavalier shape, H.L.C.
Caveany (Castleton) Shenango C.
Celadon, Harker P.
Celadon, G.M.B.
Celebron, Albright C. Co.
Celest, Lenox, Inc.
Celeste (Syracuse C.) Onondaga P.
Celia, Jackson C.
Centennial, Anchor P.
Century Shape, H.L.C.
Century Shape, Salem C. Co.
Century Ware, Salem C. Co.
Century White, Hall C.
Ceramex, Pfaltzgraff P.
Ceylon, Royal C.
Chalet (hotel) Walker C.
Chalet, Lenox, Inc.
Chalet, Pickard, Inc.
Champion, Burford Brothers
Champion, U.S. Pottery (E. Liverpool, Ohio)
Chanson, Lenox, Inc.
Chanticleer, B.J. Brock Co.
Chantilly Lace, Gorham Co.
Charlene Shape, Pickard, Inc.
Charmaine, Lenox, Inc.
Chateau, H.L.C.
Chateau Chantilly, Gorham Co.
Chateau France, Limoges C.
Chatham, C.C. Thompson P.
Chatham, H.L.C.
Chatham (hotel) Walker C. Co.
   (Remember: There is also a pottery
   named Chatham Potters.)
Checks and Daisies, T.S.T.
Chefsware, H.F. Coors Co.
Cherry, Salem C.
Cherry Blossom, Salem C.
Cherry Line, Brush P.
Chester, Brunt P.
Chesterton Series, Harker P.
Chicago, Brunt P.
Chi Chi Poodle, Glidden P.
China Rose, Limoges C.
Chinese Garden, Pickard, Inc.
Chinese Red Kitchenware, Hall C. Co.
Chinese Season, Pickard, Inc.
Chinoiserie, Gorham Co.
Chippendale shape, Royal C.
Christmas Eve, Salem C.
Cinderella, Lenox, Inc.
Claremont shape, Canonsburg P.
Classic Heritage, T.S.T.

Clifton (majolica) Chesapeake P.
Clio, Steubenville P.
Cloud Burst, W.S. George P.
Clover, H.L.C.
Clover, Southern Potteries
Cock o' the Walk, Southern Potteries
Cocoa Rose, Flintridge C. Co.
Coin Flora, Salem C.
Coin Leaves, Salem C.
Colonade, Lenox, Inc.
Colonial Dames, Crown P.
Colonial Fireside, Salem C.
Colonial Garden (Poppytrail) Metlox Potteries
Colonial Gold Band, H.L.C.
Colonial Heritage (Poppytrail) Metlox Potteries
Colonial Heritage, Royal C.
Colonial Homestead, Royal C.
Colonial shape, H.L.C.
Colonial shape, Lenox, Inc.
Colonial shape, Southern Potteries
Colonial Star (hotel) Walker C. Co.
Colorama, Cronin C.
Colorama, Stetson C. Co.
Colortone, Paden City P.
Columbia, East Palestine P.
Columbia China, Harker P.
Columbia, Mayer C.
Columbus, East End P.
Comet, Limoges C.
Comet, Salem C.
Command Performance, Lenox, Inc.
Community Ware, W.S. George P.
Confetti, Paden City P.
Contempo, Bauer P.
Constellation (Castleton) Shenango C.
Continental, Flintridge C. Co.
Conversation shape, T.S.T.
Cook and Serve Line, McCoy
Coorsite, H.F. Coors Co.
Coral, Burford Bros.
Coralbell (Syracuse C.) Onondaga P.
Coralitos, Pacific P.
Coral Reef, Vernon Kilns
Cord Edge shape, Mayer C.
Corinthian shape:
    Harker P.
    Sebring P.
Cornell, K.T.K.
Corn Flower Blue, T.S.T.
Corn King, Shawnee P.
Corn Queen, Shawnee P.
Corn-shaped lines:
    American P., Marietta, Ohio
    Brush P.
    Brush McCoy P.

Corn-shaped lines (cont.)
    J.W. McCoy P.
    Shawnee P.
    Standard P. (McNicol)
    Stanford P.
    Terrace Ceramics
Corona shape (Castleton) Shenango C.
Coronado, Crown P.
Coronado, Lenox, Inc.
Coronet, H.L.C.
Coronet (service plates) Sterling C.
Coronet (Syracuse C.) Onondaga P.
Corsage (Castleton) Shenango C.
Cosmopolitan, Wellsville C.
Cotillion Eggshell, H.L.C.
Countess Eggshell, H.L.C.
Country Classics, Haeger P.
Country Craft, Chatham Potters
Country Garden, Lenox, Inc.
Country Garden, Royal C.
Country Garden, Stangl P.
Country Garden of Fruit, Chatham Potters
Country Kitchen (hotel) Shenango C.
Country Lane, B.J. Brock Co.
Country Lane, Lenox, Inc.
Country Life, Stangl P.
Country Manor, H.L.C.
Country Scene, Hadley P.
Countryside, Harker P.
Country Side, E.M. Knowles C. Co.
Country Side (Poppy Trail) Metlox Potteries
Countryside, Royal C.
Coupe Shape:
    H.L.C.
    Lenox, Inc.
    Onondaga P.
    Pickard, Inc.
    Scio P.
    Walker C. Co.
Crab Apple, Southern Potteries
Crackle Ware, Dedham P.
Crescendo (Castleton) Shenango C.
Crescent, Pickard Inc.
Crest-O-Gold, Sabin Industries
Crestone, Hull P.
Crestwood, T.S.T.
Cretan, Lenox, Inc.
Crocus, Hall C.
Cronin Casuals, Cronin C. Co.
Cross-stitch decals
    Cronin C. Co.
    Crooksville C.
    Harker P.
    W.S. George P.
Crotan Leaves, Santa Anita P.

Crown, Robinson Clay Products
Crown Brand, Robinson Ransbottom P.
Crown Wreath (Castleton) Shenango C.
Cuckoo, Smith Philips C. Co.
Cumberland, Southern Potteries
Cupid, French C.
Curiosity Shop, Royal C.
Currier & Ives:
  Canonsburg P.
  Crooksville C.
  Harker P.
  H.L.C.
  Royal C.
  Scio P.
  T.S.T.
Cynthia Southern Potteries

Daffodil, Hall C.
Dahlia, Southern Potteries
Dalrimple, W.S. George P.
Dartmouth, Crooksville C.
Dawn (Hallcraft) Hall C.
Dawn, Lenox, Inc.
Day, Steubenville P.
Daybreak, Lenox, Inc.
Daybreak, Mayer C.
Debonair (kitchenware) Hull P.
Dehaura, Denver China Co.
Della Robbia (Vernonware) Metlox Potteries
Deloris, Vernon Kilns
Delphian shape, T.S.T.
Del Ray, T.S.T.
Del Rio shape, W.S. George P.
De Luxe, Pope-Gosser C. Co.
Denura, Denver China Co.
Derby, Ford China Co.
Derwood shape, W.S. George P.
Desert Mist, B.J. Brock Co.
De Sota, Wellsville C.
Detroit, K.T.K.
Devon Point, Leigh Potters
Dewey, East End P.
Diamond China, E. Bennett P.
Diamond, International P. (Trenton)
Diana shape:
  K.T.K.
  E.M. Knowles
  Limoges C.
  Pickard, Inc.
Dimension shape, Lenox, Inc.
Dixie Harvest, Southern Potteries
Dogwood, California Ceramics
Dogwood (Franciscan) G.M.B.
Dogwood (hotel) Buffalo C.
Dogwood (hotel) Syracuse C. Co.

Dogwood, Royal C.
Dogwood, Stangl P.
Doily Petit Point, Salem C.
Dolly Madison (Castleton) Shenango P.
Doloris, Vernon Kilns
Domino Black, G.M.B.
Domino, W.S. George P.
Don, Steubenville P.
Dorian (Syracuse C.) Onondaga P.
Doris, Mayer C.
Doris, (Syracuse C.) Onondaga P.
Dorset, Scio P.
Dresden Bouquet, Warwick C. Co.
Dresden Eggshell, H.L.C.
Dresden (hotel) Buffalo C.
Dresden, Warwick C. Co.
Drexel, C.C. Thompson P.
DuBarry Gray, Lenox, Inc.
Du Barry, H.L.C.
Dubois, Mayer C.
Dura Print, H.L.C.
Duratone, H.L.C.

Early California, Vernon Kilns
East Wind, T.S.T.
Eclipse, Lenox, Inc.
Eclipse, T.S.T.
Econo Rim (hotel) Syracuse C.
Edgemore, Pope-Gosser C. Co.
Edgewood shape, Mayer C.
Effeco, Florentine P.
Eggshell Countess (shape) H.L.C.
Eggshell Georgian (shape) H.L.C.
Eggshell, H.L.C.
Eggshell Nautilus (shape) H.L.C.
Eggshell Swing (shape) H.L.C.
Electric, Brunt P.
Electric Burford Bros.
El Cid, T.S.T.
Elmhurst, W.S. George P.
Elsmere, Cartwright Bros.
Embassy, H.L.C.
Emerald Ivy, H.L.C.
Empire (Castleton) Shenango C.
Empire (Lamberton) Scammell C. Co.
Empire (Syracuse C.) Onondaga
NOTE: There were also four Empire Potteries
Empire Green, H.L.C.
Enchanted Hour, Lenox, Inc.
Essex Maroon, Lenox, Inc.
Eternal Gold, Lenox, Inc.
Etruscan (granite) Maryland P.
Etruscan (Majolica) Griffin, Smith, and Hill
Etruscan (Taylorstone) T.S.T.
Eugenia, Amer. C. Co. Toronto, Ohio

Eureka, Hall C. Co.
Evangeline shape, Amer. C. Co. Toronto, Ohio
Even Bake, Watt P.
Evening Flower, Southern Potteries
Evening Mood, Lenox, Inc.
Ever Yours, T.S.T.
Exotic White, T.S.T.
Expresso (Concord Series) Harker P.

Fairfax, H.L.C.
Fairfield, Lenox, Inc.
Fair Lady, Lenox, Inc.
Fairlane, Steubenville P.
Fairmeadows, Gorham Co.
Fairmont, Lenox, Inc.
Fanciful, Lenox, Inc.
Fantasia, Vernon Kilns
Fantasy (Hall Craft) Hall C. Co.
Fascination, Universal Potteries
Feather (dinnerware) Glidden P.
Featherweight China, Jackson C.
Federal, Limoges C.
Federal, Onondaga P.
Fenix, Smith Phillips C. Co.
Fern, Hall C.
Festival, Lenox, Inc.
Festival, Southern Potteries
Fiesta, H.L.C.
Fiesta Brown, T.S.T.
Fiesta Green, T.S.T.
Fiesta Yellow, T.S.T.
Filigree, Lenox, Inc.
Finesse (carefree china) Syracuse C. Co.
Fisherman, Hadley P.
Five Banded Ware, Hull P.
Flair (Castleton) Shenango C.
Flair (Hallcraft) Hall C. Co.
Flair shape, G.M.B.
Flame Lily (Carefree) Syracuse C.
Flamingo, H.L.C.
Flamingo, Wellsville C.
Flare Ware, Hull P.
Flav-R-Bake, Watt P.
Fleur-de-lis, Sabin Industries
Fleurette, Pickard, Inc.
Fleurette shape, W.S. George P.
Flight, W.S. George P.
Flight of the Swallows, H.L.C.
Flirtation, Lenox, Inc.
Flirtation, W.S. George P.
Floral Chintz, Pickard, Inc.
Floralia, Lenox, Inc.
Florence, Pope-Gosser C. Co.
Florence, Steubenville P.
Florida, K.T.K.

Florida, Lenox, Inc.
Flow or Flown Blue:
    Buffalo P.
    K.T.K.
    Mercer P.
    Various Trenton P.
    Wheeling P.
Flower Basket, C.C. Thompson P.
Flower Basket, E.M. Knowles C. Co.
Flower Fantasy, Southern Potteries
Flower Song, Lenox, Inc.
Flower Tree, T.S.T.
Flowers of Hawaii, Santa Anita P.
    (For Hawaiian Flowers, see Vernon Kilns)
Fluted design, Amer. Bisque Co.
Flying Bluebird, H.L.C.
Fondosa, Red Wing P.
Forever, Lenox, Inc.
Formal (Amer. Haviland) Shenango C.
Fortune, H.L.C.
Franciscan, G.M.B.
French, Trenton P. Works
French Chef, Marsh Industries
French Garden (Castleton) Shenango C.
French Metallic Lustre, Ohio P.
French Provincial, Salem C. Co.
Fresh Meadow, Lenox, Inc.
Frost Flowers (Hallcraft) Hall C.
Fruit, Chatham Potters
Fruit, G.M.B.
Fruit (kitchenware) Red Wing P.
Fruit, Marsh Industries
Fruit, Stangl F.
Fruit Festival, Nelson McCoy P.
Fruits, Harker P.
Fruits, K.T.K.

Gael Plaid, W.S. George P.
Garden, Salem C. Co.
Garden Lane, Southern Potteries
Garden Nook, W.S. George P.
Garden of Eden, Hall C. Co.
Garden Party, Lenox, Inc.
Garden Rose, W.S. George P.
Gardenia (Eggshell) H.L.C.
Garland (Amer. Hav.) Shenango C.
Garland, H.L.C.
Garland, Pickard, Inc.
Gaylord, Pickard, Inc.
Geddo, Onondaga P.
Geneva, Sevres C.
Genoa, Mayer C.
Georgian shape, H.L.C.
Geranium, G.M.B.
Geranium, Vohann of Ca.

Geranium, Salem C.
Gerium, Metlox Potteries
Gingham, Vernon Kilns
Glace, Mayer C.
Glendale, Buffalo P.
Glendale, Lenox, Inc.
Glendere shape, Albright C. Co.
Glen Rose, Chesapeake P.
Glenwood, H.L.C.
Gloria (Castleton) Shenango C.
Gloria, Southern Potteries
Glo-tan, Carr China
Godey Prints, Salem C.
Gold & Turquoise, H.L.C.
Gold Band, Buffalo P.
Gold Band, Pickard, Inc.
Gold Band, G.M.B.
Gold Band, T.S.T.
Gold Band, W.S. George P.
Gold Bow Knot, H.L.C.
Gold China, Pickard, Inc.
Gold Circle, H.L.C.
Gold Crown, H.L.C.
Gold Initial and Pink Rose, H.L.C.
Gold Rim, Gorham Co.
Goldcrest, H.L.C.
Golden Crown, Salem C. Co.
Golden Gate, H.L.C.
Golden Gate, Lenox, Inc.
Golden Goosegirl, H.L.C.
Golden Harvest (Chesterton Series) Harker P.
Golden Jubilee, T.S.T.
Golden Maize, Sebring P.
Golden Melody (Castleton) Shenango C.
Golden Rose, K.T.K.
Golden Rose, Scio P.
Golden Star, Stetson C.
Golden Wedding, E.M. Knowles C. Co.
Golden Wheat, H.L.C.
Golden Wheat, E.M. Knowles C. Co.
Golden Wheat, Lenox, Inc.
Golden Wheat, Scio
Golden Wreath, Lenox, Inc.
Gotham (Amer. Haviland) Shenango C.
Gourmet, Amer. Ceramic Prdts. Co.
Gourmet Cookware, Marsh Industries
Gourmet Line, G.M.B.
Gourmet, Pfaltzgraff P.
Governor Clinton (Syracuse C.) Onondaga P.
Granada, French-Saxon C. Co.
Granada, G.M.B.
Grandeur, Pickard, Inc.
Grape Ovenware, Winfield P.
Grape Royale, Maddux of Calif.
Grape Vine, E.M. Knowles C. Co.

Gray Dawn, H.L.C.
Gray Stone, Nelson McCoy P.
Grecian Ivory, Paden City P.
Greek Key (Amer. Haviland) Shenango C.
Green Bird, Hadley P.
Greenbriar, H.L.C.
Greenbriar, Paden City P.
Green Grass, H.L.C.
Green O Gold, Sabin Industries
Green Valley, W.S. George P.
Green Wheat, E.M. Knowles C. Co.
Gypsy Trail Hostess Ware, Red Wing P.

Hacienda, G.M.B.
Hallcraft, Hall C. Co.
Hanover, Lenox, Inc.
Harkerware, Harker P.
Harlequin, H.L.C.
Harlequin (Hall Craft) Hall C. Co.
Harmony (Syracuse C.) Onondaga P.
Harvard, K.T.K.
Harvard, Mayer Co.
Harvest, B.J. Brock Co.
Harvest, Universal Potteries
Harvest Gold, H.L.C.
Harvest Time, Iroquois C. Co.
Harwood, Lenox, Inc.
Hawaiian Flowers, Vernon Kilns
Hazel, Scio P.
Heart Brand, Burley & Winter P.
Heather Bloom, T.S.T.
Heirloom, H.L.C.
Heirloom, Pickard, Inc.
Heirloom, Sebring P.
Helen, Crown Potteries
Hemlock, Pickard, Inc.
Heritage Green, T.S.T.
Heritage Line, Conrad Crafters
Heritage Mist, T.S.T.
Heritage Stoneware, Pfaltzgraff P.
Hiawatha, Stetson C.
Hidden Valley, Royal C.
Highland Fling, Stetson C.
Highland Ivy, Southern Potteries
Highland shape, Albright C.
Holiday (Hallcraft) Hall C. Co.
Holiday, Laurel P. of Calif.
Holiday, Stetson C.
Holly and Spruce, T.S.T.
Holly Stone, Hollydale P.Co.
Holyoke, Lenox, Inc.
Home Flowers, Chesapeake P.
Homespun, Vernon Kilns
Homestead, T.S.T.
Honey Locust, Crown P.

Honey Hen, T.S.T.
Honeymoon Cottage, Harker P.
Honeymoon, Pope-Gosser C. Co.
Horizon, B.J. Brock Co.
Hotoven, Harker P.
Huckleberry, Iron Mountain Stoneware
Hudson shape, H.L.C.
Huntington, Flintridge C.

Ice, Iron Mountain Stoneware
Imperial, H.L.C.
Imperial, Lenox, Inc.
Imperial, Salem C. Co.
Imperial China, Empire C.
Imperial China, Pioneer P. (Wellsville)
Imperial Geddo, Onondaga P.
Imperial Porcelain, Wheeling P.
Impromptu Line, Iroquois C. Co.
Inca Ware, Shenango C.
Independence Ironstone (See Shenango) Japanese
Indian Morn, T.S.T.
Indian Summer, G.M.B.
Indian Summer, H.L.C.
Indian Summer, Metlox Potteries
Indian Summer, T.S.T.
Indian Tree:
    Crescent C.
    H.L.C.
    E.M. Knowles C. Co.
    Maddock and Sons P.
    Mayer C.
    Royal C.
    Salem C. Co.
    Shenango C.
Informal line, Iroquois C.
Innovation shape, Lenox, Inc.
Interlude, Lenox, Inc.
International Ironstone (See Salem) English
Interplay, Iroquois C.
Ioga, Warwick C. Co.
Iona, T.S.T.
Iowa, K.T.K.
Iris, E. Palestine P.
Iroquois Casual China, Iroquois C. Co.
Iva-Lure, Crooksville C.
Ivory Franklinware, Sebring P.
Ivory Hotel, Syracuse C.
Ivory, K.T.K.
Ivory Lamberton, Sterling C.
Ivory Porcelain, Sebring P. Co.
Ivy, Harker P.

Jack Straw, Salem C.
Jacobin Ware, Sabin Ind.
Jac Tan, Jackson C.

Jade Rose, H.L.C.
Jade Ware, Sebring P.
Jane Adams, Salem C.
Japonica, International C. (Trenton)
Jefferson, Pickard, Inc.
Jefferson, Syracuse C.
Jerry the Jerk, Pfaltzgraff P.
Jewell, Crown P.
Jewell, E.M. Knowles
Jewell, Lenox
Jiffy Ware, Limoges C.
Joan of Arc, Limoges C.
Josephine, Pickard, Inc.
Jubilee, Sebring P.
Jubilee Peach, Salem C.
June Bride, Warwick C. Co.
June (Castleton) Shenango P.
Juno, Mayer C.
Juno, Syracuse C.
Jus-Rite, Bailey Walker C. Co.
Just Right (kitchenware) Hull P.

Karen, Limoges C.
Kenilworth, H.L.C.
Keystone shape, Canonsburg P.
Keystone, Vodrey P.
King Arthur (Syracuse) Onondaga P.
King Charles, H.L.C.
King O Dell, Robinson Clay Prdts. Co.
Kingsbury, Gorham Co.
Kirkwood, Mayer C.
Kitchen Kraft, H.L.C.
Kwaker shape, H.L.C.

LaBelle, Wheeling P.
Lace (Castleton) Shenango C.
La Costa (Castleton) Shenango C.
Lady Greenbrier, H.L.C.
Lady Hamilton, Sabin Industries
Lady Lee, H.L.C.
Lady Love, Lenox, Inc.
Lady Madison, Gorham Co.
Lady Stafford, H.L.C.
Lafayette, Lenox, Inc.
Lafayette Porcelain, E. Palestine P.
La Francaise, French C.
La Grande, Crooksville C.
Lamberton China:
    Scammell C. Co.
    Sterling C. Co.
La Mirada, Amer. Ceramics Prdts. Co.
Lanaware, Cemar Clay Prdts.
Lancaster (Syracuse C.) Onondaga P.
Lancaster, T.S.T.

Lansdowne, Gorham Co.
Lansdowne, Salem C. Co.
La Pomma (dinnerware) Robinson Clay Prdts. Co.
Larchmont (Royal Jackson) Jackson C.
La Rosa, National C. Co.
La Rosa, Paden City P.
La Salle, H.L.C.
Latona C., T.S.T.
Laurel, La Belle C.
Laurella, Universal Potteries
Laurent, Lenox, Inc.
Lava, California Ceramics
Lazy Bones, Frankoma P.
Lazy Susan, T.S.T.
Leaf Dance, E.M. Knowles C. Co.
Leaflike shape:
    Steubenville P.
    Universal P.
Leeds, Ford C.
Leigh Ware, Leigh Potters
Lei Lani, Vernon Kilns
Leland, C.C. Thompson P.
Lemon Blossom, T.S.T.
Lenoir, Amer. C. (Toronto, Ohio)
Lenox Rose, Lenox, Inc.
Lexington, Lenox, Inc.
Lexington, Red Wing P.
Liberty shape, H.L.C.
Lido shape, W.S. George P.
Look Out Mountain, Iron Mountain Stoneware
Lorenzo, Gorham Co.
Lorraine, Scio P.
Lotus (Cameoware) Harker P.
Lotus, International C. (Trenton)
Lotus, Red Wing P.
Lotus Ware, K.T.K.
Louise, H.L.C.
Lowell, Lenox, Inc.
Luray Pastels, T.S.T.
Lustre Band and Sprig (name for Tea Leaf, see Tea Leaf)
Lustre Spray, (see Tea Leaf)
Luzerne, Mercer P.
Lygia, French C.
Lyric (Hallcraft) Hall C.
Lyric (Syracuse C.) Onondaga P.

Madison, Lenox, Inc.
Madrid, Dresden P. (E. Liverpool, O.)
Magnolia, Harker P.
Magnolia, Red Wing P.
Magnolia, Stangl P.
Magnolia, T.S.T.
Magnolia Eggshell, H.L.C.
Main Street, Salem C.
Maine, K.T.K.
Maize Ware, American P.

Majolica:
    Arsenal P.
    E. Bennett P.
    Chesapeake P.
    Crown P.
    Faience Mfg. Co.
    Morley & Co.
    New York City P.
    Odell & Booth Bros.
    Philadelphia City P.
    Phoenixville P.
Majestic (Castleton) Shenango C.
Majestic shape, H.L.C.
Malay Bambu, Weil of Calif.
Malay Blossom, Weil of Calif.
Malay Mango, Weil of Calif.
Malay Rose, Weil of Calif.
Malibu, H.L.C.
Malibu Modern, Hollydale P.
Malmaison, Lenox, Inc.
Malvern, Pickard, Inc.
Mandalay (Castleton) Shenango P.
Mandarin, Lenox, Inc.
Manhattan, George C. Murphy P.
Manhattan shape, Limoges C. Co.
Manor, Lenox, Inc.
Mansfield, Lenox, Inc.
Maple Leaf, B.J. Brock Co.
Maple Leaf, Salem C.
Maple Wood, H.L.C.
Marchetta, Pope-Gosser C. Co.
Marcrest, Marshall Burns Co.
Mardi Gras, Southern Potteries
Margaret Rose, H.L.C.
Maria, Pickard, Inc.
Marilyn, H.L.C.
Mariposa, G.M.B.
Mariposa Modern, Laurel P. of Calif.
Marquis, Mayer C.
Marquis, Pickard, Inc.
Martha Washington (Castleton) Shenango C.
Martha Washington shape, French C.
Martha's Flowers, Iron Mountain Stoneware
Mayan, Santa Anita P.
Mayan Aztec, Frankoma P.
Mayfair (Castleton) Shenango C.
Mayfair, W.S. George P.
Mayflower, Vernon Kilns
Mayflower shape, E.M. Knowles C. Co.
Mayflowers, Lenox, Inc.
Maythorn, Carr China
Maywood, Lenox, Inc.
Meadow Blue, Scio P.
Meadow Breeze, Scio P.
Medina, T.S.T.

Meerschaum, Limoges C.
Mello Tone, Coors Porcelain
Melodie (Syracuse C.) Onondaga
Melody, H.L.C.
Melody Lane, Royal C.
Melody Lane, Salem C.
Melrose, C.C. Thompson P.
Melton, Sevres C.
Menagerie, Glidden P.
Meredith, Lenox, Inc.
Mexican Cock, Glidden P.
Microcks, Sabin Industries
Midnight Mist, Crown P.
Midsummer, Limoges C.
Millefiore, Hall C.
Mimosa, Chatham Potters
Minaret, Gorham Co.
Ming (Coupe shape) Lenox, Inc.
Ming (Temple shape) Lenox, Inc.
Ming Tree, Weil of Calif.
Minuet, Hall C.
Miramar, Flintridge C.
Miss America, H.L.C.
Mistic (Syracuse C.) Onondaga P.
Moby Dick, Vernon Kilns
Mocha Pine, T.S.T.
Modern, Bauer P.
Modern California, Vernon Kilns
Modern Classic, Paden City P.
Modern Provincial, B.J. Brock Co.
Modern Star, H.L.C.
Moderne (Royal Jackson) Jackson C.
Modular Casserole, Glidden P.
Monarch, K.T.K.
Montana, K.T.K.
Montclair, Lenox, Inc.
Monterey, Crescent P. (Trenton)
Monticello, Hall C.
Monticello, Lenox, Inc.
Moonlight Mood, Lenox, Inc.
Moonspun, Lenox, Inc.
Morning Glory, T.S.T.
Mosaic, Pickard, Inc.
Moss Rose, E.M. Knowles C. Co.
Moss Rose, Universal Potteries
Mount Vernon, Hall C. Co.
Mountain Cherry, Southern Potteries
Mountain Craft, Amer. Bisque Co.
Mountain Ivy, Southern Potteries
Mulberry (Hallcraft) Hall C.
Mums, T.S.T.
Mums the Word, Royal C.
Museum shape (Castleton) Shenango C.
My Old Kentucky Home, Salem C. Co.
Mystic, Lenox, Inc.

Nantucket, H.L.C.
Narco shape, Mayer Co.
Narrim shape (hotel) Sterling C.
Narrolite shape (hotel) Walker C. Co.
NASCO, National Silver Co.
Nassau, Mercer P.
Nasturtium, Paden City P.
Natchez, H.L.C.
Native America, Vernon Kilns
Nature Study, Syracuse C.
Nautical Ivory, H.L.C.
Nautilus shape, H.L.C.
Nautilus, Globe P.
Navare, Pickard, Inc.
Netherlands, Universal Potteries
New Avon, Scio P.
New Louvre, Pope-Gosser C. Co.
New Princess, Limoges C.
Night, Iron Mountain Stoneware
Night Flower, Southern Potteries
Nile, Mayer C.
Noblesse, Lenox, Inc.
Nocturne, Pickard, Inc.
Nocturne (Syracuse C.) Onondaga P.
Nocturne Lyric, Lenox, Inc.
Normandy, Red Wing P.
North Star, Salem C. Co.
Nose Gay, H.L.C.
Nouvelle (Castleton) Shenango C.
Nurock, Brush P.

Oak Leaf, Lenox, Inc.
Oak Leaf, Warwick C. Co.
Ochre, W.S. George P.
Ohio, Brunt P.
Ohio, H.L.C.
Ohio, Walker C.
Oklahoma Plainsmen, Frankoma P.
Old Abbey, Warwick C. Co.
Old Boston, Western Stoneware
Old Charleston, Syracuse C.
Old Colony, Robinson Ransbottom
Old Curiosity shop, Royal C.
Old English, Royal C.
Old Ivory, Onondaga P.
Old Liverpool, C.C. Thompson P.
Old Rose (Castleton) Shenango C.
Old Towne Yellow, T.S.T.
Old Virginia Fashionware, Limoges C.
Olde Orleans, Scio P.
Olde Town, T.S.T.
Olympia, Lenox, Inc.
Onion Pattern:
    Carr C.
    Greenwood P.

Onion Pattern (cont.)
    H.L.C.
    Syracuse C. (hotel)
    Most companies made Onion.
Orange Blossom, California Ceramics
Orchard, California Ceramics
Oregon, C.C. Thompson P.
Organdie, Vernon Kilns
Oriental Pagoda, Hopewell C.
Orleans, Lenox, Inc.
Oslo, Lenox, Inc.,
Oven Proof Creation, Stetson C.
Oven Serve, H.L.C.
Oven Ware, Watt P.
Over the Hills, Iron Mountain Stoneware
Overture, Pickard, Inc.
Oxford shape (cups) Warwick C. Co.
Oxford shape, Sabin Industries

Pacific Underglaze Plaids, E.M. Knowles C. Co.
Palace Court, Lenox, Inc.
Palisades, Lenox, Inc.
Palissy, Vodrey P.
Pals, W.S. George P.
Pantry Bake-in-Ware, Crooksville C.
Pantry Shelf, E.M. Knowles C. Co.
Paraside, H.L.C.
Paramount Ivory, T.S.T.
Paree shape, Mayer C.
Note: From the following list we may conclude
that Paris is a shape name.
Paris Blue, Anchor P.
Paris, George C. Murphy P.
Paris White, Crescent P. (Trenton)
Paris White, East Morrisiana C.
Paris White, New England P.
Paris White, Trenton Potteries
Parisian Border, E.M. Knowles C. Co.
Park Ave. shape, W.S. George P.
Parquet, Mayer C.
Pastel Garden, Sabin Industries
Pastoral, T.S.T.
Pasture Rose, H.L.C.
Pate Sur Pate, Harker P.
Patio, Paden City P.
Patricia (Syracuse C.) Onondaga P.
Pavlova, Lenox, Inc.
Peach and Clover, Salem C.
Peach Bloom, Iron Mountain Stoneware
Peach Blossom (Hall Craft) Hall C. Co.
Peach Blossom, Metlox Potteries
Peach Blow, Limoges C. Co.
Peach Tree, Lenox, Inc.
Pear and Grape, Hadley P.
Pearl Edge Shape, Shenango C.

Pearl White, Goodwin P.
Peasant Ware, Watt P.
Pebbleford, T.S.T.
Pegasus shape, Sebring P.
Peking, Lenox, Inc.
Pennova C., T.S.T.
Penthouse, E.M. Knowles C. Co.
Pêpe, Red Wing P.
Periwinkle, H.L.C.
Persian Garden (Eggshell) H.L.C.
Persian Gem, Cleveland C.
Persimmon, T.S.T.
Peter Terris, Shenango C.
Petipoint, H.L.C.
Petite Bouquet, T.S.T.
Petroscan, Ohio P. Co.
Phillis, Mayer C.
Picardy (Castleton) Shenango C.
Pie Crust shape, Southern Pottery
Pierrette, Universal Potteries
Pilgrim shape, Albright C. Co.
Pine Cone, Lenox, Inc.
Pine Cone (Tea Set) McCoy P.
Pine Cone, W.S. George P.
Pinehurst, Lenox, Inc.
Pinehurst, Robinson Clay Pr.
Pink Apple Blossom, H.L.C.
Pink Caladium, W.S. George P.
Pink Castle, T.S.T.
Pink Mum, T.S.T.
Pink Rose & Daisy, H.L.C.
Pink Rose, H.L.C.
Pink Moss Rose, H.L.C.
Pink Rose Garland, H.L.C.
Pink Snowball & Green Moss Fern, H.L.C.
Pink Wild Rose, H.L.C.
Pink Willow, H.L.C.
Pink Willow, Royal C.
Pink Willow, Sterling C.
Pinks, H.L.C.
Plaidware, Hull P.
Plainsman Pattern, Frankoma P.
Plantation Ivy, Southern Potteries
Platinum Swirl, Scio P.
Platinum Tulip, Hall C. Co.
Plaza, E.M. Knowles C. Co.
Plaza, Paden City P.
Plum, Los Angeles P.
Plum (Syracuse C.) Onondaga P.
Plum Blossoms, Lenox, Inc.
Pluto, French C.
Plymouth, Onondaga P.
Plymouth, T.S.T.
Poetry, Pickard, Inc.
Poinsettia, Southern Potteries

Polaris (Syracse C.) Onondaga
Polka Dot, Hall C.
Polka Print, H.L.C.
Pompeii (Castleton) Shenango C.
Pond Mountain, Iron Mountain Stoneware
Poppies, W.S. George P.
Poppy, Chesapeake P.
Poppy Trail, Metlox Potteries
Posey Shop, Limoges C.
Prairie Rose, Stetson C.
Premier, T.S.T.
Presidential, H.L.C.
Primitive Pony, Winfield P.
Primrose (Castleton) Shenango C.
Primrose, Salem C.
Princess, Lenox, Inc.
Princess, Smith Philips C. Co.
Princess Anne, Salem C.
Princeton, K.T.K.
Priscilla, Glasgow P.
Priscilla, H.L.C.
Priscilla, Lenox, Inc.
Promise, Lenox, Inc.
Provincial shape:
    Harker P. in Cameoware with Tulip decoration.
    Metlox Potteries with Blue, Apple, Fruit, Rose,
        Whitestone.
    Red Wing P.
    Santa Anita P. with Apple.
    Stangl P.
Psyche, Glasgow P.
Pumpkin (Chesterton Series) Harker P.
Puritan, Onondaga P.
Puritan shape, Walker C.
Purinton slipware, Purinton P.
Pussy Willow, Amer. Ceramics Prdts. Co.
Pussy Willow, W.S. George P.

Quaker Maid Cookware, Pearl China Co.
Quaker Maid Ironstone, Harker P.
Quaker Town (Temperware) Lenox, Inc.
Quartette, Red Wing P.
Queen Ann, Flintridge C.
Queensware shape, Royal C.

Radcliff (Syracuse C.) Onondaga P.
Radison shape, W.S. George P.
Raggedy Ann & Andy Ware, Crooksville C. Co.
Railroad china:
    Buffalo C.
    Fraunfelter C.
    Greenwood P.
    H.L.C.
    Iroquois C.
    Jackson C.

Lenox, Inc.
    Maddock P.
    Mayer C.
    Scammel C. (Lamberton)
    Shenango C.
    Sterling C. (Lamberton)
    Syracuse C.
    Walker C. (Bailey Walker)
    Warwick C.
Rainer, George Bros.
Rainer, T.S.T.
Raleigh, U.S.P. (E. Liverpool, O.)
Rambler Rose, Crown P.
Rambling Rose, Sabin Industries
Rambling Rose, Universal P.
Ranch Style, Salem C.
Ranchero shape, Sabin Industries
Ranchero shape, T.S.T.
Ranchero shape, W.S. George P.
Ranchhouse (breakfast sets) W.S. George P.
Ransom shape, Scio P.
Rapture, Lenox, Inc.
Ravelle, Mayer C.
Ravenna (Castleton) Shenango C.
Raymor, Universal P.
Raymor Contempora, Steubenville P.
Raymor Fine China, Walker China Co.
Raymor Modern Stoneware, Roseville P.
Raymor, Roseville Pottery
Real Ivory, Chesapeake P.
Reflections (Castleton) Shenango C.
Red Anthurium (Flowers of Hawaii) Santa Anita P.
Red Apple, Watt P.
Red Leaf, Southern Potteries
Red Poppy, Hall C. Co.
Red Sails, Limoges C.
Red Wood, California Ceramics
Regal shape:
    Alliance C. Co.
    G.M.B.
    Globe P.
    Mayer C. Co.
    Shenango C.
Regal Rings, Sabin Industries
Regency Bouquet, Limoges C.
Regency shape:
    Canonsburg P.
    G.M.B.
    H.L.C.
    Sterling C. Co.
    Warwick C. Co.
Regent shape, E.M. Knowles C. Co.
Regents Park (shape) Camelia, (Amer. Haviland) Shenango P.
Remembrance, Pickard, Inc.

Rena, Crown P.
Republic, H.L.C.
Republic shape, Mayer C
Reveille, T.S.T.
Rever, East Palestine P.
Revere, Akron C.
Revere shape, Walker C.
Rhodora, Lenox, Inc.
Richmond, Hall C.
Ridge Daisy, Southern Potteries
Rieti Ware, New England P.
Rim shape, Pickard, Inc.
  T.S.T
Rim Rol, Shenango C.
Rim Tone, T.S.T.
Ring pattern, Bauer P.
Rioshape, Salem C.
Rioshape, Stetson C.
Rio, Stetson C.
Riviera, H.L.C.
Roan Mountain, Iron Mountain Stoneware
Roaster, Marsh Ind.
Roca, H.F. Coors
Rochester, Wheeling P.
Rochett, Brunt P.
Rococo, Southern Porcelain
Rolled-edge shape hotel ware:
  Buffalo C.
  Mayer C.
  Shenango C.
  Sterling C.
  Syracuse C.
  Walker C.
Roloc, D.E. McNicol P.
Romance, Cronin C.
Romance, H.L.C.
Romance (Hall Craft) Hall C. Co.
Romance, Lenox, Inc.
Rondale, Lenox, Inc.
Rooster, T.S.T.
Rosa, Pickard, Inc.
Rosalinde (Amer. Haviland) Shenango P.
Rosanne (Amer. Haviland) Shenango P.
Rose & Daisy, H.L.C.
Rose Buds, Southern Potteries
Rose Garland Border, H.L.C.
Rose Marie, Limoges C.
Rose Parade, Hull P.
Rose Point, Pope-Gosser C. Co.
Roselyn, Lenox, Inc.
Royal Blue, International P. (Trenton, N.J.)
Royal Buttercup, Gorham Co.
Royal China, International P. (Trenton, N.J.)
Royal Hickman, Haeger P.
Royal Ironstone, Royal C.

Royal Ivory, Owen C. (Minerva, Ohio)
Royal, K.T.K.
Royal Mararina, Limoges C. Co.
Royal Maytime, Royal C. Co.
Royal Medallion (Castleton) Shenango C.
Royal Rose, K.T.K.
Royal Stetson, Royal C.
Royal Windsor, Salem C.
Rugby, International (Trenton, N.J.)
Rum Rill:
  Florence P.
  Red Wing P.
  Shawnee P.
Russel Wright designs:
  Harker P.
  Iroquois C.
  Paden City P.
  Sterling C.
  Steubenville P.
Rutledge, Lenox, Inc.
Russet Ware, Hall C. Co.
Rusty Rose, Harker P.

Sabina Line, Sabin Industries
Sabina II, Sabin Industries
Sakarra (Castleton) Shenango P.
Salamina, Vernon Kilns
Sand Dunes, Sabin Industries
Sandra, Salem C. Co.
Sandstone, N. McCoy P.
San Jacinto, T.S.T.
San Marino, Flintridge C.
Santa Fe, T.S.T.
Santa Rosa, Los Angeles Potteries
Santa Rosa, Stetson C.
Santa Rosa, (Syracuse C.) Onondaga P.
Santan, Wellsville C.
Sappho, Glasgow P.
Saratoga, Southern Potteries
Savannah, Pickard, Inc.
Scotch Plaid, Crown P.
Scottsdale, Stetson C.
Sculpture:
  Lenox, Inc.
  Mayer C.
  Metlox Potteries
  Stangl
Sculptura, Mayer C.
Sculptured Berry, Metlox Potteries
Sculptured Stoneware, Glidden P.
Sea Shells, Royal C.
Seaside, Laurel P.
Selma (Syracuse) Onondaga P.
Senaca shape, H.L.C.
Sequoia, American Bisque Co.
Serenade, H.L.C.

Serenity, Pickard C.
Severn, Crescent P. (Trenton)
Severn, Trenton P.
Sevilla (earthenware) Cameron Clay Prdts. Co.
Shadowtone, Syracuse C.
Shaker Brown, Salem C.
Shalimar, G.M.B.
Shalimar, Lenox, Inc.
Shalimar, Royal C.
Shalimar, Steubenville P.
Shasta, Mayer C.
Shasta, W.S. George P.
Sheffield, Pickard, Inc.
Sheffield, Pope-Gosser C. Co.
Sheffield, Salem C. Co.
Shellcrest shape, Paden City P.
Shelledge (Syracuse) Onondaga P.
Shenandoah, Crown P.
Shenandoah, Royal C.
Shenandoah Pastels, Paden City P.
Shenandoah Ware, Paden City P.
Sherwood (Syracuse) Onondaga P.
Ship Ahoy, Limoges C.
Ship & Whale, Hadley P.
Shortcake, W.S. George P.
Sienna, Crescent C.
Sierra, T.S.T.
Silhouette, Crooksville C.
Silhouette, Hall C. Co.
Silouette (Syracuse C.) Onondaga P.
Silouette, T.S.T.
Silver Autumn, W.S. George P.
Silver Elegance (Eng.) Salem C. Co.
Silver Moon, Warwick C.
Silver Poppy, Warwick C.
Silver Swirl, H.L.C.
Simplicity, Canonsburg P.
Skiffs, E.M. Knowles C. Co.
Sky Blue, H.L.C.
Sky Tone, H.L.C.
Skyline, Canonsburg P.
Skyline shape, Southern Potteries
Smart Set, Red Wing P.
Smyrna, Mercer P.
Snow Flake, H.L.C.
Snow Flake, T.S.T.
Snow Lily, Lenox, Inc.
Solid Cherry, Iron Mountain Stoneware
Sogsbee, Union Potteries
Somerset (Syracuse C.) Onondago P.
Sonnet, Lenox, Inc.
Southern Gardens, Lenox, Inc.
Southern Camellia, Southern Potteries
Southern Provincial, Southern Potteries
Spring (Hallcraft) Hall C.
Spring, Lenox, Inc.

Springdale, Lenox, Inc.
Springfield, Lenox, Inc.
Spring Frolic, E.M. Knowles C. Co.
Spring Glory, E.M. Knowles C. Co.
Spring Meadow, Gorham Co.
Spring Morn, Gorham Co.
Spring Song, H.L.C.
Springtime, T.S.T.
Springtime, Hall C. Co.
Square Gliddenware, Glidden P.
Stanford, K.T.K.
Stanford, Lenox, Inc.
Staple, K.T.K.
Star Flower, Watt P.
Starlight, Lenox, Inc.
Sterling, Pope Gosser C.
Steubenville Ivory, Steubenville P.
Stinthall, Crooksville C.
Stonecraft Java Brown, Royal C.
Stonecraft, N. McCoy P.
Stonehenge, Shenango P.
Stonewall, D.E. McNicol P.
Stratford, H.L.C.
Strawberry Blue, Royal C.
Stawberry Hill, Syracuse C.
Strawberry pattern, see Shortcake.
Strawflower, T.S.T.
Studio 10 (Hall Craft) Hall C.
Summerfield, Lenox, Inc.
Sun Glow, Kitchenware, Hull P.
Sun Lure, Crooksville C.
Sun Tone, H.L.C.
Sunflower Kitchenware, Hull P.
Sunflower, Southern Potteries
Sunglass, H.L.C.
Sunny Spray, Southern Potteries
Sunnyvale (Castleton) Shenango P.
Sunrise Brand, H.L.C.
Superior, Carrollton P.
Susan, Southern Potteries
Suzann shape, French Saxon C.
Swing shape, H.L.C. Swirl, H.L.C.
Swirl:
    G.M.B.
    H.L.C.
    Royal C.
    Stetson
Sylvan, E.M. Knowles C. Co.
Sylvan, Flintridge C.
Symphony shape:
    Lenox, Inc.
    Pickard Inc.
    Salem C. Co.
    Shenango P.
Syncopation, Arita Tabletop

Tableau, Lenox, Inc.
Tacoma, K.T.K.
Tacoma, Mercer P.
Tahiti, Limoges C.
Tara, Pickard, Inc.
Taverne, Hall C.
Taverne, T.S.T.
Taylorstone, T.S.T.
Tea Leaf:
    Buffalo P.
    Brunt P.
    Cartwright Bros.
    Cumbow China Dec.
    East End P.
    Goodwin Bros.
    Harker C.
    K.T.K.
    Mayer C.
    Red Cliff Co.
    Walker C.
    Wick C.
    Note: Preceding list courtesy of Annise Heaivilin, researcher in Tea Leaf.
Temple shape, Lenox, Inc.
Tempo, Scio P.
Tenderly, Lenox, Inc.
Terrace, Lenox, Inc.
Terres, Peter, Shenango C.
Thematic shape, Crooksville C.
Theme shape:
    Gorham Co.
    H.L.C.
Thistle, French Saxon C.
Thistle, Southern Potteries
Thistle, Stangl P.
Three Leaf Clover, Hadley P.
Three Masted Schooner & Whale, Hadley
Tiger Iris, Amer. Ceramics Prdcts.
Times Square, W.S. George P.
Toledo Delight, Sebring P.
Toulon, Mt. Clemens P.
Tourainne (Amer. Haviland) Shenango C.
Town & Country, Red Wing P.
Town & Country, Stetson C.
Town Garden, Gorham Co.
Traditional, Lenox, Inc.
Trail Hostess Ware, Red Wing P.
Trailway shape, Southern Potteries
Traymore shape, K.T.K.
Trend shape, Steubenville P.
Trend shape, Syracuse C.
Trenton China, Scammell C. Co.
Tricorn shape, Salem C. Co.
Trilby, Glasgow P. (Trenton, N.J.)
Triumph, Limoges C.

Triumph shape, Limoges C.
Tudor, Lenox, Inc.
Tudor Rose (Castleton) Shenango P.
Tudor Rose, Sabin Industries
Tudor Rose, Warwick C. Co.
Tulip, Southern Potteries
Tulip Basket, H.L.C.
Tulip decaled design:
    H.L.C.
    Hall C.
    Harker P.
    Universal Potteries
Tulip Wreath, H.L.C.
Tweed, Vernon Kilns
Twin Border, Potters Co-operative

Upico Ivory, Universal Potteries

Valera, Lenox, Inc.
Vandemere, H.L.C.
Varenne (Amer. Haviland) Shenango P.
Velve, T.S.T.
Velvet (Concord Series) Harker P.
Vermillion Rose, Limoges C.
Vernonware, Metlox Potteries
Vernonware, Vernon Kilns
Versailles, Lenox, Inc.
Versailles, T.S.T.
Verus Porcelain, Oliver C. Co.
Vesta, Pickard, Inc.
Vesta, Steubenville P.
Viceroy (Eggshell) H.L.C.
Victoria, Lenox, Inc.
Victoria shape, E. Knowles
Victoria (Syracuse C.) Onondaga P.
Victorian Rose, Salem C. Co.
Victory shape, Salem C. Co.
Vienna, Salem C. Co.
Villa, Mayer C.
Village, Pfaltzgraff P.
Village Green, Red Wing P.
Vintage, Harker P.
Violet, Stetson C.
Virginia, K.T.K.
Virginia, Onondaga P.
Virginia Rose shape, H.L.C.
Vision shape, Pickard, Inc.
Vista Series, Royal C.
Vistosa, T.S.T.
Vogue china, H.L.C.
Vogue (Syracuse C.) Onondaga P.
Vreniware, Santa Anita P.
Vue-tility (cookie jar) National Potteries

Waco, E. Liverpool P.
Wagon Wheels, Frankoma P.

Further Suggested Reading

My compulsion to share the joys of collecting American dinnerware and kitchenware produced many articles early in my research. Then the realization of the vastness of the field led me to realize the material could never fit between the covers of one easy-to-handle book. That in turn created a desire to "get it into print" somewhere. Because so many more pictures, and a more detailed history can be presented in an article, I suggest the following as added reading material to this book. Articles are listed in chronological order by magazines.

Antique Trader
"The American China Company," July 4, 1979, p. 70.
"Fraunfelter China," May 30, 1979, p. 77.
"American Dinnerware and Commercial Pottery," A regular monthly column dealing mainly with questions and answers and various small features: July 11, 1979, p. 71; September 26, 1979, p. 73; October 24, 1979, p. 72; November 14, 1979, p. 69; December 5, 1979, p. 70; January 2, 1980, p. 38; February 13, 1980, p. 58; March 19, 1980, p. 68; April, 16, 1980, p. 70.

Collector News
"American Pottery Stirs Memories," February, 1977, pp. 1, 46, 47.
"Hull or Hall? Pottery Marks Confusing," June 1977, p. 56.
"Notes on Ohio Potteries," (Roseville), January, 1978, p. 41.
"Notes on Ohio Potteries," April, 1978, p. 50.

Depression Glass Daze
NOTE: The Depression Glass Daze column was entitled "From the Desk of Lois Lehner." That was the only title. Listed below are the potteries discussed each month.
McCoy & Brush Pottery History, October, 1976, p. 37.
Homer Laughlin, April, 1977, p. 37.
Cronin China, W.S. George, decalcomania, May, 1977, p. 39.
Tulip decorated ware, June, 1977, p. 53.
Red Wing, Wellsville China, July, 1977, p. 40.
Cronin China, Pearl China, Pope Gosser, October, 1977, p. 40.
Cleveland China, Oxford Pottery, November, 1977, p. 45.
Crooksville and Sebring Potteries, December, 1977, p. 37.
Mount Clemens query article, April, 1978, p. 34.
Smith Philips, Wheeling Pottery Company, Mayer China, March, 1978, p. 37.
U.S. Ceramic Tile Co., Limoges China, May, 1978, p. 26.
Canonsburg Pottery, Universal Potteries, Uhl Pottery, June, 1978, p. 42.
Calendar plates, bird decaled plates, etc., Jan. 1979, p. 44.
Mount Clemens Pottery follow-up, February, 1979, p. 4.
Hand-painted pottery, Red Wing, Continental Kilns, Watt Pottery, Southern Potteries, Purinton Pottery, etc., April, 1979, pp. 42, 43.
Royal Copley, Technical Porcelain, etc., June, 1979, p. 40.

Questions and answers for many companies with many pictures from readers. July 1979, p. 8

A full history of Spaulding China Company that made Royal Copley. Also a discussion of "Marcrest," the mark used by Marshall Burns of Chicago, September, 1979, p. 6.

Iron Mountain Stoneware, a full page of pictures and comment. Southern Potteries, a full page of pictures with names etc. August, 1979, p. 7.

Harker China Company, a full page of pictures, with many tyes of Cameoware, December, 1979, p. 16.

The Glaze

"The Various Potteries of East Liverpool," July-August, 1977, pp. 10, 11.

"What Is Art Pottery," July-August, 1977, p. 9.

"Robinson Ransbottom of Roseville, Ohio," July-August, 1977, p. 9.

"Potpourri of Pottery," (Stanford Pottery, Southern Pottery, etc.), September, 1977, p. 5.

"Paden City Pottery," November, 1977, p. 9.

"W.S. George," March, 1978, p. 11.

"Bells and More Bells," (various potteries named Bell), April, 1978, p. 12.

"M.A. Hadley Pottery," April, 1978, p. 12.

"Gonder Ceramic Arts," June, 1978, p. 10.

"Potpourri of Pottery," (Hull, David D. in Roseville, etc.), August, 1978, p. 13.

"Cookie Jars," (four full pages, pictures of many), September, 1978, pp. 8-11.

"Homer Laughlin," Part I (contains a full page of H.L.C. dishes with shapes and decoration names), January, 1979, pp. 8, 9.

"Homer Laughlin," Part II (second page of pictures), March-April, 1979, p. 12.

"Homer Laughlin," Part III (two pages of H.L.C. pictures), June, 1979, pp. 13-18 (full pages).

"Homer Laughlin," Part IV (two pages of H.L.C. pictures), August, 1979, pp. 14, 15.

"Sabin Industries," (one page of pictures), November 1979, p. 9.

Bibliography

Books

Altman, Seymour and Altmon, Violet. *The Book of Buffalo Pottery*. New York: Crown Publishers, Inc., 1969.

Barber, Edwin Atlee. *The Pottery and Porcelain of the United States*. New York: G.P. Putnam's Sons, 1893.

————. *Marks of American Potters*. Philadelphia: Patterson and White, 1904: Reprint. Southampton, N.Y.: Cracker Barrel Press, 1968.

————. Both of the above books printed in one vol. New York: J. and J. Publishing, 1976.

Bausman, Joseph H. *History of Beaver County Pennsylvania*. Vol. 2. New York: n.p., 1904.

Beers, J.H. *The History of Armstrong County Pennsylvania: Her People Past and Present*. Vol. 1. Philadelphia: J.H. Beers and Company, 1914.

Blair, Dean C. *The Potters and Potteries of Summit County, 1825–1915*. Akron: Summit County Historical Society, 1966.

Butler, Joseph T. *American Antiques, 1800–1900*. New York: Golden Press, 1965.

Clark, Garth, and Hughto, Margie. *A Century of Ceramics in the United States, 1878–1978*. New York: E. P. Dutton, 1979.

Cox, Warren E. *The Book of Pottery and Porcelain*, 2 vols. New York: Crown Publishers, 1944; reprint, 1970.

Cunningham, Jo. *The Autumn Leaf Story*. Springfield, Mo.: Haf-a-Production, 1976.

De Jonge, Eric, ed. *Country Things from the Pages of the Magazine Antiques*. New York: Weathervane Books div. of Crown Publishers, 1973.

Dreppard, Carl. *Geography of American Antiques*. Garden City, N.Y.: Doubleday, 1948.

Duke, Harvey. *Superior Quality Hall China*, Otisville, Mich.: privately printed as an Elo book, 1977. Sold in conjunction with the *Depression Glass Daze*.

Eberlein, Harold and Wearne, Roger. *The Practical Book of Chinaware*. Philadelphia: J.B. Lippincott Co., 1925.

Evans, Paul. *Art Pottery of the United States*. New York: Charles Scribner's Sons, 1974.

Frank, Donna. *Clay in the Master's Hands*. New York: Vantage House, 1977.

Freeman, Larry, *China Classics*. Glen, N.Y.: Century House, 1959.

Fridley, A.W. *Catalina Pottery*. Long Beach: privately printed, 1977.

Guild, Lurelle. *The Geography of American Antiques*. New York, Doubleday Page & Co., 1927.

Hayes, Barbara. *Bauer—The California Pottery Rainbow*. Venice, Calif.: Salem Witch Antiques, 1977.

Heald, E.T. *'The American Way of Life.'* The Stark County Story, vol. 4, pt. 3. Columbus, Ohio: Stark County Historical Society, 1959.

Henzke, Lucile. *American Art Pottery*. New York: Thomas Nelson, Inc., 1970.

Hoffman, Donald C. *Why Not Warwick*. Chicago: privately printed, 1975.

Howe, Henry. *Historical Collections of Ohio*. Cincinnati, Ohio: State of Ohio, 1902.

Humphreys, Sherry B. and Schmidt, Johnell L. *Texas Pottery*. Washington, Tex.: Star of the Republic Museum, 1976.

Huxford, Sharon and Huxford, Bob. *Brush–McCoy Pottery*. Paducah, Ky.: Collector Books, 1978 (catalog reprints)

_____. *The Story of Fiesta*. Paducah, Ky.: Collector Books, 1974.

Kester, Walter M. *History of Toronto, Ohio, 1900–1914*. Toronto, Ohio: Toronto Tribune Publishing Co., 1969.

Kovel, Ralph and Kovel, Terry. *Guide to American Art Pottery*. New York: Crown Publishers, 1974.

Lehner, Lois. *Ohio Pottery and Glass, Marks and Manufacturers*. Des Moines, Ia.: Wallace-Homestead Book Co., 1978.

McKee, Floyd W. *A Century of American Dinnerware Manufacture*, privately printed, 1966.

McClinton, Katherine. *American Country Antiques*. New York: Coward–McCann, 1967.

Mebane, John. *Ceramics in United States*. Best Sellers in Antiques. Dubuque, Ia.: Babka Publishing Co., 1974.

Middleton, Jefferson. *Clay Products*. 1900 Census of the United States, vol. 3, 1912.

Moody. *Moody's Industrial Manual*, two vols. New York: Moody's Investor's Service, 1977.

Nelson, Maxine Feek. *Versatile Vernon Kilns*. Costa Mesa, Calif.: Rainbow Publications, 1978.

Pappas, Joan and Kendall Harold. *Hampshire Pottery Manufactured by J.S. Taft and Company, Keene, New Hampshire*. New York: Crown Publishers, 1971.

Peck, Herbert. *The Book of Rookwood Pottery*, New York: Crown, 1968.

Purviance, Evan and Purviance, Louise. *Zanesville Art Pottery in Color*. Des Moines, Ia.: Wallace-Homestead Book Co., 1968.

Ramsay, John. *American Potters and Pottery*. New York: Tudor Publishing Co., 1947.

Ray, Marcia. *Collectible Ceramics*. New York: Crown Publishers, 1974.

Revi, Albert Christian, ed. *Spinning Wheel's Complete Book of Antiques*. New York: Grosset and Dunlap, 1975.

Sandknop, Stephen S. *Nothing Could be Finer: A Compendium of Railroad Dining Car China*. Edina, Mo.: Sandknop Publications, 1977.

Schneider, Norris F. *Zanesville Art Pottery*. Zanesville, Ohio: Privately printed, 1963.

Simon, Delores. *Shawnee Pottery*, Paducah, Ky.: Collector Books, 1977.

Spargo, John. *Early American Pottery and China*. New York: Garden City Publishing Co., 1926.

_____. *The Potters and Potteries of Bennington*. New York: Dover Press, (first ed., 1926), (second ed., 1972)

Staff: written, *Time–Life Encyclopedia of Antiques*, Vol. B, Alexandria, Va., 1977.

Stewart, Regina and Consentino, Geraldine. *Stoneware — A Guide for Beginning Collectors*. Racine, Wis.: Western Publishing Co., 1977.

Stiles, Helen E. *Pottery in the United States*. New York: E.P. Dutton and Co., Inc., 1941.

Stout, W. *History of Clay Industry in Ohio*. n.p.: Ries and Leighton, around 1921. (Also published in full in the *Geological Survey of Ohio*, Columbus, 1923. Fourth Series, Bulletin 26.)

Thorn, C. Jordan. *Handbook of Old Pottery and Porcelain Marks*. New York; Tudor Publishers, 1947.

Todd, Jack H. *Porcelain Insulators, Guide for Collectors*. n.p.: Privately printed, 1971.

Winchester, Alice. *How to Know American Antiques*. New York: Signet Books, 1951.

Winchester, Alice. *The Antiques Book*. New York: Bonanza Books, 1950.

Young, Jennie J. *The Ceramic Art: The History and Manufacture of Pottery and Porcelain.* New York: Harper and Brothers, 1878.

No author. *History of West Virginia, Old and New.* n.p.: American Historical Society, 1923.

Newspapers and Periodicals

American Art Pottery News
    Staff-written. "Pisgah Forest Cameo." June 1978, p. 3.
    Staff-written. "Pfaltzgraff Not a Dirty Word." July 1976, p. 4.

American Antiques
    Allison, Grace. "A Rare Bone China in the 1890's—Lotus Ware from Ohio." January 1978, p. 1.

Antiques Journal
    Ball, Bernice. "Etruscan Majolica." September 1964, p. 24.
    Bartlett, Margaret. "Onion Is Fund to Seek." October 1969, p. 20.
    Hackley, Mamie. "Tea Leaf Lustre." April 26, 1973, p. 5.
    Johnson, Deb, and Johnson, Gini. "Peters and Reed and the Zane Pottery." April 1975, p. 12.
    Poese, Bill. "Flow Blue." March 1972, p. 13.
    Rosenow, Jane. "Peoria Pottery and How It Grew." December 1969, p. 30.
    Smith, Clarissa. "Etruscan Majolica." June 1957, p. 8.
    Thompsen, J.K. "The White House China Room." July 1961, p. 8.
    Wintermute, Ogden H. "Tea Leaf Ironstone." May 1973, p. 14.

Antiques Magazine
    Stradling, J.G. "American Ceramics and the Philadelphia Centennial." July 1970, pp. 146–158.

Antique Monthly
    Green, Janet. "White House China Among World's Best." November 1972, p. 12A.

Antique News, (New Carlisle, Ohio)
    Crutcher, Jean. "Lotus Ware." October 1964, p. 1.

Antique Reporter
    Hutchison, Jeanette Ray. "Story of Tea Leaf." November 1973, p. 16.
    Miller, Robert W. "Dedham and Rabbits." June 13, 1973, p. 15.

Antique Trader
    Bartlett, Margaret M. "Onion Is Fun to Seek." August 1, 1972, p. 37; or *Annual of Articles*, Vol. V, p. 292.
    ————. "The Early Ironstone and Its Makers." *Annual of Articles for 1976*, Vol. V, p. 292.
    Coates, Pamela. "Wheeling Potteries Company." *Annual of Articles for 1975*, Vol. IV, p. 228.
    Cook, Peter W. "Bennington's Hound Handled Pitchers." *Annual of Articles for 1976*, Vol. V, p. 332.
    Dommel, Darlene. "Dickota Pottery." *Annual of Articles for 1974*, p. 337.
    Goldblum, Nettie. "American Belleek." *Annual of Articles for 1976*, Vol. V, p. 230.
    Havens, Meredith. "The B & O Blue Railroad China." *Annual of Articles for 1973*, p. 84.
    Hoffman, Donald C., Sr. "Warwick China." *1975 Annual of Articles*, Vol. V, p. 194.
    Miller, Robert W. "Willow Ware Plates." *Annual of Articles for 1972*, p. 89.
    Nelson, Maxine. "Vernon Kilns Americana Plate Collection." *Annual of Articles for 1975*, Vol. IV, p. 161.
    Russell, Mildred. "The Simplicity of Tea Leaf Lustre." *Annual of Articles for 1972*, p. 121.

Smith, Doris W. "Pretty and Practical Bauer Pottery." *Annual of Articles for 1973*, p. 4.

Staff-written. "Ironstone China." *Annual of Articles for 1972*, p. 102.

Thompson, Donna Ashworth. "Collectables For Tomorrow from Frankoma Pottery." July 20, 1976, p. 46.

Turnbull, Margaret E. "Hounds and Pitchers." *Annual of Articles for 1972*, p. 31.

Tyacke, Marv, and Tyacker, Bev. "Watt Pottery." September 13, 1978, p. 66.

Appalachia Magazine

Harney, Andy Leon. "Applachian Stoneware for America's Tables: The Iron Mountain Story." October–November, 1973.

Better Homes and Gardens

Huttenlocher, Fae. "A.B.C.'s of Table Furnishings." In three or more issues, March 1947, p. 54; April 1947, p. 54; August 1947, p. 53.

Staff-written. "Pacific Clay Products Co.," October 1935.

Collectors News

Lynn, Ophelia. "Happiness Was Bluebird in 1900." November 1970, p. 22.

Collector's Weekly

Bretzger, Judy. "Ott & Brewer Now of Age." November 23, 1971, p. 3.

Roger JoAnn. "Mutual China Closes." February 1972, p. 4.

————. "Syracuse China Stops Production of Casual Line." June 29, 1971, p. 11.

Schmitt, Agnes. "Ohio Valley Pottery, China Gain Popularity." July 14, 1970, p. 3.

Staff-written. "The Marks and Signatures of Pickard China." June 1977, p. 13.

Country Life Magazine

Sprackling, Helen. "The Charm of China." September 1931, p. 65.

————. "The Glory of Glass." September 1933, p. 33.

China, Glass, and Lamps

Staff-written. "Oldest Pottery in America Marks Its 125th Anniversary." January 1965. (Reprint sent without page number.)

Staff-written. "American Pottery Trademarks." July 23, 1923, p. 19.

China Glass and Tableware

Staff-written. "Newsletter." August 1979, p. 17.

Crockery and Glass Journal

Betz, W. A. "It All Started in East Liverpool." April 1955. (Reprinted without page number.)

Zimmerman, M.K. "The Pottery Industry in East Liverpool." December 1924, p. 116. (Fiftieth Anniversary Issue.)

Daily Leader

Mount Clemens, Michigan Newspaper.

Staff-written. "Old Timer Gazes Back at 1914." 25th anniversary issue, May 22, 1939. pp. 1, 4, 8.

Daily Leader

East Palestine Newspaper

Staff-written. "East Palestine's First Pottery." February 1960. p. 1.

Depression Glass Daze

Bloesser, Jim. "The Mysterious Bauer." November 1977. p. 43.

————. "Vernon Gingham." July 1977, p. 40

Brink, Helen. "Bluebird China." January 1979, p. 41.

Brown, Betsey. "Russel Wright." June 1979, p. 5.

Duke, Harvey. "Chats on China." May 1977, p. 36

Scott, Virginia. "China Ad Search and Research." May 1977, p. 38, August 1977, p. 40.

Stanton, Joyce. "Syracuse China." November 1977, p. 43.

Stanton, Joyce. "Syracuse China Continued." February 1978, p. 39.

Fortnight Magazine
  Staff-written. "Daring Dishes." August 4, 1950, p. 23.
The Glaze
  Barnett, Jerry. "The Paden City Pottery Company." November 1977, p. 8.
  Bartz, Jim. "Treasures of the Dining Car." March 1978, p. 15.
  Cunningham, Jo. "And the Autumn Leaves Fell." June 1977, p. 5.
  Fridley, Al. "West Coast Pottery." November 1977, p. 7.
  Hoffman, Sr., Donald. "When Warwick Rode the Rails." December–January 1978, p. 9.
  Hunter, Bess. "Vernon Kilns." July–August 1977, p. 16.
  Jackson, June. "History of Kass China Co." April 1978, p. 13.
  Latty, Betty. "Abdingdon, U.S.A." June 1977, p. 6.
  Slack, Bonnie. "Traveling China." December–January 1978, p. 8.
Harpers New Monthly Magazine, Vol. LXII
  Staff-written. "Pottery in the United States." December 1880, pp. 357–369. (Reprinted in *Hobbies*, February 1949, pp. 104–120.)
Hobbies Magazine
  Allen, Frederick W. "More About Dedham Pottery." September 1952, p. 80.
  Farrington, Frank. "American Porcelain." November 1940, p. 53.
  Hommel, Rudolf. "Colonial Master Potters." May 1949, p. 80.
  La Grange, Marie J. "More About Makers of Majolica." June 1939, p. 54.
  Peterson, Arthur G. "Some Pottery in the 1880's." October 1973.
  Ramsay, John. "Lotus Ware." October 1942, p. 55.
  _____. "American Majolica." May 1945, p. 45.
  Ripley, Katherine B. 'Canova Pottery." January 1942, p. 58.
  Shull, Thelma. "American Scenes for the China Collector." June 1942, p. 66.
  _____. "Belleek China." July 1941, p. 64.
  Staff-written. "Presidential Plates." June 1952, p. 82.
  Varick, Vernon. "Notes on Early New Jersey Potters." July 1944, p. 64.
  No author given. "Pottery in the United States. *Harper's New Monthly Magazine*, February 1881. Reprinted, *Hobbies*, February 1949, p. 104.
  Shull, Thelma. "American Scenes for the China Collector." June 1942, p. 66.
  _____. "Belleek China." July 1941, p. 00.
  Staff-written. "Presidential Plates." June 1952, p. 82.
  Varick, Vernon. "Notes on Early New Jersey Potters." July 1944.
Home Lighting and Accessories
  Staff-written. "What Happened to Yesterday's Artistic Craftsmen?" (on Cordey China Company) May 1973. Reprinted with no page numbers.
House Beautiful
  Gough, Marion. "Sixteen Most Popular China Patterns." November 1942, pp. 48–49.
  Staff-written. "American Pottery Comes of Age." August 1943, p. 6.
House and Garden
  Brown, B.A. "The Story of American China." October 1942, p. 35.
Lincoln Courier
  Staff-written. "Stetson China Was Moved Here from Roodhouse." August 26, 1953, Section 8, p. 11.
National Glass, Pottery and Collectables Journal
  Barnett, Gerald. "Leigh Potters Inc." March 1979, p. 22.
  Staff-written. No title (on Harker Pottery). December 1978, p. 12.
New Republic Magazine
  Cowan, R. Gury. "In Defense of American China." July 26, 1922, p. 256.
  Hamilton, Alice. "Hazards in American Potteries." July 26, 1922, p. 187.
Pottery Collectors' Newsletter
  Staff-written. No title (on Rookwood Pottery). May 1976, p. 43.

Pottery, Glass, and Brass Salesman Magazine

Jervis, W.P. "A Dictionary of Pottery Terms." in many installments, 1917 through 1918.

_____. "Wanopee Pottery." September 26, 1918, p. 11.

_____. "The World's Pottery Marks," in many installments, 1913 through 1916. Published weekly.

Staff-written. "Smith Phillips China Company." December 27, 1917, p. 16.

Staff-written. "The Man Who Saw." May 31, 1917 (A.E. Hull Pottery and Buffalo Pottery Company), p. 16.

Spinning Wheel Magazine

Ballinger, Phyllis. "Chatter about Spatter." October 1976. p. 10.

Blasberg, Robert. "Twenty Years of Fulper." October 1973, p. 14.

Butterworth, Elsie Walker. "Tucker China." June 1949, p. 3.

Davis, Chester. "Cordey China." January–February 1973, p. 10.

Dommel, Darlene. "Red Wing and Rum Rill Pottery." December 1972, p. 22.

Evans, Paul. "Art Ware of the Ohio Pottery." December 1976, p. 15.

_____. "The Nixon Presidential China." July–August, 1976, p. 36.

_____. "Hampshire Pottery." September 1970, p. 22.

Fitzpatrick, Paul J. "White House China." June 1973, p. 68.

Fitzpatrick, Nancy. "The Chesapeake Pottery Co." September 1957, p. 14.

Henzke, Lucille. "Stangl Audubon Birds." March 1971, p. 10.

McClinton, Katherine Morrison. "American Hand Painted China." *Spinning Wheels' Complete Book of Antiques*, p. 84.

Ray, Marcia. "A.B.C.'s of Ceramics." June 1968, p. 21.

Staff-written. "Ohio Ironstone." June 1954, p. 26.

Staff-written. "Bennett Pottery." November 1958, p. 22.

Staff-written. "Old Sleepy Eye." January–February 1965, p. 18.

Tri State Trader

Allision, Grace. "Lotus Ware." May 6, 1978, p. 1.

_____. "Triangle Novelty Company—Juanita Ware." February 26, 1977, p. 1.

_____. "Ohio's Bradshaw Pottery." May 19, 1979, p. 1.

Lasker, Faith B. "Presidential China, Thirty-eight First Families' Best Shown in Smithsonian Exhibit." August 13, 1977, p. 12.

Postle, Kathleen. "Overbeck Motifs Drawn from Nature." July 24, 1971, p. 1.

Stefano, Frank, Jr. "Clews Pottery." (Indiana potteries.) December 13, 1975, p. 8.

Staff-written. "Fire Destroys Pennsbury, Pa. Pottery." August 14, 1971, p. 4.

Staff-written. "First Hampshire Pottery Was Made One Hundred Years Ago." December 21, 1971, p. 2.

Staff-written. "Russel Wright's Genius is Largely Unrecognized." October 6, 1979, p. 43.

Western Collector

Ady, Laura S. "Tealeaf Pattern Ironstone Ware." March 1968, p. 11.

Evans, Paul. "The Robertson Saga." May 1967, p. 7.

Hellender, Isobel. "One Hundred Years of Sleepy Eye." May 1972, pp. 4–9.

Youngstown Vindicator Newspaper

Allision, Grace. "Alliance Firm Makes Souvenir Dishes." August 20, 1975, p. 8.

American Ceramic Society Bulletins

Forst, Florence, "Directions in Dinnerware Design." XXXI, September 1952, p. 320.

Kogan, Belle, "Style Trends and Conditions in Pottery Industry." XXX, June 1951, p. 201.

Staff-written or no author given:

"Centenary Anniversary of Harker Pottery Company." XX, January 1941, p. 25.

"Charles W. Franzheim." XX, May 1941, p. 185.

"Company News." (Pfaltzgraff) XXVI, October 1947, p. 415.

"Cook, Charles Howell." VIII, August 1925, p. 48.

"Edwin M. Knowles." XXII, March 1943, p. 78.

"Eugene Hardesty." XXVII, May 1948, p. 147.

"Goldscheiders Produce New Porcelain Base." XXV, December 1946, p. 494.

"Harold Philips Humphry." VIII, February 1925, p. 50.

"Herford Hope." VIII, February 1925, p. 47.

"History of Haeger Potteries Inc." XXIV, October 1945, p. 356.

"History of Hall China." XXIV, August 1945, p. 280.

"In Memorium—Charles D. Fraunfelter." VIII, February 1925, pp. 185, 186.

"James H. Goodwin." VIII, February 1925, p. 34.

"James Macmath Smith, President of Shenango." XX, June 1941, p. 163.

"Notes for Ceramists." XX, May 1941, p. 186.

"Symposium Held at 48th Annual Meeting of the American Ceramic Society." XXV, October 1946, p. 376.

"The Overbeck Pottery." XXIII, May 1944, p. 156.

"Report of the Committee on the Definition of Term Ceramics." III, July 1920, p. 26.

"William Bloor." XVI, January 1937, p. 25.

Vodrey, William H. "Record of the Pottery Industry in East Liverpool District." XXIV, August 1945, pp. 282–288.

Watts, Arthur. "Early History of Electrical Porcelain Industry in the U.S." XVIII, October 1939, pp. 404–408.

General Directories

Complete Directory of Glass Factories and Potteries of the United States and Canada. Pittsburgh, Pa.: Commoner Publishing Co., 1902, 1903. (Referred to in text as *1902–1903 Complete Directory.*)

Directory Issue of Crockery and Glass Journal, for March 15, 1954, showing manufacturers, importers and distributors.

California

California Manufacturers' Directory. Los Angeles: Times Mirror Press, 1924, 1948, 1951, 1955, 1957, 1960, 1977.

Southern California Business Directory and Buyers Guide. Los Angeles: Civic Data Corp., 1977.

Illinois

Polk's Lincoln City Directory. Lincoln, Illinois: R.L. Polk and Co., 1924, 1929–1930, 1946, 1950, 1955, 1959, 1962, 1963, 1966.

The Fourth Annual Report of the Factory Inspector of Illinois: Chicago: State of Illinois, ending December 15, 1896.

Indiana

Twentieth Annual Report. Indiana Department of Geology and Natural Resources. 1895, p. 173.

Indiana Industrial Directory for 1946, 1948, 1954–1955, 1958–1959, 1962–1963, 1964–1965, 1977–1978, Indiana State Chamber of Commerce.

Indiana Manufacturers' Directory for 1922, 1941, 1946, Indiana State Chamber of Commerce.

Louisianna

New Orleans City Directory for all the years from 1880 through 1900.

Michigan

Directory of Michigan Manufacturers for 1959, 1963, 1967, 1971, 1976, 1977.

New Jersey

Industrial Directory of New Jersey for 1901, 1918, 1931, 1940-1941, 1943-1944.

Trenton City Directory for all years between 1900-1971 except: 1901, 1918, 1931, 1940-1941, 1943-1944.

Ohio

Alliance Directory, 1960.

Annual Report of the Factory Inspector of Ohio, 10 vols. Columbus, Ohio: State of Ohio, 1891, 1893, 1896, 1899, 1902, 1903, 1904, 1905, 1906, 1907.

Industrial Directory, 1967, 1973.

East Liverpool Directory, R.L. Polk and Co. (inc. Chester and Newell, W. Va.), 1908, 1910, 1912, 1914-1915, 1916, 1924, 1926, 1929, 1931, 1934, 1937, 1941, 1943, 1945, 1948, 1949, 1951, 1953, 1954, 1956-1957, 1958-1959, 1960.

Ohio Columbiana County Farm and Business Directory, 1948.

Secretary of State Report for Ohio, 1910.

Salem City Directory for 1906, Salem, 1906.

Pennsylvania

Annual Report of the Factory Inspector of Pennsylvania. Philadelphia: State of Pennsylvania, 1893-1895, 1900.

Industrial Directory for Pennsylvania for the years 1916, 1919, 1922, 1931, 1935, 1947, 1950, 1953, 1956, 1959, 1968, 1970, 1973, 1975, 1976.

South Carolina

Handbook of South Carolina. Resources, Institutions and Industries of the State: Columbia, S.C. The State Company, Columbia, S.C.: State Department of Agriculture, 1907.

Industrial Directory of South Carolina. Columbia: S.C. Research, Planning and Development Board, 1947.

South Carolina Industrial Directory for 1972-1973 and 1976.

Tennessee

Directory of Tennessee Industries for 1943, 1947, 1949, 1952, 1954-1955, 1957-1958, 1959-1960, 1963, 1966, 1969.

Memphis Mid-South Manufacturers Guide for 1970, 1973, and 1975.

Texas

Texas State Gazetteer. Chicago: R.L. Polk Company, for 1884-1885, 1890-1891, 1892, 1896-1897, 1914-1915.

Virginia

Survey of Hopewell, Virginia. Hopewell Va.: Hopewell Chamber of Commerce, 1938.

West Virginia

West Virginia Manufacturing Directory for 1962 and 1967.

West Virginia State Gazetteer and Business Directory, for 1895-1896, 1900, 1910-1911, 1918-1919, 1923-1924, published by the R.L. Polk Company.

Centennial and Special Publications

Carson, Edward. *Homer Laughlin, 1873-1893, The First Hundred Years.*

Dooley, Raymond. *The Namesake Town: A Centennial History of Lincoln, Illinois.* Published by the Centennial Booklet Committee, 1953.

Loar, Peggy A. *Indiana Stoneware.* Published by the Indianapolis Museum of Art with a catalog of an exhibition, April, 1974.

Madden, Bett. "Jug Towns." *The Living Museum.* Illinois State Museum Booklet, January 1968, p. 164.

Milam, Otis H., Jr., *Clay Products.* Prepared by the National Youth Administration, June, 1939.

No author. "Carrollton Pottery Company." Carrollton: *Free Standard Press*, Centennial Ed., 1915.

No author. *China and Glassware.* (Reprint of Butler Bros. catalogs for 1925, 1930.) Mentone, Ala.: Antique Research Publications, 1968.

No author. *Crooksville—Roseville* Festival Booklets. Roseville, Ohio: Privately printed by Festival Committee, 1967, 1976.

Company Printed Information

No author. *Sixth and Eleventh Annual Tri State Pottery Festival* Booklets for the years 1973 and 1978.

No author, *Sebring, Ohio, A Brief History*, 65pp. printed by Anniversary Committee, 1949.

No author. *Heritage of a Century.* Privately printed by Mayer China Co. around 1915.

No author. *History of Maddux of California.* Privately printed by Maddux of Calif., 1977.

No author. *History of the Canonsburg Pottery Company.* Printed and furnished by the company, June 20, 1972.

No author. *Stangl, A Portrait in Progress in Pottery,* privately printed booklet by Stangl Pottery, 1965.

No author. *Sterling China, How It's Made and Suggestions for Proper Use.* East Liverpool, Ohio, no date (around 1950).

No author. *Story of Genuine Fiesta Dinnerware. 1936 to 1973.* Printed by the Homer Laughlin China Company.

Index of Factories

(Page numbers for history in dark print)

B

LINCOLN CHINA CO., Lincoln, Ill.,   100, **143**
LINCOLN POTTERY, Trenton, N.J.,   **100**, 113
LION'S VALLEY STONEWARE, Lemon Grove, Calif.,   **100**
LOS ANGELES POTTERIES, Lynwood, Calif.,   **100**
LOUISIANA PORCELAIN WORKS, New Orleans, La.,   100, **112**
LOWRY BROTHERS, Roseville, Ohio,   **100**

M
MACOMB POTTERY, Macomb, Ill.,   **167**
MADDOCK, JOHN & SONS, Trenton, N.J.,   100, **101**
MADDOCK POTTERY COMPANY, Trenton, N.J.,   **100**, 131
MADDOCK, THOMAS & SONS, Trenton, N.J.,   10, **101**
MADDUX OF CA., Los Angeles, Calif.,   19, **101**
MARSHALL BURNS, Chicago, Ill.,   **102**
MARSH IND., Los Angeles, Calif.,   **102**
MARYLAND POTTERY CO., Baltimore, Md.,   **102**
MARYLAND QUEENSWARE FACTORY, Baltimore, Md.,   **102**
MAYER CHINA, Beaver Falls, Pa.,   81, **103**
MCCOY, J.W., Roseville, Ohio,   **105**
MCCOY, NELSON POTTERY, Roseville, Ohio,   **104**, 110, 129
MCFARLAND, WILLIAM, Cincinnati, Ohio,   9, **105**
MCNICOL POTTERIES (three potteries),   **105**, 113
MEAD, DR., New York City, N.Y.,   9, **106**
MELLOR AND CO., Trenton, N.J.,   **45**, 106
MERCER POTTERY, Trenton, N.J.,   **106**
METLOX MFG. CO., Manhattan Beach, Calif.,   19, **106**
MIDLAND POTTERY, Roseville, Ohio,   **105**, 109
MILLER, ABRAHAM, Philadelphia, Pa..   9, 109, **152**
MILLINGTON, ASTBURY, & POULSON, Trenton, N.J.,   101, **109**
MITCHELL, JAMES, Middlebury, Vt.,   **57**, 109
MONMOUTH POTTERY, Monmouth, Ill.,   109, **166**
MORGAN BELLEEK CHINA CO., Canton, Ohio,   **109**
MORLEY & CO., Wellsville, Ohio,   **109**, 121, 165
MORRIS & WILLMORE, Trenton, N.J.,   10, **44**, 109
MORRISON & CARR, N.Y. City,   9, 109, **113**
MOSES, JOHN & SONS, Trenton, N.J.,   **67**, 109
MOUNT CLEMENS POTTERY, Mount Clemens, Mich.,   104, **109-110**, 129
MURPHY POTTERY, E. Liverpool, Ohio,   **111**
MUTUAL CHINA CO., Indianapolis, Ind.,   **111**
MUTUAL POTTERY, Trenton, N.J.,   **152**

N
NATIONAL CHINA, E. Liverpool, Ohio,   **111**
NATIONAL POTTERIES CORP., Cleveland, Ohio,   **111**
NATIONAL SILVER CO., New York, N.Y.,   106, **111**, 130
NEW CASTLE C. CO., New Castle, Pa.,   **111**, 136
NEW ENGLAND P. CO., E. Boston, Mass.,   **112**
NEW JERSEY P. CO., Trenton, N.J.,   **112**
NEW MILFORD P. CO., New Milford, Conn.,   **112**
NEW ORLEANS PORCELAIN CO., New Orleans, La.,   **112**
NEW YORK CITY P., N.Y. City,   **100**, 113
NORRIS, JAMES E., Trenton, N.J.,   **113**
NORTON AND FENTON, Bennington, Vt.,   9, 113, **154**
N. CAMBRIDGE C., N. Cambridge, Mass.,   **113**
NOVELTY POTTERY WORKS, E. Liverpool, Ohio,   105, **113**

238

About the Author

Lois Lehner, Radnor, Ohio, graduate of Ohio State University, former school teacher, proudly presents her second book, which deals with American dinnerware. Lois feels this is something that has touched the life of almost every American who has lived, even if they only ate from the ware. Everybody used dishes, and at least some that passed through the hands of each family were made in America. Her first book, *Ohio Pottery and Glass Marks and Manufacturers* brought forth so many questions along this line that Lois decided a second book was in order. Letters from all over the country have prompted her to write many articles on dinnerware for several publications, and she is currently writing a monthly column for the *Antique Trader*. A list of Lois's articles can be found in this book in the section entitled "Further Suggested Reading."

Photograph: Wayne Cubberly